ATLANTIS

PROF. ARYSIO SANTOS

ATLANTIS
THE LOST CONTINENT FINALLY FOUND

ATLANTIS
PUBLICATIONS

Published by Atlantis Publications, Inc.
Lynnwood, WA 98037 U.S.A.
contact@atlantispublications.com
www.atlan.org and www.atlantislinks.com

Distributed to the book trade by North Atlantic Books and Random House, Inc.

Logo and Cover Design: Rodrigo Friche
Line Art and Graphic Editing: Ney P. Junior; Tatiane Lima
Text Editing and Proofreading: Pradip Purtej Singh

Library of Congress Cataloging-in-Publication Data
Santos, Arysio.
  Atlantis : the lost continent finally found / Arysio Santos.
     p. cm.
  Originally published: [United States] : Atlantis Publications, 2005.
  Summary: "Cracking the riddle of Atlantis with a new set of tools, scientist and scholar Santos presents his groundbreaking theory of the lost civilization, definitively locating Atlantis near Indonesia"—Provided by publisher.
  ISBN 978-1-55643-956-8
  1. Atlantis (Legendary place) I. Title.
  GN751.S276 2011
  001.94—dc22
                        2010040876

      1 2 3 4 5 6 7 8 9 MALLOY 16 15 14 13 12 11

Contents

DEDICATION

This book is dedicated to all those who believe, like myself, that the legend of Atlantis is something more than just a fable or a moral tale invented by Plato or some other ancient mythographer. I hope that the three decades which I have joyfully dedicated to the research of Atlantis were not altogether lost, and that at least some of the seeds which I have scattered far and wide will fall on fertile ground and grow to bear further seeds, turning this type of research into a reputable academic discipline serving the welfare of all mankind.

ACKNOWLEDGEMENTS

This book is the result of some 30 years of research. Over these many years, several people have helped one way or another. Some people helped with expert advice, some with suggestions of themes for research and clarification, others by providing answers to our specialized questions, still others by pointing out errors of substance, and so forth.

Above all, I want to thank my many readers and fans for the support they have provided reading my site and my books and publications, and for the many questions they posed, which forced me to dig deeper. Among these early supporters I name Frank J. Hoff and Renato R. Carneiro, who provided both help and encouragement.

This research would not have been possible without the unfailing help of my wife, who became the "man of the house" while I was lost navigating the South Seas in the wake of Ulysses, Jason, Hercules, Aeneas, Gilgamesh, Alexander, and a host of other ancient explorers. And I also want to thank all my four children, each of whom helped in a great many ways: Bernardo, Carlos, Antonio and Andrea. My blessings and my thanks to them all.

Arysio Nunes dos Santos, February 2005

PREFACE

"What became of the Black people of Sumer?" the traveler asked the old man; for ancient records show that the people of Sumer were Black. "What happened to them?" "Ah," the old man sighed. "They lost their history, and so they died."

<u>Runoko Rashidi, The Ancient Sumerians</u>

Thousands of books have been written on Atlantis since its existence was first disclosed by Plato, the prince of philosophers, some two and a half millennia ago. One may well wonder whether a new book on the subject is really needed. Can anything new actually be said about Atlantis?

The answer is a most emphatic yes!

After all, the riddle of Atlantis has <u>never</u> been solved thus far to the satisfaction of most people, the academic experts in particular. Hundreds of possible locations have already been proposed as the site of Atlantis. Some authorities think that Atlantis is located on an island such as Crete, the Azores, Ireland or Espartel, or even the Canary Islands or the Antilles, the Florida Keys, etc..

Other people think that it is a continental location such as Africa, America, Western Europe, Antarctica and so on. More recently – after we pointed out in detail the fact that Plato specifically speaks of Atlantis as definitively having sunk under the sea – some researchers have concentrated on submerged locations such as the Celtic Shelf, the North Sea Shelf, or sunken regions off Spain (Tartessos), off Cyprus, off Gibraltar and so on.

We have also long been pointing out – for the first time ever in connection with Atlantis – that the sea level rose by 130 meters and more ever since the end of the last Ice Age and that, in consequence of this reality, Plato might well be right, after all. As a result of this enormous rise in sea level, several regions, often of a continental extension, sank in several regions of the world: in Indonesia (Sunda Shelf), in Europe (Celtic Shelf, North Sea Shelf), in the Americas (the Antilles Shelf), and so forth.

Plato also gave the specific date of 11,600 BP [Before Present] for the Atlantean cataclysm of long ago. And this date exactly corresponds to that of the catastrophic end of the last Pleistocene Ice Age and the so-called Younger Dryas event. Now, such exact coincidences are highly unlikely in practice, as all physicists well know, notwithstanding the contrary opinion of many geological experts, who stolidly cling to the now sorely outdated Uniformitarian theories of Darwin and Lyell.

It therefore stands to reason that it is in these now sunken regions of the world that people must begin their quest for Atlantis, if they really want to find it. This is far more logical than just relying on the ever-changing though often negative opinions of experts on the many disciplines directly or indirectly related to Atlantis: Geology, Climatology, Evolution, Anthropology, Archaeology, Linguistics, Comparative Religion and Mythology, Paleoanthropology, etc..

In other words, we must heed scientific facts and reason rather than mere opinions, no matter how authoritative. Scientific theories and expert opinions are no more than mere speculation, often very poorly founded and suggested as a mere working hypothesis of a tentative character. As Plato teaches in his remarkable <u>Critias</u>, one of his two dialogues on Atlantis, these opinions keep changing with time, and are hence unreliable, in contrast to Tradition, which is perennial.

This constant evolution is really the essence of the Scientific Method, the one recommended for doing Science by epistemologists and philosophers such as René Descartes and a host of others.

To put it otherwise, where Atlantis and its location are concerned, we must first look for and list all the possible candidates. Then, and only then, we must retrofit them to Plato's words and statements, in order to verify if the two can be reconciled in some way.

The non-conformities must be deemed unexplained paradoxes or anomalies, to be studied further and clarified with additional research and more reliable data.

Do this for every possible candidate, and let the best candidate stand up, becoming the tentative starting point as the best prospect. Then, begin to gather further data, both traditional and new, and see which candidate best fits the new evidence. Then, try to predict what telltale features will probably be found.

Repeat this over and over again, until all entries are exhausted. Above all, look for the confirmation of these specific predictions: past tropical climate in the Ice Age; Pleistocenic fauna and flora; archeological and geographical evidence, immense mineralogical and gemological riches, and so forth. Eventually, when the right candidate is finally found, all items will start to fall in place, as if by magic.

In a sense, the present book is a dramatic break with the past reality where academics carefully avoided the subject of Atlantis. It is an attempt, by a professional scientist trained in the Scientific Method and in

Epistemology – the philosophical science concerned with the framing of theories and their scientific analysis – to systematically study, perhaps for the first time ever, the various existing theories on Atlantis' location and its unavoidable scientific reality.

What is even more curious is the fact that my original intention was to dispel the physical reality of the myth of Atlantis and related traditions such as the reality of the Flood, of Eden and other such mythical Paradises which I, like most of my academic colleagues, deemed the result of religious zeal or sheer superstitions held by backward natives or extremely ignorant ancients.

Much to my surprise, the vast sunken continent which I discovered in the region of Indonesia turned out to be the only candidate which consistently withstood all attempts at dismissal, even after all the other alternative candidates had been thoroughly eliminated for one or more reasons impossible to overcome in any reasonable way.

In order to find the truth, you must first prepare yourself to cope with it. Otherwise, you will not be able to believe even your own findings. Truth might be so utterly unbelievable as to require an entirely new paradigm in both Science and Religion. In order to accept such novel truths, you must make your mind a razed board where new ideas might be written.

This vast sunken continent, which we might call Sundaland or Australasia – or, even more appropriately, Atlantis or Eden – endured and refused to go away. This after a series of consistent failures to find discrepancies with either known geological facts or the traditional descriptions such as the ones given by Plato, Homer, Virgil, Pindar, Diodorus, Pliny, and a host of other authorities, from Greece and other places both European and otherwise.

Suddenly, as if by magic, the pieces of the giant jigsaw puzzle all began to fall in place. The more facts I adduced, the more I researched this region of the world, the more the predictions of Plato and other mythographers started to come out as true: a tropical climate in the Ice Age; a vast continental extension now sunken, but formerly subaerial, inhabited and crisscrossed by many rivers and canals, etc..

Even the Four Rivers of Paradise – running along the Four Cardinal Directions as they should – were present there, in the very location I discovered, the Sunda Shelf. This unique site also had an abundance of canal networks built in order to control these torrents; a luxuriant agriculture of most extreme antiquity; vast forests and fauna and flora; abundant mineral resources including gold, silver, tin, copper and precious gemstones of all sorts, and so on.

Moreover, this unique location also included a huge agricultural plain of exactly the rectangular shape and enormous size given by Plato; as well as coconuts, bananas, elephants and other resources both biological and mineral described by the great philosopher in his remarkable dialogues. Above all, the actual topography of the region exactly conformed to Plato's detailed description in every essential detail.

Even the names and the local traditions on Paradise and its destruction invariably matched Indonesia, once properly decoded and properly understood and translated. Moreover, the whole region is attended by all sorts of submarine supervolcanoes and tsunami-engendering earthquakes fully capable of causing the terrible events described by Plato, as the recent Indonesian earthquake cogently attests.

When I first proposed my theory and my Indonesian location, as well as the possible connection of the Flood with giant volcanisms and earthquakes, my fellow scientists merely scoffed and walked away hurriedly, under some ill-cooked excuse or the other. Nowadays, they listen with utmost seriousness when I speak of Atlantis-Eden and its demise, or whenever I mention the word "tsunami".

The great philosopher himself connects the Atlantean events with the Flood or Universal Deluge. The reality and date of this event I have scientifically proved in a way that no one can validly deny anymore, according to both Science and Religious and Mythical Tradition.

And it is this fascinating story that, after fully thirty years of dedicated study, I now offer to the dear reader in the present book and in the sequels of books and documentaries already programmed to follow it.

The recent earthquake and tsunami in Indonesia and other nations in its vicinity – one of the greatest such human tragedies ever to occur with perhaps as many as 400,000 fatalities – compels belief that such huge catastrophes of global extent are an inherent feature of Nature, contrary to what many academics even today stolidly maintain.

Oddly enough the Indonesian disaster took place precisely at Christmas time, when the Dies Natalis Solis Invicti ("the Birthday of the Invincible Sun") has been universally feasted since remotest antiquity. As we shall see, the Dies Natalis commemorates not the Day Star itself, but its terrestrial counterpart, the ferocious volcano of Atlantis-Eden.

After all, Indonesia lies at the very heart of the "Pacific Fire Belt", the world's most active tectonic region. Indonesia is located at the boundary of three converging Continental Plates whose motion causes terrible stresses in the earth's crust, leading to the frequent disasters there. As such, Indonesia harbors hundreds of active or quiescent volcanoes, and is seismically most active.

It is quite possible that the Indonesian tsunami was ultimately caused by atmospheric pollution due to the unbridled burning of fossil fuels such as coal, gas and petroleum. This type of pollution leads to an increased CO_2 level in the atmosphere, which leads to global warming.

This global warming in turn results in the melting of the circumpolar glaciers, so that the sea level rises and increased stresses are induced on the earth's crust by a process the specialists call "positive feedback". A rise in sea level of a mere meter or so results in an overload of 1 ton/m^2. Over 1 km^2 this overload becomes 1 million ton/km^2, a huge pressure, even by geological standards.

These stresses further trigger a great series of huge earthquakes and volcanic activities such as the several aftershocks currently witnessed in Indonesia. These events occur as the earth's crust moves in order to accommodate and support this increased loading. And they may again lead to a supervolcanism or a giant earthquake large enough to start a chain reaction of volcanisms and earthquakes of global extent.

These volcanisms may also be explosive and able to darken the atmosphere sufficiently to drive the earth into a new Ice Age, killing so many people as to literally render humans "as rare as the gold of Ophir".

And this is no sheer metaphor. This kind of thing has happened several times in the past, and certainly will again, in the course of geological time. Ask any competent geologist or climatologist and see for yourself. Or read the Internet on supervolcanoes and giant tsunamis.

Dear reader, while reading this book please remember what Max Planck once said of scientific theories. This genial German scientist – the discoverer of the quantization of radiation – pointed out that all revolutionary theories sound a bit ridiculous when first presented. It was thus with Heliocentrism; with Columbus' proposed western navigation to the East Indies; with Relativity and Quantum Mechanics; with the Nuclear Bomb, and so forth.

In time, people get used to the novel ideas presented by the fresh theories, which often grow to become the new scientific paradigm for the younger generations. We are quite sure that this is what will happen to Atlantis, now that its reality and true location are pointed out in detail here and in other works of ours, and now that the Indonesian catastrophe has hopefully sobered us all considerably to the dire consequences of polluting the planet as unreasonably as we are currently doing.

The Author

INTRODUCTION

A pleasant village lies at the surface of the ocean.
May its king be merry and enjoy splendid feasts,
Down to the time when the sea turns fierce and bold...
A wave will suddenly cover the entire region...
A pleasant village, full of people, lies over a lake,
A fortress impregnable, surrounded by the sea.

Book of Taliesin, Poem 21

A Note of Caution on Internet Links

This book contains hundreds of links (about 400) to Internet sites bearing figures and texts related to the theme of Atlantis or illustrating and documenting certain specific topics referred in the main text. This is a revolutionary innovation which will, we believe, become the future trend in books, since it blends the advantages of both the print media and the Internet in a serendipitous way.

The Internet now contains about 10 billion sites readily accessible and searchable via robots such as those of Google. So, this medium offers an indispensable tool for providing independent data about topics on which the reader may desire more information. Though readily accessible, Internet sites are often difficult to sort and select, precisely because of the huge number of possible answers that come in response to any specific query.

Most of the sites returned – often by the thousands or even millions – are of little interest either because they are commercial or amateurish or committed to odd views which seldom interest the ordinary viewer. Hence, it is next to impossible in practice to sort out the information desired in any way other than by trial-and-error, a very annoying and time-consuming activity.

On the other hand, it is impossible to add to books the active links to URL addresses in the Internet. Besides, these addresses are normally very long and quite intolerant to even minor typos. So, we devised the novel technique used in this book of providing reference numbers like this one, following, where the arrow indicates that the readers must go out of the book itself, the way they would normally do in order to access the Internet or, for that matter, other books and journals. ↑xxx

In practice, the readers read the book normally. When they have the time and the inclination, they turn on their PCs in order to consult the Internet at leisure. However, instead of going to the desired sites directly, they head for our Atlantis site, to the page specifically dedicated to this end (www.atlan.org/links). There the reader will also find detailed instructions on how to proceed, should these be required.

Actually, all that is needed is to click on the desired reference number in my site, which is actively linked to the desired site or page. When more than one entry is embodied in the reference number, the active links are incorporated in the specific words which figure in the book as text underlined with dots, as exemplified here.

Another advantage of the hybrid technique introduced by this book lies in the fact that the linked sites are backed up (mirrored) in mine, so that they never go dead. Moreover, only the specific pages or passages or figures are selected and reproduced, sparing the reader from a lot of idle talk.

Besides, the site's Webmaster is charged with constantly updating the links, and extending them, adding more material at the measure that new, interesting information becomes available in the Internet. Again, the figures in the present book are also reproduced in my site, often in color or in far more detail than is possible here, for several technical reasons.

Introduction

Atlantis! Few words evoke a deeper feeling of wonder, of mystery and of an utter, sense of irreparable loss than the name of the Lost Continent. And this fascinating mix of feelings has lasted since the times of Plato, the great philosopher who wrote about Atlantis some two and a half millennia ago, when Greece was still the main center of culture in the Western World.

But is Atlantis just a myth? A moral fable? A Science Fiction creation? Or is it indeed an actual history, somehow restored to the realm of reality by the magic pen of the prince of philosophers? There is a certain something in the story of Atlantis that captures human imagination and instantly fascinates everyone who reads Plato's masterful account of the lost prehistoric empire of global extent.

Perhaps this something is Plato's insistence on the fact that he is speaking truthfully, and that the story of Atlantis is an absolute reality. Or maybe it is Atlantis' immense wealth in gold and gemstones, which Plato describes as being "never before possessed by any kings or potentates, and is not likely ever to be again". Perhaps some adventurers dream of all this fabulous wealth lying there in wait for a lucky researcher wise enough to really believe that Eldorado was something more than just a fable.

Many thousands of books have been written on Atlantis during the twenty five centuries that have elapsed since Plato's time. However, the matter of Atlantis is far from exhausted. In fact, the mystery of its where-abouts has never yet been satisfactorily settled, despite the hundreds of different locations proposed for it just about everywhere in the world: the entire Mediterranean region; the North Sea; the Atlantic coasts of Europe and Africa; the mid-Atlantic region; the Americas, and so on.

As a matter of fact, experts on the subject have been unable to agree even on whether Atlantis really existed or was no more than a figment of Plato's imagination; a moral fable devised by the philosopher to provide an ethical background for the ideal Utopian republic he had postulated in his other dialogues, the Republic in particular.

Some prefer the middling line, and conclude that Plato's report on the Lost Continent is a wild exaggeration of normal, everyday events. Accordingly, they propose that Plato's Atlantis was in fact the same as Minoan Crete, or Mycenian Greece, or Hissarlik's Troy, or the island of Cyprus, or some other petty Bronze Age civilization turned into a veritable Paradise by the wondrous pen of the great sage.

But the fact is that if we remove the wonderful element from Plato's narrative we are left with essentially nothing. Few of us, if anyone, are re-ally interested in the trivial demise of a small culture which was born and disappeared somewhere, leaving little or no imprint of its former existence. After all, such vanished cultures number in the hundreds nowadays.

However, Atlantis is clearly much more than that. To believe Plato, Atlantis was the mother of all civilizations. Atlantis was a vast empire of continental size and worldwide extension. It had mastered navigation and naval commerce, invented metallurgy and stone-dressing, and excelled in the arts and offices of all sorts, including dance, theater, music and sports.

Moreover, the Atlanteans amassed such vast amounts of wealth that Plato himself marvels at it, as we mentioned above. Said otherwise, Atlantis was literally the same as Eldorado and Golden Cipango; as the fabulous Ophir of King Solomon and the paradise of Havilah and Tarshish, "the land where gold is born". The mere mention of Eldorado's name sufficed to set the minds of the early adventurers such as Columbus, Pizarro and Cortez aflame with gold fever.

Notwithstanding their wealth, the Atlanteans were a noble, virtuous people, who despised riches and only pursued wisdom and piety. In time, however, they fell from grace and grew ambitious and covetous. The gods, gathered in council, decided to punish them so that they might again improve. For this purpose they sent cataclysmic floods and earthquakes, and unreservedly destroyed the shining empire, which became a sort of moral scarecrow to all who misbehaved in a similar way.

Truthfully, the story of Atlantis strikes me as being closely similar to a dozen others told in the mythologies of all peoples, the Judeo-Christians in particular: the story of Sodom and Gomorrah; the narrative of the Flood; the fall of Adam and Eve and that of Lucifer, and so forth. The Celts also had very similar traditions on sunken places, witness the poem of Taliesin quoted in the epigraph above or the Legend of Ys, etc..

Homer too tells a similar story of the Phaeacians and of the dire consequences of their disobedience to Poseidon, their patron god and founder. Ghostly Phaeacia closely evokes Atlantis in Homer's picturesque description. The Incas of South America too have similar stories on the Atumurunas, the fallen giants who were punished and exterminated by the Flood sent by God due to their habits of sodomy.

Plato himself identifies the Atlantean cataclysm with the Universal Flood. And he also adds several interesting details which unequivocally lead to the conclusion that this cataclysm was triggered by a titanic volcanic activity attended by ground subsidence and caldera formation; pumice release; giant tsunamis and earthquakes, and so forth. We will return to this theme in more detail later, in the main text.

Moreover, the date given it by Plato – of 11,600 BP [Before Present] – <u>exactly</u> coincides with the one of the end of the Pleistocene Ice Age, as well as of the so-called Meltwater Pulse 1B [MWP1B]. Both of these geologic phenomena were in reality giant cataclysms of global import and of catastrophic consequences far larger than the recent tsunami and earthquakes which currently afflict disaster-prone Indonesia.

Since such global geological events are fortunately rather infrequent, we are compelled to apply Ockham's Razor, and try to unify them all into a single event. Put otherwise, it seems that the cataclysm of which Plato speaks is actually the same as the one to which all sacred traditions of the world also refer. There are literally hundreds of legends on the Flood and on Paradise Lost in virtually all cultures of the world, both primitive and advanced.

The fact that such legends also abound in the New World bespeak their hoary antiquity. In fact, according to the standard doctrines currently taught in essentially all academies the world over, contact between the Old and the New World ceased soon after the end of the Ice Age, when sea levels rose, closing the Beringian Passage, the sole possible communication link between the two worlds, according to scholarly wisdom.

Since the legend in question did in fact reach the New World from the Old, the only way in which this diffusion might have happened was, according to current academic wisdom, via Beringia. This means the contact was effected during the Ice Age or soon after, before that passage definitively closed. We are hence led to conclude that whether it is a legend or actual reality, the event in fact dates from the very epoch in which it is said to have taken place, that of the catastrophic end of the Ice Age.

What this means is that Plato apparently knew precisely what he was talking about, and was in fact inventing nothing at all. It is only recently that the reality of geologic and climatic cataclysms of global import have become accepted by academicians specializing in these and related disciplines, for instance: Archaeology, Anthropology, Paleoanthropology, Paleontology, Evolution, Climatology, and so forth.

Indonesia, the Remnants of Sunken Atlantis

Today, the evidence of Catastrophism is overwhelming, and cannot be denied anymore even by the most diehard of academics and experts of all sorts. Until recently, the possibility that continents may sink was unanimously rejected by all kinds of scholars and scientists, the geologists in particular, as we shall discuss in greater detail in the main text below.

However, we have managed to show that this view, though still prevalent, is false. We have also demonstrated that a whole sunken continent – truly "larger than Libya (North Africa) and Asia (Minor) put together" just as Plato affirmed – actually exists in the region of Indonesia and the South China Sea, in the East Indies, the true site of Atlantis-Eden.

The myriad islands of Indonesia are in fact the mountain tops and highlands of the sunken continent, which was immersed when sea levels rose and its lowlands foundered, at the end of the Pleistocene Ice Age, some 11,600 years ago. This is the exact date given by Plato in his dialogues on Atlantis. And Ockham's Razor requires that we scientists attempt to unify these cataclysms.

Actually, this region of the world has been little explored down to the present date. Geologists had based their understanding on the results they had obtained for the Atlantic Ocean and the Mediterranean Sea, the only areas really studied thus far. But all such generalizations are fraught with perils of all sorts, just as the philosopher Hume warned us. Induction is not a valid procedure, either philosophically or scientifically speaking.

The negative results the scientists had obtained for the Atlantic Ocean or the Mediterranean Sea – where no sunken continents or even islands of any substantial size could ever be found – do not prove that different conditions might not prevail in either the Indian or the Pacific Oceans, not to mention the Arctic and the Antarctic Oceans.

The fact that the specialists all gave up then, instead of looking further away, is highly revealing of the myopic views of Western scholars, who firmly believe that Civilization originated in their part of the world, and nowhere else. The reality is that deep under the waters of the Indo-Pacific Ocean – and more exactly, at their very divide – there lie the remains of a sunken continent of huge size, just as reported by Plato in his two dialogues on Atlantis, the Timaeus and the Critias.

We had the privilege of discovering this sunken continent in Indonesia and of charting it out for the first time ever some twenty years ago. This was far before other would-be researchers started claiming the same discovery, which they very obviously only did after my own detailed writings on the subject had appeared.

The sunken island-continent – for such is literally the meaning of the world nêsos used by Plato – I discovered in the region of Indonesia is truly of enormous size, as can be seen in the maps of the region which I present in my Atlantis site and in the present book.

We might in fact call it a "New World" (Mundus Novus), much as did Amerigo Vespucci when he finally realized that the "islands" discovered by Christopher Columbus were in fact a formerly unsuspected continent, the world's Quarta Pars ("Fourth Part").

We also might, along the same lines, call this new Indonesian continent the world's Quinta Pars ("Fifth Part"), the fifth continent, the one which completes the quincunx so often embodied in the quaint symbolism of Mt. Meru, so extremely important throughout antiquity.

Actually, the new world I discovered is the same as the Taprobane (Tamraparna) of the ancient traditions, also known by traditional names such as Terra Australis Incognita, Antichthon, Antilia, Antipodes, Antiporthmos, Atala and so forth. These names all convey the idea of "Counter-Earth", or "Earth Antipodal", just as does the name of Atlantis itself. And the knowledge of their existence dates from times immemorial.

We will be discussing these matters in greater detail in the main text. But the fact is that these fabled lands were deemed to be far more than mere myth by the ancients. Such was particularly the case with Taprobane, known as the site of Hades and the "Otherworld" (<u>Mundus Alterius</u>) ever since the times of Alexander the Great, and even before.

However, the glory of discovering Atlantis-Eden and its true location and reality is not really mine, after all. All I did was to study the sacred traditions of many peoples, until I was really able to finally understand what they were all about: Greek, Roman, Egyptian, Mesopotamian, Phoenician, Amerindian, Hindu, Buddhist, Judeo-Christian, and so on. In time they all started to make sense.

And it was from them that I eventually came to the true location of Paradise as well as the reality of the Universal Flood and the correct nature of the geological phenomena which triggered the event. The rest of the task was comparatively easy. All I had to do was a sort of "reverse engineering", looking for the scientific data which supported and explained the ancient traditions.

Returning to Indonesia's sunken continent which we have identified with Atlantis-Eden: in contrast to this region of the world, which is rather shallow, the Atlantic and the Indian Oceans are strewn with volcanic islands such as the Azores and the Canaries, which rise directly from the seafloor.

These islands generally belong to the Mid-Oceanic Ridge. As such, these volcanic islands rose rather than sank, and were never part of any sunken continent or even large islands. This is in contrast to the naïve conviction of earlier Atlantologists like Ignatius Donnelly, Lewis Spence, Pierre Termier, Mme. Blavatsky, W. Scott Elliott and several others.

The origin of these ridges and these islands is today fully accounted for by Plate Tectonics Theory. And this shows that <u>they are rising</u> from the seafloor, rather than sinking into it in any possible way. The islands there are mere volcanic peaks formed from basaltic magma characteristic of the seafloor material and are in no way associated with continental material, generally silicic in nature.

It was this realization that led to the widespread skepticism of scientists concerning the possibility of Atlantis ever having been located in these regions of the world. The same thing holds in relation to the Pacific Ocean, where similar conditions prevail.

So, one may also say goodbye to Pacific continents, sunken or not, such as Lemuria and Mu, at least in the terms proposed by the above researchers, among several other now outdated proponents.

The only exception to this geological rule seems to be the region of Indonesia itself. It lies at the intersection of three Continental Plates, which are all three converging into the region, creating enormous stresses on the earth's crust. The result is that the crust is locally pushed up, forming extensive shelves (the Sunda Shelf, etc.) and several mountain ranges of impressive altitude.

These shelves are rather shallow, and become exposed (subaerial) during the Ice Ages, when the sea level drops by well over a hundred meters. This happened during the last Ice Age, the period when Atlantis flourished, according to Plato's detailed report.

This entire region is very prone to huge earthquakes and explosive volcanic activity, often resulting in major disasters, which are well attested in geological records. The recent lethal Indonesian tsunami and earthquake are only the latest of a whole series extending throughout history and prehistory, as witnessed in the geological record of the region.

The recent Indonesian tsunami was only 10 meters or so in height. Despite this fact, it was able to kill 400,000 people, or perhaps even more, according to some estimates. Imagine the destruction caused by a mile high wave of the type described in a great many legends of the Flood the world over. [001]

The island arc of Indonesia actually forms the boundary or divide of the two great oceans, the Pacific and the Indian. During the Ice Age, the whole region was exposed, forming a vast continent attached to Southeast Asia and the Malay Peninsula (formerly called Lanka or Taprobane).

When the sea level rose by 130 meters or so, the very extensive lowlands of the Indonesian shelf became submerged and permanently disappeared under the sea. Only the highlands and the volcanic peaks remained as some sort of mute witnesses of the cataclysm.

And these highlands and volcanic peaks became the myriad islands of Indonesia, a name which means something like "insular India". The few people who survived were forced out, and moved to India proper and other places such as Southeast Asia, China, Polynesia, the Americas, the Near East, and so forth.

Eventually, they reached Europe and other Far Western locations, where they founded the ancient civilizations we presently know about. Of course, the clearest records of this pristine sunken land are preserved in India's sacred traditions on places such as Lanka, Kumari Kandam, Tripura, and so forth. After all, they are the direct inheritors of that great antediluvian culture.

The Word "Island" in Plato

We believe that the Greek word "island" (nêsos) used by Plato actually refers to the islands and the region of Indonesia itself. This word also embodies a sense of "submerged land" and apparently corresponds to what the Hindus call dvipa. This Sanskrit noun specifically refers to paradisial lands now sunken, very much as was also the case with Atlantis.

And this word is generally translated as "island-continent", given that the Hindu dvipas are also said to be of continental size, just as was the case with Atlantis itself. But, as Strabo and other Classical geographers and mythographers expound, the word "island" (nêsos) often designated what we nowadays call "continent". In a rather improper manner, by the way, since these continents in fact "contain" nothing.

Actually, both the Latin word insula and its Greek counterpart nêsos ultimately derive from the Dravidian inču meaning "watery land, marsh". According to Diodorus Siculus, Atlantis sank away in the Tritonides Marshes. This is a remarkable disclosure which tends to confirm our conclusion that Atlantis was a continent now sunken.

Moreover, this mythical region was often identified to the former location of the Garden of the Hesperides (or Atlantides), another well-known metaphor for Atlantis-Eden itself.

The Greek word nêsos underwent metathesis (inču >*niču > *nêsu > nêsos). But this Greek word is visibly the same as the Latin and the Dravidian forms. The Dravidian origin of both the word and the myth cogently suggest a Hindu origin of the whole myth of Atlantis – especially when we also note that the Sanskrit word dvipa literally means "two waters" (dvi-ap), a strange coincidence at best.

We believe that, rather than meaning "having water on two sides" as is so often inferred, the real allusion here is to "two levels of water", one exposed and prevailing during the Ice Ages, and the other one submerged and prevalent in the Interglacials such as the present one.

But this is just a further hypothesis, offered here as food for thought for our dear readers. No matter what, in Plato, the word "island" (nêsos) actually meant what we now improperly dub "continent".

Moreover, it is now becoming quite clear that a great civilization indeed developed in this vast equatorial continent during the Ice Age, at least enough to compel belief in Plato's detailed disclosures or those made by several other ancient authorities, both classical and otherwise.

Among these other Classical authors referring to the story of Atlantis we mention Diodorus Siculus, Theopompos, Homer, Hesiod, Pindar, Apollodorus, Virgil and several other Greek and Roman mythographers and rhapsodes. Then, we also have the similar sacred traditions of practically all peoples on earth, which use other names but clearly refer to the same location, the sunken continent of Atlantis-Eden.

To believe these ancient traditions, this great civilization spread to several distant regions of the world, eventually becoming an empire of worldwide extension.

It is only through diffusion that we are really able to understand the sudden appearance of remarkably advanced technologies such as agriculture, stone-dressing, metallurgy, religion and, above all, of language and the alphabet all over the world during the so-called Neolithic Revolution.

And it is only through the agency of a worldwide empire that we may account for the worldwide diffusion which occurred soon after the end of the Ice Age, the great cataclysm which destroyed Atlantis-Eden, and sent the scant survivors away, in a great diaspora.

As we have managed to show in great detail, most of these advances contain unmistakable clues of having originated from India and, even more exactly, from the now sunken vast region presently called Indonesia ("Indian islands"), formerly an integral part of India itself.

For instance, most human languages embody unequivocal traces of having had a common origin in the sacred tongues of India, such as Sanskrit and Dravida. Such is perhaps the reason why all human languages – including those of the most primitive nations in the world – are so remarkably advanced in both grammar and semantics.

Again, take the instance of the alphabet, one of the most seminal human inventions ever. The alphabet also includes many unmistakable "Indian fingerprints". For instance, the first letter of the alphabet is called aleph (or alpha, etc.). And this word closely evokes the name of the elephant (elephas, in Greek) and, above all, of Ganesha, the elephant-god whose name is by the Hindus placed at the start of any undertakings whatsoever.

We also note that the shape of the Greek alpha: α – the Greek counterpart of the Semitic aleph – closely evokes not a bull, but the head of a bull elephant with its tusk sawn off (like Ganesha, the Hindu elephant-god). If you want to see that fact, draw the "eye" inside the glyph where it would be located on an elephant's head. The Hebrew word aleph does not mean "bull" as often stated, but "cattle, oxen", that is "castrated bulls".

Such is also the reason why it is represented by an inverted bull's head (A), a telltale symbolism. [002]

So do, by the way, the earliest forms of the Semitic aleph. This fact evokes the story of the Golden Calf and its ousting from Israel, as reported in <u>Exodus</u>. Note also that the word aleph is not originally Semitic. Now why would a Semitic letter be baptized with a foreign word? And why would the Semitic alphabet start with an ousted deity, a demonized one?

Besides, the Semitic alphabet also ends with a bull (taw), showing its initiatic Hindu character. Why? These examples could be multiplied at will. And they all show that the standard academic views on the development of civilization in the Near East are utterly in error. For instance, they have dozens of theories on the alphabet's origin, but no clear idea of when, where and how this development occurred: Egypt, Israel, Phoenicia, India, Crete, Mycenae, Turkey, and so on. [003]

We well realize that these uncanny claims may seem far-fetched and even impossible to most people, both expert and lay. But we are prepared to prove these assertions. And we have in fact done so in several detailed documents produced during the many years of detailed research we have dedicated to the problem of Atlantis, and which we plan to publish soon.

It was from the "seeds" planted by the survivors of the cataclysm – the civilizing heroes, gods and angels of which all traditions speak – that the great civilizations of the historic and the prehistoric past ultimately arose: the Indus Valley Culture, Egypt, Mesopotamia, Hatti, Greece, Minoan Crete, Rome, the Incas, Mayas, Aztecs, and so forth.

It is certainly more than a coincidence that all these great civilizations speak of these pristine civilizers, instead of claiming for themselves a glory that would be well deserved, had they in fact invented agriculture and the other arts and techniques that characterize civilization.

For instance, it took several million years for Man to pass from simple flint-knapping to the polished stone characteristic of the Neolithic. And both these techniques and their advancements only spread by diffusion, rather than by independent reinvention. [004]

In one form or another, all these ancient peoples just named – along with several others – also spoke of Paradise as the cradle of Mankind and of Civilization. How could they all independently reinvent exactly the same myth, as unanimously affirmed by today's academic scholars?

The ancients often used names which closely assonate with the ones for Atlantis, another uncanny coincidence: Atlantis, Tala, Attala, Atala,

Patala, Talatala, Thule, Tollán, Aztlán, Aztatlán, Tlaloc, etc.. Moreover, these names mostly mean "the Land Antipodal", an etymology preserved in names of mythical lands and continents such as Antilia, Antichthon, Antiporthmos, Antœci, etc..

What this means is that the ancients well knew that the Paradise Lost was located in the opposite hemisphere, on the other side of the earth. As such, they often referred to Paradise as being located on either the Farthest West or the Farthest East.

Given the fact that the earth is round, one extreme is actually co-terminous with the other, and hence vicinal and actually common. This region of the world to which the ancients allude really corresponds to Indonesia, the actual divide both of the Ocean and of the two hemispheres of the earth: East and West. It was there that, in antiquity, the day started by convention and, hence, the place where the sun was born every day (International Dateline).

It is at the very least curious that the ancients should develop such a sophisticated concept, unless they somehow had a need for it. And this need speaks of the reality of an empire of worldwide extension, spanning the world's countries and oceans. What other reason could there be for coordinating time between distant regions of the world?

The "White Island" of the Universal Traditions

Indonesia was also identified with the so-called "White Island", the actual name of Paradise in several ancient traditions. This name corresponds to the one of Sveta-dvipa (or Saka-dvipa), the paradisial "White Island" of Hindu traditions. It was there – in this "island of the whites" – that the white races (Sakas) originated, in the dawn of time.

These Sakas were also called Yavanas ("Whites"). And the Yavanas are the same as the Ionians (or Iaꜰones, as in Homer). And this name – which is alternatively spelled Javanas – actually derives from the island of Java, one of the main Indonesian islands.

Another of their names was "Ethiopians". The name of the "Ethiopians" was facetiously interpreted as meaning "burnt-faces" by the ancient Greeks. But it really meant "purified by fire", as interpreted in the ancient Hindu sacred texts on the agnishvatthas ("purified by fire"). This ethnonym normally designated both the Berbers and the Libyo-Phoenicians of North Africa.

But it also applied to other white or red races of the Far East (Indonesia), the Tocharians in particular. Homer already referred to "the Pious Ethiopians, located one half in the Far East, where the sun rises, the other half in the Far West, where it sets." These Eastern peoples were the "blond Chinese" of Pliny and Solinus, the "Long-Lived Ethiopians" of Herodotus, and so forth.

In actual terms these Ethiopians correspond to the Tocharians, the Avars, the Sakas, the Hephthalites and other such "White Huns". Rather than "whites" (or Aryans) these White Ethiopians were in fact Chamites. And this means they were "reds" rather than really "whites". In Hindu terms they correspond to the Dravidas rather than to the Aryans proper. As we shall be arguing later on, these peoples from the Far East were part of the Sea Peoples who in fact invaded and settled in the European region as the Greeks, the Etruscans, the Libyans, and so forth.

The Dravidas have, even today, red as their heraldic color (Skt. varna = "caste, color"), whereas the Aryans have white for their own. The present dark color of most Dravidas is due to racial mixing with the local melanoid races (Mundas, Negritos, Melanesians, Australoids).

More or less the same thing happened – except that it was in reverse – with the Aryans. They crossbred with the fair local Alpine races of Europe and the Near East, and became fairer themselves. And this is how the pristine Chamitic Dravidian "reds" of Atlantis engendered both the melanoid race of South India and the fair, white-skinned races of modern Europe and the Levant.

Long considered an idle invention on the part of the Classical writers, the reality of these "white Ethiopians" cannot be doubted any longer. Their well-preserved mummies have recently been discovered in great numbers in the deserts of Mongolia and the Tarim Basin region, the site of the Chinese province of Xinjiang. Some of these mummies are so perfectly preserved that their red or fair hair and even their blue-eyes and tall stature can still be observed in perfect detail.

And so can their wool clothes, often consisting of tartans quite like the ones of the Irish and other nations of Celtic Britain. It is perhaps worth remarking that the word "tartan" ultimately derives from Tartary (Tatary or Mongolia). This fact attests that, in earlier epochs, this type of material came from the Far East, being in all probability produced by the Seres or Tocharians.

These White Huns were also called Hephthalites, an ethnonym of obscure meaning and origin. This name is, according to experts, perhaps related to the one of Naphtali, the son of Jacob. This Hebrew word means "wrestler, warrior", and perhaps alludes to the role they had as mercenary soldiers in the Indian and other Far Eastern courts, Chinese included. [005]

If so, this etymology corresponds to the name of the Jews, apparently derived from the Sanskrit radix yudh, meaning exactly the same as in Hebrew. We will return to this important subject later on.

This type of linguistic evidence leaves little room for doubting the Far Eastern origin of the white races, probably from (Far Eastern) Atlantis itself. From there these survivors of the cataclysm eventually passed to Southeast Asia, and then to China, and finally to Europe and the Near East.

The term "White Island" has, as usual, a dual meaning. It refers both to the fact that the white races originated there and that this land was purified by fire, so that their denizens might improve and be restored to their pristine piety. To put it otherwise, we see that these peoples are the same as the Pious Ethiopians and, even more exactly, the Atlanteans in their pristine, unsullied purity.

The name of the "White Island" is frequent in the traditions of many peoples. The Hindus called it Sveta-dvipa or Saka-dvipa, as we just discussed. And they also referred to their denizens as pitris ("dead ancestors") or, more commonly, as agnishvatthas. This name refers to "those who sat too near the fire" and got burnt by it, becoming purified, more or less as happens to gold.

The "fire" in question here is of course the mighty volcano of Indonesia, the ferocious Krakatoa which conflagrated the whole region of Indonesia in the dawn of time. And it is of course the same as the one which scorched the Ethiopians, the Berbers and the Libyans, as well as other such white or red races originally from the Far East.

Many of these peoples were in fact restored to piety, just as seems to have been the case of the Tocharians and the Celts, to name just two. But most persisted in their vices and their barbarisms. Such seems to have been the case with the barbarous Berbers and the Yüeh-chi, a name that also means "barbarian" in Chinese. This name applied to the Hsiung-nu, the barbarians known in the west as "Huns", and as Huna in ancient India. [006]

The name of the Yüeh-chi also seems to be related to the one used for the Jewish people, if one observes the close assonance of the two ethnonyms. These "barbarians" made persistent attacks against the Chinese, who were forced into building the famous Chinese Wall to protect themselves from the periodic, unprovoked raids and attacks of these ferocious horse-riding nomads and their fierce Mongolian allies.

The word "barbar" ultimately derives from the Sanskrit, and refers to the "balbutiating" tongue these barbarians spoke. And this term invariably applied to the speakers of Dravidian based tongues such as Berber (Tamazight), Guanche, Etruscan, Pelasgian, and so forth.

Some experts even identify these bellicose peoples with Gog and Magog, also said to have lived in the very same region of the world, as attested in the Alexander Romances, etc..

We also encounter "White Island" or "White Land" in the name of Sukhavati, the Western Paradise of Buddha Amitabha. Its western location of course implies the idea already argued that it is placed at the world's divide, between the East and the West.

Sukhavati literally means "abounding in delights". But these "delights" are in fact sweetmeats, the Sanskrit word sukha playing with śukra ("sugar, white"), of which it is a corruption. Ultimately, the meaning of the name Sukhavati plays with the word Kandhava ("candy bar"), another name for Paradise Destroyed in the ancient Hindu traditions.

The name of Aztlán, the Aztec Paradise, is also said to mean "land of purity"; "white land" by several experts. And the same is also true of Yvymaraney, the "Pure Land" or Paradise of the Tupi-Guarani Indians of Brazil. The Navajo Indians of North America also refer to a White Island in connection with Paradise, as I comment in my Atlantis site. And so did the ancient Greeks with the Leukades ("White Islands"), which they too equated with Paradise Destroyed.

This list could be increased further. But the above should suffice to prove the diffusion of the myth of Paradise Lost to all corners of the world: India, China, Tibet, Mongolia, America, Europe, Oceania, and so forth. And, as we just commented, this universal diffusion could only have happened in Pleistocenic times or shortly after, when the Beringian Passage was still open, allowing this type of intercommunication.

Plato's Atlantis Was a Tropical Paradise Even During the Ice Age

It is true, as several researchers have claimed, that Atlantis was in fact located to the west of Gibraltar, very much as Plato affirmed. But the philosopher did not specify how far to the west. In fact, Plato apparently meant the far shore of the Ocean which, to the ancient Europeans, included the Pacific Ocean and invariably meant the East Indies.

Even though Plato may be ambiguous in his statement of this fact – actually a double entendre – Diodorus Siculus is very explicit on the subject. So were the ancient Celts, who invariably sited Paradise on the far bank of the Ocean, in Defrobani (Taprobane) itself.

However, we must also keep in mind the "western" location of the Paradise of Buddha Amitabha, as well as the western route chosen by Christopher Columbus when heading to the East Indies. Columbus' belief was based on many ancient authorities, and should not be easily dismissed.

And it is a fact that the farthest west is coterminous with the farthest east, so that both lie in one and the same location, at "the farthest fringes of the world". Where the East ends, in China and Indonesia, the West begins, and vice-versa, as is clear.

Nor should we forget the detailed references and quotations we make when discussing this crucial issue further in the main text of the present book. It is this propensity of overlooking such obvious facts that has led to the persistent failures of all or most Atlantologists so far, who insist on looking for Atlantis in the vicinity of Gibraltar, as if Plato's words could not be interpreted otherwise.

Moreover, it is important to keep in mind the fact that the ancients – the mendacious Phoenicians in particular – created a whole lot of phony Atlantises just about everywhere in the world, the region around Gibraltar in particular.

These phony Paradises mainly served to confound the competition about the real source of the precious merchandise they peddled to the west: the East Indian commodities such as ivory, precious woods, metals, gemstones, dyes, drugs, perfumes and so forth.

Besides, the secret kept on the true location of Paradise's remains also served to prevent the greedy from desecrating the sacred place. This was the site of Eden, of Paradise turned into the much feared Hades, the Land of the Dead. Only the initiates knew it truly to be in Taprobane, also the site of the Otherworld of the Hindus and the Islands of the Blest of the Greeks, the Celts and the Phoenicians, among other peoples.

In his dialogues on Atlantis, Plato left us such a convincing description of this primordial paradise that few people are able to believe that he was inventing or even embellishing some more ordinary everyday events and locations.

Though Plato's texts are unfortunately short and his planned trilogy or tetralogy was left unfinished, the two short pieces that remained abound in detailed geographical and geological facts, in very precise dates, in architectonic details, and so on.

Anyone who reads Plato's fascinating texts on Atlantis, the Timaeus and the Critias – a few dozen pages only, available on the Internet links just given, both in English and in the Greek original – will probably become convinced that they cannot but refer to anything other than the description of a land that once actually existed, apparently during the Ice Age, when global temperatures were fully 15° cooler than today, and the present temperate regions were unbearably cold. [007]

Despite this circumstance, Plato's Atlantis is a tropical paradise abounding in all sorts of wonders and riches: extensive plains and beautiful fields, dales and mountains; gemstones and metals of every sort, both precious and common; scented woods, perfumes and dyes of a very high value; abundant rivers, lakes and irrigation canals; a most productive agriculture; golden palaces and silvery walls and citadels; elephants and wild animals of all kinds, etc..

But how could Atlantis be deemed a tropical Paradise actually existing during the Ice Age except by being located at the equatorial region, given the fact that earth's now temperate regions were then either covered by ice or totally desiccated due to the absence of rain?

Plato also speaks of temples of unsurpassed richness and beauty, made of solid gold and silver and of hoards of these precious metals and of gemstones which no other nation would ever match.

When we look closer into this matter, it is easy to realize that most of these riches were characteristic of the East Indies, and, specifically, of Indonesia. Indonesia is actually the site of the fabulous "Spice Islands" (or Moluccas), a name whose mere mention caused the brows of the ancient adventurers and explorers to burn with gold fever at the mere thought of the enormous profits to be made there.

It is strange that no researcher ever pointed out these close parallels between Atlantis and the East Indies (Paradise) before. Perhaps people are all blinded by the obsession that "If it is Atlantis, its gotta be located somewhere in the Atlantic Ocean". But is this true?

The fact is that we must clearly understand what the ancients really meant by names such as "Ocean of Atlantis", the real name of this ocean or sea. As we shall see, this name encompassed both the Atlantic Ocean proper and its two main extensions, the Indian and the Pacific Oceans of modern times, one towards the west, the other one towards the east.

In antiquity – and down to the times of Christopher Columbus himself – the modern Atlantic Ocean was considered the Pacific's western extension, and the Indian Ocean its eastern extension. In the figures section of this book we demonstrate this fact with both actual maps and ancient texts such as the well-known world charts owed to Eratosthenes and Strabo, the famous Greek geographers.

As reported in some detail by Plato, the mighty Atlantean empire came to a sudden end in the course of their great war against the Athenians, who were apparently allied to other Greeks, to the ancient Egyptians, and to several other ancient peoples.

During the course of these battles, the ground caved in – probably due to a giant volcanism – and opened up, engulfing the two contending armies en masse, as reported by Plato. All this happened "in the course of a single night and a day of pain" according to the great philosopher.

In consequence, the whole island sank away and disappeared permanently under the waters of the sea. Ever since that time – some 11,600 years ago, as affirmed by Plato – Atlantis has lain on the bottom of the ocean that once bore its name, of Atlantic Sea.

But this name was later transferred, through a great series of mistakes and confusions, to the oceanic water body that now bears it and is located between Europe and Africa on one side, and the Americas on the other, the modern Atlantic Ocean.

The disappearance of Atlantis was so thorough that even its former existence became utterly forgotten. But its memory survived in the sacred oral traditions of all or most peoples on earth, especially the Phoenicians, the Egyptians, the Greeks and the Hindus.

It fell to Plato to restore the legend to the realm of reality, perhaps basing himself on the secret traditions of the Mysteries. These secrets were only told to the initiates themselves, vowed to secrecy under pain of death. This crime – called "impiety" – consisted in divulging to the profanes the real contents of the secret of the Mysteries.

And a great many people paid with their lives for this crime of breaking the code of secrecy. The most notorious of these were Socrates and Cicero, who both paid the ultimate price. Even Plato himself had to flee Athens in order to escape the death penalty due to his unauthorized disclosures. And so also Aeschylus, Seneca, Alcibiades, and even Aristotle, to name only a few of the many victims of the ancient code of conduct.

It is quite likely that the anti-Atlantis stance of most scientists and intellectuals ultimately derives from this ancient legislation which somehow seems to be still in force today one way or the other. With the advent of Christianity, this sort of ferocious censorship was pursued by the Holy Inquisition and its many counterparts all over the world.

In a way, the "heresy" of people such as Leonardo da Vinci, Giordano Bruno, Tommaso Campanella, Pico de la Mirandola, Galileo Galilei and a host of other such intellectuals of the Renaissance was ultimately connected with the theme of Atlantis. And so were the "heresies" of Gnostics such as the Cathars and the Bogomils, not to mention the Amerindians themselves, exterminated by the millions.

The resurgence of Atlantis started during the Renaissance, with the foundation of Plato's Academy in Florence by Marsilio Ficino and Pico de la Mirandola. And this revival of Classicism eventually led to the proposals of adventurers such as Christopher Columbus and other heirs of the Gnostic traditions who well knew that the remains of Paradise Lost were located in the East Indies.

However, no one who really studies the story of Christopher Columbus and his "accidental" discovery of America will fail to realize the obvious fact that he was inspired by the ancient reports on Golden Paradises such as Marco Polo's Cipango; Plato's Atlantis; Solomon's Ophir; the fabulous Atlantic Islands of the medieval geographers, the Eldorado of the Amerinds, and so on.

As we just said, the great Renaissance explorer never doubted that these fabulous islands and partly sunken continents lay in the East Indies, the real focus of Columbus' and other navigations. No matter what, no wise academic or professional expert ignores that the theme of Atlantis is taboo, and can only be treated negatively, with scorn and haughtiness.

Very few academics, if any, are willing to risk their careers, their positions and the cozy grants they get in pursuit of this type of tabooed research, ill-favored by the entire community. Indeed, who has ever heard of a serious scientific expedition being mounted or funded by scientific or academic institutions or government funding agencies in order to research Atlantis and its vicinal seas?

Their justification – no one ever admits cowardice or greed as a reason – is that the very possibility of accepting the reality of Atlantis would inevitably result in the need of a thorough revision of human sciences such as Anthropology and History, not to mention the many ancillary disciplines such as Linguistics, Archaeology, Evolution, Paleoanthropology, Mythology and perhaps even Religion itself.

These academic disciplines are all neatly separated into several different isolated niches, and hardly interact one with the other anymore. So, they never come in conflict among themselves, creating a very comfortable assurance to all who labor in teaching or in research, as I myself did for so many years before I finally retired in order to dedicate myself fully to the research of Atlantis-Eden.

Well, it now seems that the story of Atlantis has finally come full circle, returning to its very start, and beginning anew. If the extremely fertile plains and the golden temples and palaces of Atlantis really existed – as affirmed by Plato and Diodorus, among others – they must exist somewhere on earth, either below the ground or beneath the waves of the ocean.

More hopefully, some remains of Atlantis will be found in the former highlands of the great empire, the ones which remained above the waters after the great cataclysm that ended the Ice Age and caused its enduring demise. And if they exist, they can be found, provided we start looking in the right places, instead of the wrong ones, as we have all been doing so far.

My discovery of the true location of Atlantis and of the actual geological mechanism which caused the submersion of the Lost Continent in the Great Flood is admittedly only a start.

But every journey, no matter how long, starts with the first step, as the philosopher Lao Tzé once taught. Well, I have taken that first stride. And I hope that at least some of my readers will bear with me and read my words attentively and with an open mind, accepting at least some of them in whole or in part.

Atlantis has gained a lot of public recognition lately. A great plethora of new books and researches – some valid and serious, some no more than obvious scams intended to make a fast buck – have recently been published on the subject of Atlantis. And its name is now very often in the press and in the media, as is easy to verify directly.

The Internet has about ten million sites bearing the word "Atlantis" or its equivalents in other languages (Atlántida, Atlântida, Atlantida, Atlantide, and so forth). And its myth has undergone a revival, perhaps stirred by my own publications on the issue. My Atlantis site on the Internet alone has received over 2.5 million visits within the last few years, since it was posted.

In the past 12,000 years or so which have elapsed since the end of the Ice Age, we humans have again managed to rebuild Civilization. And this reconstruction was essentially from scratch, so utter and so global was the destruction triggered by the Atlantean cataclysm.

Of course, the "seeds" left us by Atlantis-Eden greatly speeded this process of recovery. The establishment of the original Civilization must naturally have taken a far greater lapse of time. Inventions are difficult to make and costly to implement. They are hence few and far between. And such was particularly the case in antiquity, when cultures were far more conservative than today.

In the past two centuries we humans had the luck of discovering a great many lost civilizations which had left no visible records nor visible remains: Sumer; Troy; the Indus Valley Culture; Tartessos; Angkor; Minoan Crete, Mycenian Greece, Tocharia, Dvaraka, Chichén Itzá, and so forth.

Most of these lost civilizations were only mentioned in the mythological records and were found by romantic amateur researchers such as Heinrich Schliemann and A. Le Plongeon, who took the ancient traditions as verbatim fact, and followed the ancient texts to the letter.

Why would the traditions on Atlantis-Eden as the site of the Terrestrial Paradise be false if they are told over and over again essentially by all peoples on earth? Why would the ancients all lie, when they should far more likely attempt to appropriate the seminal discoveries such as Agriculture and Metallurgy as their own, had these discoveries really been made by their own people?

Quite likely, the interest in Atlantis is fostered by an instinctive belief that we humans are something more than mere beasts of the field that deserve little more than the daily swill, the <u>panis et circenses</u> of which the Roman rulers spoke with flagrant contempt.

Perhaps it is really true that we humans indeed came from Paradise in the very distant past, and just forgot our divine origins there. And perhaps we just stumbled and fell, more or less like Adam and Lucifer and Atlas, and other such corrupted gods and heroes.

But are we now finally ready to get up again and resume the path that leads to the more heavenly pursuits of which Plato and other ancient sages spoke? Or, perhaps, we are merely all afraid that the cataclysm which once was may be again. So, we willingly feign that it never really happened and that Atlantis-Eden never really existed except in the minds of certain moralists and Bible-thumpers, Plato included among them.

However, no one can sanely deny anymore that the world now again stands at the brink of destruction due to a hubris and arrogance no lesser than that of the Atlanteans themselves; one that drives us all into endless wars fed by endless greed. Nor can anyone sanely deny anymore the reality of past cataclysms of the type described by Plato, despite the contrary assertions of Darwin and Lyell.

The Quest for Lost Atlantis
Is Only Now Feasible

In the last few decades, the search for vestiges of Lost Atlantis has become a far more promising prospect than was ever possible in the past. We now possess scuba-diving equipment which allows the exploration of the shallower sections of the sea. We also now have equipment such as minisubs, sidescan sonars and ROVs which allow us to peek into the deeper seas.

And we also possess well-equipped oceanographic ships and even space satellites which allow us to film or map the oceanographic bottoms down to any depth and to any scale and detail one might possibly desire in the quest for elusive Atlantis.

Additionally, these ships and these institutions have highly qualified technicians and professional scientists, trained in Oceanography and related sciences, who are able to scan and interpret the often elusive vestiges of a sunken civilization of long ago.

Moreover, these scientists now have far more realistic views on Climatic Changes, Catastrophism and on Evolution, which are a far cry from the Victorian doctrines of Darwin and Lyell.

These foolish, Panglossian doctrines are unfortunately still prevalent in the academic curricula of all nations on earth. But they are fast falling in general discredit and will be soon trashed, I am sure, despite the ferocious opposition of reactionaries of all callings and all specialties.

And so will also die out a host of current academic disciplines founded on outright lies dating from Victorian times, the so-called "splitterisms" in particular. Their sole, exclusive intention was the one of providing a pseudo-scientific justification for Colonialism, White-Supremacism and other such now outdated doctrines. [008]

All that is really needed now is to put this formidable paraphernalia to the service of a good cause instead of merely using them for bellicose purposes such as warfare, conquest, domination and espionage.

Again, human and earth sciences such as Oceanography, Geology, Climatology, Seismology, Anthropology, Linguistics, Paleoanthropology, Comparative Religion and Mythology have made enormous strides over the last decades despite the usual conservatism of their academic masters.

Hence, these and other related disciplines may now be put to the service of Atlantis. All that is lacking is the enthusiasm to do so, and to honestly start the quest for Paradise Lost. This quest is, as I have found out, quite akin to the one for the Holy Grail. It is hence the most important research anyone can ever think of, bar none.

The study of sunken coastlines, of the shallower marginal seafloors, and the use of new equipments such as the research sonars and ROVs just mentioned have revolutionized the whole proposition. These techniques have become so precise that they are now used to prospect for ancient shipwrecks and to hunt for submerged treasures, including objects as small as metal coins, statues and ceramic vases such as amphorae and rhytons.

Within the last few years – perhaps stimulated by my own researches on the subject – the whole subject of Atlantology has again gained considerable respectability and interest both among the general public and even within some academic circles. Certain Greek scholars of a high repute are in the process of organizing a worldwide conference of the reality of Atlantis, and have already obtained the following of a great number of participants from all over the world, myself included. [009]

As is clear, the entire situation is currently starting to change. The pieces of the gigantic jigsaw puzzle bequeathed us by our elders are finally beginning to fall in place. It is true that the completion of the whole pattern – the crowning piece, so to say – would be the finding of submerged temples, palaces, walls, statues, roads, smaller artefacts and other such archaeological items.

Hopefully, these artefacts will be reliably dated and unequivocally ascribed to Atlantis itself and no other civilization or colony of later epochs. But this type of find will only occur when we start looking in the right spots, rather than in the wrong ones, as up to now.

It is a pity that so many amateur researchers cry "Atlantis" or "Eureka" whenever any piece of rubble or any impossible artefact, real or not, is found, either on the ground or at any depth.

These finds are often impossibly deep, as is the case of Sarmast's Cyprus and Zelitsky's Cuba, to name just two. Or they are placed in unlikely sites such as Antarctica, Brazil or the Bolivian Andes, which very obviously never sank, at least in the times of Man. But these more obvious frauds are fast being exposed by the experts, and are hence short-lived even in the sensationalist media.

We have ourselves already unequivocally located some archaeological artefacts in the shallow seas of the Indonesian region. Some of these were photographed from outer space by NASA's and NOAA's spy satellites; some observed from the surface by more local methods.

So clear are these vestiges that we are currently in the process of organizing an oceanographic expedition to their site, in order to take a closer look at them. We want to run no risks of over-optimism. And we do not want to risk having sensationalists or ambitious treasure-hunters rushing to the place and claiming my finds as their own, as has unfortunately already happened in the recent past.

Some people are extremely greedy. The mere mention of "Atlantis" or "Paradise" is sufficient to set their brows burning with gold fever, just as it did in the times of Columbus and other conquistadors. And they will stop at nothing for the sake of gain.

I beg my dear readers to be patient, just as I have been myself. I well know that it is frustrating to have to wait until reliable evidence develops. But it is better this way. Better than being frustrated by false finds and false claims, as has been so often the case with Atlantis. Besides, this type of scientific research is extremely costly and hence quite difficult to undertake.

Dozens of sites and dozens of evidences, sunken or not, have been discovered over the past years off the coasts of Florida, Mexico, Cuba, Venezuela, the Bahamas, the Bermudas, and so on. The same is also true even of India, where very promising sites and artefacts have been discovered by Indian archaeologists: in Dwarka, in Mahabalipuram, and other coastal locations.

This is also true of Spain and Portugal. Even remote Japan – this specific spot quite near my own Far Eastern site – has yielded submarine features which many mistakenly believe are artificial, but which are no more than mere geological artefacts of a natural origin. These alleged finds are all illusions, and have not withstood the test of time or of a more thorough scientific scrutiny.

One should not be misled by the fact that unequivocal vestiges of Atlantis are found just about everywhere in the world. Very often, this is the result of over-optimism on the part of the proponents of impossible sites. But sometimes, these vestiges are quite real.

After all, Atlantis was indeed a worldwide empire, despite the widespread incredulity of most academics. So, Atlantis left its cultural and religious imprints just about everywhere in the world. And it is often this indirect diffusional influence that is found, rather than Atlantean artefacts proper.

A Major Scientific Revolution in the Making

The crucial parameters in the search of Lost Atlantis are the dates and the submergence depths. If the archaeological objects can be dated – and they often can, if really authentic and really crucial work is done – the date has to be consonant with the Pleistocenic ones of Plato.

And their depth has also to be correct, and should lie at around 50 meters or so, the depth which corresponds to the right date given by sea level rise. All the rest is sheer illusion and must not be accepted unless they can be verified and validated in some independent way.

If these two parameters – time and submersion depth – are not acceptable, the artefact must be dismissed as a priori impossible by all serious researchers. This, unless some reliable explanation is offered for the discrepancy. And this has to be compelling enough to convince the scientific community at large, if we in fact want to earn both their respect and their recognition.

Unbiased scientific recognition for Atlantis and related issues is extremely difficult if not impossible to get nowadays. But it is ideally required, unless the find is so compelling and so unequivocal as to be irrefutable and convincing by itself.

The science of Atlantology is fast becoming a politically-correct academic discipline. And it has already started a revolution which cannot be stopped anymore. This revolution promises to radically change the whole outlook of the Human Sciences in general, and of Anthropology and Religion in particular.

As is clear, what was once deemed sheer legend is fast turning into hard scientific fact, given the recent advances in marine archaeology and in reliable radiocarbon dating, etc.. We can only anticipate that even more remarkable finds will be made in the forthcoming years, now that the true location of Atlantis is known for sure, at least to believe the many adherents of my theory.

No one has any doubts today that these finds and these advances could be of crucial importance to mankind as a whole. They would force us humans to change the current paradigm on what we take to be the whole prehistory of mankind.

Above all, we will have to revise the stupid notion that our ancestors were all semi-morons incapable of any advance down to a mere 10,000 years or so ago, as if some sort of magic event had happened then, allowing the start of the Neolithic Age.

What actually happened was the catastrophic end of the Pleistocene. And all specialists well know that such catastrophic events set back the species, rather than improve them.

So, how could this terrible global cataclysm be an exception to this well-known evolutionary rule? This was also the case with humans, who apparently underwent a considerable reduction in both physical size and brain size, both of which reached as much as 30% in the average.

A far more logical explanation is the one I gave over two decades ago. The cataclysm caused Atlantis to sink away under the waters, forcing the scarce survivors out.

In their diaspora, these scant survivors moved to other places in the world, the Americas included. And they brought along the "seeds" of Civilization, the agricultural ones included, which they transmitted to the peoples they encountered in their newly adopted homelands.

Since this event – reported in the sacred traditions of essentially all peoples on earth – occurred soon after the catastrophic end of the Pleistocene, the fact that the Neolithic Revolution also started at about that date should come as no surprise to those who accept this far more logical account of facts.

Moreover, this date also closely coincides with the one of 11,600 BP for Atlantis' demise, as given by Plato. And this is again an uncanny co-incidence, particularly when we consider the fact that the very possibility of global cataclysms is even today vehemently denied by the academic scholars.

As I just said, this revolutionary proposal of mine also agrees with the sacred traditions of essentially all peoples on earth concerning the Civilizing Heroes who came down from Paradise and brought to them the seeds of Civilization. Why would they all lie, particularly considering the holy character of this sacred tradition which figures even in the Bible?

Why would all human advancement be stymied for the millions of years during which humans have existed and, above all, for the last million years, when we humans have existed in essentially the modern form of Homo sapiens and then start all of a sudden a mere ten thousand years ago? The a priori odds against this eventuality are simply overwhelming.

And the explanations so far offered are all essentially shallow and scientifically untenable. One such is that Agriculture was actually impossible during the Ice Age, and hence never developed till this age was over. But this allegation is now known to be false.

The Chinese archaeologists and other such researchers have now demonstrated by actual finds of antique artefacts such as grains and tools that rice agriculture was already developed in the Far East as early as 15,000 years ago (in Korea, etc.), and probably much earlier than that, and hence during the Pleistocene Ice Age itself. We will enlarge on this important issue in the main text, further below. [010]

These researchers also managed to prove that wild rice cropping started as early as 25,000 years ago, and probably even earlier. So, it is now archaeologically proved that, contrary to what is presently held in the West, Agriculture first arose in the Far East, rather than in the Near East.

Now, this is the very region where I found Atlantis-Eden to have flourished during the Ice Age. As is clear, the scientific evidence keeps piling up. And a great many sacred traditions on the rise of Agriculture actually speak of Paradise, of the Garden of Eden as its actual source.

Now, this garden or grove was obviously a cultivated region, just as its name implies. The word "garden" implies a "cultivated ground", a "grove" or "orchard". This etymology further suggests that the name of the Garden of Eden is actually due to agriculture arising there.

It is very probable that most traces of this early agriculture have been effaced by the Flood, or permanently buried under the sea. This effacing happened at the end of the Ice Age, when sea level rose by an enormous 130 meters, flooding all coastal locations on earth for a width of 200 kilometers and more. But these sunken locations may still be found when we start to look in the right spots, particularly under the seas of Indonesia and the vicinal spots.

Once this truth is realized, these prehistoric locations will start to be found by the dozen or even the hundreds, as is already starting to happen in China, Japan, Korea, India, Indonesia, Southeast Asia, and so on. The next step would consist in attempting to learn to communicate with the ancient Atlanteans and to really understand the sacred messages they bequeathed us in their myths, their rites and their holy books.

PART I - THE TRUE HISTORY OF ATLANTIS

> *Men occasionally stumble over the truth. But most of them pick themselves up and hurry off as if nothing ever happened.*
>
> <u>Sir Winston Churchill</u>

CHAPTER 1 – INDONESIA AS THE TRUE SITE OF EDEN

Indra... killed the Dragon,
And unleashed the waters,
And split open the bellies
Of the mountains.

The Rig Veda (I:32)

Forewarning Note

The cataclysms of fire and water of worldwide extent of which we speak in this chapter are strictly scientific in nature and extent, in contrast to other proposals such as Pole Shift and a warm Ice Age Antarctica, which are both a geological and a physical impossibility.

Other recently proposed hypotheses, such as the one of the Mediterranean Sea being dry as recently as 11,600 years ago, or of Antarctica being warm during the Ice Age, also do not accord with what is known of earth's geological past.

These unscientific hypotheses collide frontally with all sorts of empirical observations of the local marine sediments which have been conducted by thousands of experts over the last several years. Sedimentology leaves no doubt about the nature – marine or subaerial – of the seafloor deposits, refuting what these authors insistently affirm in their claims.

The definitive ruling of these scientific researches is that the Mediterranean Sea has been full for the last 5.2 million years or so, and that Antarctica has been under ice for the last million years and more, as directly attested by ice cores drilled in situ, and currently studied on a year-by-year basis. I know of no serious scientist who would ever support such scientifically preposterous proposals.

Actually, proponents of the recently dry Mediterranean Sea or the warm Ice Age Antarctica quote no valid sources whatsoever – either scientific or traditional – on these uncanny, scientifically impossible "facts". The only such source that proponents of the dry Mediterranean theory quote is a piece of science fiction written by H.G. Wells (Outline of History, New York, 1921).

But Wells was neither a scientist nor a historian, but only a gifted story-teller full of inventiveness. And he has long been denounced as such by the more serious researchers of these issues. The assertion of the author in question here that "at the moment scientists do not have the technological capability to definitively date... the highly complex geological activities... of the Mediterranean [Sea]" is both false and misleading.

Methods such as Radiocarbon Dating and others based on isotopic analysis or on radioactivity are both highly reliable and extremely accurate, in contrast to what this author claims. The same is also true of the hypotheses which attribute the Atlantean cataclysm to giant meteoritic impacts due to comets and asteroids. Such is the case, for instance of Otto Muck (The Secret of Atlantis, New York, 1976).

Muck was a brilliant German scientist, and his book is wonderfully argued. Alas, his genial hypothesis – even today followed by many other authors – ultimately proved to be utterly wrong. Comparatively speaking, extra-terrestrial impacts are orders of magnitude less frequent than supervolcanic eruptions.

Meteorites and comets invariably leave giant impact craters behind, particularly when they are as big as required for the wiping out of an entire continent, as postulated by Otto Muck. And they also leave behind layers of dust and soot which can be unequivocally identified and dated by researchers, much as is the case, say, of the extinction of the dinosaurs, believed to have been caused by this type of disaster.

Even when they impact the seas, giant meteorites leave behind detectable vestiges, for instance, gravitational anomalies, which are easy to detect by outer space satellites and similar techniques. What is more important, such impacts also leave behind dust layers of an anomalous nature (rich in rare metals such as iridium and osmium, etc.) which may be discerned in the marine sediments.

No such layers exist anywhere in the Atlantic Ocean which may date from such a recent event. This fact is attested by myriad samples collected in situ, and is hence now incontrovertibly established. These giant cataclysms are normally also attended by supervolcanic eruptions, and are widely attested in both the geological and the climatological records.

Even though originally resisted by many experts, these global consequences are now generally accepted by modern geologists. This is in sharp contrast to what occurred some 20 or 30 years ago, when I first started my detailed scientific researches on the Lost Continent of Atlantis, which, I am very sure, were instrumental in leading most people to accept the reality of the Sunken Continent.

Likewise real are also the massive extinctions of all sorts of species of organisms, particularly the large mammals, which took place at the end of the Pleistocene Ice Age, some 11,600 years ago. On that terrible occasion, some 70% of the then prevalent species of great mammals, which existed in the Pleistocene, became extinct.

And these extinct human species included, in all probability, two or three species of humans, such as the recently discovered "hobbits" of Flores island, which became extinct at about that time. In Europe and the Near East the Neandertals and the Cro Magnons also became extinct then. In all probability, the first were the dwarfs, and the second the giants of which most mythologies speak. And it is certainly more than a sheer coincidence that both these "hobbits" and these "giants" lived in Indonesia, the site of Eden. [on]

In the Far East – for instance in Java and in China – Homo erectus also became extinct at about this time, even though he had by then attained a remarkable development both in physical size and in cranial capacity. His body and his brain, like the ones of both Neandertals and Cro Magnons, were fully 30% larger than of today's humans, be they either modern or primitive. [1] *

As we just said, the reality of the Flood cataclysm – which we correctly identified with the catastrophic end of the last Pleistocene Ice Age, date and all – is widely attested in both the climatological and the geological records, and cannot be denied anymore.

Only the proposed mechanism which we believe to have caused the end of the Pleistocene Ice Age – which is a certain fact, but one which remains unexplained by Science so far, despite the enormous interest it attracts – is new and is actually our own.

It is also one which is now fast gaining acceptance by the scientific community at large as a possible cause, since scientists have now come to realize the reality of, and the climatic danger posed by, giant volcanoes such as, say, the Krakatoa, the Toba and the Yellowstone supervolcanoes.

Some twenty years ago we publicly proposed that the dramatic end of the Ice Age was triggered by the huge supervolcanic explosion of the Krakatoa volcano (and perhaps of other vicinal volcanoes as well). This huge explosion actually opened up the Strait of Sunda, separating the islands of Java and Sumatra in Indonesia, and let in the oceanic waters which flooded the interior lowlands of paradisial Atlantis.

---

*   See endnote 1 and others at the end of the book.

This giant explosion is also widely referred to in all sorts of worldwide myths and traditions concerning the Flood, Atlantis and Paradise, which was indeed located in this very region of the world. This giant cataclysm is also universally remembered as the explosion of the Holy Mountain of Paradise – alias Mt. Atlas, Sinai, Zion, Alborj, Qâf, Golgotha, Meru, Mashu, and so on.

The supervolcanic explosion of Mt. Krakatoa also caused a giant tsunami which ravaged and permanently submerged the lowlands of Atlantis, causing their disappearance under the waters. This explosive eruption also triggered the end of the last Ice Age by covering the continental glaciers with a layer of soot (fly ash) which accelerated their melting by increasing the absorption of sunshine.

This mechanism of Ice Age termination – which I originally proposed some twenty years or so ago – has now been dramatically confirmed by NASA's space satellites, which found it to be responsible for upwards of 25% of the global warming and over 70% of the melting of earth's remaining glaciers, both continental and maritime. Its importance cannot be challenged any longer, since the validation is the result of direct observation from outer space. [012]

The giant tsunami caused by the volcanic explosion also resulted in a maritime invasion of the continents surrounding the Pacific region and, above all, in the Antarctic region which faces it at the far south. The result was that the Antarctic glaciers were broken up and lofted by these invading waters and then carried back into the ocean when these invading waters returned to it.

This type of geological process has recently also been confirmed by climatological and oceanographic research, and is now called "Heinrich Event", after its discoverer, Hartmut Heinrich, the German oceanographer who first observed it in the maritime record of the North Atlantic Ocean in 1988.

Heinrich Events – in particular the one called H0 [H Zero] – seem to be directly associated with the cataclysmic end of the Pleistocene Ice Age, and are generally sudden and brutal. This event, H0, apparently occurred at the right date of 11.6 kya (calendrical years) or 10.5 kiloyears (radiocarbon years), terminating both the Younger Dryas and the Ice Age at the exact date given by Plato. [013]

The meltwaters of these enormous, mile thick continental glaciers – either covered by soot and melted away or carried off back to sea as icebergs – flowed back into the oceans, raising the sea level by as much as 130–150 meters. This huge rise in the sea level created tremendous strains and stresses on the crust of the earth due to their extra weight on the seafloor.

On the opposite side of the world, the isostatic rebound of the continents, relieved of the colossal weight of the mile-thick glaciers which formerly covered them, also added to these huge crustal stresses. Earth's crust then heaved and cracked open in the weak spots, engendering further volcanic eruptions and huge earthquakes and giant tsunamis.

This activity feeds back positively into the process, furthering it to completion by means of a chain reaction no different than the seismic paroxysm recently observed in the Indonesian catastrophe, except being far larger in import. Here, the initial earthquake triggered a series of other similar events, fortunately of a smaller size than the first one. But this chain reaction was dramatic enough to suggest that, under appropriate conditions, it may grow indefinitely, much as happens in a nuclear chain reaction.

The result then was the sudden and dramatic end of the Pleistocene Ice Age as well as the causation of the so-called Quaternary Extinctions, which caused the extinction of a great many species of large mammals, certain human ones included. And Man then became "as rare as the gold of Ophir" just as narrated in the Bible and similar sacred traditions of most peoples on earth, the distant Americas included.

Introduction

All nations, of all times, believed in the existence of a Primordial Paradise where Man originated and developed civilization for the first time ever. This story, real and true, is told in the Bible and in Hindu Holy Books such a the Rig Veda, the Puranas, the Ramayana and many others.

The very universality of the myth of the Terrestrial Paradise bespeaks its hoary antiquity. Otherwise, how could the myth have diffused to the distant Americas, if the Beringian Passage became permanently closed soon after the end of the Pleistocene, some 11,600 years ago?

That this Paradise which lay "towards the Orient" was real no one doubts anymore, excepting perhaps some diehard scientists who even today stolidly hold that the different civilizations on earth developed independently from one another.

This, even in such unlikely places as Europe, the Americas, the desertic Near East, or the middle of the Atlantic Ocean, foolishly ignoring the fact that these spots were generally either utterly isolated or covered by ice or dismally desertic during the Ice Ages.

These scientists shut their eyes to the very considerable contrary evidence that has developed from essentially all fields of the different human and earth sciences, particularly the linguistic, the anthropological and the geological and the climatological.

It is mainly on these sciences that we base our arguments in favor of the reality of a pristine Far Eastern source of human civilization traditionally called Atlantis, Eden, Paradise, Elysium, Hades, etc.. [2]

Even in the traditions which speak of a Western Paradise really mean the Far Orient. This is merely the result of – the earth being round and all that – the fact that beyond the farthest east lies the farthest west, and vice-versa. Since the site of Atlantis-Eden really lay beyond the Far East, in Indonesia, it can rightfully be said to lie in the Farthest West.

It was in the Far Orient – and beyond, towards the east – that agriculture (of rice and other grains) and animal domestication were originally invented and developed. These two crucial inventions allowed Man's fixation to the soil, and the resulting prosperity led to civilization and the founding of the first cities ever. It is from there that these remarkable inventions eventually diffused to the rest of the world.

This is a logical conclusion, based on the sacred traditions of most peoples on earth, as well as on application of ordinary scientific commonsense to the probability of such remarkable inventions occurring independently a whole series of times in succession. This is a result of the so-called Bayes' Law, one of the basic tenets of the Mathematical Theory of the Calculus of Probabilities.

This fundamental Law of Nature seems to have been forgotten or simply dismissed by the many supporters of Nicholai Vavilov (1887–1942). Vavilov – whose theories are even today accepted by most investigators – was the great Russian naturalist who introduced the now outdated theory of independent "genecenters" distributed all over the world where agriculture was locally reinvented over and over again, soon after the start of the Neolithic Age, some 10,000 years ago.

It is exactly the opposite sort of thing that is related in the Bible, which attributes the foundation of the first city – and hence the invention of agriculture – to Cain (cf. Gen. 4:17). This first city is there called Enoch (or Henoch or Chenoch = "the Abode of the Pure", in Dravida, the actual language originally spoken in paradisial Atlantis).

The name of "Pure Land" given to this very first of all cities is the same in Hindu traditions of enormous antiquity (Sveta-dvipa, Sukhavati, Atala, etc.). Its end and destruction at the completion of the allotted time of an era is what is meant by Enoch's lifespan of 365 years, "a year of years", an era. [014]

Similarly, the name of the Mesopotamian Paradise, called Dilmun, also means the same thing in Dravida, where the name ultimately originated. Even in the Amerindian traditions, Yvymaraney "the Land of the Pure", is the legendary birthplace of the Tupi-Guarani Indians of Brazil.

And so do the names Aztlán or Aztlatán, the land of origin of the ancient Aztecs of Mexico, and Tollán, the one of the Mayas of Yucatan, both also mean the same thing in their respective tongues. That all these Paradises be named "pure land" is certainly more than sheer coincidence. All in all, it refers to Atlantis itself and its purification by fire and water at the end of its allotted time.

Indonesia as the True Site of Eden

Man – or, more exactly, the anthropoid simians who were our ancestors – apparently first arose in Africa some 3 million years ago. But these primitive hominids soon spread all over Eurasia and beyond, reaching the Far Orient and Australia at least about 1 million years ago or perhaps even more. And it was there that these pristine humans originally developed Civilization.

It was in Indonesia and in the neighboring lands that Man – after emigrating from the semi-desertic Pleistocenic savannas of Africa and from the then fully desertic Middle East – first found the ideal climatic conditions for his full development. And it was there that these pristine humans actually invented agriculture and civilization, innovations which turned us into more that just ordinary animals endlessly engaged in the search of food.

Despite the current views on this matter, these developments actually took place during the last Ice Age, in the Pleistocene. The Pleistocene was the last of the major geological eras, the one which began some 2.7 million years ago and ended only a scant 11,600 years ago, a mere eye's blink insofar as geological time itself is concerned.

The Pleistocene – a name which is Greek for "most recent" – is also called Anthropozoic Era or Quaternary Era or, yet, more loosely, the Ice

Age. During the Pleistocene – and, more exactly, during the glacial episodes which happen at intervals of about 100 thousand years each – the sea level dropped by about 130 to 150 meters (430 to 500 feet) below its present value.

With this, a large coastal strip – the so-called Continental Platform, with a width of about 200 km (= 125 miles) – became exposed, forming land bridges that interconnected many islands and regions. What was by far the most dramatic of such exposures took place in the region of Indonesia, precisely the spot where human civilization and agriculture first flourished.

This vast exposed expanse of the South China Sea then formed an immense continent, indeed "larger than Asia (Minor) and Libya (Africa) put together". This is, as we shall see below, precisely what Plato affirms in his dialogues on Atlantis, despite the contrary allegations of many researchers, both academic and lay.

These so-called researchers prefer to bend facts and words in favor of their pet theories rather than holding to truth and reality, the aims of the true scientific investigator. Their teachings are generally based on now sorely outdated Victorian doctrines such as Uniformitarian Geology and Evolution, which stolidly reject realities such as Catastrophism as a major factor in human evolution and cultural development.

With the end of the Pleistocene Ice Age, the immense glaciers that covered the whole of the northern half of North America and Eurasia soon melted away. Their meltwaters drained off to the sea, whose level rose by the estimated amount of about 130–150 meters just quoted above. With this enormous rise, Atlantis sank away and disappeared for good, along with most of its formerly huge population.

Eden Was in Fact Lemurian Atlantis

Based on Plato's own data, we estimate the population of Atlantis at the time of its catastrophic end to be about 20 million people in the Great Plain alone. This is of course a huge number of people for the early epoch in question here.

This great concentration of humans would only be possible with a highly advanced agriculture, with two or three crops a year, just as reported by Plato. And this great agricultural productivity is even today typical of the whole region, the islands of Java and Sumatra in particular.

Even more precisely, this vast sunken continent was the same as Lemurian Atlantis, the older of the two Atlantises mentioned by Plato. Plato's relation is somewhat garbled in this context, and must be closely read in order to discover this fundamental dualism. The second Atlantis succeeded the first in the same spot, that is the Indonesian region.

Lemurian Atlantis – which we often call Lemuria for simplicity's sake – was the vast plain which the Greeks called Elysian Fields and which the Egyptians named "the Field of Reeds" (Sekhet Aaru). And it is quite likely that the "reed" in question here are really rice growing in marshes (paddies), as it does even today in the whole region. This plain – which Plato describes in great detail in his Critias – was submerged and presently forms the Java Sea, just to the north of Java island.

This Lemurian Atlantis of ours should not be confused with the purely fanciful counterparts of the Theosophists and other such followers of Mme. Blavatsky. Their "Lemuria" is a hypothetical sunken continent of the mid-Pacific region, one which never existed at all. [3]

The Egyptians also called their former homeland "the Ancestral Land" (To-wer), the overseas Paradise where they formerly lived, in Zep Tepi ("Primordial Time"). In contrast, the name of Egypt proper – derived from the Egyptian Het-Ka-Ptah – may be interpreted as meaning "second abode of Ptah", the great god who personified the Egyptian paideuma.

In that tongue, het means "house, abode", whereas ka means "second, double", being considered the soul and counterpart of an individual. The ka or double is more or less like the Guardian Angel of Judeo-Christians and the genius of the Greco-Roman traditions.

In other words, Egypt was really the second abode of the Egyptians. The Egyptians themselves claimed to have originally come from Punt, the Land of the Gods, their first abode on the far side of the Indian Ocean, before it sank and disappeared under the waters of the sea.

As we demonstrate below, Punt was actually located in the East Indies (Indonesia). This sunken continent in Indonesia later became, after its destruction, the "Land of the Dead", the dreadful, forbidden region where no mariner ever ventured to go, as it was in fact "the Land of No Return". This terrible place the Egyptians also called Amenti; the Greeks Hades; the Jews Sheol ("Hell"), and the Hindus Tamraparna.

This Sanskrit name passed into Greco-Roman traditions as Taprobane, alias "the Islands of the Blest" (Makaron Nesos in Greek, and Fortunatae Insulae in Latin). Tamraparna is the Sanskrit name of Taprobane (Sumatra). This name means "Golden Peninsula" in that tongue. Its Dravidian equivalent is Tamaraparana, meaning the same.

Amenti is the Egyptian hell. Amenti is also called Duat, and its meaning in ancient Egyptian is "Westerner". Otherwise said, Amenti is the Western Paradise turned into the Land of the Dead by the cataclysm. The idea of "Westerner" is here connected with the setting of the sun, its daily "death" in the west. [o15]

Its location was in the farthest west, beyond the Ocean, in the same location as Tamraparna. In this sense, the idea of "Westerner" referred to Indonesia, placed beyond the Far East, and hence in the farthest west, as we shall be arguing in more detail in later sections of this book.

Later, these blessed islands came to be known as "Atlantic Islands", not because they were placed in the Atlantic Ocean, as most people think, but because they were known to be the remainder of sunken Atlantis. The highlands remained above the water line when the lowlands were submerged by the rising waters of the oceans at the end of the Ice Age, as we just discussed above.

Interestingly enough, Taprobane, "the Peninsula of Gold", is the very island or continent where the Hindus placed their pristine Paradise, also said to have been sunken in a global cataclysm. They also called it Kumari Kandam, the primordial sunken homeland of the Dravidian Hindus, which is also the same as Lanka or Tripura, the sunken city of the Ramayana traditions.

The gloomy, pestilential marshland which remained above the water was later named Amenti by the Egyptians, Hades or Tartarus by the Greeks, Patala by the Hindus, and Sheol or Hell by the Judeo-Christians.

In the few spared spots which remained paradisial, Taprobane was also dubbed Elysium – or "Islands of the Blest" (Makaron nesos) or Hades – by the Greeks; Punt by the Egyptians; Dilmun by the Mesopotamians; Hawaiki by the Polynesians, Svarga by the Hindus, Sukhavati by the Buddhists, and so on. So we see that the otherworld of Taprobane was believed to exist in three parallel dimensions superposed one upon the other: Terrestrial, Celestial and Infernal.

The Celts – whose legends embody perhaps the most detailed recollection of this sunken golden realm – called this destroyed place by names such as Avalon, Emain Abbalach or, yet, Ynis Wydr ("Island of Glass") or Flath Ynis ("Island of the Heroes"). The Celts also associated this eerie region of the world with the Holy Grail and the resurrection of their dead heroes.

As we already mentioned above, this half-sunken Paradise is also the Yvymaraney of the Tupian Indians of Brazil, as well as the Aztlán (or Aztatlán or Atitlán) of the Aztecs of Mexico, and the Tollán of the Mayas of Yucatan.

This Paradise is the submerged land from which these Indians were obliged to flee when it vanished under the seas, disappearing from sight. This sacred tradition on the Terrestrial Paradise is absolutely universal, so that its reality cannot be doubted anymore.

The Seminal Exodus

The greatest of all colonies of Atlantis was founded in India, perhaps already during the heyday of Lemurian Atlantis, its former counterpart and "mother" of the Atlantean empire. The scant survivors of the Toba cataclysm that destroyed Lemuria were forced to flee their Paradise Destroyed. Apparently, India temporarily became the main refuge and sanctuary chosen by the survivors of the Indonesian Toba cataclysm.

But when conditions in the Indonesian continent eased enough, most people again returned to this paradisial region. Eventually, Mother Atlantis' wondrous "son" – the junior Atlantis again founded in the Indonesian region – reached the apex of human grandeur. But a new catastrophe – again of global extent, but this time caused by the Krakatoa volcano – eventually caused the end of the Pleistocene Ice Age.

And the melting of the huge Himalayan glaciers which resulted also caused huge floods of the great rivers of Asia and rendered the whole region unfit for human habitation for a very large period of time afterwards. These floods also ravaged this remainder of Atlantis, already greatly destroyed by the original volcanic cataclysm itself and the huge earthquakes and tsunamis it caused.

The melting of the huge Himalayan glaciers eventually ended up in the desertification of the whole region they formerly irrigated, in Tibet, the Tarim Basin region, Inner and Outer Mongolia, and so forth. Once again this doomed people was obliged to flee their formerly paradisial homeland.

Throughout the ensuing millennia, when the desiccation worsened, they emigrated to remoter places such as Southeast Asia, China, Mongolia, and so forth.

But the local inhabitants drove them away, and they were forced into nomadism and pillaging, becoming "barbarians" such as the Yüeh-chi, the Tocharians, the Hsiung-nu (or Huns), and so forth. And so, over the millennia, they again emigrated to found the great civilizations of Egypt,

Mesopotamia, Palestine, North Africa, Europe, North Asia, the Near Orient and even distant Oceania and the Americas.

Some of this people came on foot, in huge hordes like those of the Israelite exodus. Others came by ship, like Noah in his Ark or Aeneas with his fleet, to found the great civilizations of the ancient world. And these luciferine wanderers became known by names such as Fomoré, Pelasgians, Etruscans, Hyksos, Berbers, Ethiopians, Libyans, Sea Peoples, and so on.

These names were often associated with the idea of a sunken land turned into a marsh or "island": the Sekhet Aaru, the Tritonian Marshes, and so forth. This "island" was the "island of Atlantis", the <u>nêsos</u> so often mentioned by Plato. And this word corresponds to the Sanskrit <u>dvipa,</u> itself meaning "island-continent" and literally referring to Paradise Sunken.

The great civilizations that we know of, in the Indus Valley, in Egypt, in Mesopotamia, in Asia Minor, Greece, Rome, and even the Americas (Mexico, Peru, etc.) were mostly Atlantean colonies founded by these survivors of the cataclysms which twice destroyed the twin Paradises of Atlantis proper and Lemurian Atlantis, at the start and the end of the last Ice Age and in their wake.

These colonists of course attempted to recreate their Garden of Eden in their new homelands scattered all over the entire world. And, just as reported in the ancient myths everywhere, they naturally civilized the savages they met everywhere, teaching them the arts of Agriculture, Stone Dressing, Metallurgy, Writing, Religion, Mythology, Law, Language, and so forth.

And they also named each local topographical feature after the archetypes of their pristine abode, just as immigrants will normally do everywhere even nowadays. Such is the reason why we keep finding nominal vestiges of Atlantean features everywhere, from Brazil and North America to Spain, Crete, and even Africa and North Europe.

Geographical features named Pillars of Hercules, Mt. Atlas, Tartessos, Gadeira, Hesperia, the Isles of the Blest, Atlantic Islands, Dilmun, Eden, Punt, and so on exist just about everywhere in the world, to the great confusion of the researchers of the elusive Lost Continent of Atlantis.

Such was precisely the intention of the original mythographers: of confounding the inquisitive profanes. Similarly, all the ancient civilizations invariably spoke of Civilizing Heroes such as Quetzalcoatl, Kukulkan, Bochica, Manu, Noah, Aeneas, the Oannés, Hotu Matua, etc..

And, of course, this list also included twin semi-divine heroes such as Atlas and Hercules, or Shiva and Vishnu. These duos of heroes are the omnipresent Twins who founded civilizations just about everywhere, according to the ancient mythologies of essentially all peoples on earth.

Such traditions occur both in the Old and in the New Worlds. And this universal diffusion of the paradisial traditions unequivocally proves that these traditions can only date from the Pleistocenic epochs or soon after, when the Beringian Passage was still open, allowing this intercommunication.

When sea level again rose, after the end of the Pleistocene, all further intercommunication between the Old and the New World became impossible, according to the standard theories on the matter. So, of necessity, these pristine traditions can only date from this remote epoch or earlier, when the Beringian Passage was still open. And this brings us back to paradisial times, the time of Atlantis itself.

CHAPTER 2 - ATLANTIS AND THE "ATLANTIC OCEAN"

A pleasant city sat over the seas,
Its king happy, its feasts splendid.
But the sea rose in great audacity...
And a giant wave covered its entirety.
The pleasant city is now a lake,
An invincible citadel submerged
Deep beneath the sea.

Taliesin

Interestingly enough, the only place so far unclaimed among the literally hundreds of sitings (localizations) of Atlantis is Indonesia. Even more exactly, the place we have in mind here is the now sunken lowlands of the region, better called Sundaland or Austronesia. And this huge sunken continent actually lies in the shallow seas located to the south of Southeast Asia, in the region that presently corresponds to Indonesia.

As commented next, the myriad scattered islands of Indonesia are in fact the highlands and the volcanic peaks which remained when its vast lowlands sank away at the end of the Ice Age. This happened when the sea level rose globally by the huge margin of 130–150 meters, as already mentioned above.

Curiously enough, no one ever thought – before we did so ourselves – of looking for Atlantis in the now sunken region of Indonesia, where we in fact have a huge land of continental proportions.

No one ever dreamed that a real sunken continent once existed there, at least since the "Lemuria" of Hæckel and Sclater was ruled out of existence by better alternatives such as Plate Tectonics Theory. Besides, all researchers so far thought – and in fact still do – that Civilization could only have arisen in the Mediterranean region, the realm of white man.

Of course, no solid evidence of the existence of Atlantis and, even more so, of Lemuria, has ever before surfaced in any serious way through the efforts of former proponents. All the maps and all the evidence so far presented by these earlier Atlantologists is purely conjectural, more or less like the one produced by Heinrich Schliemann in his quest for Troy.

Troy is, as some experts have already proposed, really another alias of elusive Atlantis. Schliemann's Troy is nothing but an illusion, a mere "embodiment of desire" (kamarupa). And so is Blavatsky's Lemuria, its counterpart in the Pacific Ocean. This, despite the many conjectural maps which have been shown in the great many books authored by Theosophists and similar investigators of all shades.

The reason for this absence of realistically acceptable locations is easy to understand: these experts have all been looking for Atlantis on the wrong side of the world. All they ever find, therefore, consists of mirages and falsities such as the ones they often propose.

Most experts generally place Atlantis around the Atlantic Ocean, where it never was. In this they forget that the ancients generally ignored the existence of America, and hence reasonably deemed – like Columbus and other Medieval and Renaissance geographers – that the Atlantic Ocean we know as such today was merely the eastern extension of the Pacific Ocean.

The Pacific Ocean is in fact the "true ocean" (alethinos okeanos or alethinos pontos) of which Plato and other initiates spoke as the one where Atlantis was really located. The Greek word pontos meant the same as "high sea, ocean" in antiquity. We have discovered, and here expound, perhaps for the first time ever, that this "true ocean" of Plato is indeed the Pacific Ocean of which the Atlantic and the Indian Ocean were deemed to be the extensions towards the east and the west, respectively.

By this name Plato and all others invariably designated the "Atlantic Ocean" as the "Ocean of Atlantis" which they all thought to extend all the way to the East Indies, just as Columbus himself did.

Besides, these modern researchers of Atlantis all fail to take into account a basic fact mentioned by Plato and his peers: the huge continent of Atlantis actually sank away and disappeared in the sea. Hence it is under the waters, rather than on earth's surface, that we must effect our quest for Atlantis. This, rather than, say, in subaerial locations such as Bolivia, Amazonia, Cyprus, Florida, Mexico, Antarctica, Morocco, Spain, Crete, and so forth.

The "Atlantic Ocean" of the ancients figures in many maps such as the ones of Eratosthenes and Strabo, to name just two of several such ancient charts dating back to Classical times. These two maps are reproduced and commented in our figures section (Part II), to which we direct the interested reader.

In antiquity, the Atlantic Ocean corresponded to the world-encircling Ocean. Moreover, the description of this ocean – the one we presently misname as "Atlantic Ocean" – figures in a great many reliable authorities: Aristotle, Herodotus, Strabo, Pliny, Seneca, Solinus, Avienus, and so forth. And it had several names: Western Ocean, Outer Ocean, Mare Magnum, or, more usually, simply Ocean.

Some of these authors were Plato's contemporaries or predecessors, and there can be no doubt that the philosopher also partook their views in one way or the other. Such is also the case of more recent authors, for instance the ones of the Middle Ages and the Renaissance.

As we all know, Columbus himself shared these concepts of the ancient authorities just named. And so did the geographers and explorers of his time or earlier: Martin Behaim, Paolo Toscanelli, Pierre d'Ailly, Marco Polo, Sir John Mandeville, Henricus Martellus, and so on.

So, if anything at all is incontrovertibly established it is the fact that the ancients believed that the "Atlantic Ocean" included the Pacific Ocean, and hence extended all the way to the East Indies. It is hence extremely strange that most researchers who believe that Atlantis was located either in Europe or next to it ignore – or at least pretend to ignore for public consumption – this unavoidable reality which is too well documented to be contested by anyone who studies the issue in depth.

And this reality in turn allows us to look for Atlantis – as well as the "Atlantic Islands", their sunken remainders – in the whole of the Outer Ocean, which actually includes the Pacific Ocean. This is precisely the reason why all the ancient explorers actually believed – just as Columbus himself also did – that this ocean extended all the way to the East Indies.

There, they knew – or at least thought they knew – that these fabled islands were actually located, as per the written report of early explorers such as Marco Polo and a myriad such who had visited the region of the Far East from the eastern side, where they got to know the Pacific Ocean itself from its western end.

And they quite logically thought – since they ignored the existence of the interposed Americas – that this vast ocean extend all the way to their own shores, in Europe and Africa. There, they reasoned, based on the traditions of former times, the "island of Atlantis" and its visible remains – the loftier portions which remained behind when sea level rose at the end of the Pleistocene – were truly located.

This fact is now apparently ignored by all or most researchers of the lost continent of Atlantis. But this is sheer folly since, as we now know, the very name of the "Atlantic Ocean" and the "Atlantic Islands" it was fabled to contain ultimately derives from its connection with Atlantis. This fact is explicitly affirmed by Plato himself, and should hence never be lightly dismissed by any true Atlantologist.

The Reality of the Civilizing Heroes

The legends of all peoples invariably tell of Civilizing Heroes, Angels, Gods, or even Demons and Monsters who were their civilizers and who taught them religion, law, agriculture, metallurgy and even the alphabet. Rather than Extraterrestrials or Gods, these Luciferine civilizers are the Fallen Angels; the same all too human heroes who, according to the <u>Bible</u>, fell desperately in love with the beautiful native girls, the Daughters of Men (<u>Gen.</u> 6:1 ff.).

These fallen angels or demi-gods were neither gods nor pure sprites, as most people think. The reality of such spiritual beings is ruled out insofar as Science is concerned. They were the saintly men who came as missionaries from Atlantis, preaching the pristine religion from which arose all the others we now have all over the earth.

How else could these Fallen Angels have successfully mated with human females and bred children, as the passage of <u>Genesis</u> just quoted explicitly affirms, if they had not been human beings themselves? Only a simpleton who utterly ignores the most basic realities of Genetics would believe that some alienigen ufonaut could ever successfully mate with a human male or female.

The a priori odds against this possibility are simply too enormous to be contemplated by any serious scientific researcher. Even genetic manipulation would never solve the problem, as all or most geneticists well realize. Ask any of them, and see for yourself, is the best counsel we can give the dear reader.

To put it bluntly, the theories of authors such as Erich von Däniken and Zechariah Sitchin are sheer Science Fiction, with no support whatsoever in reality or in Science, let alone in Tradition. The sacred traditions of all peoples on earth clearly speak of the human nature of all such angels and heroes, fallen or not. At best, they shared a spark of divinity, no doubt due to their paradisial origin, in Atlantis-Eden, that is, in the Terrestrial Paradise.

In fact, the mysterious "Sons of God" (<u>ben Elohim</u>) of <u>Gen. 6</u> are precisely the same ones identified by Plato with the Atlanteans. The great philosopher explicitly dubs the Atlanteans as "Sons of God". Their sin with the Daughters of Men – and, more probably, the rejection and enslavement of their own hybrid offspring – was apparently the same as the sin which ultimately led to the Flood, at least in the belief of essentially all the ancient nations, the Jews and the Christians included.

This unforgivable sin was also apparently the same as the mysterious "Original Sin" which ultimately resulted in the destruction of Paradise

(Atlantis) and in the Fall of Man. This sin is also visibly the one ritually "washed away" by the Baptism. And Baptism is itself an allegory of the Flood, as St. Jerome and several other Church Patriarchs explicitly acknowledge.

Significantly, all nations on earth have similar beliefs and similar rituals of purification from this primordial taint. This type of sin is apparently similar to the one committed by the masters of slaves of all times who often fornicated with their female slaves in order to engender "improved" slaves whom they of course deemed sub-human and inferior, rather than real human offspring.

Plato actually states precisely this very cause – "too much admixture with mortal blood" – as the reason for the destruction of Atlantis by God (Zeus) in his (unfinished) dialogue on Atlantis, the Critias.

And the same story, generally disguised under some allegoric form such as "pride" (hubris), is also told by Homer concerning the Phaeacians, whom he likewise dubs "Sons of God".

The mysterious Phaeacians and their ghostly tropical island are in fact a disguised replica of Atlantis-Eden itself. Hence, the Lost Continent of the South Seas – the one really sailed by Ulysses and his men – was described by the genial bard several centuries before its real existence was finally disclosed by Plato in his two seminal dialogues on the lost continent of Atlantis.

This tradition also figures in Celtic myths such as the one concerning Mererid, the sinful, corrupt daughter of King Gradlon. Her scabrous conduct actually led to the sinking of the land of Ys. In the Americas we also have several identical myths.

For instance, we have the Colombian myth of Bochica, their Civilizing Hero whose corrupt daughter or wife, Chia, the causer of the Flood, is the visible counterpart of Princess Mererid, the daughter of virtuous King Gradlon, the Flood hero of the Breton Barzaz Breitz.

The Bible Is Right After All

If we read the Bible attentively we will note that it also speaks of two Creations (cf. Gen. 1 and 2). And these two Creations apparently correspond to the two Atlantises commented further above.

In fact, the Bible's chronology as established by both the Jewish rabbis and the Christian theologians establishes the date of Creation at about

3,761 BC (lizira), which some experts such as Bishop Ussher have amended to about 4,004 BC.

This date amounts to about 6,000 years BP [Before Present]. Both these dates are merely approximate, and vary greatly from codex to codex (Talmud, Septuagint, Samaritan, Vulgate, etc.). When considered in tandem, rather than in parallel, as usually done, these two intervals add up to about 11,600 years ago, the very date given by Plato.

Plato also tells of two different Atlantises, one corresponding to Atlantis proper, and the other one to pristine "Greece", of which only a "skeleton" remained after the Flood, the second Atlantis.

This "skeleton" are the highlands of Atlantis which remained emerse when the lowlands had sunk away under the sea. And they presently form the myriad islands of Indonesia, as well as the Malay Peninsula, the main feature of ancient Taprobane.

As we already commented above, these two Atlantises actually correspond to the Virgin Mother and her Wondrous Son. These two universal personages are really personifications of the two Atlantises destroyed in the two sequential cataclysms, the one of Toba volcano in 75 kya [kiloyears ago] and the one of the Krakatoa volcano, 11.6 kya, the one that coincides with the catastrophic end of the Pleistocene Age.

The last date is also exactly the one mentioned by Plato in both the Timaeus and the Critias, give or take a decade or so. This uncanny coincidence – which several authors unduly attempt to distort – leaves no room for doubting that Plato knew exactly what he was talking about.

It is also worth mentioning that, up to the present time, most people wrongly believe that cataclysms of global extent such as the ones of the Universal Flood and the demise of Atlantis are geologically impossible. Many experts also do, following the specious geological and evolutionary doctrines of Darwin and Lyell which are still currently taught in essentially all schools everywhere.

But this view is grossly wrong, as we already showed above. And it is now fast changing, as the reality of Catastrophism has been shown to be an inescapable fact of Nature, one which we cannot dodge, willingly or unwillingly. Foolishly playing the ostrich or wearing pink eyeglasses in order to hide from the unavoidable catastrophe will never work, as we are all fast learning nowadays.

Moreover, the Bible itself tells of two serial destructions of the world by the Universal Flood. These two different narratives of the cataclysm are quaintly embroidered together on each other in the confused narrative of <u>Gen.</u> 6. These two comprise the Elohist and the Jahvist accounts of the Flood.

And these two relations visibly refer to two different events. For instance, in one version, the rains lasted 40 days and 40 nights, in contrast to the other, where they lasted fully 150 days. In one version Noah saves a single couple of each species in his ark, whereas he saves seven such in the other, and so on.

We also note that the tradition narrated by Plato embodies two different cataclysms, which exactly coincide with the Biblical lore, once this tradition is correctly interpreted. Moreover, as we just said above, these two different traditions also exactly agree with the prehistoric events actually observed in the geological and in the ethnological records of all nations on earth.

These two tragedies were caused one by the Toba and the other by the Krakatoa volcanoes in what were in fact the greatest such catastrophes ever experienced by humans in the course of their existence on earth. And, when we trace these worldwide legends to their source, no matter where we actually start from, we invariably end up with Indonesia and the two sequential Atlantises of legend.

First, we have Lemurian Atlantis proper (the "Virgin Mother"), located in Indonesia and destroyed by the Toba cataclysm of 75 kya. Second, we have Atlantis proper (the "Son"), destroyed by the Krakatoa volcano in 11.6 kya, at the close of the Pleistocene Ice Age.

We might even include the third one, the Indus Valley Atlantis, in India, destroyed by the desiccation and foundering of the Indus delta region which set in at the start of the Kali Yuga, in 3,102 BC, as told in the Hindu traditions concerning Dvaraka (Dwarka) and its demise.

These three Atlantises are the ones corresponding to the three former Eras of Mankind of which so many sacred traditions speak. We currently live in the fourth era, the Kali Yuga. And our demise will complete the cycle of four yugas, the Mahayuga, and will be followed by a return to the Golden Age (Satya Yuga).

These three eras also correspond to the divine Trinity (Trimurti) formed by Brahma, Shiva and Vishnu, the archetypes of all such triads we find just about everywhere in the world. In volcanic terms, the three volcanoes correspond to the Toba, the Krakatoa and the Dempo volcano, all three located in the region of Sumatra.

The Elusive Sunken Continent Revealed

As is clear from the above arguments, continents don't really sink. It is really the sea that rises, flooding and submerging entire continents. This is what happened in Lemurian Atlantis and, to a great extent, also in the Indus Valley, the site of the second (or more exactly the third) Atlantis.

Relativists will say that both events – sea level rise and continental sinking – are one and the same thing, at least from the point of view of the local observers. And I agree, being a relativist myself, though by no means a strict follower of Einstein's seminal doctrines.

But geologists will hotly debate the issue, and claim – as they have long been doing – that actual sunken continents are a geological impossibility. It is all a matter of perspective, of relativistic illusions of sundry sorts. But the best ancient sources in fact speak of the sea level rising rather than of continents actually sinking like some sort of giant ship.

Such is the case, say, of that magnificent Hindu saga, the Mahabharata, which tells of the demise of Dvaraka. Dvaraka – which many mistake for Dwarka, its later replica in the Indus Delta region – was the legendary capital of Krishna's worldwide empire, according to the magnificent Mahabharata.

There are in fact two great Indian epics that are patently varying accounts of one and the same historical event. One seems to be the Dravidian account of the great war (the Ramayana), whereas the other one (Mahabharata) seems to correspond to the Aryan one, that of their opponents.

Rama is an alias of Krishna, and Dvaraka is likewise the replica of Lanka, its counterpart in the Ramayana. Or perhaps the two great epics might actually refer to two different geological events, one considered as the repetition of the other.

The legend of Lanka was transferred not only to the region of Dwarka, but to several other regions of ancient India. One such is the island of Sri Lanka which most people even today mistake for true Lanka and true Taprobane. But this identification is merely a mistake, as we show in more detail later, in Parts II and III of the present book.

As in the Ramayana, Dvaraka was also flooded out of the map by the rising waters of the sea. But both accounts are confused, and the two inimical factions are quite close relatives. Very much the same thing also apparently happens in Plato's account of the Great War of Atlantis, where both sides are treated with like sympathy by the prince of philosophers.

More or less the same story is also told of Lanka, in the <u>Ramayana</u>. Here, the ocean is released from its unusual bounds by Rama's arrows, and rises to submerge the golden city, itself just another alias of Atlantis. The hero's fiery arrows are visibly the allegories of a giant volcanism. That fact can be seen in the <u>Mahabharata</u> too, or in some Hindu sacred texts which also describe these events.

Anyone who examines a detailed chart of the oceanic seafloor in the region of Indonesia – for instance the Ice Age Map of the Indonesian region shown in the figure further below – will readily concede that the South China Sea there encircled by the myriad islands of Indonesia indeed formed a region of continental extension during the last glaciation, when the sea level was 130 meters lower than is presently the case.

As is now known, the Ice Age actually ended most abruptly some 11,600 years ago. And this is also the exact date given by Plato in his two fascinating dialogues on the sunken continent which we had the honor of discovering in Indonesia.

Moreover, this is also the exact date of Meltwater Pulse 1B (MWP1B), a sort of Flood event occurring in the region of Indonesia. We will return to this important geological event later on.

Now, how could the great philosopher ever have guessed this crucial date to such an uncanny accuracy if even the reality of such global cataclysms was deemed a geological impossibility down to the times I started arguing its reality, and is even now deemed so by most geologists?

This chart – which we present in <u>Fig. 1 in our Atlantis site</u> for several years now – is based on strictly scientific data which I painfully collected over the last 30 years or so. This, in contrast to most other such sub-surface maps, which are sheer inventions of Theosophists and other such researchers. And it very clearly shows the huge sunken continent of Atlantis in the now submerged region of Indonesia. [016]

This map of ours also shows the extensive sunken strip of Indian Atlantis at the Indus Delta region, in the west coast of India. This is the region of Dwarka, the modern counterpart of Dvaraka, the legendary capital of Krishna already commented above.

Real Dvaraka, in Indonesia, was sunken in the Flood, in the way just commented above. This, in contrast to Dwarka, which was sunken by an earthquake long after, in a later cataclysm. As we just commented, true Dvaraka is really an alias of Lanka, the capital of Ravana's worldwide empire according to the <u>Ramayana</u>.

Many experts mistake Dwarka and Dvaraka even today, since their fates are so similar. But this identification is purely exoteric in character, and should not be deemed real.

Our chart just linked should be compared to the recently published map of the region of Sundaland shown in the below figure. This map was compiled and charted by Dr. Harold K. Voris, Ph. D., Curator and Head of the Department of Zoology of the Field Museum of Chicago (IL). Dr. Voris and the Field Museum – which actually owns the copyright to the maps – were kind enough to allow the publication of their map here in this book, whose main scope, though unconventional, is purely educational. [017]

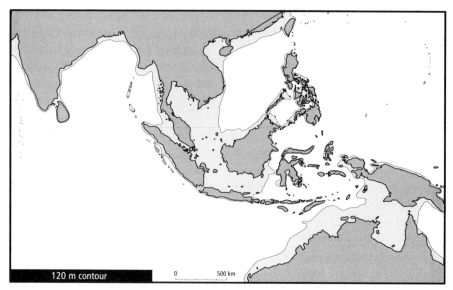

120 m contour   0   500 km

This accurate map leaves no room for doubting the reality of what we are affirming here. It unequivocally demonstrates the reality of sunken Atlantis-Eden beyond reasonable doubt.

And it also shows that our own original map was rather accurate, as can be seen by a direct comparison of the two versions: our own and Dr. Voris'. The Lost Continent proper is the now sunken region of Sundaland, in Indonesia. This whole region was exposed during the Ice Age, forming a vast land of continental proportions.

We are currently planning – and actually in the process of organizing and obtaining the required funds for – an expedition to search the region of Indonesia, where we have already located some artefacts which seem to be connected with Atlantis-Eden itself. As is clear, great events and great archaeological finds are already starting to happen in the East Indies, the very region where we have located Atlantis.

We once again remark that this map of ours – in contrast to most charts presenting other proposed sites for Atlantis and/or Lemuria, etc.

– is strictly scientific and geologically accurate, rather than an invention or a mere replication of the work of earlier researchers, as is normally the case with all such maps of Atlantis Lemuria.

Our map is based on the detailed geophysical reconstruction of the seafloor of the regions in question here. It portrays areas of depth under the isobath of 120 meters or so, and which were obviously exposed during the Ice Age, when the sea level dropped by this much and even more.

In fact, several other similar, strictly scientific maps actually exist. One of these maps was published in the National Geographic Magazine (vol. 174, No. 4, Oct. 1988, pg. 446-7) and is reproduced, for synoptic comparison, in our Atlantis site, linked here. This map shows the world as it was some 18,000 years ago, at the height of the Ice Age. [o18]

This date corresponds to the peak of the last glaciation of the Pleistocene Age, which started about 70 kya or so. This glaciation was probably caused by the giant Toba volcanism which occurred a few millennia before. And its onset was as sudden and brutal as the one which characterized the catastrophic end of the Pleistocene, some 11,600 years ago. [o19]

As can be seen, the map of Fig. 2 illustrated in our site also corresponds quite closely with our seafloor map, which is shown as Fig. 1 in our Atlantis site. Quite recently, NOAA, the National Oceanographic and Atmospheric Agency – the American agency that is a counterpart of NASA for the oceanic underworld – has published detailed maps for the global seafloor which also most exactly confirm our map shown here.

We originally charted the above map some twenty years ago, and it has now been validated to a remarkable accuracy by these recently released NOAA researches, as well as those of Dr. Voris just illustrated. Our map was originally compiled from detailed oceanographic data obtained by oceanographic ships and subs, equipped with sidescan sonar and other such advanced research methods.

This coincidence demonstrates the meticulous care and exactitude we employed not only in the original compilation of the map of our site's Fig. 1, but more generally in all of our revolutionary scientific researches on Atlantis. These maps from NOAA were only recently released to the public, and were not available to anyone before.

They were till now classified for military purposes, and were hence unavailable both to me and to the other researchers at the time I started my own work on the lost continent of Atlantis.

The very fact that they so closely confirm my own maps in almost every detail leaves no doubt about their reality and the huge expanse of the sunken continent of Atlantis in Sundaland. The existence of Sundaland, often confused with Lemuria itself, was first hypothetically proposed by 19ᵗʰ. century naturalists as some sort of landbridge connecting Africa to Indonesia.

This hypothetical landbridge was postulated by Ernst Hæckel and others in order to justify the distribution of lemurs in these two regions of the earth. Such landbridges were later dismissed with the discovery of the reality of Continental Drift, and finally came to be largely discredited by all researchers except perhaps by some Theosophists pursuing the now outdated proposals of Mme. Blavatsky.

But the real existence of this enormous sunken continent in the region of Indonesia – right where Plato and other ancient authorities placed it all the time – proves that, at least in this case, these ancient traditions were all mainly founded on actual fact.

So, the reality of the words of the great philosopher Plato cannot be doubted anymore by those informed on such matters, or by those who take the trouble to verify the facts which we are presenting here and in other chapters of the present book.

In particular, please note in the above map the huge chunk of land – of continental dimensions – to the south of Southeast Asia, which became sunken when the sea level rose at the end of the Pleistocene.

Another sizable hunk of land in the Indus Delta, the site of the second Atlantis, also disappeared then, at the end of the Ice Age, some 11,600 years ago, which, as we have already commented, is also the exact date given by Plato in his seminal dialogues on Atlantis. Another portion of this region disappeared later, at the start of the Kali Yuga, some 5,100 years ago.

No other region in the world displays a similar feature: an entire semi-submerged land of continental extension. And this includes the region of the Americas (not shown) as well as several others. The only logical conclusion is that Atlantis could only have been located in the Indonesian region of the world. This, unless Plato was in fact speaking lies in his very detailed description of the Lost Continent, and was wildly exaggerating the dimensions of sunken Atlantis.

But if Plato was wrong or lying or inventing, his dialogues are worth very little, and should in fact be ranged alongside certain charming novels and romances of antiquity which speak of similar fairylands: the Epic of Gilgamesh; the Ramayana, the Mahabharata, the Odyssey, the Iliad, etc., etc..

By the sheer weight of the scientific evidence confirming many of the descriptions Plato gave of Atlantis, we can safely assume that what Plato wrote may have been slightly embellished by his poetic brain, but was not altogether mere fiction or invention or lies. To think otherwise would be to believe in the far more improbable series of coincidences that our detailed researches of this theme have brought to light.

As the several maps illustrated above show, a huge extension – visibly of continental size and as large as Australia itself – prolonged Southeast Asia all the way down to Australia, to which it was attached in the Ice Age. This continent-sized land was indeed "larger than Asia [Minor] and Libya [North Africa] put together", exactly as Plato affirms.

Plato's usage of the term "island" (nêsos) to describe the Lost Continent was in consonance with his times, and really referred to what we nowadays improperly call "continents", since they in fact contain no oceans and are entirely surrounded by sea water on all sides, just as islands actually are.

This usage of the word "island" is actually instanced in Plato himself, and in the Platonics of later times. An example is Cicero, who utilizes the word in this connection in his remarkable Scipio's Dream. Even Aristotle, the most famous of Plato's disciples, uses the word nêsos (Greek for "island") thus in his famous De Mundo. And so does Theopompos, another Greek author contemporary of Plato.

This sunken continent is here seen to have been about two or three times larger than India, itself a large expanse of land of continental size. And it was also far larger than the continent of Australia itself, here shown somewhat exaggerated due to the peculiarities of the cartographic projection (Mercator's) utilized in this map of ours.

The Great Rift and Hesiod's Khasma Mega

The Indonesian Islands and the Malay Peninsula that we nowadays observe are really the unsunken relics of Atlantis. They are in fact the lofty volcanic mountains which became the volcanic islands of this region, the true site of Paradise spoken of in all ancient traditions.

The sunken portion of continental extension now forms the muddy, shallow bottoms of the South China Sea and the Java Sea in the Indonesian region. It is encircled by the islands of Indonesia and forms the boundary of the Indian and the Pacific Oceans.

Indonesia is part of the volcanic "Fire Belt" which serves as a sort of wall or fence separating the two oceans (Indian and Pacific) and the two worlds (East and West) which they delimited.

Then, as now, Indonesia formed the divide of the New and the Ancient Worlds. Indonesia was also what the ancients called the Ultima Thule ("Ultimate Divide"). Thule also corresponded to what our elders named the "Pillars of Hercules", which, according to Plato, were placed "just in front of Atlantis".

The "Pillars of Hercules" in Gibraltar and in the Bosphorus (or Bosporus) are of course no more than mere replicas or copies of the real Pillars of Hercules (and /or Atlas). The true "Pillars of Hercules" are those of Sunda Strait, the one leading to the interior of the Atlantean continent, in Indonesia. Sunda Strait is the very location of the Krakatoa volcano.

And the Krakatoa is the "pillar of heaven" whose giant explosion caused the demise of Atlantis and also triggered the catastrophic end of the last Pleistocene Ice Age.

The other "Pillar of Hercules", its dual, was in fact Mt. Dempo, the other volcano flanking Sunda Strait, in the region between Java and Sumatra, in Indonesia. But in a former era, this other "pillar of heaven" was the Toba Volcano, which likewise destroyed the world when it exploded and collapsed into its giant caldera.

These Pillars of Hercules were also the impassable frontier between the Old and the New Worlds, separating, as they then did, the Ocean in two separate halves: the Indian in the west, and the Pacific in the east. These two separate world-halves are often mentioned in the Rig Veda. And they were also long called "Orient" and "Occident" in the ancient traditions.

These two "worlds" (or rather, "world-halves") of antiquity are in fact sundered by the volcanic island arc of Indonesia. These volcanic islands are truly the boundary of the Tectonic Plates that form the continents of the region. And they were often personified by "heroes" such as Purusha, Vishnu, Shiva, and, of course, Atlas and Hercules, their Greco-Roman counterparts.

This impassable barrier to navigation, in the region of Atlantis is also insistently mentioned by Plato and several other ancient sources on Atlantis, often under disguises as the ones of the Odyssey (Scylla and Charybdis), the Vadavamukha (or "Submarine Mare") of Hindu traditions, etc..

These pillars or pylons actually flanked the strait which allowed the passage of ships from one side of the world to the other. We will return to this subject in more detail in Part III of the present book.

The myth of Hercules ripping open the Strait of Gibraltar during the course of his tenth labor (the rustling of Geryon's cattle) is really a copy of identical Javanese myths of an extreme antiquity and of other Hindu myths, which can be traced back to the <u>Rig Veda</u> itself.

This Javanese legend is told in detail in the <u>Pustaka Raja Purwa</u> ("Book of the Ancient Dynasties") and there refers to the opening of Sunda Strait by a prehistoric eruption of the Krakatoa Volcano followed by ground subsidence and the formation of the strait. [020]

The very fact that this book's title is in Sanskrit unequivocally betrays its Hindu origin, and attests the fact that Indonesia was still part of India's empire when it was originally written, probably a very long time ago. The event even figures in the <u>Rig Veda</u>, in the verse quoted above on Indra having "split open the belly of the mountains" like some volcano.

Some researchers, for instance David Keys and Ken Wohletz, to whom we will return later on, believe that this giant eruption corresponds to the one which, in 535 AD, caused the demise of the Byzantine Empire. But this claim is actually impossible, as this legend on Sunda's opening is far prior to that date, dating from Classical antiquity or even before.

In contrast to the opening of Gibraltar Strait – which was not formed by any volcanoes and actually dates from far before the times of Man (5.2 million years ago) – the opening of Sunda Strait by a giant volcanism was real, and really dates from relatively recent times such as the Late Pleistocenic dates in question here.

The great rift that came to separate the islands of Java and Sumatra was caused by the subsidence of the Krakatoa volcano, which turned into a giant submarine caldera. This submarine caldera – which the Hindus equate with the Vadavamukha – presently forms the so-called Sunda Strait.

This great rift separating (or linking) the two world-halves was very well known to the ancients. Hesiod called it <u>Khasma Mega</u> ("Great Rift"), a designative he somehow learnt from the ancient Hindus. This people called it (in Sanskrit) by names such as <u>Abhvan</u> ("Great Abyss"), <u>Kalamukha</u> ("Black Hole"), <u>Aurva</u> ("Fiery Pit") <u>Vadava-mukha</u> ("Fiery Submarine Mare"), and so on.

This Great Abyss is also the same one that the Egyptians called <u>Nun</u>, and which the Mesopotamians named <u>Apzu</u> ("Abyss"). Hesiod and several other ancient authorities place this <u>Khaos</u> ("Divide") or <u>Khasma Mega</u> at the world's divide, at the very entrance to Hell (Tartarus). And Hell – or Hades or Tartarus, or Cimmeria, etc. – was the name applied by the ancients to the region of Paradise Destroyed. There were located, as Hesiod mentions, the three realms of space: Heaven, Hell and Earth, coexisting side by side, in different dimensions.

Hesiod also places, in his <u>Theogony</u>, Atlas and his Pillar (Mt. Atlas) in the gloomy spot where the ancient navigators such as Ulysses and the Argonauts all met their doom. As we said above, this terrifying Black Hole – the archetype of all such that haunt Man's imagination since remotest antiquity – is indeed the Krakatoa's fiery caldera, ready to revive at Doom, at least in Hindu traditions on the <u>Vadava-mukha</u>.

A famous <u>Jataka</u> (Buddhist collection of traditional tales) tells the story of Supparaka, the best of sailors, himself one of the many avatars of Buddha. In the course of his navigations in the South Seas, Supparaka one day reached the region known as the Vadavamukha, the fiery Gate of Hell.

The Vadavamukha is in fact the giant submerged caldera of the Krakatoa volcano, the one lurking inside the Strait of Sunda, separating Java and Sumatra. And Supparaka and his ship were miraculously saved at the last moment, when escape already seemed impossible.

This story somehow early reached ancient Greece, where it was converted by Homer into the saga of Ulysses and his navigations in the South Seas region, the masterful <u>Odyssey</u>. In the course of his navigations, Ulysses also met a similar feature, which Homer names Charybdis, the Maelstrom of Death.

Ulysses' ship was wrecked, and his crew were all killed. But the hero himself was also saved by a miraculous intervention of Ino or Leucothea, the White Goddess who herself personifies Atlantis' paideuma. Similar maritime features, the Symplegades or Cyanean Rocks, were also met by Jason and the Argonauts, who were apparently sailing the same Far Eastern region of the world as Ulysses.

Anyone who bothers to compare the details of Homer's poem with the <u>Jataka</u> tale just named will not fail to realize that both originated from a common source of immense antiquity.

And since the actual geographical feature – the Vadavamukha – really exists in the region of Indonesia, and not in the Mediterranean or the Atlantic Ocean, it is rather logical to suppose that the charming tale originated there, and somehow got transferred to Greece in very pristine times, the ones of Homer and Orpheus.

We also find a very similar relation in the so-called <u>Tale of the Shipwrecked Sailor</u>. This tale, which figures in the very early traditions of ancient Egypt, is both strange and traditional. As is clear, these sacred traditions originated in the region of Indonesia, diffusing to the whole of the Old World quite early in time. And only a civilization capable of roving these distant seas would be able to carry out this early process of diffusion of sacred traditions on former paradisial locations.

CHAPTER 3 - WHAT REALLY HAPPENED DURING THE LAST PLEISTOCENIC ICE AGE?

In the Beginning the Golden Womb arose...
And held sundered Earth and Sky...
He propped up the skies, creating space...

<u>The Rig Veda (10:121)</u>

Let us here recapitulate briefly what actually happened during the Pleistocene Ice Age, for its true significance seems to have escaped the notice not only of scientists but also of all Atlantologists so far. This is how Ice Ages start. Converted into clouds by the sun, sea water is carried (as clouds) into the continents by the wind, where it pours down as either rain, hail or snow.

If conditions are right, as they were then, during the Ice Age, this rain water is then retained in glaciers which end up covering the temperate regions of the world in a shroud of ice that is generally one or two miles thick. Deprived of so much water, sea level consequently drops by the huge amount of 130–150 meters and even more, exposing the shallower seafloors all over the world. Normally, this fall amounts to a few millimeters or less.

This exposure was the case of the South China Sea, whose depth seldom exceeds 60 meters or so, as shown in the map of page 46 above or the global one of Fig. 1 and 2 in our Atlantis site. When the Ice Age ends, this process is reversed. The glaciers melt away, and their meltwater quickly drains off into the sea. In consequence, the previously exposed bottoms which had turned into dry land become submerged once again.

As is easy to see, the world works as some kind of electronic flipflop or swing, forever oscillating between these two extremes of cold and heat. Interestingly enough, it is Life itself that re-equilibrates the balance, introducing a negative feedback that counteracts the tendency for the world to freeze or to sizzle, much as happens, say, in Venus and Mars, our two nearest neighbors in the Solar System.

For instance, if carbon dioxide (CO_2) increases in the atmosphere, the temperature tends to go up with the so-called Greenhouse Effect. This is precisely what we observe in sizzling Venus, whose present atmosphere is almost pure CO_2. And this extra CO_2 may well have been introduced by the fall of a comet whose body consisted of this gas, perhaps mixed with water and other substances.

In contrast, in gelid Mars, whose atmosphere (and Life) was very probably all lost in a tremendous cataclysm – seemingly caused by the fall of a meteorite of planetoidal size – the opposite swing apparently took place, again permanently killing all life there.

Wherever Life exists, as on Earth, increased CO_2 content of the atmosphere also results in increased photosynthesis. Plants grow more luxuriantly, fixing and removing the excess of atmospheric carbon dioxide inside themselves, and thus alleviating the situation of excess CO_2.

The opposite process happens if the CO_2 content of the atmosphere is catastrophically reduced for some reason. Photosynthesis is consequently reduced and plant matter – mainly the plankton in the seas, rather than really the tropical forests, as most experts think – decreases, liberating the excess CO_2. This release increases its atmospheric content, tending to restore earth's temperature back to its normal value.

However, this negative feedback compensation by Life only works within very narrow limits, and any excessive perturbation can trigger an Ice Age or a Hot Age, as is fast becoming apparent to experts now that we have discovered how these things really work.

As with flipflops and balances, this transition is enhanced by positive feedback, and quickly leads to the extreme situations which are, once again, stable and permanent until triggered back on again.

For instance if the seas warm up, the solubility of CO_2 in them is strongly decreased, and its atmospheric content increases, tending to further increase earth's temperature, and vice-versa. Moreover, an ice cover effectively reflects sunlight back towards outer space, reducing the amount of solar heat absorbed by the earth. Its temperature consequently drops, the glaciers further increase, until they cover all the temperate regions of the whole earth.

The Actual Cause of the Ice Ages

In the absence of Life, we have the two extremes instanced by our two neighboring planets, Venus and Mars. The causes of the Ice Ages and of the periodic advance and retreat of the continental glaciers is not presently well-known. But, at least to believe the ancient myths, the end of the Pleistocene Ice Age was in fact triggered by the cataclysmic explosion of Mt. Atlas, the one which wiped Atlantis out of the map.

Mount Atlas – "the Pillar of Heaven" which was the pride of Lemurian Atlantis – was an immense volcanic peak in the region that now corresponds to the island arc of Indonesia. To be more precise, this volcanic peak was first the Toba, then the terrible Krakatoa. Both supervolcanoes are still very much alive and highly active even today, despite their monumental explosions and cave-ins in Atlantean times.

Similar huge cataclysms of global import in this remote region of the world are also testified by the tektite belt and the volcanic ash layer that cover most of the South Indian Ocean, Australia, Indonesia and Southeast Asia, as well as much other more local evidence. *4*

The ashes and dust liberated by the gigantic explosion of the Krakatoa volcano were carried away by the winds, eventually settling to cover the glaciers of North Asia and North America with a dark veil of ashes, carbonized matter and soot. The result was an increased absorption of sunlight and a quick melting away of the glaciers that covered all the continents beyond the tropical regions themselves.

The process of glacier melting was far from uniform, as many geologists of the Darwinian school tend to think. The meltwaters of the glaciers quickly flowed back into the seas, creating huge stresses between the overloaded sea bottom and the alleviated continents. Earth's crust cracked and rifted in many places, again giving rise to volcanoes, earthquakes and tsunamis of unprecedented proportions.

And this violent process continued, impelled by its own momentum until it was finally complete and the earth had quit the last Ice Age. In the course of this terrible event – the same one that the myths call the Universal Flood – over 70% of the species of great mammals became extinct.

Thermal Runaway and the Quaternary Extinctions

This self-sustaining, degeneratively increasing process is what we physicists call "positive feedback". And it is identical to the one that causes the transitions of electronic flipflops in electronic computers and other such contraptions.

Once triggered, this type of process literally "feeds on itself", tending to increase in an indefinite way, until some physical limit is reached. And it also corresponds to so-called "chain reactions" taking place in nuclear devices such as A-Bombs and nuclear reactors.

This paroxysmal process is currently being attested in Indonesia, where the huge earthquake which caused the lethal tsunami of Christmas Day 2004 is still giving rise to a great series of likewise terrible aftershocks six months later. And this kind of paroxysm is also observed with giant volcanisms, as attested directly in the volcanological record.

This process also corresponds to another physical process called "thermal runaway". This phenomenon often happens on a global scale, for instance, in the so-called Greenhouse Effect. Increased temperature of the earth tends to liberate the CO_2 (carbonic gas) dissolved in sea water to the atmosphere, since its solubility in water actually decreases with temperature.

This extra atmospheric CO_2 further tends to increase global warming, liberating further amounts of CO_2, and so on. This process goes on until all or most of the dissolved CO_2 is liberated to the atmosphere, and the earth becomes overheated. The reverse happens when Ice Ages start.

This process is possibly what happened on sizzling Venus, perhaps several billions of years ago. And it may well be the case that Venus also had Life, just as Mars apparently also did, as we are finally starting to learn, after NASA's remarkable in situ researches on these solar planets.

Geologists call the widespread mortality that took place at the end of the Pleistocene by the name of "Quaternary Extinctions". But though starting to admit their inescapable reality, Geologists are still far from being able to fully account for their cause. Actually, none of the literally dozens of scientific theories hereto proposed in order to elucidate the cause of Ice Ages have been consensually accepted by the scientific community as a whole.

Among the extinct species we then had several magnificent animals: the mammoth, the mastodon, the saber-toothed tiger, the cave bear, the giant sloths and armadillos, dozens of sundry species of camelids, cervids, cavalids and, very probably, the Neandertal and the Cro-Magnon men as well, who apparently became extinct at about this date for some unexplained reason that can only have been linked to the last Ice Age itself.

So did, as commented in endnote 1, the dwarfish Homo floriensis as well as gigantic Asian Homo erectus. Homo erectus was very probably the same as the very "giants" whose existence is mentioned in <u>Genesis</u> 6. And minuscule <u>Homo floriensis</u> – under 1 meter tall, and only as brainy as a chimpanzee – was probably the same as the dwarfs or goblins of which the ancient myths on Paradise insistently speak. As is clear, the ancient myths in no way overstate the universal extent and the unparalleled violence of the cataclysmic Flood.

The Collapse of the Holy Mountain

As detailed in <u>my Atlantis site</u>, Mount Atlas is the same as the Holy Mountain of Paradise represented by the Great Pyramid. Osiris dead, reposing inside the Holy Mountain, represents the corpse of dead Atlantis or, rather, the many dead of Atlantis, buried and entombed by the gigantic explosion of the Holy Mount Atlas, that is, the Krakatoa volcano. [↑021]

And so does Vishnu reposing on Shesha's coiled body, and Tlaloc, the Aztecan counterpart of Atlas as the dead god of Atlantis. Such is in fact the symbolism of pyramids everywhere. "Sleeping" is a euphemism for "dead". But it also expresses the hope or certainty that Paradise will in time resurrect, along with its many dead.

Mount Atlas is also the same as the Mount Meru of the sacred Hindu traditions, the pyramid-shaped mountain that served as the sky's support according to that mythology. Indeed, the Egyptian word for pyramid, M'R, was most probably read "MeRu", as in the Hindu name of the holy mountain simulated by this monument everywhere.

The ancient Egyptians did not spell out the vowels in their hieroglyphic writing, so that the above reading probably corresponds to the actual one of Mt. Meru (M'R), the exploded Mountain of Paradise illustrated in the so-called Kalachakra mandalas.

In Hindu traditions, Mt. Meru actually served as the Stambha (or Skambha), that is, the gigantic Pillar of Heaven. This Pillar of Heaven was also called Sthavara, essentially the same word as the word <u>Stauros</u>, the name of Christ's Cross in Greek. These uncanny parallels speak of a secret identity. Mt. Meru (or Kailasa = <u>Kav-lasa</u> = "Skull" = Calvary") also served as the support of the Cosmic Tree where the Cosmic Man (Purusha) was crucified, just like Christ, on the Cosmic Cross.

Mt. Meru is also the Holy Mountain of Paradise, endlessly portrayed in India in the very instant of its explosion, in the beautiful Hindu mandalas such as the <u>Shri Yantra</u> and the <u>Kalachakra Mandala</u>. These devices all portray the site of Paradise in the act of being destroyed by a giant confla-gration of its Holy Mountain. And that can only have been a supervolcanic explosion similar to the one of the Krakatoa volcano. ↑*022*

The Meaning of the Myth of the Primordial Castration

In consequence of its giant explosion, Mt. Meru (or Atlas), voided of its magma, collapsed underground like some sort of a punctured balloon. Its former lofty peak sunk away underseas, turning into a giant caldera, the one we already commented above.

Our researches into the ancient world legends have unequivocally shown that the real culprit was indeed the Krakatoa volcano, the same one that still periodically devastates the region of Indonesia whenever it again erupts explosively, as it did in 1883 and other similar occasions. But the same sort of thing also happened in a previous era, when the Toba volcano erupted in 75,000 years BP.

The Krakatoa is presently a giant submarine supervolcano located inside the colossal caldera which now forms the Sunda Strait separating Sumatra from Java. In Hindu myths, its explosion and subsequent fate are usually allegorized as the Primordial Castration, the one which turned the Cosmic Phallus (Linga) into the Cosmic Yoni (or Vulva). And Earth's Yoni is the same as the Khasma Mega of Hesiod, and the Vadavamukha of Hindu traditions.

We see how the apparently absurd traditions of the ancients, when properly clarified, indeed make far more geological sense than the crude attempts at explanation by the modern experts, both scientists and ama-teur researchers of all sorts. It is also precisely to this fact that the legend of Atlas, the Pillar of Heaven, actually refers.

Unable to bear the load of an earth overpopulated with too many gods, Atlas collapsed, and let the sky fall down over the earth, destroy-ing it in a giant conflagration of fire and water. This myth is also told of Hercules, another such "Pillar of Heaven". And this identity reveals the essential identity of the two divine heroes and savior demi-gods.

The name of Atlas indeed derives from the Greek radix tla meaning "to bear", preceded by the Greek negative prefix a-, meaning "not". Hence, the name of Atlas literally means "the one who was unable to bear [scil., the weight of the skies]". Such is the reason why Atlas (and other proud Titans like himself) are often portrayed with weak, serpentine legs.

This Greek name in fact derives from the similar Sanskrit one (Hindu) of Atala. Atala is the Hindu Hell, the site of their sunken Paradise. As in Greek, the name of Atala is also composed of the Sanskrit prefix a-, likewise meaning "not" and <u>tala</u>, meaning "pillar" and, more exactly, the Pillar of Heaven.

In that tongue, <u>tala</u> also means "earth, land", so that the name of Atala can also be interpreted as meaning "no-land". And this is, coincidentally enough, the meaning of the name of Utopia, created by Thomas More as a replica of Atlantis, as those versed in the Occult Sciences well realize.

As we show further below, in Dravida, this word was formed from <u>atta- ala</u>, where the first root corresponds to <u>atta</u> ("footsole, footstep, antipodes") and the second means "sunken land, lagoon, marshland, island". Hence, this Indian etymology corresponds to "the sunken land (or island or dvipa) which lies at the antipodes". This sacred etymology is of extreme practical importance, as it places Atlantis at the Antipodes, the mysterious lost continent or island which figures in ancient Mystery traditions such as the ones of the Platonics and the Pythagoreans.

Egypt, India and the Origin of the Legend of Atlantis

Plato concedes that he learnt the legend of Atlantis from Solon who, in turn, got it from the Egyptian priests. But the Egyptian priests in turn learnt it from the Hindus, that is, in India and Indonesia, where the seminal events in fact took place.

Indonesia is indeed the same as Punt which was the Ancestral Land (<u>To-wer</u>), the "Island of Fire" whence the Egyptians originally came, in the dawn of time. Expelled by the cataclysm that razed their primordial land, in Indonesia (Punt), the Egyptians moved to their Promised Land, in the Near East.

Egypt is really the <u>Het-ka-Ptah</u>, "the second abode of Ptah". Ptah is the Supreme Creator of the Egyptian pantheon. He personified the paideuma of Egypt, that is, its whole civilization and culture. From this "Land of the Gods" also came the Aryans, the Hebrews and Phœnicians, as well as the several other nations of mixed stock that founded the magnificent civilizations of olden times, the Americas included.

Such is really the reason why these nations all spoke obsessively of Paradise Lost and lands that had sunken away. It is from this Paradise Lost – from primordial Atlantis – that sprang all or most of our sacred myths and our religious traditions. And these sacred memories and traditions are in fact the very ones which allowed the ascent of Man above the other beasts of the field.

It is also from Atlantis that, directly or indirectly, issued all or most of our science and technology: irrigation, agriculture, metallurgy, animal domestication, cattle-herding, stone-dressing, astronomy, music, religion, philosophy, the alphabet, the weaving of fibers such as silk and cotton, gunpowder, paper, the magnetic compass, gemstone cutting, and so forth. Even language itself came to us from there, as I have been able to show.

These inventions are often so clever and so advanced that they seem as natural as the air we breathe and the gods we worship. But they are all incredibly advanced inventions that came to us from the dawn of time, from the twin Atlantises we so utterly forgot.

The Chinese affirm that "the fish are the ones which will last discover the existence of water". Likewise, it is no surprise that we humans are so ignorant of the inescapable reality of Atlantis, the Paradise Lost of which all our sacred traditions speak. But Atlantis is really our soul or spirit, the Soul of the World.

This connection also clarifies the Egyptian usage of the word ka ("soul, spirit") to designate their lost homeland. Punt, their Paradise Lost is no other than Indonesia, "the land of spices and perfumes" (Moluccas).

Atlantis and the Illusions of Darwinian Uniformitarianism

Darwin's Theory of Uniformitarian Evolution is a mere illusion of diehard scientists who insist on clinging to hopelessly outdated trash. What the world presents us daily is an endless series of ever larger cataclysms, ranging from atom smashing to supernovas and hypernovas and even the Big Bang itself.

We all recently watched a comet hitting Jupiter and opening a gash bigger than the whole earth on that planet. Mars too shows all signs of having been hit by a planetoidal-sized body, which opened a huge crater on one side of it while pushing up Olympus Mons on the opposite side of that planet.

Perhaps it was this very cataclysm that extinguished Life for good on the Red Planet. Venus too presents vestiges of very similar geological catastrophes, perhaps caused by the huge comet which apparently brought on the excessive CO_2 that presently renders that planet into a literal inferno.

Perhaps we are only stranded here on earth, fated to become extinct when our allotted time expires, who knows when? Life is an illusion, as all things, just as the Hindus insistently teach us with their myths.

According to the Hindus, even the gods eventually die. And when they do, they are replaced by better, more evolved godly forms. But the greatest illusion is the supremacist theory which affirms that Civilizations first arose in an Occidental Atlantis that never was, out of Europoid stock.

However, it is now known for sure that Agriculture and Civilization really evolved in the Far East, during the Pleistocene, at a time when the whole of Europe was almost all covered by mile-thick glaciers.

This prevailing cold rendered survival there very meager and scant, as attested by the geological evidence. The Near East and most of Africa were also both desertic then, due to the prevalent scarcity of rains. So humanity could hardly survive there, let alone thrive and develop Civilization, which requires a mild climate and abundant rains, and plenty of food, in order to prosper.

Plato's Atlantis is, in contrast with icy Pleistocenic Europe or the desertic Middle East of that epoch, described as a luxurious tropical Paradise of the Ice Age, one bedecked with metals, gemstones, horses, elephants, coconuts, pineapples, perfumes, incenses, aromatic and useful woods and other such features that were an exclusivity of India and Indonesia in the ancient world.

Was the great philosopher dreaming all this, or was he indeed basing himself on secret traditions and holy books now lost in the bonfires of the Holy Inquisition and other such witch-hunts so frequent in antiquity? The Atlantic Atlantis is itself a mere delusion, just as are the Cretan, the African, the American, the North European and the Black Sea Atlantises proposed by some researchers.

The Krakatoa Volcano and the "Innavigable Seas" of Atlantis

The true Atlantis, the archetype of all others, is really Indonesia, as we have been arguing. In fact, Atlantis was the extensive sunken continent rimmed by the huge Indonesian island arc now separating the Pacific Ocean from the Indian. This place was the world's divide, the Ultima Thule of which the Greco-Roman traditions so insistently spoke.

It was this primordial Atlantis that served as a model for the second and even the third Atlantis – the one of the Indus Valley – as well as for the myriad other similar Paradises that we encounter in the ancient religious traditions and the mythologies of essentially all peoples in the world.

It is exactly there, in Indonesia, that we actually had Plato's "innavigable seas" of Atlantis, the same as the one also mentioned by the ancient navigators such as Pytheas of Marseille, Himilco, Hanno, Sataspes, Ulysses, Jason, and many other ancient explorers, or by ancient geographers and mythographers such as Pindar, Plato, Strabo and Pliny.

These seas were another central, unique feature of Atlantis. They were rendered "innavigable" (aplôta) as the direct result of the colossal cataclysm, just as reported by Plato and Diodorus and other ancient authorities. As we just mentioned above, the seas of Atlantis (Atlantic Seas) were rendered "innavigable" because they were thickly covered with giant banks of freely floating, fiery pumice stone. More on that later, with actual authoritative quotations, in the next section of this book.

This pumice was ejected by the giant explosion of volcanic Mt. Atlas, the one which caused the foundering of the Lost Continent. A similar phenomenon indeed happened – to a far lesser scale, but big enough to be one of the world's largest catastrophes – in the 1883 explosion of the Krakatoa volcano which we have already mentioned earlier.

The shedding of pumice is characteristic of the Indonesian volcanoes, and is indeed the cause of their explosive eruptions of incomparable force. Their lava is normally rhyolithic (siliceous), and is hence highly viscous in nature. No other known geological process but volcanisms produces pumice stone.

The formation of pumice – that is, spumy vitreous rock – is quite similar to the "popping" of popcorn. The water-soaked siliceous magma of the submarine volcano (in this case Krakatoa) builds up tremendous pressures under the weight of the overlying crust and the seawater above it, which act as some sort of "cork" or "lid" to the molten magma below.

Eventually, this topping crust gives up and bursts, and the eruption occurs, very often explosively. This was exactly what happened when Atlantis was destroyed by the huge explosion of the Krakatoa volcano some 11,600 years ago. Thus released, the overheated water originally dissolved in the hot magma instantly turned into vapor.

As we just said, the magma literally burst like popcorn, except that on a huge scale, turning the whole magma chamber into spongy pumice stone, which was blown up in a giant fiery cloud of dust and debris.

The sea was impelled, creating the huge tsunami which was the event mythified in the Bible as "the Flood from below". Simultaneously, the ashes and soot were thrown up into the stratosphere, as volcanic smoke and fly ash.

This material eventually fell back to the earth and the seas, choking to death all life in the region. And this giant maritime volcanism also vaporized a lot of water, causing the enormous quantities of rain reported as "the Flood from above" mentioned in the Bible and other mythologies.

Further away, in the temperate regions then covered by ice, this soot and lofted dust and ashes settled over the immense Ice Age glaciers, causing their fast melting and triggering the end of the Pleistocene Ice Age, precisely as we related further above. This hypothesis of ours has now been dramatically confirmed by NASA, as commented above, and cannot be reasonably doubted anymore.

As we have demonstrated in great detail, with all sorts of scientific arguments, such was the mechanism which really led the earth out of the Ice Age some 11,600 years ago, at the end of the Pleistocene and the Younger Dryas, in one of the greatest cataclysms ever to hit humanity.

This unbelievably remote date most exactly agrees – to a matter of a decade or so, as is now known – with the one given by Plato for the Atlantean cataclysm. This uncanny coincidence cannot be purely random. The evidence is thus that Plato well knew what he was talking about, and was basing himself on sacred, secret traditions derived from Atlantis-Eden itself.

The Chimerical Atlantises

Interestingly enough, the Hindus associate this sort of stuff – this vitreous "seafroth" (really pumice stone, rather than ambergris) – with Krishna and Balarama, the real archetypes of Hercules and Atlas. Balarama is himself the alias of the Serpent <u>Shesha</u>, whose name means (in Sanskrit) "residue, scum" and, even more exactly, the kind of foam such as ambergris or pumice stone thrown over the beaches by the seas.

This etymon also coincides with that of the "mud" – or "scum, spume, froth, slime" (<u>pelos</u>) – reported by Plato as covering the seas of Atlantis after the cataclysm.

This whole story is in fact a clever allegory of the explosion of Mt. Atlas. This explosion formed the World's Pillar (or "Pillar of Heaven") which allegedly holds up the skies, ejecting the huge amounts of pumice stone and fly ash that covered the whole soil and the seas of Atlantis.

And this thick layer of fiery tephra choked out all the forms of life which existed in this previously paradisial place, the site of Atlantis-Eden. We will return to this subject in more detail in Part III of the present book, and will not repeat this discussion here.

The Titans – and Atlas in particular – were often likened to Serpents (or Dragons), and to "weak-legged", anguipedal, civilizing heroes such as Erychthonius, Erechtheus, Cadmus, Hercules, Quetzalcoatl, Kukulkan, Hephaistos, Atlas, etc.. All such Titans indeed derive their myth from the Nagas or Minas ("Serpent-people", "Dragons", "Fish-people") of India and Indonesia, the archetypes of the Titans of Greece.

As we said above, the Cretan "Atlantis" of certain authorities is actually an illusion. And so are all other sites outside the East Indies of the Far East, the poetic name of Indonesia in antiquity.

Nevertheless, the explosion of the Thera volcano closely parallels the one of the Krakatoa of 1883, as some researchers have noted. But this eruption of the Thera volcano was far too small and far too late and too wrongly sited in relation to the Pillars of Hercules for it to be the right time and the right place.

Moreover, Crete lacked the size and the importance that Plato attributes to Atlantis. Thera and Crete were puny in comparison to, say, its contemporary civilizations in Egypt, Babylon, the Indus Valley and even Mycenian Greece. And the Theran cataclysm never pushed Crete underseas, or even hampered its existence in any notable way, as is now well known.

In fact, the very name of Crete (<u>Kriti</u>) means "swept, cut off, razed", rather than "sunken one", as does the name of Atlantis in the holy tongues of India. So, although Crete was recognizedly "swept" by the Theran cataclysm, it was not really "sunken" by it, as Atlantis actually was.

The story of Crete being the true site of Atlantis is nowadays only pushed by tourism agents bent on attracting visitors to the charming site in the Greek islands. The prehistoric explosion of the Krakatoa volcano which sundered open the Strait of Sunda was, by comparison with the one of the Thera volcano, fully a million times stronger, in terms of the energy actually released and the amount of crust lofted.

If the Theran explosion could sweep away a considerable extent of Minoan Crete, we are led to conjecture that the one of the Indonesian volcano could well have wiped out an entire continental-sized civilization, as it in fact did. And it could also very likely have triggered the chain reaction of positive feedback events that culminated in the catastrophic end of the Pleistocene Ice Age.

The Mid-Atlantic Ridge and Donnelly's Atlantis

Equally illusory are the supposed Atlantises of the Bosphorus (Moreau de Jonnés); of Spain (R. Hennig); of Libya (Borchardt); of Benin in Africa (Leo Frobenius), and the even less likely one of the North Sea (Olaus Rudbeck). The same holds for the Americas (several researchers including Col. Fawcett) and Antarctica (several proponents, among them the British journalist Graham Hancock).

Even more impossible are the purely phantasmal Atlantises located in sunken islands or continents of the Mediterranean Sea (Robert Sarmast) or of the Atlantic Ocean (several proponents) and, particularly, the ones of the Sargasso Sea, as they are not even real geological possibilities.

There are no sunken continents at the bottom of the Atlantic Ocean, period. An extensive and detailed study of this region has unequivocally shown this fact, which cannot and should not therefore be doubted anymore. What this detailed research demonstrated instead is the existence of the Mid-Atlantic Ridge, a vast submarine cordillera that divides the Atlantic Ocean more or less at the middle.

This submarine feature corresponds to the rift from whence the Tectonic Plates issue, causing the continents to drift away from the ridge, at the rate of a few centimeter per year. As is now clear, this is land which is rising, rather than sinking, as Ignatius Donnelly, Mme. Blavatsky and other nineteenth century researchers originally supposed.

Hence, despite the brilliant plea of the two researchers just named, this ridge corresponds not to a sunken continent, but instead to land which is slowly rising out of the seafloor. Such rifts and ridges in fact exist in all oceans, and are not unique features of the mid-Atlantic Ocean. And their volcanic peaks sometimes rise above the sea level in certain spots, forming islands and island arcs.

This is actually what happens in Indonesia and at the Indus Valley, as well as in the Azores, the Madeiras and other such volcanic islands of the ocean. When they do, they normally cause the kind of terrible supervolcanoes and earthquakes that we have been discussing.

It is no coincidence that the two Atlantises we mentioned above are both located precisely at such volcanic spots where the Mid-Oceanic Ridges, or their branches, rise above the surface of the sea. When we inspect the map of the above figure, we also note that a sizable chunk of India actually disappeared in the Indus Delta region at the end of the Ice Age.

This region of India is nowadays known as the Rann of Kutch ("Marshes of Death") and is in fact still sinking underseas, even today. This region is deemed some sort of a Hell by the natives of the region and has been clearly flooded by some sort of terrible cataclysm that also took place at the end of the Pleistocene, just as did the one of Lemurian Atlantis.

This region is merely a replica of Dvaraka, the legendary capital city of Krishna's worldwide empire, as we already discussed above. It is <u>not</u> the site of true Atlantis, which really lies in the region of Indonesia, as we have already agued above. Dwarka, in the Indus Delta region is merely a ghostly Atlantis, a replica imitating the original archetype in Malaysia.

The legends of the <u>Ramayana</u> and the <u>Mahabharata</u> have, already in antiquity, been transferred to this region of India, as well as to Sri Lanka, which both function as reasonable replicas of Atlantis. And they have also been transferred to the Celtic Shelf, where the tradition of sunken cities also survives.

As such, these close replicas have fooled myriad researchers the world over. These legends all speak of sunken cities whose golden spires can often be seen glittering under the waters by the local fishermen.

The Indian legends on Dvaraka and Golden Lanka strikingly evoke the similar tales of the Celts on legendary places such as Ys and Avalon, which occur in the region of Britain and Brittany, and as the Nordic Vineta in the North Sea. But these legends and alleged sightings are all chimaeras, much as are the ones of Sri Lanka, Eldorado, Septe Cidades, Golden Cipango, Cibola, Tartessos, and so forth.

As we just showed, the luciferine civilization of the Indus Valley may be counted as the third avatar of Atlantis. The Indus Valley is one of the greatest and earliest archaeological sites of the present era of mankind.

Civilization was again reborn there and, at its demise, radiated to all other places on earth, as we just said: Mesopotamia, Egypt, Minoan Crete, Mycenian Greece, Etruria, Hatti, Phoenicia, the Americas, and so forth.

This serves to show, once again, that the legend of Atlantis really originated in the Far East, in the region of India and Indonesia, whence it later diffused to the whole world, in one way or the other. As the distance from the real location of Atlantis increases in either time or space, the parallels dim, and the replicas get worse and worse, until they finally fade away and disappear altogether, like some mirage.

CHAPTER 4 - INDONESIAN ATLANTIS AND THE FOUR RIVERS OF PARADISE

*There are three fountains
Under the Mountain of Gifts.
And a city that is buried,
Under the waves of the sea.*

Taliesin

The Four Rivers of Paradise

History often repeats itself. On the occasion of the end of the Ice Age, the greater part of the Himalayan glaciers melted away, pouring their meltwaters down the Indus Valley, in floods that were hundreds of times larger than the ones of today, even when the terrible monsoon storms castigate the entire region.

Such is clearly the record left by the tempests and floods that swept away the third Atlantis, if we also count the first one (Lemurian Atlantis) and its successor (Atlantis proper). This happened during what is really the third of the biblical Floods, the two previous ones being triggered by the Toba and the Krakatoa volcanoes, at the dates and events already mentioned.

This Himalayan meltwater formed the great rivers of the Indus Valley region: the Indus, the Ganges, the Sutlej and the Brahmaputra. These rivers are locally identified to the Four Rivers of Paradise, particularly in Tibetan Buddhism. These four rivers all spring in the neighborhood of Manasarovar Lake, in the region of Mt. Kailasa.

In Hindu-Buddhic traditions, Mt. Kailasa is usually identified with Mt. Meru, the Holy Mountain of Paradise, the actual source of their Four Rivers of Paradise. The replica is so perfect that I was for a long time misled into believing that this was the true source of the myth of the Four Rivers of Paradise which figure so centrally in Hindu-Tibetan traditions.

I then noted that the same thing also happened at the other side of the mighty Himalayas, whence issue the great rivers that irrigate South Asia, China and Southeast Asia, such as the Huang-ho, the Yangtze, the Mekong, and the Irrawaddy.

However, these four rivers are again mere replicas of the Four Rivers of Eden (Atlantis proper), whose sunken remains we recently discovered in Indonesia, as I will be arguing next.

There can be very little doubt that the Indonesian Atlantis – as well as its two main successors, the Indian Atlantis and the Chinese Atlantis just mentioned – are far more than just sacred traditions based on thin air.

They are real, and their destructions are based on actual geological facts such as the Universal Flood, which were in no way exaggerated by our ancestors, in contrast to the false premises of Darwin and Lyell which have fooled so many people for such a long time.

As we just said, we have at long last been able to locate the real, original Four Rivers of Paradise of which the ancient traditions so insistently speak. Through the process of diffusion, these sacred traditions became universal, a fact which explicates why we now find the traditions on these four sacred rivers just about everywhere in the world.

And this includes the Americas, as attested, for instance, in the sacred lore of the "River of Milk" of the Tucano Indians of the Brazilian Amazonia. This mythical river is clearly the same as the Pishon of the Bible, a name which also means the same thing in Dravida, the sacred Atlantean tongue in which this holy book, like so many others, was originally written.

But these paradisial rivers – in Tibet, in China, in the Americas, etc. – are all mere replicas, sheer phantasmagoria having no reality whatsoever. The actual Four Rivers of Paradise are of course now sunken, with Atlantis-Eden itself.

Fortunately, their beds still remain as clearly visible under the waters as one might possibly wish. These river beds were carved when the region was still subaerial, a fact that attests their reality during the Ice Ages, since rivers of course do not flow under the sea.

And their beds are, as just affirmed, attested in the seafloor of the region, as we have managed to discover in the maps originally due to early researchers of the region such as G. A. F. Molengraaff and other naturalists. But the best source on this is by far the detailed maps of Dr. Harold K. Voris already referenced above and reproduced in the figure below. A clearer, original color version is linked here. [1]023

This uncanny discovery we made is a very cogent proof of the reality of Atlantis-Eden and of Paradise, its mythical counterpart. One tradition reinforces and supports the other, and they all add up to establish the reality of Atlantis as the Terrestrial Paradise of which the traditions of virtually all peoples on earth invariably speak.

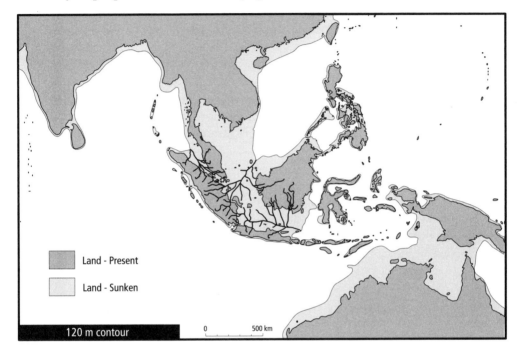

Unfortunately, the more detailed discussion of this fascinating subject does not fit here, and was left for an already planned sequel of the present book, one which centers on the theme of Paradise itself. So, we here limit ourselves to giving only the barest essentials of our seminal discovery. First of all, we note that the seafloor of the region is crisscrossed by riverbeds. This geological fact attests that the region was subaerial and well-watered during the Ice Age, the time of Atlantis.

Consider, in the map of the seafloor of the region of Indonesia just linked, the region around the islands of Java and Sumatra. This is the region at the center of the figure, the one near Australia, shown at the bottom right. Above all, note the rectangular region above Java, which presently corresponds to the Java Sea and the Sunda Strait, seen as the small dent between the islands of Java and Sumatra.

The Java Sea and Sunda Shelf formed an extensive plain during the Ice Age, when it was subaerial. Such huge plains are as rare as the gold of

Ophir. Moreover, the rectangular shelf of the Java Sea measures about 600 x 400 km, which is exactly the size given by Plato for Atlantis' Great Plain. So, it seems reasonable to conclude that the present Java Sea corresponded to the former Great Plain of Atlantis.

But the most telltale connection of this region with Paradise are the four rivers springing from the mountain at the left of Sunda Strait (Mt. Dempo, a huge volcanic peak). The largest of these rivers flows towards the west, across the whole Great Plain. A smaller river springs next to its source and flows south, into the Sunda Strait (best seen in the color version just linked)

A third river also springs in the same region and flows north, into the South China Sea. And a fourth river, born more or less at the same spot flows west, into what is presently Malacca Strait, separating Sumatra from the Malay Peninsula.

These four rivers are all born on or near Mt. Dempo, a famous volcano and huge crater lake of the region. This volcano is, as we comment in more detail further below, one of the two Pillars of Hercules, the other one being the Krakatoa volcano, actually located beneath the waters of Sunda Strait.

The Flood and the Destruction of Paradise

Now, rivers like these four, flowing along the Four Cardinal Directions are also as rare as the gold of Ophir. So, this region is visibly that of Eden and hence of Atlantis itself, its alias. What else? Why posit alternative locations, if Ockham's Razor dictates that we tend to identify these two legendary paradises and most others as well?

The super-eruption of the Krakatoa volcano – probably accompanied by those of the other neighboring volcanoes such as the Dempo due to some sort of paroxysmal chain reaction – was what really caused the destruction of Paradise. When this volcano erupted, it opened up Sunda Strait and triggered the maritime invasion known to geologists as Meltwater Pulse 1B.

The Ocean, freed of its bonds, invaded the region of the Great Plain of Atlantis and the coterminous one of the Sunda Shelf, next to it. This maritime invasion was sudden and brutal, exactly as described by Plato in his <u>Critias</u>. And it probably corresponded to the geological event known as Meltwater Pulse 1B.

This event was also the same as the one called the Flood in the universal traditions. The cataclysm in question here submerged the food sources of Atlantis (the Great Plain) and actually caused the mass exodus of entire nations which were later to form the great civilizations of the remote past: those of the American Indians, the Egyptians, the Greeks, the Minoans, the Mesopotamians, the Mycenians, the Indus Valley Culture, etc..

These early mass migrants also include the Jews, the Phoenicians, the Aryans and even the Amerinds, all driven out from their ancestral homelands in Indonesia and Southeast Asia. At first these migrants attempted to settle in India and in Southeast Asia. But they were eventually driven out by the local populations, being forced to move out to China and Mongolia and, finally, to the places they presently occupy.

Such mass migrations are the same as the ones told in the Bible (Exodus) and in similar holy books of nations everywhere. They are the legends concerning mythical heroes such Moses leading the Israelites; Aeneas leading the Roman people; Hercules leading his Greek "cattle" (hordes); the Incas leading their people, and so on.

These legends also concern the traditions on Cain's expulsion from Eden; of Quetzalcoatl's arrival in Mexico; of Viracocha and the coming of the Incas to Peru; of the Fomorians and the Tuatha Dé Danaan invading Britain, and so on. These legends generally disguise historical facts under the thin veil of allegories intended to confound the more ignorant, unwelcome profanes. Why would these peoples all invent lies which so closely correspond to inescapable realities?

The aforementioned myths personify – or rather, deify – the peoples in question under the figures of purely mythical heroes such as Manu, Noah, Moses, Hercules, Kukulkan, Quetzalcoatl, Bochica, and a myriad others. And these legends often include heroines or goddesses such as Venus, Demeter, Dana, Danu, Cybele, Vesta, Hathor, Isis, Ishtar, Shri, Astarte, Hecate, Myriam, and so on.

The above named goddesses are all personifications of Lemurian Atlantis, the first Atlantis. The Great Goddess was the same as the Great Mother of both gods and humans of which the ancient religions so often speak. The Great Mother is also the same goddess whom we know as the Virgin Mary, as many experts have those concluded.

As such, the Virgin Mother personifies Lemurian Atlantis creating Civilization all by herself, without the help of a male "seed", so to say, injected from outside, as is the case with all subsequent civilizations, bar none. They all were, in one way or the other, mere colonies founded or inseminated by other nations, much as was the case with the Americas, Australia, Tasmania, and so on in historical times.

The objective of myths is really one of creating paradoxes and aporias (dead ends), which rake our brains, forcing us to reason and to find a viable explanation which satisfies the mind.

The paradoxical virginity of the Great Mother is one such aporia. This impossible virginity actually refers to the fact that the Virgin (Kanya or Durga in Sanskrit, Mu or Mumba in Dravida, Hathor or Isis in Egypt, etc.) bore the great civilization of Lemurian Atlantis all by herself, in an autochthonous manner, without the help of any other "inseminating" civilization acting as some sort of fertilizing male.

It is in this context that the Great Mother is often compared to a queen bee, which engenders the whole colony without the help of a male, so to say. In contrast, all other civilizations invariably evolved by being "seeded" from outside by the Civilizing Heroes, the Angels, the Gods, the Devils, the Anunnaki or Oannés, the Nagas or Titans, and so on.

These seminal personages really were the Atlantean Sons of God who later illuminated the whole world with the Light of our Great Virgin Mother; heroes or angels like Erichthon, Erechtheus, Hercules, Lucifer, Adam, Sumé, Quetzalcoatl, Bochica, and a multitude of others such. Interestingly, all these heroes or gods or angels originally came from a land with sank away and disappeared under the waters, just like Atlantis.

Coincidentally, the region of the Ganges Delta is called Bengal (or rather, Bangala), a name derived from the Dravida (bang-ala) and meaning "sunken (saline) marshland", This name closely evokes the Sanskrit one of Atlantis itself as a-tala ("sunken land"), and hence leaves no room for doubting its connection with the Lost Continent itself.

Again, the name of Atala may also be interpreted (in Dravida) as atta-ala ("sunken marshland"), bringing the correspondence with Bangala even closer. The region of Bangala is near enough to the site of Indonesian Atlantis to be considered an integral part of the sunken empire, just as attested by its own name.

India – and more exactly, Indonesia, its original seat – was really our Great Mother-Father. The Father is the inseminating god known as Shiva in India. And the Mother is Durga or Kali, his shakti (or feminine shape). Like her, Shiva is a god who dates from the Indus Valley Civilization, if not far earlier, since Hinduism apparently originated in Atlantis-Eden, the actual site of Paradise.

Shiva is often portrayed horned, say, as the proto-Shiva of Harappa, his earliest known shape. Shiva would later become identified with

Dionysos in Greece; Osiris in Egypt; Tammuz in Mesopotamia; Attis in Phrygia, Jahveh in Israel; Cernunnos in Celtia; Kronos or Zeus in Greece; Viracocha in Peru; Quetzalcoatl in Mexico; Bochica in Colombia, Jurupari or Sumé in Brazil, and so on. [024]

Shiva is also the great horned god who self-castrated himself and died, but resurrected from among the dead on the third day, as whole and as virile as ever. As such, Shiva is also an alias of Kronos (Cronus or Saturn), the king of the Golden Age whose name means precisely the same as "horned" (KRN) in a great many tongues.

This image is actually an analogy of an immortal volcano such as the Krakatoa (alias Vadavamukha) which explodes and vanishes from sight, but which keeps quietly burning underneath the ocean, until the time comes for it to rise and shine again, perhaps at God's command, perhaps on its own, who knows for sure?

To be sincere, I am unable to say. Science and Religion have contrary opinions on such matters, and the decision is left for the dear reader, who may hopefully be better informed or opinionated than ourselves on such difficult matters. As for myself, I am a mere scientist trained to think in physical terms only. So, I never dare to go above these bounds, real or not, which are beyond my grasp.

But the inescapable fact is that most if not all gods and goddesses of antiquity were half-personified volcanoes. Their avatar or apparition in a fiery avatar was equated to a theophany, and was hence as widely feared as it was desired by all: "Let thy kingdom come!"

The Krakatoa volcano is really the same as the Vadavamukha of which the Hindu traditions on the Universal Flood and the Eras of Mankind (Yugas) so cogently speak. The Vadava is also often equated to the Horn-of-Plenty of the ancient traditions.

And it is really the same as the Great Mother Earth gone haywire and destroying her children and all her creation. As such, she is the Fiery Submarine Mare; the Fire of Doomsday which performs the great carnage of the Universal Flood, ending the yugas (geological eras).

When the foreordained time comes for it, and the end of the eras of mankind is at hand, the Great God (or Goddess or Androgyne) descends in a majestic avatar. Quite often the duo of heroes – the Twins of all mythologies – descend: as Shiva and Vishnu or as Krishna and Balarama in India; as the Twins in the Navajo traditions; as Lucifer and Michael in Judeo-Christianism, and so on. Very often, the pair corresponds to the two dancers of the Yabh-Yum of Hindus and Tibetans. [025]

The two (Shiva and Shakti) are, as we just said, the personification of the two volcanoes which are also the same as the Two Pillars of Heaven and the two volcanoes of Atlantis. Their wild "dance" (<u>tandava</u>) is really an allegory of the giant earthquake caused by the volcanic explosion, the one which shakes the world, both terms being synonymous in the sacred languages of India.

The two personages are often represented by their sex symbols, the <u>yoni</u> and the <u>linga</u>. Again, these two symbolize the two volcanoes, acting in "unison" and united in sex. Curiously enough, the two Pillars of Hercules (Calpe and Habila) are also represented by similar symbolisms, one suggesting a "cup" (or yoni), the other one a "cap" (or linga). Coincidences or concordances?

Far more than a simple coincidence, these symbols closely resemble the two volcanoes of Atlantis, one a lofty peak (<u>linga</u>), the other a giant caldera (or <u>yoni</u>). But this symbolism is unfortunately too complex to usefully discuss here, being left for a more befitting opportunity.

PART II - ANCIENT COSMOGRAMS, MAPS AND SYMBOLISMS

When you have eliminated the impossible, whatever remains, however improbable, must be the truth.

Sir Arthur Conan Doyle

CHAPTER 5 – ATLANTIS IN AMERICA

> *A great earthquake caused the mountains to incend. The flames ascended to the skies. The stars fell down as molten stone. The Flood ensued, and humans tried to escape by building an enormous tower.*
>
> <u>Washo Indians (California)</u>

Introduction

In the present chapter we comment upon some remarkable symbolisms coming to us from our remotest past. And we also reproduce and gloss some ancient maps embodying world conceptions which are, even today, sorely misunderstood by all specialists: the globe of Crates of Mallus, Homer's and Eratosthenes' maps of the world, Cosmas' cosmogram, and so forth.

Better resolution, vectorial versions of these figures, some in gorgeous color, are also available in our Atlantis site, where they can be perused by the interested readers.

Most of these symbols and imagery were never explained before in any way that really matters: the plan of Atlantis as a replica of the world; the circular shape of the Hindu dvipas (Sunken Paradises); the Carthaginian tophet and Tanit as the image of a volcano, and so on. But it is not originality that we sought here. Rather, we concentrated on the connections with Atlantis, skipping all others.

Moreover, the remarkable figures discussed here were chosen accordingly. We limited ourselves to the symbols which pertain to the Atlantis theme most closely.

The argute reader will no doubt find out that there is a lot of repetition in the text here. Such is also often the case with most of my writings. Some of this repetition is admittedly my own fault, and could perhaps be avoided by a more competent writer. But much of it is essentially unavoidable and pertains to the myths themselves.

However, as the ancient Romans were wont to say: *quod abundat non nocet* ("what abounds causes no harm"). It is actually the symbols themselves, and the many descriptions of them given by the different authorities that endlessly repeat each other. But each variant adds something new and often crucial, and hence has to be discussed over and over again, even at the risk of seeming prolix.

Roughly speaking, these symbolisms all refer back to Atlantis itself as a replica of the world in its many variant aspects. Over time and space one symbol passes into another in a subtle way which takes a lot of study and of familiarity with its many instances and variations, often minimal and often seemingly meaningless, but generally extremely interesting and highly informative once decoded.

Therefore, I beg the dear readers to consider these repetitions necessary, as the parallels pointed only become obvious <u>after</u> expounding. People are conditioned to believe that our remote ancestors were incapable of finer reasoning. And the discussion below aims to prove this is not true. Hence the need to comment in some detail on the finer aspects of seminal symbols such as the ones in question here.

Some of the following explanations are somewhat long, at least in comparison with usual figure captions. But we did our best to make them as exhaustive as possible in the available space. Despite their length, far more could of course be said on most of the symbols below.

Even though we Westerners are not much used to it, ancient symbolism is really a language, a wholly independent medium of communication. As such, Symbolism has the advantage of being universal, in contrast to say, language, which requires a lot of practice and study before it becomes effective. Symbolism works at many simultaneous levels, each completing and expanding the other.

Even a simple symbol such as a dot or a circle has a lot of parallel meanings, often only accessible to the qualified experts. And it takes a lot of examples and explanations before this fact becomes evident to the lay reader, normally unused to this kind of subtlety.

In these explanations we also resort to linguistic explanations. These embody not only derivations of obscure terms from the pristine tongues such as Greek, Hebrew and Latin, but above all from the two main sacred tongues of India, Sanskrit and Dravida.

We have made the remarkable discovery that these sacred tongues lie at the root of most words of non-descript origin, often mediated by Mediterranean Dravidian tongues such as Pelasgian and Etruscan. Some linguists will probably object to these derivations on the usual argument that these tongues are linguistic isolates, and that such derivations are only allowable within a given linguistic family.

But this reasoning is false. All languages on earth are necessarily cognate, since it is highly unlikely that such a remarkable human invention would be made over and over again independently. The priori odds against an independent reinvention of language – or of agriculture, metallurgy, stone dressing, etc. – are impossibly small, as any specialist in Statistics will tell you.

What the widespread idea of "linguistic isolate" – a sad misnomer, by the way – really means is that a relationship among these different languages has not yet been discovered, not that it does not exist. But this is just a consequence of the fact that these languages or families were never properly researched by specialists honestly engaged in discovering these connections.

So, rather than being placed in different, non-communicating bins, as "linguistic isolates" these languages should more properly be dubbed "unresearched", so as to invite further study. And this type of detailed linguistic study is what we actually did.

With impressive results, we add, as the connections were generally far closer than we had ever expected. This is demonstrated by the few instances discussed below. Even more, this fact is demonstrated by our results on Etruscan, Pelasgian and other pristine Mediterranean tongues, which we not only managed to decipher, but to trace back to India and Indonesia, their Dravidian cradle.

What our research also demonstrated is the fact that languages change far less than is usually supposed by the mainstream linguists. They base their claim on the observed changes from the Indo-European family. But all such generalizations are fraught with dangers, Induction not being a valid logical process, as the philosopher Hume and others pointed out long ago.

The Indo-Europeans are a bellicose, restless people. Hence, they frequently interact with many cultures, absorbing their customs and their tongues, often far superior to their own. It is thus, by absorption, and not as the result of evolution that we must account for the observed change.

For instance, English has picked up over 99% of its vocabulary from foreign tongues such as Greek, Latin, French, Spanish, Portuguese, etc.. Skeat, the reputed linguist, lists only about 3,800 pedigreed English words of Anglo-Saxon origin, whereas modern English now encompasses over one million words according to the best qualified experts.

More conservative nations maintain their languages essentially unchanged often for several millennia. For instance, the Berber language (Tamazigh) has been demonstrated to have changed only slightly over the last 8,000 years and more. So, it is not unbelievable that some words can be traced back to Atlantean, alias Proto-World itself.

We have also supplied a few Internet links in the text which follows below. We have been able to devise a simple, novel way in which the curious reader of this book may easily use this fantastic source of information on topics such as the ones discussed here.

This linking makes use of our Atlantis Site, with a page specifically dedicated to this task. Whenever the readers want to consult this medium, all they have to do is to go to this Internet page in my site, and click on the corresponding link, which is provided in active form there.

In this way we managed – perhaps for the first time ever – to make readily accessible to the readers of this book the literally billions of informative pages and illustrative figures now available in the Worldwide Web. And this access is not only essentially instantaneous, but also extremely easy to use in practice: a simple click of your mouse.

The links are kept permanently alive by caching and by an observant Webmaster. We will also be accepting further suggestions by our readers of Internet topics to cover, so as to enrich even more this important novel source augmenting and enriching bookish information. In this way, we have finally managed to serendipitously combine the great advantages offered by the Internet with the many desirable features of hard printed books, the ones we all learnt to cherish from infancy.

The information provided by the Internet has the advantage of being independent, and hence essentially unbiased. So, it can often be trusted by the more skeptical readers. And these may, if they so desire, pursue the topics further by searching through Google and others such search engines with the keywords supplied in the glosses or the Subject Index below. So, our advice to the dear reader is: please, relax and enjoy the ride...

The Foundering of Aztlán (Aztec)

The figure above, like the following two, is taken from ancient Aztec codices. They originated in pre-Columbian times and illustrate Aztlán, the primordial Paradise and sunken homeland of these highly civilized Indians of Mexico. In the first figure, the mountain at the center of the island corresponds to Mt. Atlas, also the central feature of Atlantis according to Plato. These drawings actually date from the epoch of the Conquest, but reproduce Aztec drawings and traditions from a far earlier date.

The whole island is visibly sinking in what is apparently a huge cataclysm with only the volcanic peak remaining emerse, forming an island. The seas are extremely turbulent and the picture seemingly illustrates a massive tsunami, a recurrent event in the whole region of Indonesia, as the recent disaster there attests.

But here, the cause of the cataclysm seems to be a giant explosive volcanism, rather than an earthquake proper. This fact is evident in the other two figures discussed next, where the Holy Mountain is explicitly portrayed as such a phenomenon, volcanic plume included. Both earthquakes and explosive volcanisms are frequent in the whole Indonesian region, which is part of the so-called "Pacific Fire Belt".

The male figure at the top of the mountain apparently corresponds to Atlas in Greek traditions, who also supported the skies from the peak of Mt. Atlas, the Pillar of Heaven. Here, Aztlán is shown as an island entirely surrounded by water, much as was the capital city of the Aztecs as well as of Atlantis, as described by Plato.

The four non-descript features labeled azteca ("Aztec") in the figure apparently correspond to the Four Pillars of the Earth and their four guardian gods. These four pillars also figure in most Old World traditions, such as Egyptian. In Hindu traditions they are called the Four Lokapalas ("Guardians of Paradise").

In the Aztec traditions these four guardians were called Tlalocs and played exactly the same role as Atlas. In reality, these four pillars (and their guardians) also corresponded tó the two pairs of "Pillars of Hercules" and "Pillars of Atlas", one pair located in the Far West (Gibraltar), and the other in the Far East, flanking Sunda Strait.

According to Hindu traditions, the main pair of guardians corresponds to Shiva and Vishnu or their many aliases: Krishna and Balarama, Rama and Ravana, etc.. In Vedic times, the four were identified to Indra, Varuna, Yama and Kubera, the archetypes of the later volcanic gods just mentioned.

Some versions of this interesting cosmogram are shown in several other codices, also reproduced above. In the second of the above figures (Gemelli-Carreri Codex), the holy mountain is explicitly represented as a volcano, with a lofty plume on its top resembling a giant palm tree.

This is the source of the widespread myth of the giant Tree of Life (or of Death) which grows atop the Holy Mountain. In India, this myth corresponds to the giant Jambu Tree which grows on top of Mt. Meru, in

Jambudvipa. This quaint symbolism is described in much more detail in our Atlantis site linked here. [032]

The third figure, taken from the <u>Boturini Codex,</u> also illustrates the same scene. But the Indians are here explicitly shown crossing the ocean in a boat, towards America, shown as the land encircling it. This motif quaintly evokes the map of the world of Cosmas Indicopleustes discussed further below, as well as Plato's description of the <u>Peirata Ges,</u> the Outer Continent. In this codex, the Holy Mountain is explicitly shown as a stepped pyramid with a volcanic plume (or "tree of life" or "pillar of heaven") on top and surrounded by six other islands.

This stepped pyramid evokes the ones of Indonesia or those of Mexico and Peru. But here it apparently represents the volcanic mountains of Indonesia and the agricultural terraces used for cultivation there. The seven islands (or tombs?) are the ones of Chicomoztóc ("Seven Recesses"). As such, they also correspond to the Seven Islands of the Blest, which again symbolize the same thing.

The Foundering of Tolán (Maya)

The next figure reproduces a beautiful bas-relief carved in one of the Mayan temples in Mexico's Yucatan. The perfect correspondence with the Aztec traditions illustrated in the previous figure of this list is telltale. It seems that the barbarous Aztecs actually absorbed the sacred traditions of the more civilized Mayas and added them to their own religious and sacred traditions.

Or perhaps the two great Mexican cultures were two sides of the same coin, one pious and the other barbarous, as is so often the case with Atlantean relicts. In the bas-relief we see the alias and counterpart of Noah hastily abandoning the destroyed region of Tolán, the Mayan Paradise. The dead fish and the dead person vividly illustrate the lethal nature of the great cataclysm depicted here.

And so do the solid stone temples (pyramids?) which are shown collapsing. The whole island has already sunken down, with only the top of the volcano itself remaining emerse, forming an island. The curious wisps of smoke leave no room for doubting that the Holy Mountain of Paradise was indeed a volcano and that it was its eruption that somehow triggered the fateful disaster.

Like the other Indians, both the Mayas and the Aztecs were unsure of the true location of Aztlán-Tolán. More likely, they knew it well, but were unwilling to profane the sacred traditions by revealing it to the public. The Incas – who were in all probability the true civilizers of both the Mayas and the Aztecs – were quite sure of the western location of Paradise.

In other words, the Incan Paradise lay beyond the Pacific Ocean, towards the west. Thence their civilizers came – Zumé, the Inca rulers, etc. – in the dawn of time. In contrast to the Atlantic Ocean, an empty waste in prehistory, the wide Pacific Ocean was where all the action actually concentrated, according to Leo Frobenius, the erudite German archaeologist and several other experts, Thor Heyerdahl in particular.

The Brazilian Indians sometimes place their Paradise in the east, sometimes in the west. So, it is at least risky to unreservedly believe in their sacred traditions, unless one can make sure first that they are not sheer mystifications or misinformation intended to deceive us, the profanes.

As for myself, I prefer to believe in traditions like the ones of the Incas or the Navajos and other Indians of the Pacific coast, or in the even more reliable ones of the Hindus and the Buddhists concerning the Western Paradise of Buddha Amitabha. But I also recall once again that, just as Columbus reasoned, the farthest west is actually coterminous with the farthest east, so that the two places are really one and the same. This inescapable fact was well known to the ancient mythographers, who often made use of it to baffle and confound the profanes they despised.

Quetzalcoatl and Atlas Holding Up the Skies

The first of the previous two figures reproduces an Aztec bas relief illustrating Quetzalcoatl bearing up the skies. This type of motif was recurrent in both Aztec and in Maya art, where the god is named Chibchacun. The second figure represents the mighty titan Atlas, doing the same according to Greco-Roman mythology. This particular figure is the so-called Atlas Farnese, the famous Greco-Roman statue. [033]

In Mexican art two male figures are often illustrated doing this: Quetzalcoatl and his twin brother and dual, Tezcatlipoca. Curiously enough, Tezcatlipoca's tree is called arbol espejo ("mirror tree"), much as the two Phoenician Pillars of Hercules and/or Atlas were also deemed to be mirror images of each other at the two opposite sides of the world.

The same motif also happens in Greco-Roman traditions, where Atlas and Hercules take turns bearing up heaven. One should note that the Mexican hero or god – half-human, half-divine, as so many heroic saviors of mankind – wears a long beard in the illustration, much as does Atlas, incidentally. The Bible too speaks of twin Trees, of Life and Knowledge, and so do other Old World traditions, India's included.

Beards are highly unusual with both the Aztecs and the Mayas. These natives, like most other American Indians, essentially never have beards which can be grown into a goatee such as the one illustrated here. The curved posture of Quetzalcoatl is also curious. It closely reproduces the one of Atlas just shown, bent under the excessive weight of the earth or heaven, which he attempts to keep separated, but eventually fails.

Here, these two levels (heaven and earth) visibly correspond to the floor and ceiling of the temple, which is itself an accurate image of the cosmos and its several layers of heavens and hells.

According to both Maya and Aztec traditions – as well as those of the ancient Greeks and Hindus and other peoples – an Atlas figure (atlante) supports heaven, preventing it from falling down over the earth.

When Atlas (or Hercules) succumbs under the excessive burden, the sky falls down, and becomes the new earth. A new heaven and a new earth result, more or less as told in the <u>Book of Revelation</u> about the New Jerusalem. The old heaven becomes the new earth, and the old earth becomes the new hell.

When this figure of Quetzalcoatl is compared in detail to the majestic Atlas Farnese, or the many others that exist both in America and in Greece, it is not difficult to see that the curved postures of the two heroes are identical, both bent under the excessive weight of heaven.

The parallels are so close that it is hard to deny that the two religious traditions originated from a pristine one common to both nations, since they agree in every detail. These close parallels extend to several other features: falling serial heavens, successive Creations, Civilizing Heroes and Saviors, etc..

As we have already asserted, it is only the aprioristic stance of the academics against the possibility of pristine contacts which misleads them all into claiming an independent origin of such identical cosmogonies.

Such is particularly the case when one realizes that the figures of Quetzalcoatl, like the ones of Atlas, are also visibly one and the same bearded hero. Both are the great Civilizing Heroes of Humanity and both personify Atlantis itself. Both heroes are also the aliases and archetypes of similar Saviors of Mankind, such as Jesus Christ, Hercules, Osiris, Tammuz, Attis, Mithras, Krishna, Balarama, among several others.

So are also the personages of their wicked twins and oppositors, the very incarnations of the Devil: Hercules in Greece; Tezcatlipoca in Mexico; Seth-Typhon in Egypt, and so forth. The great duel between the two brothers eventually led to the destruction of the whole world, which they were forced to recreate anew. And this duel of cosmic proportions is really an allegory of the Great War of Atlantis, as expounded by Plato in his famous dialogues on the Lost Continent, as well as by ourselves in the present book.

The Atlantes of Tula (Mexico)

The Atlas figure at left, reproduced faithfully from the famous Atlantes of Tula (Mexico), represents an atlante or telamon. Such figures were widely used in Greece and Rome, just as they also were in the Americas. The erect, stiff figure simulates a pillar. And it was indeed used as such in Greece and other Mediterranean locations. [↑034]

The same type of stiff standing figure serving as a pillar for temples and palaces was also popular in ancient Greece and Rome. There they were called atlantes (Greek) or telamones (Latin). They also had other names such as caryatides, canephores, calatophores, etc.. [↑035]

And they could be either masculine or feminine, but in every case they represented the same thing: the figure of Atlas bearing up the skies on his head. Sometimes, Atlas is represented standing like an atlante. Such atlante figures are often twins, representing Hercules and Atlas in Classical antiquity and Quetzalcoatl and his brother in Mexican traditions. This dualism may be observed in the two pillars of the figure shown. [↑036]

The term atlantes actually derives from Atlas or Telamon, his alias and counterpart. Both names actually derive from the Greek root tla meaning "to bear up, support" (scil., the world or heaven). The Aztecs also often attribute the myth of the Pillar of Heaven to the figure of Tlaloc, their great civilizer. Once again we find the radix tla- associated with an Atlas figure and with the myth of Atlantis (or Aztlán). These uncanny coincidences are of course far more than casual.

The myth of Atlas bearing up the world (or the sky) also closely corresponds to that of Quetzalcoatl, who also does the same in the Aztec traditions. So does his twin, Tezcatlipoca, as we just discussed.

In Greek mythology, Atlas and Hercules likewise function as twins, and take turns in bearing up the world. In fact, the two heroes represent the two Pillars of Hercules and/or Atlas, just as their Aztec counterparts also do. In Hindu traditions, the twin heroes correspond to Krishna and Balarama or their many aliases, including Shiva and Vishnu.

One pair of Pillars of Hercules was located in the Far West, in Gibraltar, and the other, the pair of "pillars" posted at the sides of Sunda Strait, in Indonesia, the actual entrance to Taprobane, the true site of Atlantis-Eden. They were volcanoes deemed "pillars of heaven" because their lofty plumes reached all the way to heaven itself.

Once again, we have here a perfect correspondence of the two sacred traditions on Paradise Lost, the one of the Greeks (Atlantis) and that of the Aztecs (Aztlán). It is quite obvious that the two symbols and the two heroes represented one and the same thing both in the Old and the New World. It is only the stubborn obstinacy of certain scholars that prevents us all from seeing the obvious, even when it is pointed out, as here.

Consider the parallels given below and try to estimate, as some sort of homework, the following sequential improbabilities of purely random coincidences: twin giants bearing up heaven and/or earth; twin trees of life; twin volcanoes on whose tops they grow as mirror images of each other (antipodal); heaven falling down and destroying the former world; Indians having long beards; such personages equated to flying dragons or winged serpents; trees growing in opposite directions (one upside down); twin central guardians flanked by four helpers at the four corners of the world; etc..

It is a pity that anthropologists or archaeologists or even linguists <u>never</u> consult physicists and statisticians like myself on such purely mathematical matters, much as Napoleon once consulted Poisson on the probabilities of foot-soldiers being trodden upon by cavalry horses or as insurance companies consult statisticians on the risks of loss.

They would fast conclude that the odds of such random coincidences are essentially impossible, and should hence <u>never</u> occur in actual practice. It is perhaps for this very reason that the present human disciplines are kept so widely separated from the exact ones everywhere in the modern world. This even seems to be the result of deliberate planning, so that the Illusion of Separativity may survive in this brave world of ours.

Chapter 6 – Atlantis in Ancient Cosmograms

Facts do not cease to exist because they are ignored.

Aldous Huxley (1894–1963)

The Mountain of Sunrise and Sunset

The remarkable figure below reproduces the decoration on an Egyptian vase dating from pre-dynastic times (Amratian Period, c. 4,000– 3500 BC). This figure is a cosmogram, a sort of cosmological map illustrating the inner working of the cosmos. The extreme antiquity of this motif – encountered in a great many variant forms in Egypt – attests the fact that this sacred tradition dates from extreme antiquity: 6,000 years ago, and perhaps even more.

Since their civilization had not yet developed, it is apparent that the Egyptians brought this symbolism from whatever place they originally came from, before the dawn of history. This place was, in all probability, the East Indies, where this symbolism is current ever since Vedic times, the times of Atlantis.

The two mountains shown are the Mountain of Sunrise and the Mountain of Sunset, already commented in the previous entry. The wavy lines – an Egyptian hieroglyph for "water" – represent the World-Encircling Ocean. The sun is shown entering the world from the right (the Orient), at dawn (6:00 AM), and exiting it from the left (the Occident), at dusk (6:00 PM).

The strait at the left is known to be Gibraltar Strait, alias "Pillars of Hercules". The strait at the extreme right, the extreme Orient, is really unknown up to now. But it is also known that the ancient Egyptians considered these two straits the extremities (or "fringes") of the world, one in the far occident (Gibraltar), the other one in the far orient. We have, after a very long study of the problem, been able to locate and identify these Eastern Pillars in Indonesia and, even more exactly, in Sunda Strait, in Sumatra.

Sumatra was, in antiquity, the site of Taprobane. And this site was invariably considered the site of the start of the day. It was there that the City of Lanka was located, the fabulous capital of Ravana's worldwide empire. And this great mythical empire was the alias and archetype of Atlantis itself. We will return to this subject further below, when we discuss the true identity of the White Ethiopians.

This Egyptian symbolism closely corresponds to the one of Nut in her diurnal, celestial aspect devouring the sun in the morning and birthing it in the afternoon; or, conversely, in her nocturnal (chthonian) aspect, doing the opposite. This type of symbolism is recurrent in Egyptian iconography. In alternative interpretations, the earth/celestial goddess is substituted by the Double Lion (Acker or Ruty). [037]

The idea here is that the sun is first "devoured" by the underground earth monster, which it enters when night starts. And then the sun reissues from there at sunrise, returning to the sky in this world, which it then crosses, as if in the interior of another twin monster, the celestial one.

Some Egyptian iconographies – which we discuss in the links just given – portray this curious belief with the sun entering the arched body of Nut or Hathor (the Sky) via her mouth and exiting through her vulva. It then reenters the earth, where the process is reversed. In other versions, also discussed there, the Goddess is substituted by the Double Lion (Acker) or the two pylons or the Mountain of the Orient, and so on. [038]

But the symbolism is invariably the same: the Earth Monster which is also the Earth Serpent or the Double Lion or the Vadava or, even more exactly, the Split Mountain (Mashu), etc.. Even more exactly, these two gates are the two straits illustrated in the figure above.

Actually, these two gates or portals are Sunda Strait in the Far Orient and Gibraltar Strait in the Far Occident. Alternatively, Sunda Strait is the monster's mouth, and Gibraltar its anus. All in all, these strange symbolisms represent the events which actually happened in Atlantis-Eden, in the dawn of time. Devoured by the giant volcanic caldera which opened up on the occasion of its demise, its many people resurrected in the Occident, supposedly immortalized.

In India, the enormous caldera is specifically compared to the giant mouth of the Earth Monster (the Serpent Shesha, or its alias, the Submarine Mare), or to earth's yoni, etc.. The volcanic caldera (tophet) also corresponds to the fiery dragon's mouth (or lion's mouth or hell's mouth) which we encounter in so many traditions the world over. The hero has to be devoured by the Dragon, in order to revive and to become immortal, very much as is the case of the Australian initiants just commented.

In Greece we also find the same belief vividly illustrated in the quaint Greek vase linked here. It illustrates Jason being vomited out by the dragon during his quest of the Golden Fleece. The scene is watched by Pallas Athena, herself a personification of Atlantis as the Great Mother of both gods and humans. [039]

The process of swallowing is started when the sun enters this world via the mouth (at dawn), and is reversed when it exits this world via its anus (at sunset). And this course is repeated in reverse when the sun enters the netherworld, as everything there runs in reverse, time included.

The Celestial Being corresponds to Nut, the sky goddess, and the Terrestrial Being to Geb, the earth god. Their sexes are often inverted, and so are their roles. The two gods correspond to earth's two hemispheres, separated since the dawn of time, as we comment in more detail in our Atlantis site.

This symbolism is encountered the world over. In India it often figures in the Rig Veda, where the feat is variously attributed to Purusha, Vishnu, Agni, Varuna, etc.. In Polynesia it is Tane who separates his parents, Rangi (Heaven, male) and Papa (Earth, female). In Greece, it is Kronos (Saturn) who separates Ouranos from Gaea by cutting off his father's penis. These examples could be multiplied. In Mesopotamia it is Enlil who separates Earth and Heaven in order to create breathing space for humans, who soon after emerged from the ground.

And their very universality demonstrates the hoary antiquity of the myth, which can only date from Atlantean times, when Beringia, the link between the Old and the New Worlds, was still open.

This myth has to do with the separation of the two humanities (Dravidas and Aryo-Semites) taking place after the Great War of Atlantis, in order to prevent its perpetuation. This separation of the world in two halves functioned most effectively down to the Renaissance, when it was unilaterally broken by the European conquistadors, with the terrible results we all well know.

Said otherwise, it is day here when the sun enters this world via the monster's mouth, and night when it exits, via the anus. The opposite obtains in the netherworld, where the day starts when the sun exits this world and enters the lower one, and ends when the sun exits the netherworld passing into this one. In the netherworld, time visibly passes the opposite way as here.

This concept of time reversal passed to Greece, as described, say, by Plato in his dialogue <u>Statesman</u>. But it is originally Hindu and, even more exactly, Atlantean. In Hindu traditions, time is cyclical. For that reason, Shesha is often called Ananta ("endless"). This fact is illustrated by the very shape of Shesha, which corresponds to the symbol of infinity, a recumbent figure of 8.

If this cycle is traced out with a pencil, it is easy to see that one circle runs in one direction and the other in the opposite one. This is exactly what happens with Cyclical Time. The two coils here (celestial and terrestrial) are the duals of each other. This symbol of the Serpent Shesha often becomes the caduceus, another frequent attribute of the goddess Tanit and of her male counterpart, Moloch, an alias of Atlas himself.

This form of Shesha exactly corresponds to the early shape of the caduceus held up by the goddess Tanit in her early effigies. The double monster also often forms the image of the <u>Ouroboros</u>, with each of the two monsters having its mouth at the other's anus, more or less as <u>illustrated</u> <u>here</u>. This is really a somewhat euphemized form of what would really amount to the symbolism of 69 in contemporary France. [1040]

The two straits portrayed in this remarkable Egyptian cosmogram also correspond to the two extremities of the world mentioned in Homer's <u>Odyssey</u> (I:22) as inhabited by: "the Ethiopians... who live at the world's extremities, divided in two halves, one where the sun (Hyperion) rises, and the other where he sets." We will return to the theme of the White Ethiopians in more detail further below, in our discussion of the many Pillars of Hercules and their connection with Taprobane.

Lanka – the location of Sunda Strait, the eastern passage – was also the site of the ancient International Dateline. And this is the place where the new day started by an international convention adopted by most peoples on earth (Meridian $0°$) since remotest antiquity. Now, it is interesting to ask why anyone would need to set up an International Dateline so early in time unless they already had both a good reason and the resources for doing so?

Only an international empire of global extent – a nation of great navigators literally able to rove the entire world – would really require an International Dateline. That Lanka was such a worldwide empire cannot now be doubted, as it is affirmed in Hindu holy books of an extreme antiquity. And so is also the fact that Lanka was considered to be the former site of Meridian $0°$.

Petty empires of a limited extent – the only ones allowed by the current doctrines on prehistory – would never require a global standardization of time and earth's coordinates. For what purpose would they need them? Gibraltar Strait lies at Lanka's opposite side, more the antipodes of Meridian $0°$. It was for this reason that it was chosen to be the place where the day ended by convention, and where night began.

It was also for this reason that Gibraltar was also considered the "mirror image" of the true Pillars of Atlas. The Pillars of Atlas, rather than the ones of Hercules, their European replicas, were the well-known markers of Atlantis' true geographical location, in Taprobane, on the opposite bank of the Ocean.

Hercules is the dual and twin of Atlas to whom Plato gives the codename of Gadeiros (or Eumelos) in his two dialogues on Atlantis. This symbolism also connected with the one of Tanit, the Phoenician goddess whose myth and meaning we discuss in more detail further below.

The Strait of Gibraltar was merely a phony replica of the true Pillars of Heaven, like so many others. As we just saw, "Sunrise" and "Sunset" are here connected with the Eras of Mankind, their start and their end. And this can only mean one thing. These mountains are really volcanoes or, likelier still, supervolcanoes. Otherwise, how could a mountain destroy the entire world?

These two supervolcanoes – which I have identified with the Toba and the Krakatoa, both located in Sumatra, in the region of Indonesia – are so incredibly potent that they can in fact trigger the Ice Ages on and off, both starting and ending them, as we have both discovered and proved in detail.

When the Ice Ages start, we have the "dawn" of a new era, and when they end we have its dusk, ragnarök. What else could this quaint symbolism and its connection with supervolcanoes actually mean?

The symbolism of the eras of mankind (yugas) is typically Hindu in origin. In fact, the yugas form the essence of both Hinduism and Buddhism, the two great religions of India. What is even more sobering, as we are now fast learning, is that Catastrophism and Catastrophic Evolution are the basic mechanisms adopted by Nature, instead of the pink-tinted, panglossian Uniformitarian Evolution advocated by Darwin and Lyell.

When we consider all this, it is clear that the doctrine of the Eras of Mankind originated in the East Indies. It is catastrophic in nature, and teaches that supervolcanoes such as the Krakatoa and the Toba are associated with the "Fire of Doomsday", which they also call Vadavamukha (or "Submarine Mare"). The Submarine Mare is obviously a submarine volcano, as we show further below.

And this mare is also the same as the lion or the dragon or the infernal dog which we find in worldwide legends. This ferocious volcano we have identified as the terrible Krakatoa, the main one in the Indonesian region. In a former era it was the Toba volcano, the one which literally destroyed the world some 75,000 years ago, in what was the largest explosive eruption ever to occur in the times of Man.

This giant Toba eruption triggered the onset of the last Ice Age, which was in all probability terminated by a similar giant eruption of the Krakatoa volcano (see link here) occurring some 11,600 years ago. The cataclysm described by Plato – which destroyed Atlantis and caused the Flood – is often understood to have been an earthquake, rather than a giant volcanism of the sort we have been arguing. [041]

That is a frequent misconception resulting from the mistranslation of the word seismos used by Plato in this context. Actually, this word means "commotion, jolt", rather than "quake, shake". But it was adopted in modern times to designate a seism or earthquake, and the name stuck.

However, the many details given by Plato are typical of a supervolcanism, rather than a colossal earthquake. Huge amounts of pumiceous lava were shed (Plato's ilus or pelos). The earth opened up in an immense chasm, and swallowed the entire region and all its people.

This event is typical of a giant eruption followed by cave-in and caldera formation, and never happens with earthquakes proper. Plato's disaster was attended by fire; the region had both cold and hot springs as well as red, black and white rocks, all typical of volcanoes.

So, it seems that the "jolt" and the tsunamis or floods mentioned by Plato were caused by an explosive volcanic eruption, rather than by an earthquake proper. This is a characteristic feature of the Krakatoa volcano due to its submarine location – as attested in the great tsunami of 1883, created by a giant explosive eruption of the volcano, rather than by an earthquake proper.

As is known, names change in the course of time, and often come to mean something quite different from what they originally meant. Such seems to have been the case here. The Greek word seismos – particularly the type called chasmatiae ("chasm opening") in antiquity – originally meant many types of great commotions of the ground, caused by both volcanoes and earthquakes proper.

Since earthquakes are far more common than giant volcanic eruptions of an explosive nature, the name became attached with this type of phenomenon, and in time came to mean exclusively those. Moreover, the Greeks had no name for volcanoes proper – perhaps for reasons of a taboo of some sort – and tended to avoid naming them explicitly, using all sorts of euphemisms instead.

All in all, it seems that the idea that the Eras of Mankind were caused by giant volcanisms probably arose in a region prone to this sort of phenomenon. And this region seems to have been Sumatra, the world's champion for this kind of disaster. This is attested both by the great Krakatoa eruption of 1883 as well as by the great tsunami that recently overwhelmed both this region and the vicinal countries.

It is now known for sure that the Hindus originally came from the region of Indonesia, fleeing to India when their original home sank under the sea in a giant volcanic catastrophe. Since India itself has no volcanoes, it seems probable that the Hindus developed these doctrines there, in Indonesia, and later brought them over to India, when they moved to this safer region of the word.

Given the fact that Atlantis also went under in one such major cataclysm of global import, it is not unreasonable to try to identify the two locations and the two disasters, as demanded by Ockham's Razor, the epistemological base of Modern Science. And this is just what we did in the course of our researches on the subject. Similarly, as Gibraltar has no volcanoes, it is quite unlikely to have been the site of Atlantis.

The Cross of Atlantis

The next figure represents the so-called Cross of Atlantis. This symbol is becoming current among some adepts of occultism due to its many mystic connotations. This symbol represents the three concentric strips of water (in black) surrounding the two strips of land plus the central island of Atlantis' capital city (in white). The Cross itself represents the canals which crossed the strips of land, and which were connected by bridges, as described in great detail by Plato himself.

The shaft of the cross is the great admittance canal which led to the Ocean itself, some 10 kilometers away from the city, according to Plato. The Cross of Atlantis is in fact a schematic map of Atlantis. But there is a lot more to this curious symbol, this being the reason why we chose to illustrate and comment upon it here. In simplified form, this symbol also corresponds to the one of the Crossed Circle ⊕ .

This simpler symbol dates from an extreme antiquity. It was used in ancient Egypt as an hieroglyph whose meaning was "city". This symbolism also represented the sacred bread which the ancient Egyptians used as some sort of a Eucharist, in holy communion. It also symbolized the body of dead Osiris, himself an image of the Great Sacrifice and of the Eucharist as well. In India, the Great sacrifice is Purusha, the Cosmic Man.

The Great Sacrifice is itself a personification of Atlantis-Eden, the site of the great human sacrifice provoked by the Flood in the region of Indonesia. All human sacrifices pale and wane in comparison with this great one. Even the recent disaster which devastated the disaster-prone region of Indonesia, killing as many as 400,000 people and perhaps even more, is puny in comparison.

Osiris was an alias of Atlas as both the Pillar of Heaven (djed) and the bearer of the world, which he was said to support over his back or his spine. Simply put, the god Osiris represented Atlantis itself, much as did Atlas, and his Vedic archetype, Purusha.

Purusha, whose myth dates from the Rig Veda and earlier is both the Great Sacrifice and the Cross personified. Purusha was the real archetype not only of Osiris, but also of Atlas, Hercules and several other such Savior Heroes whom we find just about anywhere in the world. Hence their connection with the Crossed Circle, itself the symbol of Atlantis, the City which required no naming, except within initiatic circles.

In time, the Crossed Circle came to represent the planet earth both in Astrology and in Astronomy. This symbolism survives to date, and is used to represent the earth in both these sciences. The Crossed Circle and the Cross of Atlantis also correspond to the Celtic Cross. [042]

The Celts synchretized their original beliefs to those of Judeo-Christianism, when this became the official, mandatory religion of the whole Roman Empire. And it was in this way that the Crossed Circle, the symbol of Atlantis became changed into the Celtic Cross, itself a replica more of the Cross of Atlantis than of the Christian Cross itself, as can be seen in a direct inspection of this remarkable symbolism.

It took me a great many years of diligent research before I was able to decode the real meaning of the Cross symbolism. So, with the related ones of Tanit, the Ankh, the Crossed Circle and the Cross of Atlantis itself. We take this opportunity to explain the hidden meaning of another obscure religious symbolism of great importance, the Jewish menorah. The menorah is the seven-branched candlestick. But it may also have nine arms, a fact that shows it is not really related to the number seven itself. [043]

When we look closely at this remarkable symbol, it is easy to discern its close connection with the Cross of Atlantis. All that is required is to complete the circles to obtain the second symbol, the cross of Atlantis. We also note that this dissection of the Cross of Atlantis was standard in antiquity. Perhaps it alluded to the division which took place in the empire, separating one of its racial moieties (Aryo-Semitic) from the other (Dravidian).

No matter what, the half circle also became a standard representation of Atlantis. Such was the case, for instance, of the Island of Satanaxio, one of the "Atlantic Islands". These islands were considered the remains of sunken Atlantis, so that the connection is essentially inescapable.

It is now known for sure that the use of the Cross symbolism for religious purposes dates from far before the advent of Christianity itself. Besides, the Cross symbolism was also used in the same sacred context both in the Americas and the Old World. In both of the two places the Cross was used to mark the position of the Center, the actual site of the Terrestrial Paradise.

This symbolism is pregnant with meaning, and directly relates to the actual location of Atlantis. To put it bluntly, the Cross represents the crossing of the two axes of earth's Coordinate System, as used by the ancient Atlanteans. The crossing of Parallel 0° (the Line of the Equator) with Meridian 0° (the one of Lanka, alias Atlantis) occurs just over the center of Sumatra (Taprobane), the site of the Terrestrial Paradise.

This curious geographical fact is told in a great many Hindu traditions, and can hardly be doubted anymore. It is true that Lanka – the real archetype of Atlantis – is often confused with Sri Lanka, its Indian replica and counterpart. But this is sheer exoterism, one which must be ignored by the true adepts interested in fact rather than fiction. As is clear, the intersection of Meridian 0° with Parallel 0° (Equator) forms a Cross.

And so it does today, when this meridian has been moved to London. These coincidences are all too perfect to be attributed to chance, and the sole possible explanation lies in accepting the reality of our remarkable discovery. And why not, if it is the only one which sheds light on the murky issue of human origins and the origin of civilization?

Curiously enough, this Cross is also explicitly represented in the stellar map of the Atlas Farnese, linked here. This figure of Atlas corresponds to the one already discussed above. The constellations intersected by this meridian (Canis and Argo) are both the celestial counterparts of Atlantis. [044]

For instance, the Argo – sunk down to the bottom of the Celestial Ocean – is itself a visible replica of Atlantis, which also suffered a similar fate. So, the above interpretation is also confirmed by the figure of Atlas Farnese, curved under his monstrous burden, in a posture which closely evokes the similar one of Quetzalcoatl.

The Plan of Atlantis as a Replica of the World

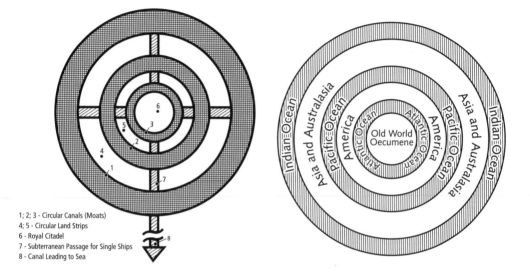

1; 2; 3 - Circular Canals (Moats)
4; 5 - Circular Land Strips
6 - Royal Citadel
7 - Subterranean Passage for Single Ships
8 - Canal Leading to Sea

As we commented in the above figure, Atlantis' capital city was shaped like a cross, the Cross of Atlantis. This conclusion prompted us to look deeper, in an attempt to find the real meaning and origin of this curious geometry. And we think we have succeeded after much research.

Let's suppose we were Ice Age sailors, with no clearer idea of the world than the one offered by Homer and his contemporaries. After we left the œcumene, the central "island", and actually crossed the ocean (Atlantic), we would reach the Americas and find it to be an impassable barrier of land.

Suppose further that we were able to cross this barrier, say, by carrying our ship on our backs, just as the ancients often did, or by finding a secret canal in Panama or Costa Rica built by, say, the ancient Atlanteans; we would then meet the Pacific Ocean. After we crossed this wide ocean, we would again meet an impassable strip of land formed by Asia, Indonesia and Australia, with any possible passages sealed off by ice down to and including Antarctica, more or less as represented by Ptolemy on his map.

Suppose that we again managed to overcome this impassable barrier, reaching the Indian Ocean, which we then crossed. We would now get to Africa, which we again traverse, in order to get back to our starting point.

The overall picture that emerges is hence the following: || Oecumene || Atlantic Ocean || America || Pacific Ocean || Asia || Indian Ocean ||

Africa ||. Hence, three or four strips of land (four if we count Africa again and the outer strip of land of Atlantis) and three of water.

All told, we have here exactly the same distribution as the one shown in the plan of Atlantis city: three strips of water and three strips of land. If we explored these strips, we would find them more or less concentric, due to earth's sphericity. It is this, we believe, that the plan of Atlantis really represents: a stylized map of the world, with its three main continents and its three main oceans.

Well, *si non è vero, è bene trovato*. But this is just an exercise of imagination which is really marginal and unimportant for our theory of Atlantis. It has only a secondary connection with the themes discussed here, which function regardless of the reality of the present hypothesis.

Actually, we present this proposal to the dear readers as mere food for thought and as an inquest on matters never before researched. However, my example – regardless of being realistic or not – also shows that only a people of navigators, capable of roving the whole world, could be capable of devising such a schematic world model. The very idea of global oceans and continents would never arise in a people confined to a small region of the earth, regardless of its location.

Besides, why would the ancients also develop and implement the concept of an International Dateline if they lived confined to a small region of the earth, as supposed by the current doctrines on human development and on human prehistory? Moreover, the very fact that this pristine International Dateline was placed in Indonesia (Lanka) singles this place out as the true site of the capital city of Atlantis' worldwide empire.

And we further note that the Hindu dvipas are also concentric like the ones of Atlantis, which they closely evoke. These dvipas are known to represent the paradisial continents and the seas surrounding them. What this close geometric identity tends to show is the fact that the Greek symbolism expounded by Plato actually derives, one way or the other, from the Hindu paradisial dvipas just illustrated. [045]

The Sacred Geometry of Atlantis in America and Elsewhere

The drawing below shows the ruins of a temple of the Pueblos, the most ancient Indians of Colorado, in the USA. Before the arrival of the first whites, the region was inhabited by these Indians. The Pueblos had agriculture, and were remarkably advanced.

The Pueblo Indians left many ruins of their remarkable temples (ki-vas) and of their cave habitations in the mountains, which probably served as refuges and citadels, rather than everyday homes and temples. Many of these fortified houses were built with bricks, and several such ruins survive even today.

These Indians were later driven out by the Spaniards, and other wild, nomadic Indian tribes moved into the vacuum left by their predecessors. This region of the USA was long associated with the Seven Golden Cities of Cibola, which the greedy conquistadors soon identified to the ones of Eldorado.

Eldorado ("Golden One", in Spanish) is of course an alias of Atlantis, and other such golden realms including Cipango, Ophir, Taprobane, Chryse, and so on. In fact, the very name of Cibola can be traced back to the Dravida civ-pola ("golden city"). The legend of the Golden Realm had somehow reached the Americas already in pre-Columbian times via cultural diffusion.

The mythical Seven Cities of Cibola are also visibly the same as the Seven Islands of the Blest, also often associated with the legend of Taprobane. The name of Taprobane derives from the Sanskrit tamra-par-na and the Dravida tamara-parana, and means the same as "golden peninsula". As is clear, all these names and all these mythical locations are one and the same: the fabled golden realm of Atlantis-Eden.

The curious shape of the temple herein illustrated leaves little room for doubting its direct connection with Atlantis and its triple circular walls described by Plato. We also find such triple enclosures all over the Old World, for instance in the famous megalithic ruins of Stonehenge and Avebury (England).

Actually, the Pueblos' temple shape is a stylized map of the world, illustrating the three concentric oceans and the three strips of land which contain them. We already commented this important issue in the above entry, to which the interested reader is now directed.

CHAPTER 7 – ATLANTIS IN ANCIENT MAPS

> *You are young, my son, and, as the years go by, time will change and even reverse many of your present opinions. Refrain therefore awhile from setting yourself up as a judge of the highest matters.*
>
> <u>Plato (427 BC–347 BC)</u>

The Idealized Maps of Atlantis

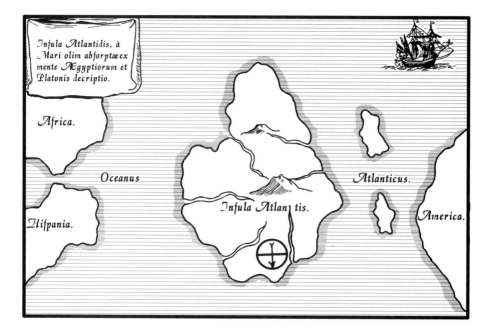

The above quaint map shows an idealized rendering of the "island" of Atlantis as conceived by Athanasius Kircher, the famous Renaissance Jesuit. It illustrated his book on sunken lands and global disasters, entitled <u>Mundus Subterraneus</u>, published in Amsterdam in 1665 AD. This map is typical of the many ones found just about anywhere. All such "maps of Atlantis" or of "Lemuria" are purely imaginary and only show idealized concepts which only exist in the minds of their authors.

Kircher was a very well informed polymath, who dabbled in many sciences, both occult and exact. Among his many scientific endeavors lies the attempt to decipher the Egyptian hieroglyphs, long before other sages attempted to do so, Champollion included.

The reader should please note that Kircher's map is inverted, so that south is up and north is down, just as indicated by the compass' needle there. This convention was usual in antiquity, and was later inverted for a series of reasons. Due to this inversion, Gibraltar, along with Africa and Spain (Hispania), lies to the left, and America to the right. The Latin legend on top the map reads: "Site of the island of Atlantis, anciently swallowed by the sea, as conceived by the mind of the Egyptians, according to Plato's description."

We note that Kircher's ideal Atlantis consists of a huge island or continent in the mid-Atlantic region. More recent oceanographic research has indubitably shown that no such lands or even any large islands ever existed in this region of the world, which has been most thoroughly studied for military purposes. The only islands in the mid-Atlantic Ocean are the Azores, which some researchers have in fact identified to Atlantis. But this identification is impossible, as is easy to show.

The Azores rise directly from the ocean floor, more than three thousand meters below. The Azores are an integral part of the Mid-Atlantic Ridge, and consist of semi-submarine basaltic matter created by the upwelling magma that rises, rather than sinks from the boundaries of the plates meeting there.

Kircher's map was shown here as a vivid testimony that the mid-Atlantic placement of Atlantis, like the one of Spain, is centuries old and that people such as Ignatius Donnelly were just reviving far older proposals. But this mid-Atlantic location, like those in the Mediterranean Sea, or off or on the coasts of Spain, Morocco and so forth, was mainly the result of a gross misinterpretation of Plato's text.

As just stated, all such maps are no more than sheer idealizations, free creations of the mind of their researchers. They are based on no geological or geographical evidence whatsoever, and have no foundation in fact or evidence of any kind.

So, they must be rejected by the savvy readers, at least until more solid evidence is provided by their proponents, very much as we did ourselves. The possibility of mid-Atlantic locations has been thoroughly refuted by all sorts of scientific investigations, including the recent ones obtained by means of outer space satellites. These satellites are now quite capable of spying the seafloor in detail, directly.

In contrast to Kircher's map and others such, my detailed map of the sunken continent of Atlantis was derived from several oceanographic studies of the region of Indonesia, where I succeeded in locating Atlantis. These studies included the earlier ones done by oceanographic ships and subs, as well as the more recent by the NOAA's and NASA's spy satellites just mentioned.

Hence, regardless of the existence of Atlantis there or elsewhere, my maps of the seafloor of the region of Indonesia are both reliable and accurate, and must be accepted by all. The fact that my maps also firmly establish the reality of Plato's claim in both date and continental extension, as well as on the actual nature and worldwide extension of the Atlantean cataclysm, is also a strong confirmation that the great philosopher in fact well knew what he was talking about.

Homer, Crates and the Map of Hecatæus of Miletus

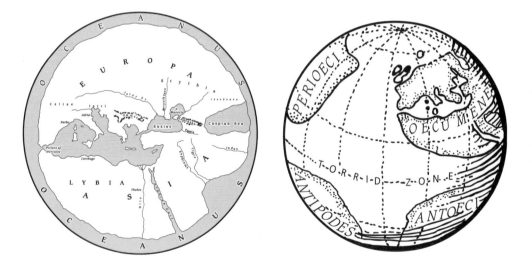

These figures reproduce both the map of Hecatæus of Miletus (c. 500 BC) and the famous globe of Crates of Mallus (170 BC). This globe was perhaps the first such ever to be fabricated. Hecatæus' geographical work was freely ripped by Herodotus in his <u>History</u>. So, it was quite familiar to the educated Greeks of Plato's time, including the philosopher himself. [046]

As the map of Hecataeus shows, there was no island – great or small – before Gibraltar Strait, here called Pillars of Hercules. So, how could Plato affirm precisely the opposite, and foolishly place immense Atlantis at this mouth to the Ocean without giving any explanation for this strange notion? Would Plato so risk being taken for a fool?

Hecatæus' world conception also closely parallels Homer's. Homer was of course a poet and no geographer, and cared little for such technicalities. Hence, Homer limited himself to describing the world as it was then conceived, in a somewhat idealized form full of poetic license.

This description of the world was by him masterfully done in the famous passage of the <u>Iliad</u> (18:478). According to it, Hephaistos, the divine smith and artificer, fashioned the shield of Achilles as a replica of the world itself: a flat disk of earth completely surrounded by water, the Ocean.

Some ancients – among them Plato, Eratosthenes and Cosmas (see next two entries) – placed a strip of environing land on the far side of the Ocean, in order to prevent its waters from spilling over into space.

In this picture, the world consisted of a circular island at the center, surrounded by the Circular Ocean, having a concentric strip of land on the outside. This strip was the <u>Peirata Gês</u> ("Encircling Land") which most experts believe to be the Americas. This picture of the world closely resembles the inner portion of the plan of Atlantis' capital city, as discussed in the entry for its map shown above.

The land is shown as limited to the œcumene and is almost perfectly circular. It is entirely encircled by the Ocean (Oceanus, its Latin name). The œcumene (or Old World) is, as shown in the map, composed of Europe (Europa), Africa (Libya) and Asia (Asia). Africa has been foreshortened to the portion above the equator. And Asia has been even more reduced, to little more than Arabia and India.

In reality, the map of Eratosthenes does not represent the whole world, but only one of its quadrants. This fact can be seen in the globe of Crates of Mallus illustrated above, where the Classical Greek conceptions are far more clearly represented. Here, the world is composed of four quadrants or "islands": the Œcumene, the Perioeci, the Antoeci and the Antipodes.

The word "island" which I used here literally corresponds to the Greek <u>nêsos</u>, rather than its usual English meaning. The Greek word embodies the ideas which we nowadays express as either "islands" proper and "continents", in the sense of large extensions of land entirely surrounded by water.

The idea is apparently derived from the fact that the four "islands" shown are in fact separated from each other either by the line of the equator or by oceans. It is also precisely in this sense that Plato referred to Atlantis as being an "island", even though the philosopher unequivocally affirms its continental size as being "larger than Asia and Libya put together." "Put together", and never "midway", as some suggest.

The above usage of the word was also adopted by several other Platonists: Cicero, Seneca, Plutarch and Macrobius, among others. Even conservative geographers such as Strabo – who specifically calls the oecumene (or Old World) an "island" (nêsos; Geogr. I:1:8.) – used the term in Plato's context. And this concept probably derived from the fact that Crates' four quadrants were in fact deemed absolutely isolated from each other by impassable barriers formed by water or by dismal deserts (cf. I:2:24f.). [047]

Strabo apparently refers to this fact in the above passage when he says that, even though "It is unlikely that the Atlantic Ocean is divided into two seas, thus being separated by isthmuses so narrow as to prevent the circumnavigation; it is more likely that it is one confluent and continuous sea." The ships which attempted this crossing departing from one side or the other (east and west) gave up and desisted, "because of their utter destitution and loneliness."

Moreover, the ancient relations all converge on the fact that the Ocean could not be crossed in any way, except in a supernatural way. This tradition figures, among others, in the Rig Veda and in the Epic of Gilgamesh, both of which are among the oldest texts now extant. Crates' world view is crucial for reconstructing these ancient conceptions of the world which are so often misinterpreted by everyone.

The southern portion of Africa is here deemed separated from the northern one at the equator, and visibly corresponds to the Antoeci ("those who live opposite the Oecumene").

The Antœci correspond to the black Africans, separated from the white Africans (Libyans) by the Sahara Desert. This is probably the "torrid zone" illustrated by Crates. The same conception was adopted by other ancient geographers, for instance Strabo and Pomponius Mela. Mela specifically identifies the Antœci with the Antichthones, as can be seen in his map. [048]

In fact, this term (Antœci) was also loosely used to designate the Antipodes in general. A close reading of Strabo's text on the name of "Ethiopian" being applicable to all peoples living south of the equator suggest that the Antipodes were in fact identical with the Ethiopians in general. If so, the Atlanteans – who also lived in the Southern Hemisphere, as we have shown – were Ethiopians, regardless of being easterners or westerners.

The Periœci ("those who live near the Oecumene") probably correspond to the Americas. This is easy to see in Crates' globe illustrated above. Finally, the Antipodes ("those who have the soles of their feet opposite ours") apparently corresponds to the now sunken continent of Atlantis, alias Australasia. Again, this fact is easy to deduce from Crates' remarkable globe, given that Australasia is actually antipodal to Greece.

Australasia was placed at the southern hemisphere, just as is the case of the sunken continent of Atlantis which I discovered to lie in the region of present-day Indonesia, a part of it. So, at least geographically speaking, my siting of Atlantis makes far more sense than the usual ones, at least in a Platonic context.

Several Platonic philosophers actually identified the Atlanteans with the Antipodes or Antichthones. For instance, Thomas More actually places his Utopia – an obvious alias of Atlantis – in an antipodal region close to the East Indies. More, a close friend of Erasmus, was also a fervent admirer of the Platonics Marsilio Ficino and Pico de la Mirandola, whose works he translated into English.

So, it is quite easy to deduce whence More drew the inspiration for his famous initiatic short novel. Very much the same thing can be said of Francis Bacon who places his New Atlantis in the Far East, beyond the Pacific Ocean. So, Tommaso Campanella, who places his City of the Sun – another Utopian Atlantis – right in the middle of Taprobane. It was facts like these that led me to seek Atlantis in this part of the world. After all, who but the Platonics of all times should know more about the Lost Continent?

Curiously enough, the problem of whether the Antipodes existed or not as a physical reality ultimately derives from the similar controversy on whether Atlantis really existed or not. The Antipodes are, as we now know, the Atlanteans themselves. Even the name of Atlantis is intimately connected with the ones of Antilia, Antipodes, Antoeci, Antichthon, etc., all of which mean "antipodal".

The suffix -<u>anti(s)</u> of its name suffices to demonstrate this fact when the surplus -<u>s</u> is eliminated. So, Atlantis is really the paradisial "land opposite" mentioned by Cosmas Indicopleustes in his map. The main idea of the word <u>anti</u>- corresponds to "opposite, antipodal".

Moreover, the very name of Atlantis is actually synonymous with it, being ultimately derived from the Dravida <u>attal-anti</u> meaning "having the feet (<u>attal-</u>) opposite (<u>anti</u>)". Put otherwise, the name of Atlantis literally means the same thing as "antipodal".

As can be seen in this excellent <u>monograph on the globe of Crates of Mallus here,</u> the Ethiopians are also intimately connected with the antipodal location of Atlantis. Crates, who was a great expert on Homer's <u>Odyssey,</u> placed the Ethiopians near the line of the equator, on both sides of it. Like Homer, Crates also spoke of twin Ethiopias. And Homer placed them one in the Far East, the other one in the Far West. [1049]

In order to exegetize Homer's passage: "The Ethiopians who dwell sundered in twain, the farthermost of men", Crates supposed that they lived at the two opposite shores of the Ocean, one on the farthest west, the other one in the farthest east. Crates' description is intentionally garbled since, as a Platonic, the illustrious grammarian was prevented from speaking clearly on these forbidden matters.

By "farthermost", Homer specifically meant the fringes of the world, one on the far west (at Gibraltar), the other one in the far east (Indonesia or Taprobane). And this agrees with Diodorus Siculus' text on Atlantis which we comment in detail in the main text. Diodorus too places the Atlanteans at the farthermost fringes of the world, on the banks of the ocean.

If one looks at Crates' globe, it is easy to see that the Eastern Ethiopians were located on the far side of the ocean, at the Antipodes, whereas the Western Ethiopians were located in west Africa, more or less in the region corresponding to present day Morocco and Mauritania. If this is right, we see that these Ethiopians are the Libyans and Berbers, etc., that is, whites, rather than blacks.

In turn, the Eastern Ethiopians actually are the Tocharians (or Yüeh-chi, etc.) of China and Taprobane. These peoples are also called Hephthalites or White Huns. They are tall, blond and blue-eyed, and look like Nordic Aryans or Guanches in essentially all features. But they are actually partly Dravida in origin, despite their looks and their language (Tocharian), which is part Aryan, part Dravida.

These Tocharians (or Eastern Ethiopians) in turn correspond to the Atlanteans themselves, the Pious Ethiopians of whom Homer and others spoke. And, as Plato related, these Pious Ethiopians later decayed and turned into nomadic barbarians (Berbers) instead of settled agricultors, like their noble ancestors.

All in all, the whole geography expounded in these extremely ancient maps closely corresponds to an idealized picture of the world having to do with Atlantis and its reality.

The Map of Eratosthenes

The figure below reproduces the map of Eratosthenes (fl. 3rd. cent. BC). Eratosthenes is the reputed Greek geographer and head librarian at Alexandria who is said to have first measured earth's circumference. Eratosthenes is, roughly speaking, a contemporary of Plato, who lived about a century earlier, but shared the same cultural ambience of Classical Greece.

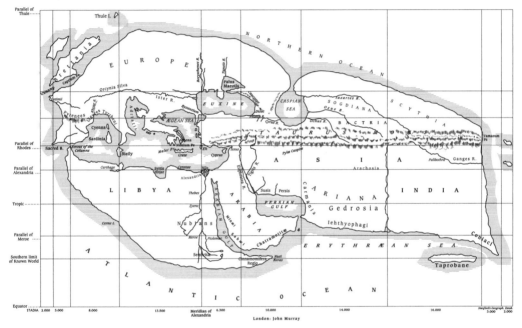

Eratosthenes' map shows the earth (Eurasia and Africa) as a disk of land fully encircled by the Ocean. If we discount the distortions due to the stylized projection shown, this map is a rather accurate depiction of the Greek œcumene, the Old World shown in the globe of Crates of Mallus just discussed.

At the far left we have the Strait of Gibraltar and the *Mare Internum* (the Mediterranean) separating Europe and Africa (Libya). Africa is foreshortened, and ends just below the Arabian Peninsula. Asia extends to India and Taprobane, and then turns up towards the land of the Seres (Chinese), beyond the Ganges river. At India's tip live the Coniaci, perhaps a metathesis or a scribal error for the Concani, even today the people of South India.

But what really interests us here is the Outer Ocean. This ocean is here called Atlantic in its southern portion, and extends all the way to Taprobane and beyond. In other versions of his map, the Atlantic Ocean is separated in two halves: the *Mare Atlanticum Occidentale* and the *Mare Atlanticum Orientale*. These two moieties correspond to what we nowadays separate into Atlantic Ocean (proper) and Pacific Ocean.

It is hence quite clear from this map that Taprobane – which we have specifically identified as the site of sunken Atlantis, in Indonesia – was located, for all practical purposes, in the "Atlantic Ocean" of the ancients, at least in the view of the Classical Greeks such as Plato himself, Crates and Eratosthenes.

Strabo too shared the same views, and mapped the world very much in the way that Eratosthenes had previously done. Therefore, it is foolish to limit the quest of Atlantis to the ocean now so named, since the ancient Greeks understood an entirely different thing by that name. To wit, they dubbed "Ocean" or "Atlantic Ocean" the Atlantic, Pacific and Indian Oceans, all three taken together, as one really should, since all three oceans are really coterminous.

The idea here is that the Ocean (or "Atlantic Ocean" or "Ocean of Atlantis") of the ancients is the sea which surrounds the whole earth (the Old World or Oecumene) rather than the present-day Atlantic Ocean. And we again emphasize the fact that the Outer Ocean was also called "Atlantic Ocean" all the way to the Far East, the island of Taprobane (Sumatra) included.

This belief prevailed down to the Middle Ages and the Renaissance, until the time when Amerigo Vespucci realized the fact that the Americas were in fact a new continent, something wholly unsuspected thus far, and that it effectively separated the two oceans which had been deemed coterminous down to these times.

Strabo lived a few centuries later than Plato, but his map too embodies names and concepts which date back to the times of Eratosthenes and Plato, and even earlier. As also does the map of Herodotus (5th. cent. BC), who might be considered a contemporary of Plato for the present purposes.

All in all, we conclude that when the ancients spoke of the "Atlantic Ocean", they really meant the "Ocean of Atlantis", the one called Pacific Ocean nowadays. This ocean comprised both the Atlantic Ocean and the Indian Ocean of modern days.

We may also conclude that the ancients believed, much as did Columbus and his many predecessors, that the present Atlantic Ocean extended all the way to the East Indies. Conversely, they also believed that the Pacific Ocean – which they well knew from the Far East since the earliest epochs – also extended eastwards all the way to Europe and Africa, where the Greeks resided.

But the ancients never dared to cross that vast expanse of water, which they deemed deadly. And hence they never discovered America, as Columbus and Vespucci would later do. In terms of Atlantis – which, as Plato affirmed, was located in the "Atlantic Ocean" of the ancients – we again repeat that this ocean should never be confused with the water body now improperly so named.

The ancients did not ignore, as we now do, that the "Atlantic Islands" were the remains of sunken Atlantis and were hence located in the "Ocean of Atlantis". This ocean is the very one bathing the coasts of Taprobane and the East Indies.

The confusion only arose later, when people finally realized that the Americas effectively separated the Ocean in two moieties, one eastern, one western. With this, the Pacific Ocean, the "Ocean of Atlantis" – so named because Atlantis was known to be located there – got an entirely new name given it by the Spaniards.

And the ancient name got stuck with the Atlantic Ocean we so know today, where Atlantis never was. This type of thing often happens with geographical names. It is for this reason that names such as the ones of Gades and Tartessos, Calpe and Habila, etc., are highly unreliable, and should never be trusted as reference points.

The old name is given to a new location, perhaps a colony of the former city, and then the old one dies out, and becomes utterly forgotten in the course of time. As an example, consider the name of America. This name was originally given Brazil, early explored by Amerigo Vespucci, and was later extended to the whole of South America.

Eventually, all three continents became thus named, by extension. But nowadays, the name "America" has become firmly attached to the United States, in North America, and very few people ever recall that it originally applied to Brazil or even South America. It was precisely this that happened to Atlantis, mythically transferred to the Gibraltar region by virtue of a similar process of false naming.

The World Conception of Cosmas Indicopleustes

Γῆ πέραν τῦ Ωχεανῦ ἐνθα πρὸ τῦ χαταχλυσμῦ χατωχουν οἱ ἄνθρωποι
Terra ultra Oceanum, vbi anté diluvium habitabant homines

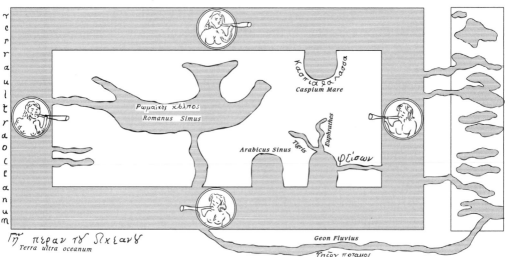

This early world map is due to Cosmas Indicopleustes, the famous author of the <u>Topographia Christiana</u>. Cosmas was an Egyptian monk from Alexandria who had been an international merchant in his earlier days. Charged by the Pope, Cosmas set out to discover the true site of Paradise, which he correctly sought in the East Indies.

Cosmas' surname is really an epithet meaning "sailor of the Indian Ocean", since he had become highly familiar with the region in his merchant days. The geographer firmly believed in the reality of Atlantis, and affirms in his book that Plato's story of the sunken continent is a garbled account of the Universal Flood, which the philosopher somehow cribbed from the Bible.

In his map, Cosmas shows the world (œcumene) surrounded by the uncrossable ocean, outside which there is another earth which he calls <u>Ge peran tou Okeanou</u> ("Earth beyond the Ocean"), adding that this was the Paradise which Man inhabited before the Flood.

The earth is irrigated by four rivers whose four headwaters are in Paradise, just as shown in the map. One of these four rivers is the Nile, here identified with the Geon and shown crossing the ocean subterraneously, in the south. The other three rivers are also shown doing the same, and are identified with the Phison, the Tigris and the Euphrates. From the map, it seems that the Phison is the river identified with the Ganges.

This accords with Flavius Josephus, who also affirms the same. This strange world conception is connected with the ancient traditions on the Terrestrial Nile and the Terrestrial Ganges, etc. having their Celestial counterparts. And what this means is that the terrestrial rivers are really the "mirror images" of the Celestial ones of Paradise, their true archetypes.

The fact that the rivers are said to run under the ocean apparently suggests that the four Celestial rivers are now submerged, just as we have discovered to be the case in Atlantis-Eden.

The "earth beyond the ocean" encircles the Ocean all around. As such, it closely evokes the <u>Peirata Ges</u> of Plato, which also does the same according to Greek traditions, and the names also mean the same thing. One should note that the square geometry adopted by Cosmas is merely conventional, just as is the circular geometry adopted by Homer and others. Discounting these distortions, the world here charted is remarkably accurate. At the center, we have the Mediterranean Sea; the other three seas are the Caspian, Red, and Arabian.

To sum it up, the world picture presented by Cosmas closely resembles that of Plato and other ancients. Paradise is the "land of many waters" where the Four Rivers of Paradise are born. It is surrounded by a wall or fence, also a widespread tradition.

Though radically against the notion of "antipodes", Cosmas' world vision closely corresponds to the Greek, with Paradise being a sort of Land Antipodal (Antichthon). Actually, Cosmas objected to the existence of antipodes on religious reasons rather than geographical grounds.

The Map of Grazioso Benincasa

The following quaint early Italian map shows the mythical islands of the Atlantic Ocean: Antilia, Salvaggia, Satanaxio, San Brandan, Fortunata, Cipango, and so on. It is said that Columbus possessed a copy of this map, and took it on board on his trip to America, along with several others which he had collected over the years, mainly during his stay in Portugal.

The names of these islands derive not from the ocean itself but from their connection with Atlantis. In fact, it is this ocean that derives its name from the ones of Atlas and Atlantis. The Medieval, and later the

Renaissance explorers and geographers eagerly strove to discover these mythical islands, long associated with the remains of sunken Atlantis.

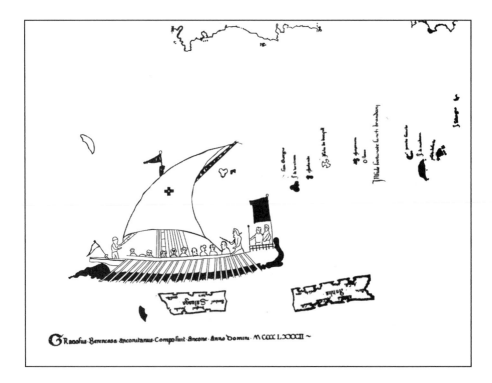

Columbus was no exception to the rule, and avidly hoped to discover Cipango, "the land where gold is born". Columbus had learnt of this fabulous golden realm from the famous writings of Marco Polo. In his book, Polo describes the fabulous island of Cipango in great detail, and places it just off the coast of China and the East Indies, describing it as a sort of Eldorado, where gold and gemstones abound.

Columbus had also learnt of golden Cipango from other sources such as Toscanelli, Behaim, Pierre d'Ailly and even Plato and other ancient mythographers. He used this knowledge to impress the monarchs of Spain and the ambitious financers of his expedition, avid for the immense gains to be made in the East Indies.

Like most, if not all, of his contemporaries, Columbus firmly believed that the Atlantic Ocean (now so named) extended all the way to the East Indies, being coterminous with the Pacific Ocean. So did the ancient explorers and geographers who also believed the same and hence thought that the islands they discovered in the mid-Atlantic were all part of the remains of sunken Atlantis turned into islands when sea level rose by an enormous amount after the end of the Ice Age.

Since most people in the region died in the terrible cataclysm, these islands became known as the Isles of the Blest (or Elysium, Taprobane, Paradise, Hades, and so forth). "Blest" is really an euphemism for "dead", so that this region is really the "Realm of the Dead". But these islands were also explicitly called Land of the Dead, or Hades, or Hell, Tartarus and so on. In fact, the ancients believed, like the modern-day Hindus and the American natives, etc., that the site of Paradise encompassed all three realms of space: Heaven, Hell, and Hades.

These three realms coexisted one inside the other, in parallel dimensions. Taprobane also corresponds to the site of Mt. Meru, the Whirling Mountain at the center of the world. Around it the whole world whirls, as if around the pole. And this axis mundi is also the same as Mt. Atlas and other such Holy Mountains everywhere.

The Whirling Mountain is also the same as the Mountain of Sunrise and Sunset, whose myth we have already commented upon above. And this twin mountain (split) further corresponds to Mt. Atlas or Meru, and to the Pillars of Atlas and/or Hercules.

The very fact that this important myth diffused worldwide is proof of its hoary antiquity. In fact, its diffusion to the distant Americas proves that it dates from before the end of the Ice Age, or shortly after, before the sea level rose, closing Beringia and effectively separating the two worlds. As such, this tradition can only have had an Atlantean origin, before the dawn of the present era.

The Map Presented King Henry VII

This curious British map — dated at 1500 AD — is rather similar to several others originating in the times of Columbus and earlier. It was probably done by a British spy placed in the Spanish court, and embodies the widespread geographical conceptions concerning the Atlantic Ocean and its direct connection with the East Indies.

This map visibly predates the exploits of Amerigo Vespucci and his realization that America was an entirely new continent or world (Mundus Novus) which quite effectively separated the Pacific Ocean (long known from the east) from the Atlantic Ocean now so named.

The whole ocean was variously named Outer Ocean, Atlantic Ocean, Cronius Mare, Mare Magnum, and so on. Cronus (or Kronos), called Saturn in Latin, was an alias of Hercules and/or Atlas, so that the name also expressed the identity of the modern Atlantic Ocean with the Pacific Ocean now so called.

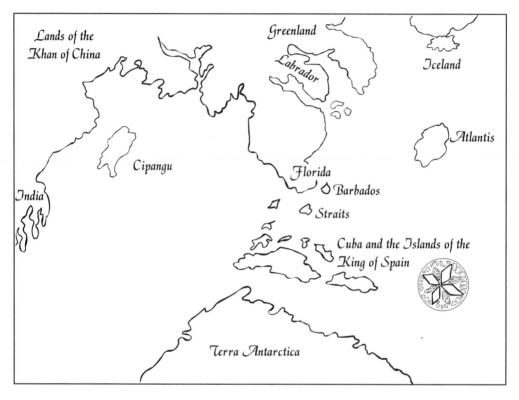

We see that the present cartographer believed, like so many others, that the island of Atlantis was located somewhat before the Americas, more or less next to the Caribbean islands. But he and others, Columbus included, also believed that the ocean was open and unimpeded all the way to the East Indies, the island of Cipango (Japan?), China and India included, as actually shown in the map.

In fact, the lands of North America – Florida, Labrador, etc. – are shown attached to China and to India, and hence as parts of the Asiatic continent. This map thus portrays the western Atlantic Ocean as it was formerly conceived down to the times of Christopher Columbus and Amerigo Vespucci. And it was thus charted by earlier geographers such as Martin Behaim and Paolo Toscanelli to name just two of a great many such cartographers.

By then the Caribbean islands – discovered by Columbus in 1492 – were well known, and widely identified with Antilia and Atlantis by all sorts of early geographers and chronists, Father Las Casas included.

The <u>Terra Antarctica</u> (or <u>Terra Australis</u>) is also explicitly illustrated in the map. This fabulous Southern Land should not be mistaken with Antarctica proper and even less with Australia, as many experts currently believe. Here, its location and size suggest an identification with Brazil, discovered (but unnamed) in this very year by the Portuguese. South America is a southern continent, being mainly located below the line of the equator. Hence, it would well deserve the name of <u>australis</u>, which means exactly this in Latin.

This mysterious southern continent already figures in the famous map of Claudius Ptolemy, one of the earliest ancient maps to survive down to the present. In my opinion this southern land originally also corresponded to Atlantis, another southern continent. Atlantis was really located in the South Seas, where the Alexandrine geographer correctly placed it.

And the South Seas, also named <u>Prasodum Mare</u>, that is "Sea of Sargassos" is really no other than the South Pacific Ocean. In the Ice Age, Australia was more or less coterminous with the Indonesian Continent, forming a single huge land extension. It was probably in this connection that Australia too earned its name of "austral", that is, "southerly". But this is a difficult subject, whose discussion does not fit here.

CHAPTER 8 – THE MANY PILLARS OF HERCULES

Facts are facts and will not disappear on account of your liking.

Jawaharlal Nehru (1889–1964)

Ptolemy's Map of Taprobane

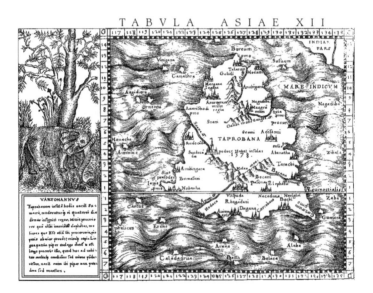

The above figure reproduces Ptolemy's Map of Taprobane. This map dates from 150 AD or so, but is based on far earlier data available in Alexandria's famous library. This particular version of the map, based on his, is due to Sebastian Münster (1522), in his edition of Ptolemy's Geography.

The legend in this curious map of Taprobane reads (in Latin): "The island of Taprobane is nowadays called Sumatra. Four crowned kings rule over it at the same time. It exports elephants that are larger and nobler than any found anywhere. Its yield of the long pepper – locally called Malaga pepper – is likewise richer, and is indeed wonderful in its abundance."

This name of the long pepper is preserved even today, in certain languages, for instance, Portuguese. And it derives from Malacca, the name of the famous strait separating Sumatra and the Malay Peninsula in Indonesia. This alone would serve to indicate that Sebastian Munster, like so many other geographers, is right in identifying Taprobane to Sumatra, rather than to Sri Lanka.

Taprobane was often confused with Sri Lanka, a confusion that persists even today. But this is sheer exoterism, and Sri Lanka is merely a facsimile of minor importance, just as are several other places, Gibraltar included. True, Taprobane is also the same as Lanka, the golden city of the Ramayana, and the capital of Ravana's worldwide empire.

Taprobane seems to be the same as the golden Cipango described by Marco Polo. Both the details and the location match. And so does the profusion of gold and gemstones, said to abound in both. Taprobane (Lanka) was also the site of the International Dateline of antiquity, a place which singled it out as "the land of sunrise".

And such is precisely the meaning of the name of Cipango both in Dravida and in Japanese (Ci-pan-kuo). According to the Ramayana, Lanka was destroyed, fired and subsequently sunk under the ocean in the course of the great war waged by Rama and Hanumant against Ravana, its great king who had abducted Sita, Rama's wife.

Several other features also confirm this identification: the equatorial location, the enormous size of the island, its shape, and so forth. But the ancients were reluctant to divulge in public the true location of Taprobane, and much preferred that the merchants went to the wrong island (Sri Lanka) and there bought the spices from the hands of the local Indian intermediaries, who thus realized an enormous profit with this ruse.

Another reason was the need of hiding away the true whereabouts of Paradise Lost, lest pirates and conquistadors and other such greedy adventurers invade the place and desecrate it. We note that the elephants of Sumatra are actually bigger and fiercer than any others, the African and the Indian included.

The Sumatran elephants were widely used in warfare, and were highly appreciated by foreign kings for both their enormous size and their ferocity in combat. These majestic elephants were formerly exported in large numbers, just as reported by Ptolemy, Onesicritus, Pliny and several other ancient authorities. And this exportation continued down to modern times, before ecological reasoning dawned on the world.

Sumatran elephants also produced the large amounts of ivory for which the whole region was famous in antiquity. And this place was also renowned for the gold and gemstones it produced in abundance. In fact, the very name of Taprobane means "golden peninsula" (<u>tamra-parna; tamara-parana</u>) in both Sanskrit and Dravida. This etymology also applies to the name of Cipango, again proving its identity with Taprobane.

The name of Taprobane also literally corresponds to the Greek one of <u>Chryse Chersonesos</u> and its Latin equivalent <u>Aurea Chersonesus</u>. These names all mean the same thing: "Golden Peninsula". And this was precisely the ancient name of Indonesia, but never of Sri Lanka.

Sri Lanka of course never produced any gold, even though it too produces gemstones such as rubies and sapphires. And it is in fact a real island, rather than a peninsula. This in contrast to Taprobane, a name which covers both Sumatra and the Malay Peninsula and which is really a giant peninsula. So, how could Sri Lanka ever be called by a name meaning "Peninsula of Gold"?

All in all, it is now clear that the fabulous Taprobane of which the ancient traditions speak as the site of Paradise (and of Hades, etc.) and the "land where gold is born" corresponds to the site of Indonesia and Southeast Asia, rather than to Sri Lanka, a poor island at best, and fully devoid of the precious metal.

We have also managed to show that true Taprobane – called Serendip ("Island of the Seres") by the Arabs, and Seylan ("land of gold") by other nationals – was in fact the true location of Eden, as well as of Atlantis itself. Both these names derive from Dravida, the pristine tongue of the whole region.

It is worth noting that the connection with both gold and ivory (elephants) is again reminiscent of Atlantis, which Plato describes as abounding in both of these precious commodities.

Plato also mentions several other commodities characteristic of the region of Sumatra: coconuts, bananas, precious woods, spices, perfumes, dyes, gemstones and minerals of all sorts, metals, and so forth. It also seems that Pallas Athena – the great goddess of the Athenian Greeks – is really an alias of the Hindu goddess locally known as Kanya Kumari ("the virgin princess"), the patroness of the whole region.

Kanya Kumari is also associated with the sunken continent whence the Dravidas are said to have come in the dawn of time (Kumari Kandam). Pallas Athena too is said to have come from the Tritonides Marshes, a place long associated with Atlantis in the Greek traditions, for example the ones told by Diodorus Siculus.

Pallas Athena was also associated with both gold and ivory, as attested by her giant chryselephantine statue in the Parthenon created by Phidias, the greatest of Greek artists. This statue was wholly made of gold and ivory (chryselephantine). And this is a most strange feature, as both materials were characteristic of Sumatra, and are both utterly missing in Greece. [1050]

These two precious commodities were formerly imported from the East Indies (Sumatra) at an enormous cost and clearly had a symbolic religious character in Greece, which seems to be connected with Atlantis and the Tritonides Marshes. There, Atlantis was said to have sunk in the dawn of time. Not in Libya, but in the Far East, where, as we now know, Atlantis was truly located.

We also note that the Libyan counterpart – so often mistaken for Atlantis – is a mere replica, as is so often the case. The true Libya or Ethiopia in question here is actually Taprobane, in reality sunken by the Flood and turned into a dismal wasteland, an enormous pestilential marshland.

The Tritonian Marshes were associated with both Triton (Trita Aptya) and the Garden of the Hesperides. And this wonderful garden where the fabled Golden Apples grew, and provided the Elixir, is in fact no other than the Garden of Eden.

It is interesting to note that Hercules is originally a Hindu hero. So is also Dionysos, his dual and counterpart. In fact, Hercules and Dionysos closely correspond to Vishnu and Shiva as well as to Gadeiros and Atlas. Gadeiros – whose name corresponds to Govinda (Vishnu) is the Good Cowherd (or Shepherd) who led the hordes of survivors away from the site of Paradise Destroyed, at the dawn of the present era.

It is hence no big surprise to note that we have two heroes (Hercules and Atlas or Shiva and Vishnu) one on each side of the world, just as we also have two Ethiopias; two pairs of pillars of Atlas and/or Hercules; two Gardens of the Hesperides; two Pole (or Morning) Stars, and so forth.

Megasthenes – who was more or less a contemporary of Plato and who based himself on independent traditions – affirms that both Hercules and Dionysos were born in the East Indies. Many other traditions support this belief. Others affirm instead that these heroes were precursors of Alexander, who invaded the East Indies several millennia before the Macedonian hero did so. [1051]

In actuality, the figure of Hercules is itself dual, as brilliantly demonstrated by Marcel Bréal in his Hércule et Caccus (Paris, 1873). The Greek Herakles is the visible dual of the Roman (or Etruscan) Hercules (or Hercle). One hero was Aryan, the other one Pelasgian or Etruscan, and hence pre-Greco-Roman in origin.

This one also corresponded to the Phoenician Baal or Melkhart, who in turn visibly corresponded to Bala, his Hindu archetype. Bala is the same as Bali, the mighty giant defeated by the dwarf Vamana.

Many Greco-Roman authorities concur on the foreign origin of Hercules. Herodotus speaks of several Hercules. And so does Homer, who places one avatar of the dead hero in Heaven (Olympus) and another one in Hades, where he is met by Ulysses. Cicero speaks of as many as seven different Hercules.

In reality, this profusion of heroes corresponds to the proliferation of his pillars, or those of Atlas, also to be found just about everywhere: Gibraltar; Phoenicia; the Indies; Ethiopia, and so forth. It may even be that Pandaia, the daughter of Hercules and ruler of the Indies may be his own feminine avatar.

No matter what, her name closely evokes the one of the Pandus, the celebrated heroes of the majestic Mahabharata. The name of the Pandus means "pale, white, rice, golden" in Sanskrit, suggesting a similar Greek etymology (pan-dia). This etymology corresponds to that of the name of Java and the Yavanas or Greeks. The word derives from the Dravida and has to do with the myth of the White Island (Svetadvipa), one of the many names of Paradise Lost.

The Many Pillars of Hercules

This map parallels the one made by José Imbelloni, the famous Argentinean anthropologist, in his book on Atlantis. Imbelloni was a careful, competent researcher, and his finds can hardly be put to question. In this careful compilation Imbelloni gathered together the various attributes of the Pillars of Hercules, Mt. Atlas and sites of Atlantis made by the ancient authorities.

The objective of this proliferation of Pillars of Hercules and/or of Atlas in antiquity was to confound the profanes on the true whereabouts of Paradise (Atlantis). And this was done for a series of reasons; the foremost of these was of course the fear that the greedy adventurers and conquistadors would desecrate the place, in their insatiable thirst for gold.

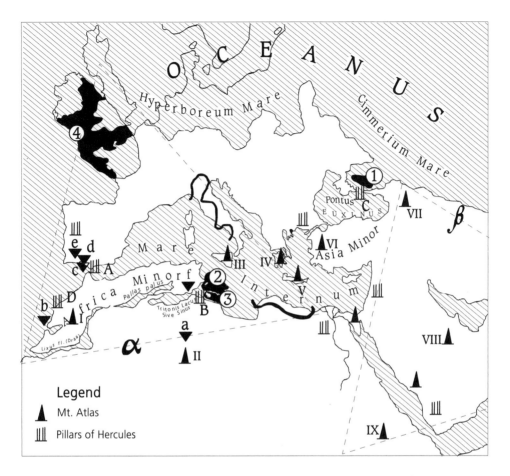

But there was only one real pair of pillars: the ones which flank Sunda Strait in Indonesia, allowing ingress to the interior of Taprobane, the real site of Paradise, in the Far East.

We have also embodied in this map the researches of more modern Atlantologists enjoying a good scientific reputation, such as Moreau de Jonnés, A. de Paniagua, P. Borchard, A. Schulten, R. Hennig, L. Frobenius, and so forth. The areas in black represent the now sunken portions of several proposed sites of Atlantis. The inverted triangles correspond to those parts of proposed sites of Atlantis which, these experts claim, remained emerse in whole or in part down to the present time.

The respective Pillars of Hercules are indicated by the twin pillars, and the several Mt. Atlas by the sharp tipped triangles in black, which are indicated by the Roman numerals and explained in his seminal text: I) the Atlas in Morocco; II) the Saharan Atlas (called <u>Mons Tale</u> by Ptolemy);

III) the Sicilian Atlas (also called <u>Mons Aetna</u>); IV) the Arcadian Atlas, and so forth.

Most of these attributions directly derive from ancient sources. They were often explicitly identified either with Mt. Atlas itself or with the Pillars of Hercules. To Imbelloni's chart we have also added some of the best known Pillars of Hercules of the ancient authorities (unnumbered): the Bosphorus Thracicus; the ancient Strait of Suez and the Bab-el-Mandeb, which the great researcher omitted for some reason.

Several other known "Pillars of Hercules" lie in other regions of the world, of Indonesia in particular. For this reason, they do not fit here and are not shown in this map. We have been able to locate at least four major instances in the region of Indonesia: Sunda Strait; Malacca Strait; Lombok Strait and the Nicobar Strait, plus several others of lesser importance.

In general, these straits were named in homage of Hindu gods such as Shiva, Balarama, Krishna and Vishnu, rather than their Greek counterparts such as Dionysos, Hercules, Atlas, Kronos and Alexander. But the meaning and context is exactly the same. So, these straits and their pylons can be considered further legitimate instances of "Pillars of Hercules".

As is clear, there was a whole multitude both of "Pillars of Hercules" and of "Mt. Atlas" in antiquity, just as indicated in Imbelloni's map. The main objective of this profusion was the usual one of confounding the unwelcome attention of inquisitive profanes.

Of course, only the true Pillar of Heaven of Atlantis, the central one, really counted. The others were just illusions of no meaning or importance. But this pillar was double, being formed by Mt. Mashu, the Split Mountain of Paradise.

This name of "Pillar of Heaven" was generally applied to volcanoes such as the Krakatoa and the Aetna, whose volcanic plume in fact simulated a fiery pillar stretching all the way to heaven itself. Several other volcanoes were also named accordingly: the Aetna, the Vesuvius, the Thera, the Teyde, and so forth. And so were several volcanoes of the Far East, Indonesia in particular, where they are most abundant.

The remarkable symbolism of Tanit is the real reason for the name "Pillars of Hercules". Tanit was indeed a symbol representing a triangle topped by a crossbar and a circle, and often two paps, as shown here. The triangle is the sacred cone of the Goddess, and represents a mountain and, even more exactly, a volcanic peak or island. ↑*052*

The circle is the sun shining on her head, much as it did in Hathor's and other aliases of Tanit. And this "sun" is really the volcano. The crossbar represents the two raised arms of the <u>ka</u> symbolism of Egypt. And the two raised arms are those of Atlas and his far famed pillars at the two sides of the world. The two "paps" yielding "milk" are frequent representations of the twin volcanoes of Paradise shedding abundance.

The two pillars or arms also correspond to the mountain said to have been ripped into two pylons or pillars by the hero, on his return from Erythea, with the cattle he had stolen from Geryon, his own former self. Said otherwise, we see that Tanit is an alias of Atlas in the castrated (or feminine) shape.

The volcanic peak also corresponds to the linga, turned into a lowly yoni or vulva after its "castration", which turned the lofty peak into a giant caldera and the mighty god into a mighty goddess.

With this cleaving, Hercules allegedly created the twin pylons, as well as the passage, the strait which they delimited at the two sides. But this event never happened at all in the region of Gibraltar, which has been open since long before the times of Man. But it is in fact real in the region of Taprobane, where the mighty Krakatoa Volcano actually cleft open Sunda Strait, separating Java from Sumatra.

The Hindus also spoke both of twin Merus as well as of its five peaks. These five peaks formed a sort of quincunx, with the main peak at the center, and the four others at the Four Cardinal Directions (the Four Pillars of the Earth). This configuration is often attested in the Kalachakra mandalas, themselves an image of Mt. Meru. [1053]

The ancient Egyptians and several other early peoples, the Mayas and the Aztecs included, also had similar traditions. Actually, the Four Pillars of the Earth corresponded to the two pairs, one located in the far orient, the other one in the far occident. The fifth pillar is the one at the center, the true Pillar of Heaven.

We illustrated and commented on this pristine Egyptian world conception in a figure shown further above in the present section. One of these straits corresponds to Gibraltar, and the other one to Sunda Strait, in Indonesia. There the day star was said to start its daily trip, which ended in Gibraltar Strait, where the day ended.

Once there, the sun entered the Ocean, which he crossed in his golden goblet during the night. In his nocturnal voyage, the sun went back to the East Indies, reaching it just in time to start his new daily voyage across the sky (the Celestial Ocean). Of course, these are only charming metaphors, allegories intended to account for the actual phenomena.

The two straits portrayed in the remarkable Egyptian cosmogram discussed further above also correspond to the two extremities of the world mentioned in Homer's Odyssey (I:22) as inhabited by: "the Ethiopians...

who live at the world's extremities, divided in two halves, one where the sun (Hyperion) rises, and the other where he sets."

We will return to the theme of the Ethiopians in more detail further below, in our discussion of the globe of Crates of Mallus, to which the interested reader is now directed.

Quite clearly, these world extremities inhabited by the Ethiopians are the two straits portrayed in the Egyptian vase. And so, the tradition in question here is far older than even Homer himself, who wrote at about 1,000 BC or so. Hence, the Greeks might well have obtained the story of Atlantis and these Ethiopians from Egypt, just as Plato affirms in his dialogues on Atlantis.

It is true that the region around Gibraltar Strait is in fact inhabited by "white Ethiopians": the Berbers, the Libyans, the Phoenicians, the Guanches, and so forth. And so is the region of Taprobane, also inhabited by other such "white Ethiopians": the Tocharians, the Seres, the Yüeh-Chi, the Hsiung-nu (Huns), etc..

The existence of these "blond, blue-eyed Chinese" was well known to the ancients. They are the "Pious Ethiopians" of Homer (Il. I:7; Od. I:22; V:288, etc.) and the Long-Lived Ethiopians of Pliny, Solinus and Herodotus, among other ancient historians and geographers.

The historian Ephorus (405–330 BC), a contemporary of Plato, mentioned an early tradition on the Ethiopians having invaded and conquered Libya (North Africa) as far as the Atlas Mountains, and later settling there. This early tradition was certainly also known to Plato, very well informed on such matters.

Herodotus (Hist. VII:70) and Strabo (Geogr. XV:21) also speak of two Ethiopias, one eastern, the other western. One of these was placed in Africa, whereas the other one ranged with the Indians, whom they closely paralleled. Strabo (Geogr. I:2:27) further affirms the following on the Ethiopians: "I assert that the ancient Greeks, in the same way as they classed all the northern nations with which they were familiar as Scythians, etc., so, I affirm, they designated as Ethiopia the whole of the southern countries toward the ocean.... If we moderns have [wrongly] confined the appellation 'Ethiopians' to those only who dwell near Egypt, this must not be allowed to interfere with the ancient meaning". Strabo's view is supported by historical fact, as expounded here, etc.. [054]

This lesson must be kept in mind by all of us. The ancient Greeks called "Ethiopia" all the countries south of the equator. These correspond to what Crates of Mallus called "Antœci" and "Antipodes" in his globe. These peoples are often confused with the Blacks. But this is wrong. The

Ethiopians in question here are in reality the White Ethiopians. The modern mistake of identifying them with the Black peoples is a result similar to the confusion just denounced by Strabo.

Ephorus further adds that: "The Ethiopians were considered as occupying all the south coasts of both Asia and Africa, divided by the Erythraean into Eastern and Western Asiatic and African." These two regions correspond precisely to those actually occupied by the White Ethiopians of Homer and others, if we interpret the Erythraean as the Global Ocean, as we should here.

Plug in the Indian Ocean, and you come out with the wrong answer which places Ethiopia in the country formally called Abyssinia, in East Africa, which recently usurped the name of Ethiopia. It seems, from the text of Herodotus just linked, and others, that the Ethiopic invasion in question here is the mythical one attributed to Osiris, but in reverse: from Egypt to the East Indies.

Diodorus Siculus (<u>Hist</u>. III:2:4), specifically affirms: "They (the Ethiopians) also say that the Egyptians are colonists sent out by the Ethiopians, Osiris having been the leader of the colony."

This relation is extremely curious, as it reverses the usual traditions on Osiris – or Dionysos (his alias), Hercules, etc. – having invaded India, a fact which never occurred. Perhaps the ancient Greeks mythified the real events, inverting them in order to reduce the humiliating defeat they actually suffered at the hands of the Eastern Ethiopians according to these unequivocal reports.

This early invasion by the Ethiopians is also very probably akin to the one reported by Theopompos, another contemporary of Plato. Though Theopompos places the event in mythical terms, his tradition on the Eusebes is very obviously the same as the historical one just told.

And this tradition is very clearly based upon reality, the two "Ethiopias" being now known for sure to have both existed, just as affirmed by Homer. Moreover, the White Ethiopians (or Seres) very obviously came from the Far East, just as told by Ephorus.

Philostratus (<u>Vit. Apol</u>. II:33f), affirms that "The Indians are the wisest of mankind. The Ethiopians are a colony of them, and they inherit the wisdom of their fathers." The Ethiopia in question here is really Indonesia, in fact early settled by the Indians, who apparently originated there. In fact, the Dravidian colony mentioned here is due to their return to the region, during the Middle Ages.

Plato's source was most probably the same as those of Ephorus and Theopompos, among others. And these sources visibly date from the times of Homer, if not far earlier still. This tradition harks back to the times when the Libyo-Phoenicians first settled in Africa, in prehistoric times, which is certainly prior to the rise of dynastic Egypt, as demonstrated by the Amratian vase illustrated here.

So, the recent attempts by some Atlantologists to identify Plato's account of the Atlantean invasion to the one of the Sea Peoples in about 1,300 BC is wrong, as it is irremediably too late to account for the far earlier traditions on the Ethiopian invasion reported by both Ephorus and Diodorus.

However, this myth of the twin Ethiopias also allegorized the dualism of Atlantis and its famous pillars. One of these pairs was located in the Far Orient, the other one in the Far Occident. The western pillars were those of Gibraltar, and the western Mt. Atlas was the well-known one of Morocco. Both these features were purely metaphorical, and were simple "mirror images" of the true ones, located in Taprobane.

Taprobane, the former site of Lanka, is the same as Indonesia. There the new day started by convention. The true "Pillar of Heaven" was located there, inside Sunda Strait. It corresponded to Mt. Krakatoa, the ferocious volcano, whose giant plume can be seen in this magnificent computer simulation here, made by an expert volcanologist working in the famous national research institute at Los Alamos. [055]

The huge size and shape of the "pillar of fire and smoke" created by Krakatoa's giant explosion allow us to understand why such unique features were called "Pillar of Heaven" in antiquity. And the real two Pillars of Hercules were the two sides of the island or mountain which flank the volcano, the Split Mountain of Paradise.

This strait (Sunda) is often compared to a gate or door (Gate of Dawn) and its two side islands (Java and Sumatra) are compared to its two pylons or pillars. This gate with its two swinging doors and its two pylons, is just as illustrated here. This swinging gate is the counterpart of the Split Mountain (Mt. Mashu), the mountain of Shamash (the Sun). We discuss this important subject in the main text, and will not repeat this discussion here. [056]

This name also applies to the two volcanoes which flank Sunda Strait, the Dempo and the Krakatoa. Sometimes the Toba volcano is substituted for one of the pillars, even though it belonged to a former era. In even earlier times, in the Ice Age, before Sunda Strait was opened, the strait leading into Atlantis – the real Gate of Paradise – was the strait between Bali and Lombok (Lombok Strait).

This strait is part of the famous Wallace Line, the passage which remained open even when all others closed out. When the Ice Age ended, and the Krakatoa exploded, opening up Sunda Strait, both the name and the function was transferred to this new Gate of Dawn and its two pylons, the two volcanoes just named.

This disastrous supervolcanic explosion of the Krakatoa actually triggered the catastrophic end of the last Ice Age. In some way, the tradition of this Indonesian event passed to Greece as the myth of Hercules opening up Gibraltar Strait after he crossed the former isthmus during his return from Erytheia driving the cattle he had stolen from Geryon, his former elder self (Grk. geryon = "elder, older").

One should keep in mind the many millennia which elapsed since these myths were first composed, perhaps in Atlantean times. People moved a lot and one civilization succeeded the other as time inexorably flowed. But they invariably carried along their sacred traditions, the very foundation of the ancient Mystery Religions. Hence, a lot of change would naturally result, no matter what.

Myths are often transferred from one place to another in this way, leading to a terrible confusion which few if any experts manage to overcome in practice. We have already discussed this subject in the main text, and the interested reader is directed to it, as well as the related glosses of the Classical maps discussed further above.

The Global Extent of the Former Atlantean Empire

This remarkable figure reproduces the map of Leo Frobenius (1873– 1938). Leo Frobenius is the great German archaeologist who specialized on Atlantis. He left behind many thousands of written pages and similar numbers of archaeological artefacts he had uncovered during the great many expeditions he personally led around the whole world, Black Africa in particular.

The great researcher came to the surprising result that Atlantis was formerly located in Benin, in West Africa. Frobenius was also able to trace the vestiges of what he believed to be the Atlantean Culture extending all the way to the most distant places in the world, the Americas included, as shown in the map below.

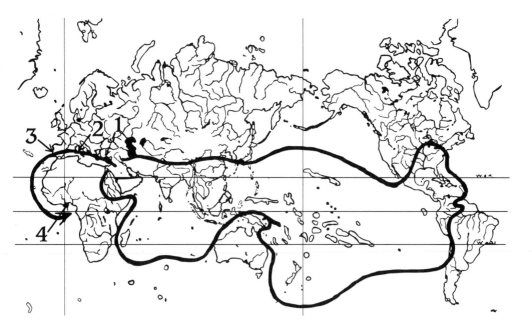

Still another important contribution made by Leo Frobenius consisted in demonstrating the fact that contacts between the Old World and the New were effected via the Pacific Ocean, rather than across the Atlantic Ocean, a dead region insofar as ancient navigation was concerned.

This reality has now been abundantly confirmed by several expert researchers. The crossing of the wide Pacific Ocean has now been shown to be viable even in primitive vessels, such as the ones used by Thor Heyerdahl and several other adventurers and explorers.

The greatest contribution made by Leo Frobenius was his courageous research of tabooed subjects such as Atlantology, which he turned into a reputable academic discipline.

The numbers 1 to 4 in Frobenius' map trace out what the great researcher called the "Poseidonic Culture". It was apparently born in Asia Minor (1), next diffusing to Etruria (2) and then to Spain (3), next passing to the region of Benin, in West Africa (4). It is interesting to note that, with the possible exception of Black Africa, all these places were ruled by "red" races of Dravidian origin: Pelasgians, Etruscans, Phoenicians, Celtiberians, Guanches, Berbers, Libyans, Ethiopians and so forth.

It is quite possible that all this is no more than a chancy coincidence. But when such coincidences start to pile up, the astute investigator is forced to pause and to ponder the matter, starting to search for a cause-

and-effect relationship; a global diffusion of the myths rather than a series of random coincidences.

It is also interesting to quote here a strange ritual once observed by another field anthropologist working in the region of Benin, the one marked by the number (4) in the map. This investigator personally observed a curious ritual where a native, dressed in long clothes and with the whole body painted white, landed from a boat and then started instructing the dark natives into the arts of agriculture, metallurgy, astronomy, and so forth.

I believe that this strange ritual somehow imitated events that really took place in the dawn of time: the instruction of the Benin natives, whom Frobenius found to be far more civilized than their neighbors.

Let me make it clear that it is not my intention to denigrate the contributions made by Black Africa to civilization: quite the contrary. All I want is the truth itself. Ethnic pride is a poor counselor both to blacks and whites. I do not claim that we whites actually invented all things. Actually, the opposite seems to be the actual case, at least insofar as the rise of humanity itself is concerned. The reds did it, not the whites.

One culture and one race influences the others, so that change and evolution, and hence progress results. Otherwise, what we have is stagnation, despite the foolish claims of Darwin and others. Ask any plant or animal breeder and they will tell you. In order to have evolution, crossbreeding is absolutely required. It is only thus that change results, permitting selection to work: natural, sexual, artificial, etc..

In this context, we humans are all mongrels, with some of us black and better adapted for Africa's sunny climate, and some white and best adapted for the cooler regions. And these include the densely forested, shady regions of Southeast Asia and Amazonia, where the sun is blocked out by the trees and is hence very scarce at ground level.

Such was particularly the case during the Ice Age, when the weather was normally clouded and cold, and sunshine quite inadequate. It was for this reason that the pale-skinned races developed in Asia whereas the dark-skinned races developed in Africa's savannahs, sunny and dry, particularly during the Ice Age.

The most interesting feature of Frobenius' research is the fact that the Atlantean culture he charted (see above map) is <u>typically tropical</u>, and is mainly delimited by the two tropics. This is an extremely curious find, since most Western experts firmly believe that Civilization arose in the temperate regions of the world, and hold that the tropics are fated to be backwaters of the far more advanced temperate cultures.

These experts perhaps forget the fact that world development started, to believe Plato, during the Ice Age, when earth's presently temperate regions were covered by mile thick layers of ice which prevented not only agriculture but even the development of humanity in substantial numbers.

We also observe that the true site of Atlantis – the one which we have recently discovered in Indonesia and Southeast Asia – is located right at the center of the vast expanse covered by the seminal culture revealed by Frobenius' exhaustive research. Moreover, Taprobane, its heart, was located right at the Line of the Equator.

This widespread diffusion seems to have occurred via the wide expanses of both the Indian and the Pacific Ocean, with the Atlantic Ocean being no more than an empty desert which no one dared to sail. It is natural that cultures diffuse departing from the center towards the periphery, rather than depart from an extremity, as proposed by the great researcher in the present connection.

So, it seems that our own hypothesis is far more consentaneous with actual reality than is Frobenius' proposal of a center in Benin, at the empire's western fringe. Benin was a very good guess, given the early date and the state of the science of Archaeology at the time when it was proposed. But the advancement of Science has been enormous since then, so that it is natural that this view be superseded and changed now.

Atlantis and Its Great Plain

As disclosed by Plato, both the empire and its capital city were named Atlantis. In the map below, we present a detailed chart of the Great Plain of Atlantis as described by Plato and by the quaint illustrations typical of the Jaina sect of Hinduism. Above all, note the huge size of the Great Plain, its rectangular shape, and the uncanny similitude with the seafloor of the Java Sea region discussed further above.

An attentive examination of this map will reveal the fact that its central peak corresponds to a replica of Mt. Atlas (or Meru) with its four "heads" descending down the four faces of this central pyramid. These features are explicitly shown in the Jaina Cosmogram linked here. [057]

This symbolic replica represents real Mt. Atlas, which is the central feature of Atlantis City shown in successively enlarged forms in the next two figures. This is the shape actually described by Plato, which is also shown in certain Jaina Cosmograms of Jambudvipa, the Hindu Paradise.

Atlantis City is located at Sunda Strait, the one sundering Java and Sumatra and allowing the ingress to Atlantis' Great Plain via the huge canal leading to the sea in front along what is now the Sunda Strait.

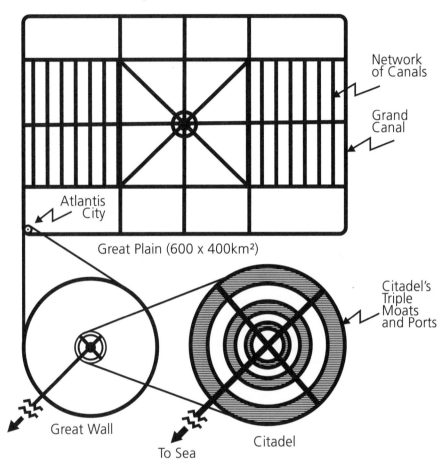

Network of Canals

Grand Canal

Atlantis City

Great Plain (600 x 400km²)

Citadel's Triple Moats and Ports

Great Wall

To Sea

Citadel

Atlantis' Location and Geometry

This huge canal was fully 50 km long, according to Plato. The city proper was built on the volcanic mound (Mt. Krakatoa) which was later transformed into the giant caldera known as the Vadavamukha, the "Mouth of Hell" when the volcano erupted and exploded, caving in, and opening up Sunda Strait.

When all such details are compared, one is unavoidably led to conclude that the two traditions originated from a common source. And since both traditions so closely coincide with the actual geographical features of the Indonesian region, we are also compelled to conclude that these sacred traditions are ultimately based on real events. We are presently in the process of organizing an oceanographical expedition to research this location in detail for relics of these singular features.

CHAPTER 9 – ATLANTIS IN MINOAN SYMBOLISM

I am the Sun who arose in the Primeval Waters.
My soul is God, I am the All-Creator...
I am the Word, the Immortal Spirit;
In this my name of "Soul of the World".

<u>Coffin Texts, Spell 317</u>

The Logo of Atlantis Publications

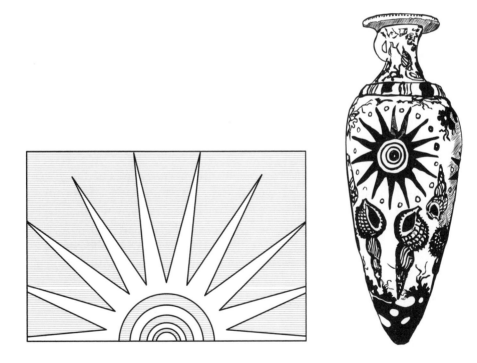

Our logotype (illustrated above) represents Atlantis as a sort of sun rising from the waters of the ocean to herald the dawn of a new age to the world. This motif is not originally ours, but is based on one from the elegant rhyton from Minoan Crete also illustrated above.

This Late Minoan vase dates from about 1,500 BC, and is hence prior to the cataclysm which destroyed Crete soon after that date. This type of decoration is of the so-called "marine style" which was obsessively used in Minoan Crete at that time. We strongly suspect that this type of decoration has everything to do with Atlantis, as the triple concentric circles of the odd starfish at the center are characteristic of the lost continent.

Needless to say, no real starfish bears such a curious decoration. Moreover, this starfish looks like a shining sun with 15 rays. As such, Atlantis is here portrayed as the terrestrial sun shining under the waters. And this sun is in turn connected with Atlantis' downfall, as we shall see next. It is also the "sun" shown shining on top of Tanit's head.

If this reasoning is right, and this symbolism is really connected with Atlantis, we can draw two conclusions from this quaint Minoan vase. First, since it is over a full millennium prior to Plato himself (428–348 BC), in no way could the great philosopher have invented the story of Atlantis or, even less, have based himself on Crete's demise in order to compose his tale of a great civilization submerged by the Flood.

Second, since the decoration necessarily predates the demise of Minoan Crete by the Thera volcanism, it is also clear that in no way could the Minoan Cretans themselves have derived the Atlantean symbolism from their own tragedy, which actually finished them off for good. Consequently, alternative explanations for the Minoan obsession with Atlantean motifs must be found.

Excluding the possibility of foresight, of divine revelation or of universal archetypes as unscientific, we are left with the hypothesis of diffusion. And this diffusion could only have come from Atlantis itself. Or can anyone offer a better explanation than ours for these uncanny coincidences?

We also note another interesting feature of this type of "marine style" decoration typical of Minoan Crete. Even though the symbolic connections with Atlantis are somewhat obvious to those familiar with this type of thing, these motifs are invariably disguised in some way: as a starfish, a giant octopus, a murex shellfish, a dolphin, sargasso weeds, the rising sun, and so on.

Hardly could the Minoan artist have intended to represent a real starfish in this curious decoration, since these organisms never display the triple circle feature depicted here. Had he intended to do so, he would choose a more natural decoration observed in real starfishes, as these creatures actually abound in Crete.

As is clear, this odd "starfish" closely resembles a "submarine sun". And this sun is visibly an image of Atlantis itself as a now submerged realm hidden under the waters. It was this connection which inspired us to use this quaint marine symbolism as an image of the rising sun.

The other features illustrated in this remarkable Minoan vessel are also very characteristic of Atlantis as well. The kelp or sargasso – which does not exist in the Mediterranean Sea – is characteristic of the South Seas (South Pacific), the very region where we have located Atlantis. In fact, these seas were formerly called <u>Prasodum Mare</u> ("Sea of Sargassos"), the name actually used by Claudius Ptolemy.

Columbus – who firmly believed himself to be navigating this far off sea – actually named the Sargasso Sea of the Caribbean region after the original East Indian one. The story of this archetypal Sargasso Sea is closely tied with the one of Atlantis, as we discuss in our Internet site. They were mentioned by several ancient authors, among them Aristotle, Pliny, Himilco, Scylax, Avienus, etc..

These sargassos were said to be so thick as to be able to tie up the ships, dragging them down and causing them to wreck. And they were also attached to the legend of the "Hand of Satan" which issued from the sea to carry ships under, directly to Hell itself.

This thick vegetation was also said to be connected with the now submerged trees of Atlantis, turned into seaweeds. In one way or another, this tradition on the "Hand of Satan" and the terrible sargassos associated with it got transferred to the Atlantic Ocean, where it survived down to the times when the explorations of the Age of Navigation had combed this ocean all the way to the Americas and beyond.

The murex shellfish was the source – real or alleged – of the precious purple dye so appreciated by the ancients in general. The purple color was the very emblem of royalty. And this symbolism is also directly associated with Atlantis itself. The Phoenicians, whose name is directly associated with this purple dye – called <u>phoinix</u> in Greek – were the exclusive suppliers of this precious commodity, which they actually fetched from the East Indies, its true source.

Finally, the dolphin is also closely associated with Atlantis. The dolphin is the sacred emblem of both Poseidon and Dionysos, the Greek counterparts of Shiva. Dionysos is the Greek Mystery god often said to have been born in India (Nysa). Poseidon is in turn the founder of Atlantis and the father of Atlas and Gadeiros, his successors as the twin rulers of Atlantis.

Shiva, the "Pillar of Heaven" (<u>Sthanu</u>, <u>Stambha</u>) is also the Hindu archetype of Poseidon and hence of Atlas, the first ruler of Atlantis. Shiva's emblem is the trident (trishula). And the trident is also the emblem of Poseidon. This charming coin from Sicily (330 BC) shows Poseidon in the obverse and his trident flanked by two dolphins in the reverse. [058]

This curious symbol, together with the anchor, are both precursors of the Cross of Christ. Some iconographies explicitly show the dolphin impaled on the trident. And this quaint imagery was adopted by the early Christians as an alias and disguise of Christ's Cross when their nascent religion was still a well-guarded secret. [059]

In fact, the twin dolphins correspond to the twin saviors, themselves aliases of Hercules and Atlas or, if you prefer, Shiva and Vishnu or Apollo and Dionysos, etc.. In this context it is interesting to compare the two dolphins with the falling figures of Solomon and Hiram of Arcane #17, the Tower, commented further above.

The vase itself (rython) is another emblem of Atlantis. The sacred vase is, in many ways, an alias and precursor of the Holy Grail. The footless shape of rhytons and amphoras is also ritual in character. It derives directly from the Svayambhu Linga of India. The linga represents Shiva as the "Pillar of the World". Even more exactly, the linga is the symbol of Atlantis, again in the same connection. [060]

The word svayambhu signifies "existing of itself; self-originated" in Sanskrit. The idea here is that Atlantis existed of itself, and did not originate, like all subsequent civilizations, from the diffusion of other cultures, arts and techniques. This idea is vividly represented here, through a curious inversion of the symbolism, by the vase or the egg which cannot stand of itself.

In this context the Svayambhu linga is often identified to the Cosmic Egg from which all things originally developed. The egg or linga often turns into the mandorla, its feminine counterpart. In fact, the two symbols are often represented together, by the yoni-lingam, the two sex symbols in intimate union. [061]

These symbols in turn represent the twin volcanoes of Atlantis, the Toba and the Krakatoa. These two volcanoes – the Krakatoa in special – also correspond to what the Hindus call the Vadavamukha (or "Submarine Mare"). The Submarine Mare is also called the "Doomsday Fire", which periodically destroys the world, when the respective eras are to end.

The aforementioned symbolisms are all closely linked and ultimately derive from a common source of extreme antiquity, probably Atlantean in origin. Their meaning is somewhat complex, particularly in their connection with the Flood. This connection is instanced by the figure just linked of Vishnu quietly asleep over the coiled body of the Serpent Shesha, itself an allegory of the Flood.

When traced to its origin, this symbolism is visibly derived from the Hindu ones just commented. And its very universality proves both its hoary age and its probable connection with Atlantis, the sole possible conveyor of this worldwide diffusion to distant overseas locations.

Curiously enough, the "starfish motif" is also characteristic of the Australian Aboriginal sacred traditions on the Flood. So is the dolphin itself, often associated in Atlantis type decorations in Australia, precisely as they were in Minoan Crete and other locations. Such is the case of the rhyton in question here or the "dolphin and trident" coins just discussed above.

One of these Australian illustrations is shown in the above figure. The seven concentric circles correspond to the Seven Isles of the Blest and the Seven Dvipas of Hindu traditions. But these often become three, in correspondence with the "Atlantis Plan motif" instanced here. [062]

The four dolphins in turn correspond to the Four Guardians (Lokapalas) of Hindu traditions, themselves aliases of the two main ones. In Australian symbolism, the dolphin often becomes the "Rainbow Serpent". And the Rainbow Serpent is himself an alias of the Serpent Shesha in his quality of sea serpent, a creature which abounds in the whole of the South Seas region and essentially nowhere else. [063]

Shesha is often specifically compared to the rainbow as a marker of the Universal Flood. And his myth is particularly important and widespread in the whole of the South Seas region, where Atlantis sank down.

The "Atlantis plain motif" is often portrayed sunken underseas in Australian paintings, such as the ones illustrated below. The resemblance is too close to require further comments, and the two traditions, Minoan and Australian, obviously originated from a common source, very probably Atlantean.

The motif of the "submarine sun" is also as old as it is widespread. As we already mentioned, it corresponds to the Vadavamukha, the "Fiery Submarine Mare" of Hindu traditions. The Vadavamukha, also called Aurva, is considered to be the "Fire of Doomsday". This because of the fact that it destroys the world when the time comes for it. [064]

In Hindu traditions, the tenth and forthcoming avatar of Vishnu – or of Shiva, according to Shivaite beliefs – is called Kalkin. Kalkin will come about riding the Vadava, and destroying the world with its fire.

The name of Kalkin is more or less synonymous with that of the Serpent Shesha, showing their esoteric connection. Both these names mean "scum, spume, froth". And it closely corresponds to the Greek word ilus or pelos, the scum or froth which, according to Plato, covered the seas of Atlantis after its destruction, rendering them innavigable.

This "froth" is actually pumice stone, which is in fact volcanic spume (Latin pumex = "spume, froth"). And these parallel traditions attest, better than anything else, the volcanic nature of the Atlantean cataclysm of fire and water.

Some texts even identify Shiva, in his Kalagni shape, with the Vadava itself. And Kalagni means "Fire of Doomsday". Another passage in the majestic Mahabharata (12:348) identifies the Vadavamukha with Vishnu (Narayana) himself, rather than his horse. And it tells of the destruction of the world by a giant volcanism, which covers all lands and creates an utter universal darkness which leads the world into a global death. [065]

The Mahabharata (I:180-4) also tells the story of the genesis of the Vadavamukha, alias Aurva. This name means "born of the thigh", because of the fact that, like Dionysos, Aurva was born out of the thigh of his mother, where she had hid his fetus, for fear of the Kshatryas. These had killed all of Aurva's race, the Bhrigus, excepting Aurva himself. [066]

Aurva's rage was so great that from his eyes poured forth a fire, which became the Vadavamukha. This was later enclosed within a mare's skull, and confined to the Ocean, on whose bottom it burns quietly until the time of Doomsday. Come this time, the Vadava goes haywire, and grows without limit, destroying the world with Fire and Water (supervolcanisms and giant tsunamis).

There are a great many variants of this legend in the Puranas and other holy books. But all describe the Vadavamukha in terms that can only refer to a submarine supervolcano such as the Krakatoa. As such volcanoes are extremely rare, the odds of the legend referring to the Krakatoa volcano are overwhelming.

Moreover, the Mahabharata text just linked, and several others of enormous antiquity, explicitly identify the Aurva with the Submarine Sun, the second such: "And the son of Saktri, like the Sun just emerging from the clouds, illuminated the whole firmament by that stainless sacrifice of his [of the Rakshasas] into which the large libations of clarified butter were poured. Then Vasishtha and the other Rishis regarded that Muni blazing with his own energy as if he were the second Sun."

The Mahabharata further affirms that the fire of Aurva destroyed the Rakshasas in their totality. And the Rakshasas are the semi-demonic people of Lanka, whom we have identified with the decayed Atlanteans. This quaint symbolism of the Submarine Fire or Sun as a submarine volcano is so exact that it leaves little room for doubting its direct connection with Atlantis, destroyed in just this way.

Finally, we note that the island of Lanka, the former abode of the Rakshasas, was also called Vadavamukha. Lanka is also the same as Taprobane or Sumatra, the abode of the Krakatoa volcano, which lies inside the waters of Sunda Strait, its frontier with Java. Now, Taprobane is the very place which we have identified with Atlantis.

It is also worth remarking that both Shiva and Vishnu are often identified with volcanoes. As such, they are also identified to the two "Pillars of the World". This imagery dates from the Rigvedic times, and hence long predates the similar ones of the Greeks, Phoenicians, and other Mediterranean peoples.

It is strange to see one's gods and heroes identified with volcanoes and cruciform celestial pillars. But this identification can be explained. Religion started out as Naturism, and gods and heroes were originally natural sprites (genii or angels) controlling natural events: volcanoes, earthquakes, winds, tempests and so forth.

It is hence natural that the two supreme gods of India would be identified to supervolcanoes, the supreme natural disaster. In this role, Vishnu and Shiva correspond to the twins of all mythologies.

These omnipresent Twins are the ones who bring about Doomsday when they start to quarrel: Atlas and Hercules, Zeus and Poseidon, Ahura Mazda and Ahriman, Solomon and Hiram, the Two Dolphins, and so forth. Even in the Americas these two figures are often found: Nhanderykey and

Tyvyry in South America, Quetzalcoatl and Tezcatlipoca in Mexico, the Twins of the Mayan <u>Popol Vuh</u>, the ones of the Navajo Indians commented in my site, and so forth.

The two volcanoes in question here are the ones of Atlantis, the two Pillars of Hercules and/or Atlas. The two are both volcanoes or, alternatively, the two pylons flanking the volcano inside Sunda Strait, the Gate of Dawn. As such, they also correspond to the Split Mountain discussed above (Mt. Mashu), the one from which the sun rises every morning, in the Orient. Hence its other name of "Mountain of the Orient (or of Sunrise)"

In more realistic terms, this quaint symbolism originated from the twin volcanoes heralding the new "day" that the terrestrial sun in fact inaugurates, the new era of the world. As the eras change, these twin volcanoes also change: the Toba and the Krakatoa in Sumatra; the Krakatoa and the Dempo in Sunda Strait and so on. It is natural that the presiding gods change residence when their former abode is destroyed as the eras come and go. Only the last two eras count, forming Heaven and Earth.

Originally, these two volcanoes were the Gunung Agung and the Gunung Rinjani, the two majestic volcanoes flanking Lombok Strait, near Bali. These two volcanic peaks – towering at 3,726 meters (Mt. Rinjani) and 3,142 meters (Mt. Agung) – were the original Pillars of Hercules – and/or Atlas or, more exactly, Shiva and Vishnu, their Hindu archetypes.

These two volcanoes formed the two pylons of the original Gate of Dawn which led to the interior of Paradise during the Ice Age. As such, Lombok Strait corresponded to the very start of Wallace Line, the only maritime passage open to the interior of Atlantis during the Ice Age.

This was before Sunda Strait and Malacca Strait were opened – one by the Atlantean cataclysm itself, the other by the rise of sea level which took place after this catastrophic event. This rise turned the River of Paradise into the narrow channel which now separates Sumatra from the Malay Peninsula, Malacca Strait.

PART III - THE MANY SITES OF ATLANTIS

> *There is no place for dogma in Science. The scientist is free to ask any question, to doubt any assertion, to seek for any evidence, to correct any error. Where Science has been used in the past to erect a new dogmatism, that dogmatism has found itself incompatible with the progress of Science; and in the end, the dogma has yielded, or Science and Freedom have perished together.*
>
> J. Robert Oppenheimer

CHAPTER 10 - THE ATLANTIC
OCEAN OF THE ANCIENTS

> *If anyone can show me that I am wrong in thought or*
> *deed, I will gladly change. I seek the truth, which has never*
> *yet hurt anybody. It is only persistence in self-delusion and*
> *ignorance which does us harm.*
>
> <u>Marcus Aurelius</u>

Introduction

In the present section (Part III) we discuss in some detail the several sites that have been thus far proposed for Atlantis over the two and a half millennia that have elapsed since Plato slightly lifted the veil of secrecy which has impenetrably surrounded the Lost Continent since remotest antiquity. In Part IV we comment, in some detail, our proposed localization, the one of Sundaland, under the seas of Indonesia.

We also here argue the identity of Eden with Atlantis, and demonstrate its true location in Taprobane (Indonesia). There, we have discovered the former existence of a huge continent, now sunken under the seas presently called Java Sea and South China Sea. And we have also discovered that this now sunken continent was the actual source of Civilization, where agriculture and other such seminal inventions were made long ago.

Even today, Atlantis remains the greatest enigma posed to humans since the beginning of history. And the myriad experts who have so far attempted to discover its true site cannot agree even on fundamental matters such as the ocean in which Atlantis is located, whether the Atlantic, the Indian or the Pacific Oceans, or even if Atlantis was wholly sunken or not.

Strangely enough, the sole obstacle that still remains in accepting the fact that the true site of Atlantis now lies under the Indonesian seas lies in the fact that people often grossly misunderstand what Plato really meant by words such as "island", "island of Atlantis"; "Atlantic Ocean", "Pillars of Hercules", "seism", "earthquake", "flood", "mud shoals", etc..

People – regrettably including most academic experts – normally believe that these words had the same meaning in Plato's time that they have today. Plato lived some 2,500 years ago, an enormous span of time, by linguistic standards.

One should not forget that Plato specifically affirms that the original names of the Atlantean localities and personages were actually translated into Egyptian from the unknown equivalents in the original language, whatever this mysterious Atlantean tongue might have been. [5]

From the Egyptian tongue they were next translated into ancient Greek and then, two and a half millennia later, into the modern languages such as English, French, etc.. It is unlikely that Solon – who did the re-translation into Greek – was actually an expert in ancient Egyptian.

It is equally improbable that either the ancient Egyptians, or the Greeks themselves, were skilled in Atlantean, a tongue spoken 9,000 years earlier than their own time. Even ancient Egyptian and ancient Greek changed so much as to often become unrecognizable in practice today, particularly in esoteric contexts.

Most fortunately, I was lucky enough to discover that the original Atlantean tongue was a form of proto-Dravida, a language that has partly survived in the dialects of South India as well as in its many holy books and traditions. This lucky trove of ours allowed us to linguistically reconstruct the etymology of many toponyms whose meaning had otherwise become utterly lost.

Many of these words actually passed into Sanskrit, the other sacred tongue of ancient India. Sanskrit is actually an artificial tongue, derived or reconstructed from Dravida itself, as we have shown in great detail. In this way, these theonyms and toponyms were sometimes preserved in a recognizable way in that sacred tongue of India.

The Case of Ys Brazil

Ask any competent linguist, and he/she will tell you that languages and words change so much in the course of millennia as to become unrecognizable in both sound and meaning (semantics and phonetics). So do toponyms and onomastics, particularly when they pass from one language to another, often through translation. The examples I give below demonstrate the truth of what I just said.

For example, the name of Brazil changed from the original one of Ilha de Vera Cruz to Terra de Santa Cruz and then to America, which is today only associated with the USA and almost never with Brazil. The land's name finally became Brazil, nowadays more correctly spelled Brasil. This name was adopted from the one of Hy Brazil (or Ys Brazil, Island of Brazil), a mythical "Atlantic Island".

These islands were believed to be a remainder of sunken Atlantis itself, and to be located in the Pacific rather than the Atlantic Ocean. All these changes in perception about Brazil and its name happened within a matter of just a few centuries, instead of ten thousand years and more. Similar changes also occurred in the United States and other locations in both the Old and the New Worlds.

Hence, it seems reasonable to concentrate on the geographical features themselves, rather than on the place-names which often change, in the course of time. Except for sea level rise, geographical features normally take millions of years to change substantially. This, in contrast to geographical place-names, which normally change a lot even in a matter of a few centuries only.

Is it hard, then, to believe that what happened to Brazil in a few scant centuries could also have happened to the Atlantean Island itself (hê Atlantis nêsos), since we know so little of what Plato really meant by that curious name? Hence, it is clear that the usual view that the above toponyms (place-names) apply verbatim to the features presently so named is erroneous. [1067]

First of all, by "Atlantic Ocean" the ancient Greeks normally designated the whole of the world-encircling ocean. By "island" they often meant what we nowadays improperly call "continent".

The Greeks and the Phoenicians habitually named any important strait connecting two different seas in which they roved as "Pillars of Hercules". In order to justify this name, they often erected temples decorated by such twin pillars there.

We well realize that our claims may seem vaunted or even frivolous to many, experts or not. But we are fully prepared to prove what we just affirmed. Given the inescapable fact of locational and toponymical confusion, we are free to look for Atlantis just about anywhere in the world, and then work backwards to prove the connection with the many geographical features of the Lost Continent listed by Plato.

These characteristic geographical and geological features include: Pleistocenic date; being sunken; a continental extension; a tropical climate in the Ice Age; a prodigious fertility; a great abundance of minerals and gemstones of all sorts; violent maritime volcanoes, tsunamis and earthquakes; a huge population and so forth.

In the present book – addressed, above all, to the general public – we have divested our original text of the impressive scientific paraphernalia that we had to use, and often develop or improve ourselves, in the sciences both human and exact.

We plan to publish this more extensive research of ours in the near future, in technical journals and Internet sites, so as to place it at the disposal of all the interested public, the scholars in particular. In the present publication, we have also skipped for the sake of simplicity the more obscure arguments we have produced over the years, concentrating only on those understandable to the lay reader.

However, we quote here in this book a host of authoritative references on these specific issues not only by Plato himself but also by his Classical contemporaries such as Aristotle, Theopompos, Diodorus Siculus, Herodotus, Pliny the Elder, Strabo, Pomponius Mela, and many other ancient Greco-Roman authors.

The reader who finds these original quotes difficult is advised to simply skip them. But the interested reader will find here an extensive list of Internet links to these Classical authors both in their original tongues and in their English translation.

These links are given as numbered notes in this book which can be accessed directly via our Atlantis site by merely clicking on these numbers there. In this novel way we are able to provide not only access to these obscure sources, but to an impressive apparatus of erudite commentaries, explanatory notes, dictionaries, glosses, and so forth.

Our strategy was to post this material – in whole or in part – in our Internet Homepage on Atlantis, so that it is readily available to all readers desirous of verifying my quotes in more detail, and/or to check my sources, references, maps and charts, all abundantly presented there.

Another strategy I am presently pursuing is the direct collaboration with some fellow scientists from the different specific disciplines involved, using this combined experience to further examine my find of Atlantis for the purpose of advancing the several sciences concerned, many of which will require a thorough revision.

Again, my purpose both here and in other pursuits is to submit my results to the scrutiny of independent research and empirical confirmation, the very essence of scientific methodology.

Some of these researches are being conducted in the open, and some secretly. This is because Atlantis is a jinxed subject for scholastic investigation and funding institutions, making researchers very reluctant to stake their reputations and careers until they have achieved very solid results which cannot be easily refuted by other scholars.

Setting Out to Disprove Atlantis

Our own views on the issue of Atlantis have been masterfully expressed by the two authors quoted in the above epigraphical quotations at the head of the present chapter. I believe my conclusions on the matter of Atlantis to be the truth, and nothing but the truth. But my finds are far from being the whole truth, as I have barely managed to scratch the surface of the complex problem posed by Atlantis.

A lot of ground has yet to be covered in the near future, now that the reality of the Lost Continent has, I hope, been scientifically established. Scientific opinion on this sensitive subject has been negative up to now, for several reasons.

But, as Plato himself affirmed, opinion – scientific opinion included – is just opinion, and is bound to change whenever new facts develop, as is the case now that we have reconstructed the secret history of Paradise Lost perhaps for the first time ever.

Actually, I set out originally to disprove what I then believed, as a scientist, to be no more than a series of sheer fads and fallacies: Däniken's "Astronaut Gods"; Velikovsky's "Biblical Catastrophism"; Blavatsky's ghostly Lemurians; the geological possibility of "sunken continents" and global cataclysms of the Flood type, etc..

Above all, I attempted to disprove the reality of Paradise Lost and that of its two main geological corollaries, Atlantis and Lemuria. Alas, I soon found that a solid core of fact invariably remained when I cleared the piles of pseudo-scientific garbage accumulated by the above named researchers and many others over the course of centuries.

When I dug deeper, I started to find, first of all, the many jewels and gold nuggets embedded in the mythologies of all peoples. I finally came to realize that these pearls of wisdom could not possibly be mere coincidences or sheer accidental invention.

This is now quite clear, given the universality and the astounding internal coherence of myths everywhere. I was accordingly compelled to make an about face in my former beliefs, much as I hope that the dear readers will also do when they are confronted with the vast evidence I amassed over the two and a half decades since my conversion occurred.

I firmly believe that what I expound next is the truth of the matter, as I just affirmed. But I am prepared to be proved wrong, just as I presumed to point out the errors of the researchers who preceded (or followed) me in the never-ending quest for Truth.

Science, as is well known, actually progresses by the process of trial-and-error. Scientific theories are freely posited only as provisional working hypotheses. In the words of Einstein, theories are only a preliminary attempt to explain known facts and empirical observations as well as is humanly possible.

At the measure that more data are gathered, better theories are formulated, in an uninterrupted, unending succession. No scientific theory is ever final. As with human beings, one generation of theories succeeds the other, hopefully with some evolutionary improvement.

So, my own theory on Atlantis' location and reality is perhaps destined to be eventually superseded by better-argued and better-founded data and hypotheses. More details on Atlantis-Eden will be gathered, and my data will be refined in both time and geographical space. But I do not believe my theory will undergo any serious revision in the forthcoming years. Its essence will endure, I am sure.

This book is the result of thirty years of dedicated research. The proofs it presents are scientifically solid and, I hope, convincing. But truth, like beauty, often resides in the eyes of the beholder.

However, there is no place for dogma in Science, just as J. Robert Oppenheimer affirmed in the quotation with which we opened this chapter. Rigidity and dogma oppress and inevitably lead to error and injustice. We must never believe that any hypothesis, theory, dogma, notion or principle – no matter how logical and how compelling it may look at any one time – is ever final and definitive.

Even less should we believe that scientific views and principles are ever to be considered final, or even too well established to be discarded or replaced. They seldom are. Take for instance the usual academic consensual view that "continents cannot possibly sink".

This is what most if not all geologists unfortunately believe even today, and in fact teach down to the present time. This belief is the result of the fact that most of them were taught to trust the uniformitarian views of Darwin and Lyell, the currently standard doctrine on the matter. And bad habits die hard, as we all know.

This widespread belief was recently reaffirmed, for instance, by Dorothy B. Vitaliano in what is probably the best and latest book on Atlantis to be written by academic scholars (Edwin Ramage (ed.), <u>Atlantis, Fact or Fiction</u>, Indiana Univ. Press, Bloomington, 1978):

> "In the light of what is known today about the ocean floors we can definitely rule out the possibility of a sunken landmass of any appreciable size in the Atlantic or, for that matter in any other ocean basin."

Vitaliano is a professional geologist, working for the reputed US Geological Survey. She specializes on volcanology and tsunamis, and has written extensively on the matter of Atlantis and related legends and traditions. Her view on the matter is typical of the negative scientific attitude which prevailed at the time when I started my researches on the matter of Atlantis and down to a long time afterwards.

But these canonic views were soon to be proved wrong not only by my own pioneering finds but also by the geological and climatological data we present here and in other works of ours. The truth of the matter is that continents can sink, and indeed have repeatedly done so in the course of geological time, exactly as Plato asserted.

And this sinking was not a gradual, smooth, uniform process, as most academic experts currently believe. This process was often violent and cataclysmic. This was particularly the case in the region of Indonesia, the real location of Atlantis, and of the date given by Plato (11,600 years BP), the one marked by <u>Meltwater Pulse 1B (MWP1B)</u>, a dramatically sudden rise in sea level. [068]

This perfect coincidence in both date and nature is certainly more than just fortuitous: It is a powerful indicator of some major catastrophe of global import, one probably related to the Universal Flood and the catastrophic end of the last Pleistocene Ice Age. [6]

The reality of the Flood cataclysm is the very essence of our revolutionary find of Atlantis. This sobering find – currently fast becoming standard knowledge – was actually what set me on the right track for locating the lost continent of Atlantis hiding away in the fabulous South Seas where it really lies. Several other clues – the Lemurian tradition included, and the one on Kumari Kandam, and so on – also confirmed my suspicions, which soon became certainty. [7]

Another "commonsensical" scientific belief similar to this one that "continents cannot possibly sink" is the scientific wisecrack that "stones cannot possibly fall from heaven". But this was also proved to be wrong in practice. They not only can, but in fact often do. And they come in all sizes, some even of planetoidal size, as we now know for sure.

This naive belief – widely held by the "no-nonsense" scientists of the Paris Academy down to the end of the nineteenth century – was hastily revised and considerably improved when a gigantic shower of sizeable meteorites literally rained down over their illustrious bald heads, formerly impervious to this rather ordinary piece of commonsense.

It is precisely this type of dogmatic science that Erasmus denounces in his magistral <u>In Praise of Folly</u>. This book earned Erasmus his excommunication, since it so sorely offended both the priests and the arrogant scholars of his time. His close friend, Thomas More, fared even worse, and ended up losing his head, certainly because of his association with Erasmus and other such "Atlantean utopists".

Atlantis is presently universally held to be a preposterous unscientific notion not only by the media, but also by the illustrious would-be sages who now fill our academies and our research institutions and who are no less stupid and arrogant than the ones of Erasmus' time.

But their view on this is merely <u>dogma</u>, with no foundation whatsoever in facts, only on opinion. The same is also true of other similar traditional views on the reality of the Terrestrial Paradise, the Universal Flood, Catastrophic Evolution, and so on. Absence of evidence is no evidence of absence, just as several experts have remarked.

Fortunately, these obsolete views and these misleading paradigms are fast being revised, now that Darwinian Evolution and the Uniformity Principle on which it is founded have both been proved to be no more than Victorian buncombe. They both derive from sheer unscientific bias and are actually unsupported by any kind of evidence whatsoever.

Science has often been used to perpetuate dogmatism, so that today, to a large extent, it has replaced the traditional inquisitional role that Religion often had, in antiquity.

This posture is, however, incompatible with the progress of Science, of Religion, and even of Humankind as a whole. Just as Oppenheimer pointed out, whenever intellectual liberty to pursue <u>any</u> line of reasoning is threatened, it is Freedom itself that is threatened. No subject should ever be tabooed in Science, or forbidden to anyone, as some actually were in the Middle Ages.

Academic freedom includes – or should include – the liberty to research even "damned" subjects such as the one of Atlantis without putting one's career and personal safety in jeopardy, as is currently the case. I am sorry for having to insist on this ugly theme as a precursor for my purely scientific work on the sunken continent, one which I have several times been recommended to abandon, as it threatened the reputation solidity of my academic institution.

But I want my readers to follow Plato's advice; to come out of the Cave, and dare to face sunshine head on. Those who are not prepared to undertake this crucial step had better abandon ship now, when it has not yet progressed out of the port. To those who stay on board, my hearty welcome. And don't fret. All you risk losing are your fetters, as Plato once said...

"Like Oil, Atlantis Is Wherever It May Be Found"

Put simply, we are hence allowed to look for Atlantis just about any-where in the world. This is what a detailed study of Plato's texts on the Lost Continent actually reveals. In fact, a close analysis – one which took us some twenty five years to complete and to compile the confirmatory evidence for – reveals the following facts, which we demonstrate in detail next in this and other chapters of this book:

1) The "Atlantic Ocean" of the ancients is not the ocean we presently call by that name. Instead it is really the Outer Ocean which encircles the entire world all around, and which is composed of the Atlantic, the Indian, and, above all, the Pacific Ocean, of which the former two were deemed mere extensions, one towards the west, the other one towards the east.

And this world-encircling ocean was anciently called not only "Atlantic Ocean" but also had names such as <u>Atlanticus Mare</u>, <u>Kronius Mare</u>, <u>Mare Externum</u>, <u>Mare Magnum</u>, <u>Alethinos Pontos</u>, <u>Mare Oceanus</u>, <u>Occidentalis Oceanus</u>, <u>Eous Mare</u> and, more simply, <u>Oceanus</u>. **8**

2) "Pillars of Hercules" was the name invariably applied by the Phoenicians and the Carthaginians not only to Gibraltar, the Bosphorus and the Kertch Straits in the Black Sea, but to any important strait leading from one sea to another or from one region to a neighboring one. Such was the way in which the name was used in antiquity, and such was also the idea that Plato had in mind when he wrote the <u>Timaeus</u> and the <u>Critias</u>, his two fascinating discourses on Atlantis.

But the real identity of the "Pillars of Atlas", the ones of Atlantis, was a closely kept secret never told anyone but the most trusted disciples. In consequence, wherever we may find Atlantis, we will also automatically find the true Pillars of Hercules and/or Atlas of which Plato spoke.

3) By the words "Island of Atlantis" (hê Atlantis nêsos), Plato really meant the same thing expressed by the Sanskrit word dvipa, which is its exact Hindu equivalent. The Greek word nêsos, like its Sanskrit counterpart, dvipa, signifies not only "island", but any flooded land or continent, as can be verified here. And the word dvipa in fact means the same thing, and specifically applies to what we presently call "continent", implying the idea of "sunken". [069]

Plato – or perhaps Solon, as the divine philosopher specifically declares – was apparently reporting hoary Egyptian traditions. And the Egyptian word yu means, like its counterparts just mentioned, not only an island, but any flooded land even of continental size like Atlantis.

4) Plato's allusion to the fact that the "island of Atlantis" lay in front of the Pillars of Hercules is in fact a double entendre intended to confuse the profanes. The Greek word he actually uses (pro) meant more or less the same as Greek anti- and Latin ante-, as in the names of Antilia, Antichthon and Antipodes. And it is also embodied in the name of Atlantis itself, perhaps meaning the very idea that Atlantis was in fact the Land Antipodal of which many traditions spoke. [9]

This Greek word is often rendered as "opposite, facing"; as such, it could well mean "antipodal", in the sense of "opposite". And it could also express the idea that Atlantis was located in the opposite shore of the Ocean, which, for the ancients, extended all the way to the East Indies. Diodorus Siculus in fact locates Atlantis on the opposite bank of the Ocean, "at the outer fringes of the world".

So, while the more gullible profanes understood that Atlantis was located just outside Gibraltar Strait, the better informed epopts knew that it lay on the opposite bank of the Ocean, opposite Gibraltar. But since one side of the world was actually the "mirror image" of the other, one could also consider that Plato was actually speaking of the opposite shore of the ocean, the archetypal one, with its own Pillars of Hercules (Sunda Strait) and its own "island" (Taprobane or Atlantis).

5) The Greek traditions on Atlantis were actually obtained from the Hindu ones on the Island (dvipa) of Taprobane. These also applied to its alias, Jambudvipa, the site of the sunken Paradise according to the ancient Hindu traditions. Taprobane, which we discuss in some detail below, was the Hindu archetype and exemplary model of all or most such traditional paradises. In practice, true Taprobane also corresponded to the site of Kumari Kandam, the sunken continent whence the Dravidas originally came, when it sank away at the end of the Ice Age, ending the first sangam. [10]

Among these we have: the Greek Elysium, the Egyptian Punt, the Mesopotamian Dilmun, the Hindu Patala or Atala, the Judeo-Christian Eden, the Aztec Aztlán, the Maya Tollán, and so on. Moreover, Taprobane (Tamraparna) was really located in Indonesia, at the Line of the Equator, rather than in Sri Lanka, its mere replica, like so many others such everywhere in the world.

We well realize that the above claims might seem far-fetched and even erroneous to most people, particularly the experts. We all have been so indoctrinated into believing that Atlantis never existed at all that it is hard to pay any unbiased attention to contrary arguments.

But lend me your ears for a moment, as I hope I will be able to convince you, dear reader. The very fact that this tradition on the reality of the Terrestrial Paradise was able to diffuse to all places on earth so early in time is proof sufficient that a nation capable of carrying out this worldwide diffusion once necessarily existed. Otherwise, who carried out this universal diffusion? Angels? Devils? Heroes? Saviors?

Three Proofs of the Above Conclusions

In what follows, we provide three arguments derived from the ancient traditions which we believe to prove our case beyond reasonable doubt that Atlantis-Eden lay – if it was at all a geographical reality – in Indonesia, in the East Indies, and nowhere else in the world.

My first proof concerns the true nature of what the ancients understood by the word "Ocean", which has nothing to do with what we currently understand by this word. The second argument concerns the oriental location of Paradise in the traditions of all peoples, the Jews and Christians and the Mesopotamians in particular. Both these arguments are commented upon in more detail further below.

They are presented here as a preview, in order to whet the appetite of my dear readers. Most experts have now come to realize that Atlantis was Paradise itself. Moreover, the ancients – Plato included, perhaps, and Diodorus Siculus for sure – also placed Atlantis on the opposite shore of the Ocean, at the outer fringes of the world, in the East Indies themselves.

These arguments should be closely read and pondered, as they shed a lot of light on the murky issue of Atlantis' whereabouts and on its undeniable identity with the site of Paradise Lost.

Since it is already difficult to have to believe in the reality of one Paradise Lost, imagine having to believe in two, one in the east the other one in the west. This is one of the main factors which led us to serendipitously conclude that Atlantis and Eden are one and the same location, in the East Indies.

We will now present an actual historical document – one of the several confusing ones we have amassed in the course of our researches – proving that the "Ocean" of the ancients was in fact the Pacific Ocean, and that both the Atlantic and the Indian oceans were deemed its "arms" or "branches", that is, their extensions respectively to the east and the west.

Thus, whenever the ancients mentioned the "Ocean" they were normally referring to the Pacific Ocean, unless they named a specific body. Since they were ignorant of the existence of America, the ancient Mediterraneans believed that the Atlantic Ocean extended all the way to the East Indies, just as Columbus and other conquistadors also did.

They also knew the Pacific Ocean from the east, and believed it to extend all the way to western Europe and Africa. In the east, the Ocean was named "Eastern Ocean" (Eoos Okeanos) and in the west it was known as "Western Ocean" (Hesperios Okeanos). But it was also known as "Atlantic Ocean" (Atlantikos Okeanos), a name meaning the same as "Ocean of the Atlanteans" since sunken Atlantis and the "Atlantic Islands", its remains, were known to be located there.

As is now clear, the ancients of Plato's time and later believed that the Outer Ocean extended from the Far East all the way to the European and the African west coasts and, conversely, all the way from there to the Far East. This belief prevailed down to the times of Marco Polo (1254–1324 AD), who speaks of the Mar Ozeano ("Ocean Sea") as doing so.

This belief is quite reasonable. It survived down to the times of Christopher Columbus and even later, until Amerigo Vespucci discovered the fact that the interposed Americas were in fact a coterminous continent separating the two oceans.

So, when Diodorus Siculus – and probably also Plato and other mythographers place Atlantis on the far side of the "Atlantic Ocean" what they mean is that the Lost Continent was formerly located in the East Indies (India and Indonesia) and in Serica (China), the "Land of the Seres" right where we finally succeeded in locating it.

The document we have in mind here is the Libro del Conoscimiento, which dates from about 1350 AD. This book embodies the geographical knowledge to that date, more or less as do others such as Marco Polo's Book of Wonders and Sir John Mandeville's Travels. [070]

Discounting some obvious fables contained in it, the geographical knowledge this book embodies is rather reliable, and is taken directly from older authorities. It is based on the accounts of Classical authors such as Pliny, Strabo, Mela and Solinus, to mention just four.

What interests us here is the view it expresses on the Pacific Ocean, the Mar Oceano of Christopher Columbus. In fact, this book, along with several others, was the source which inspired Christopher Columbus to attempt to reach the East Indies by sailing westwards, into the Atlantic Ocean, which he, like most other ancients, believed to extend all the way to the East Indies. This text, in quaint Old Spanish, reads as follows:

> E sabet que **este mar de Jndia es vn braço que entra del grant mar oriental**. E dizen algunos que atrauiesa toda la tierra fasta el mar occidental. **E los sabios dizen le el mar meridional.** E deste mar fasta el polo antartico es vna grand tierra que es la deçima parte de la faz de la tierra. E quando el sol es en el tropico de capricornio pasa el sol sobre las cabeças de **los pobladores a los quales llaman los sabios antipodas.** ["Know that the Indian Ocean is an arm of the Great Oriental Ocean [Pacific] penetrating into that region. Some say that it crosses the whole earth up to the Occidental Ocean. And the sages call it the South Sea. And from this sea down to the Antarctic Pole there is a great land which forms the tenth part of the face of the earth. And when the sun is in the Tropic of Capricorn, it passes overhead above the natives of this region, who are called Antipodes by the sages."]

This passage, which should be carefully studied, deserves an explanation. The Great Oriental Sea is the Pacific Ocean, alias the Mar Oceano of which Columbus, as well as several other ancient experts in geography, spoke. Here, the Indian Ocean is deemed to be merely an arm of the Pacific Ocean, which it in fact is, as can be seen in the World Map of the figure below. This map uses a peculiar curvilinear projection which is most convenient for our present purposes.

The Occidental Ocean (Mar Occidental) is the Atlantic Ocean of today. And it is here made the eastern extension of the Pacific Ocean itself, which the author calls the Great Oriental Ocean (Gran Mar Oriental). This curious book predates Columbus by well over a century, and there can be no doubt whatsoever that its disclosures are not due to the Age of Navigation, but are in fact owed to Antiquity itself.

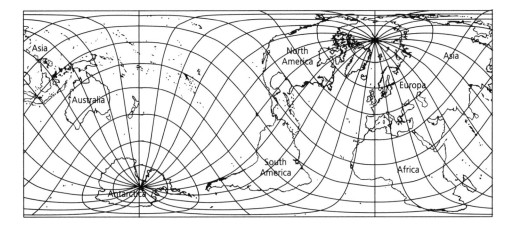

Like Marco Polo, it called the Pacific Ocean by the name of <u>Mar Oceano</u>, since it was deemed to encircle the whole earth, with the Atlantic and the Indian being its arms or extensions. As one can observe in the map shown above, the World Ocean forms a continuous, unbroken band around the entire world globe.

This coterminous world ocean is spotted by islands and continents, but its continuity is never really broken, not even by the Americas. The dominating feature is the Pacific Ocean, the others being its mere extensions or "branches", as they were often called. This is the reason why the ancients spoke of a Global Ocean, the "World Ocean" of today.

Contrary to popular belief, the ancients of course knew the Pacific Ocean very well, mostly via the east, the region they sailed the most then. And the ancients also well knew that the "Atlantic Islands" or "Islands of the Blest" lay in that eastern (or western) ocean, a fact that has now been utterly forgotten by most if not all researchers of such matters.

These islands were the remains of sunken Atlantis, the great southern, equatorial land of which the book just quoted is actually speaking. This land is also called Antichthon ("counter-earth") in Pythagorean traditions and is the same as the Antilia (idem) of the corresponding Latin ones.

This name refers to the land inhabited by the Antipodes, placed antipodally from us, as the Indonesians really are. Note that this land is located in the Tropic of Capricorn, that is, in the southern hemisphere of the earth. Excluding Africa and the Americas, we are left with Indonesia and Australia, the very site where we have located Atlantis-Eden.

The True Location of Paradise

With this, we pass to our second proof of the Indonesian location of Atlantis and hence of Eden which we also find most compelling. This proof again concerns the equatorial location of the site of Paradise. And it is taken from a very reliable Jewish source, the Jewish Encyclopedia.

The Jewish Encyclopedia is a mine of information on obscure passages of the Bible and other such Jewish sources. This encyclopedia has the advantage of having been written by orthodox Jews, whose faith and accuracy cannot be seriously doubted by anyone.

So, the words of this encyclopedia can be trusted by both Jews and Christians alike. In their description of the Garden of Eden, these illustrious authorities affirm: [071]

> Saadia Gaon, in his Arabic translation, **renders "Phison" as the Nile**, which Ibn Ezra ridicules, as: **"it is positively known that Eden is farther south, on the equator."**... Obadiah of Bertinoro, the commentator of the Mishnah, in a letter describing his travels from Italy to Jerusalem in 1489, relates the story of Jews arriving at Jerusalem from **"Aden, the land where the well-known and famous Gan Eden is situated, which is southeast of Assyria"**...

This opinion of rabbi Obadiah of Bertinoro that "the well-known and famous Gan Eden is situated... southeast of Assyria" is also in accordance with the ancient traditions. For instance, it is supported by the Tale of Sindbad the Sailor which we comment in more detail in our specialized work on this charming initiatic tale.

And it is also supported by the ancient Mesopotamian traditions which placed Dilmun, their version of the Garden of Eden, in the South Seas, to the southeast of Mesopotamia. We note that the Aden in question here is really Eden, rather than the Gulf of Aden, which the Jews never inhabited.

When one consults a world map, for instance, the one shown in the figure below, it is easy to see that the site of Indonesia in fact lies directly to the southeast of Mesopotamia, just as rabbi Obadiah affirmed. In fact, Obadiah did not say how far to southeast the Garden of Eden in fact lay. A whole lot, we note. All the way around the Indian and then across the Eastern Indian Ocean, to Indonesia, that is. But this distance could be sailed rather easily, and in fact was from deepest antiquity, as is now fast becoming obvious to all specialists ever since we pointed it out.

When the above information is plotted in a world map, we obtain the results shown in the above figure. The line drawn from Mesopotamia (Assyria) downwards is due southeast, just as rabbi Bertinoro recommended. And the line along the Line of the Equator again corresponds to the information supplied by rabbi Ibn Ezra, himself supported in this view by the exploits of rabbi Nahamanides, the supreme Jewish authority on such matters.

As shown, the two lines intersect in the region of Indonesia, and in no other. This region also corresponds to Taprobane, which was precisely the site where both the Hindu and the Greco-Roman traditions converged in placing the site of Paradise and the Islands of the Blest ever since remotest antiquity. It is clear that the ships went around the obstacles, rather than over them, as illustrated, for reasons of simplicity.

These paradisial islands, known as Elysium to the Greeks, Eden to the Jews, Dilmun to the Mesopotamians, Taprobane (Tamraparna or Seylam) to the Hindus, and as Punt to the Egyptians are all the same as sunken Atlantis. And Atlantis was truly the site of Paradise Lost, as we have long been arguing and have demonstrated in detail for the first time ever.

Moreover, the geographical charts such as the one just presented leave no room for doubting the Indonesian location of Atlantis as the site of Paradise. This is precisely the location we have now established at long last, after three decades of very dedicated research.

The third proof we want to present here is from the Suda Lexicon, this marvelous encyclopedia which summarizes Classical Greco-Roman thinking in such a remarkable way. The Suda is now available online, in both the ancient Greek original and English, so that the interested readers can conveniently consult it by themselves. [072]

The Suda (or Suidas) is the only such encyclopedia to reach us from Classical antiquity. Though somewhat late, the Suda obtained its information from far older Greco-Roman sources now utterly lost. It is hence an invaluable document on what the ancient Greeks such as Plato actually thought when they used words such as "Atlantic Ocean", "island", "continent", "Flood", "sea", "ocean", "Pillars of Hercules", "Asia", "Libya", and so forth. [073]

Unsurprisingly, these concepts changed a lot since the two and a half thousand years that have elapsed since Plato wrote his piece on Atlantis. And if we really want to understand the words of the great master, we have to learn the meaning of the technical vocabulary he used.

The Suda is perhaps the sole ancient document that really glosses these concepts in a reliable way. All the rest – particularly the hasty translations and the interpretations made by those who have an axe to grind – should be distrusted and subjected to verification from the original sources themselves.

With this we pass to the definition of the Atlantic Ocean in the Suda, one which the interested readers can check for themselves via the link to it just given. Knowing what Plato actually meant by his use of the name is essential for the search of Atlantis.

As we already said, it is obvious that "if it is Atlantis it's gotta be located in the Atlantic Ocean". After all, it was Atlantis that gave the name to the Atlantic Ocean, the "ocean of Atlantis", rather than the other way around. Otherwise, we could find a different sunken civilization – for instance Lemuria – and mistake it for Atlantis. So, an Atlantic location is crucial for the localization of Atlantis.

But this location must be consentaneous with Plato's vocabulary, rather than the modern usage of the term, which, as we just said, changed a whole lot in the course of the almost three millennia since Plato wrote his piece on the Lost Continent. This ancient world conception survived down to the times of Christopher Columbus as we explain next, as a clarifying preamble to the Suda's definition.

Columbus and the Interposed Americas

As we will now undertake to show, the name of the Atlantic Ocean – which really means "Ocean of Atlantis" in Greek (<u>Atlantis Okeanos</u>) – originally applied to the Pacific Ocean, known (from the east) since remotest antiquity, rather than to the Ocean now so named.

When the Greeks moved from wherever they originally came from to the Mediterranean region, they thought – just as did most of the ancient European peoples with perhaps a few exceptions – that what we know as the Atlantic Ocean stretched all the way to the East Indies, more or less as did Christopher Columbus and the other conquistadors, geographers and experts of all kinds.

The existence of the Americas separating the three Old World continents (Europe, Asia and Africa) was of course generally ignored in antiquity. So, this supposition was rather logical, as adduced by Strabo and a host of other ancient geographers and experts since the times of Homer. In fact, Homer, in his <u>Iliad</u> (18:478), describes the Ocean as encircling the whole earth.

Accordingly, Columbus' attempt to find a western route to the Indies was rather logical, even though it failed in a more or less serendipitous way. As the result of his logical reasoning, the former name of the Pacific Ocean – the one of "true Ocean" or "Ocean of Atlantis" – was also extended to its eastern extension, the European ocean now so named. And the name stuck.

With the advent of the dark Middle Ages, the naval contact of the Europeans with the East Indies became lost, and the very existence of Atlantis and its enormous ocean became utterly forgotten in the course of time. The only contact then was by land, via the Silk Road.

So, when Balboa rediscovered the Pacific Ocean (from the west) during the Age of Discovery, it was named anew. All memory of its former importance had become utterly effaced and forgotten, except perhaps in the minds of a very few initiates who of course never told their secret to anyone who might improperly divulge it to profane ears.

In this way, the name of the "Atlantic Ocean" of the ancient geographical traditions became finally transferred from the right to the wrong ocean. And this transference ultimately led to the desperate but vain search of the Renaissance explorers for the "Atlantic Islands", the remains of sunken Atlantis itself, in the wrong area instead of where they truly lay, in the myriad islands of Indonesia, in the "veritable ocean" (alethinos pontos) of which Plato speaks as the site of Lost Atlantis in his dialogues.

Back to the Suda

After this necessary preamble we return to the Suda and its glosses on the ancient Greek concept of "Atlantic Ocean". As we already said, this famous dictionary derives from the Classical sources themselves, and cannot hence be doubted in any valid way.

These glosses are representative of Plato's sources, and are validated by a host of other Classical authorities whose lessons we discuss in more detail in this book and in other works of ours. The Suda glosses are copied verbatim from this useful source, which we link again here for the readers' convenience. Our comments to these two glosses (headwords) are made within the square brackets, and speak for themselves. We also give the original Greek entry in LSJ for those skilled in this tongue. [074]

"**Headword:** Atlantika pelagê – **Translated headword:** "Atlantic seas"

Greek Original: *Atlantika pelagê: hesperios ôkeanos kai heôios kai panta ta aplôta pelagê. kai Atlantis thalatta, ho ôkeanos.* **Translation:** "The western ocean and the eastern one and all the innavigable seas." Also *Atlantis thalatta* ["Atlantis sea"], "the ocean".

[This entry from the Suda is highly enlightening. This Byzantine lexicon summarized the whole of the ancient Greek culture, standardizing it. First of all, we note that the Greek names of the ocean were both *Atlantika pelagê* and *Atlantis thalatta* ("Atlantic seas" and "Atlantis Sea").

Note the plural used here. Hence the two "Atlantics" of the next entry. One entry actually complements the other. The Greeks hence had two "Atlantic Oceans", one in the west (the present one) and one in the east (the modern Pacific Ocean). Please note the Atlantic's identity with the Ocean.

We also note that the Greeks included as "Atlantic Sea" any innavigable sea such as the Sea of Atlantis described by Plato. And this sea seems to be the South China Sea and the Java Sea, both extremely dangerous due to the many shoals and reefs, not to mention the terrible Malay pirates who infested the region, helping in rendering it innavigable. See also the next entry.]

"Headword: Aplôta pelagê – **Translated headword**: "Unsailed seas"

Greek Original: *ta Atlantika kai hesperios ôkeanos kai eôos. Aplôton gar to apleuston.* – **Translation:** "The Atlantics [are] both western ocean and eastern. For *aploton* [means] un-navigated."

[This enigmatic reference to the two "Atlantic Oceans" (in the plural) was already glossed in the previous entry, also from the Suda. The ancient Mediterraneans normally called the modern Atlantic by the name of Western Ocean (Hesperios Okeanos). And they likewise normally called the Pacific by the name of Eastern Ocean (Eôos Okeanos). In fact, the word eôos means not only "oriental", but also "Orient". As such, this name applied, as it does even today, to the Far Orient. In particular, Indonesia was itself called Eôos, and so was its sea or ocean. Hence, the two "Atlantics" of this gloss here actually refer to the Atlantic proper and the Pacific Ocean, considered its westernmost extension.

The ancients also considered the Pacific Ocean to be the True Ocean (Alethinos Pontos or Okeanos), with the modern Atlantic Ocean deemed its eastern extension or "arm". This arm departed eastward from the Far East, and the Indian Ocean was its western extension considered from there. Accordingly, the Pacific Ocean then becomes the "Atlantic Ocean" of the ancient Greeks, being divided into its two modern moieties, the Pacific and the Atlantic Oceans. The South Pacific was also known as South Sea, Prasion Pelagos ("Sea of Sargassos"), etc.. Hence the use of the plural here. The foolish attempts on the part of certain modern Atlantologists to identify the Atlantic Ocean of the ancients with the Mediterranean Sea are just that: sheer folly, as this entry as well as innumerous others unequivocally demonstrate.

The ancients usually thought – down to the end of the Age of Navigation when they finally learnt otherwise – that the Pacific Ocean and the Atlantic Ocean were coterminous, since they generally ignored the existence of the interposed Americas. It is for this reason that they sought in the (modern) Atlantic Ocean the so-called "Atlantic Islands". This is how they called the insular remains of sunken Atlantis they knew to be located in the Far East. Columbus was no exception to this rule, and also attempted to reach those islands, which he deemed, like all other conquistadors, the actual precursors of the East Indies: Cipango, Ys Brazil, Kattigara, Satanaxio, Sanbrandan, etc..

We note that the term used by the illustrious translator: "unsailed seas" is somewhat misleading. It implies that these seas are not sailed, and not that they are "innavigable", as actually affirmed by Pindar, Plato and several other ancient authorities. Though seemingly slight, this difference is crucial. The [modern] Atlantic Ocean, in contrast to the ancient version, may have been "unsailed" in antiquity for a series of reasons. But it was not "innavigable" in any sense of the word. Once more we observe the fact that translators very often betray the authors they translate.]

CHAPTER 11 - THE TRUE PILLARS OF HERCULES

Science is one thing, wisdom is another. Science is an edged tool, with which men play like children, and cut their own fingers.

Sir Arthur Eddington (1882–1944)

In what follows, we describe a very simple method that we have devised in order to allow the direct intercomparison of Atlantis' proposed localizations with its main features given in the passage of Timaeus 24e-25a. This passage is perhaps the most crucial in the whole work of the great philosopher, at least in what concerns the subject of Atlantis.

And this feature is really the main connecting thread of Plato's whole work. Our device acts as some sort of a mandala or yantra which forces us to keep the mind fixed in the essential features, avoiding the many slips and pitfalls normally encountered by most researchers investigating the slippery enigma of Atlantis.

We have, after a very long study, reached the conclusion that the "Pillars of Hercules" mentioned by Plato in his dialogues on Atlantis could never be those in Gibraltar. In fact, these pillars there seem to be phony, and were never accepted as true by any specialists.

Moreover, there were a host of "Pillars of Hercules" posted both in the region of Gibraltar, as well as in other straits: the Bosporus, the Syrtis, the Bab-el-Mandeb, the Cimmerian Bosphorus, and so on. So much so, that innumerous experts have reached the conclusion that Atlantis could never have been located just outside Gibraltar, and have sought the elusive sunken continent somewhere else.

In the figures section earlier in this book we reproduced a map, due to José Imbelloni, the great Argentinean anthropologist, showing several dozens of "Pillars of Hercules" and "Pillars of Atlas" located just about everywhere in the Old World region.

Moreover, it is quite possible that Plato really used the word "opposite; facing" in the sense of "antipodal" rather than "in front" or "just ahead". The Greek word he used (pro) in fact bears the two senses, so that it is quite possible that Plato was deliberately playing on words here, in order to preserve the secret of Atlantis. Other ancient authorities also did the same, for reasons we now adduce.

In the present chapter we will be discussing in detail the various locations which have so far been proposed for Atlantis. And we will show – we hope to anyone's satisfaction – that Plato in fact referred to the opposite side of the world, the antipodes, in Taprobane. Here is the passage of Plato we just mentioned, here in Benjamin Jowett's translation, one of the best available:

> **Plato's Tim. 24e–25a** – Many great and wonderful deeds are recorded of your state in our histories. But one of them exceeds all the rest in greatness and valor. For these histories tell of a mighty power which unprovoked made an expedition against the whole of Europe and Asia, and to which your city put an end. This power came forth out of the Atlantic Ocean – for in those days the Atlantic was navigable – and there was an island situated in front of the straits which are by you called the Pillars of Heracles. This island was larger than Libya and Asia put together, and was the way to other islands, and from these you might pass to the whole of the opposite continent which surrounded the true ocean. For this sea which is within the Straits of Heracles is only a harbor, having a narrow entrance. But that other is a real sea, and the surrounding land may be most truly called a boundless continent. [075]

The above passage of the genial philosopher is somewhat dense and difficult. But it is perhaps the single most important and the most controversial in both of Plato's dialogues on Atlantis. Please follow, if you so want, the links given above in order to access another translation, as well as the Greek original with detailed glosses by erudite commentators to every word in Plato's remarkable text on Atlantis.

Taken verbatim, this remarkable passage of Plato fails to make any geographical sense whatsoever. So, anyone wanting to interpret this passage literally – as so many experts have attempted in the past – is doomed to failure from the start.

That fact becomes clearer when we compare the geographical data included here with the geographical reality. This intercomparison – which is so simple that the readers can do it for themselves for any site thus far proposed for Atlantis or any other they may choose – is perhaps the most important of all analyses that can be made while attempting to locate Atlantis as a geographical reality that exists or existed somewhere on the physical earth.

This intercomparison can be done by anyone who takes the trouble to peruse a globe of the earth or a world map such as the one we showed above. In what follows next, we will also discuss the real meaning of the actual terms used by Plato in his Greek original.

The following discussion is somewhat erudite and may seem obscure to the average reader. We suggest that those of our readers who find this commentary difficult to follow, just skip it and go directly to Table III.1 next, and to the discussions which follow it.

These readers may return later to the arguments given here whenever they feel it is necessary. But, please, do try to follow the main trend of the argument, as it is in fact quite simple and easy to understand in its essence. Just skip the difficult words and arguments.

Actually, this intercomparison may be done far more easily than it may seem at first sight. These formidable Greek and Latin and Sanskrit and Dravidian words are all referred back to familiar everyday English words. We have done most of the dirty work of deciphering Plato's obscurities such as the ones pointed out above and below.

We have puzzled over and over again on the above enigmatic passage of Plato, and believe to have at last solved the puzzle posed by the philosopher to all the many experts who have earlier attempted to crack this difficult enigma. So, the rest is relatively easy to follow.

First of all, one has to keep in mind that such initiatic texts are posed by the hierophant precisely as some sort of charade or riddle to be deciphered by the audience, both initiated and profane. In other words, Plato is appealing to one's cunningness in solving the enigma of Atlantis. The solution of the riddle is absolutely fascinating, as it teaches us to reason clearly and to gain insight in the matter.

Second, for the present purpose, we must forget the usual place-names and hold to the actual geography alone. In other words, we should forget the usual interpretations of toponyms such as "Pillars of Hercules" or "Atlantic Ocean" or "Island", and stick to the actual geographical features given by Plato and by Diodorus, etc..

This, regardless of the name they may have in their own time or in ours, in Greek or in English, etc.. Above all, keep in mind that names such as "Pillars of Hercules", "Hesperia", "Libya", "Phoenicia" and so forth had a double identity: the usual one and the secret, antipodal one. Moreover, several of these had multiple identities, and were used over and over again.

Once a place that fits Plato's description – or Diodorus', etc. – is discovered, we then work backwards to try to find whether Plato could really have had it in mind when he affirmed what he did.

One must keep in mind the inescapable fact that sacred toponyms and theonyms are applied over and over again to different places and different gods and heroes. Hence, they seldom if ever mean anything at all by

themselves. We now comment several instances of this dualism or plural-
ism at work in antiquity.

One is <u>not</u> allowed to believe that Plato meant, by the above geographical features and by the place-names (Greek toponyms) he actually
used, the same that we do nowadays. In fact, it is quite obvious that <u>he did
not</u>, for his data fails to make any sense at all in this hypothesis.

Plato was very obviously far from stupid. And he was also far from
ignorant on the initiatic matters he was disclosing to those of us who are
open-minded and open-hearted enough to profit by them.

There were simply too many "Pillars of Hercules" and/or "Pillars of
Atlas" in antiquity to allow us to conclude that Plato specifically meant
Gibraltar. Instead, it is obvious that he did not. Gibraltar is just one of the
several dozens of such instances of the widespread toponym. In myths,
as in symbolism, the obvious solution is <u>never</u> the solution of the riddle,
whose role is precisely one of titillating our intelligence and our powers of
reasoning to seek further.

As we said above, by "island" the great philosopher normally meant
what we nowadays improperly call "continent". This word is really a misnomer, which in antiquity was confined to the "true continent", the one
said to "contain" the ocean on the outside, and which the experts unanimously identify as America.

By "Atlantic Ocean" the sage clearly meant the "Ocean of the Atlantis",
as he himself explains; the place where it actually foundered, in the South
Seas. And this ocean or sea is clearly the one where the Lost Continent is
actually located, rather than the one we now so name.

This accounts for the fact that Atlantis could not be found in the
Atlantic Ocean up to now, despite the insistent efforts of a great many
explorers, mariners and skilled geographers. Their error lay in not real-
izing that Plato's words should not and cannot be taken literally, for his
idea was precisely to confound the profanes, that is, the public in general,
including the experts themselves.

In myths, as in sacred disclosures of all sorts, the evident is <u>never</u>
what is really intended, and the truth is always mystical and secluded, and
reserved for the initiates alone. Consider, for instance, the obvious internal contradictions of Plato's text when taken literally.

> • **First**, there was never any large "island" of continental size in
> front of Gibraltar Strait. This region has been carefully charted and literally
> combed for Atlantis or otherwise both in antiquity and today, when we
> enjoy the help of outer space spy satellites of all sorts. And only puny
> islands such as Espartel and the Azores have ever been found there by the

many thousands of explorers of the wide region.

    • **Second**, the Atlantic Ocean was never "innavigable" in the region of Gibraltar or indeed almost anywhere that really matters, the Sargasso Sea and the Caribbean Sea themselves included.

    • **Third**, it is obvious that neither Egypt nor Greece existed as nations at the distant Pleistocenic date in which Plato's Atlantis is said to have flourished, according to the words of the philosopher himself. This epoch was the Ice Age, when no known civilization whatsoever has been discovered yet. But Agriculture already existed then, so that the possibility is there.

    • **Fourth**, there were – or, even less, are – no islands great or not on the way to the "opposite continent", which most people identify with the Americas. So, Plato was very obviously referring to another region, unless he were talking idly, like a fool.

    • **Fifth**, the "real ocean" is obviously not the Mediterranean and clearly not even the Atlantic Ocean, but the Pacific Ocean. This fact will become more clear next, when we comment Plato's text in its connection with actual geographical reality and with ancient beliefs on this issue, which is of utmost importance in understanding the myth of Atlantis.

The Tabular Comparison

After the above explanatory preamble, we now finally turn to the comparison of Plato's data with the actual geographical reality mentioned above. For the purpose of this comparison we must forget, at least for the time being, the geographical place-names that the philosopher actually used, and concentrate on the geographical features themselves. Otherwise, we will be utterly misled and stray from the correct route leading to Atlantis.

Besides, who can guarantee that Plato was not allegorizing or playing on words in order to confound the profanes, as he so often does in several of his texts? Hence, forget the names, and concentrate on the actual geographical features alone, as we already recommended above.

For the purpose of performing those comparisons, we have devised and present below Table III.1, where the main geographical data given by Plato in the above quoted passage are summarized. When we do a tabular comparison, it immediatly becomes evident that none of the many sites previously proposed for Atlantis in reality "fits the bill".

The only exception to this rule seems to be the one I discovered over twenty years ago: Indonesia and the Sunda Shelf located beneath its seas.

We will leave this comparison for the end, as some sort of dessert for the magnificent banquet offered us all by Plato, the great philosopher.

We leave this intercomparison for the end purposefully. We hope that, after these preliminary comparisons, the reader will have got the hang of the procedure's power when this important collation is finally done. After this, the reader can always return to his favorite choice at any time, to try to redo it all over again with the tricks of the trade learnt along the way.

In our other books and articles, we comment these crucial matters in far more detail than is possible here, given the time and space we have allowed ourselves. The telltale geographical data given by Plato in the above quoted passage of his <u>Timaeus</u> are summarized in <u>Table III.1</u> below. We left these features unnamed in order to avoid introducing any biases whatsoever, either pro or con.

We leave it up to the readers to decide for themselves whether the sitings in question or some others they may propose are acceptable, both geographically and toponymically. And we ask the dear readers to keep in mind the fact that toponyms such as "Pillars of Hercules" or "Gades", etc. were used over and over again in many different parts of the world, and hence mean very little on their own.

In what follows, these geographical data will be applied to all or most sites so far proposed by myself and by the other researchers and authorities. These results will be shown in the other tables that follow. It will be demonstrated, we hope, that all these sites, with the sole exception of my own proposal of true Taprobane, grossly misfit Plato's data.

The readers are encouraged to verify and check my conclusions and arguments to avoid being deceived or misled, for such is not our intention at all.

And we will be glad to stand corrected and amend our conclusions if they are found to be specious or false. After all, this is the correct procedure in Science. Science is sheer guesswork. In doing Science, we scientists arbitrarily frame hypotheses – sometimes quite absurd – and then test them out against reality.

Mistakes quite often occur in such matters, for we humans are unfortunately often prone to self-delusion. Such was apparently the case with Christopher Columbus, since he apparently chose to ignore Plato's statement that the <u>Peirata Ges</u> encircled and closed the Ocean in the far west, impeding the passage to the East Indies. Had he heeded Plato, he would have spared himself a lot of pain.

Sometimes the desire to solve a difficult riddle is so great that people fall into the grip of Illusion. This type of illusion is what the wise Hindus call <u>Maya</u> ("Illusion") or, yet, <u>Kamarupa</u> ("the embodiment of desire"). Maya and Kamarupa are what makes us see ghosts, apparitions, UFOs, greens, headless mules, and even beauty which, as Shakespeare once said, "resides in the eye of the beholder".

With reference to <u>Table III.1</u> below, it includes the main features of Plato's text in the crucial passages of his <u>Timaeus (24e–25a)</u>, quoted and commented above. We have also avoided, as best we possibly could, giving names or interpretations to these geographical features, except insofar as they may embody reality in themselves. [076]

These features will next be applied to the several sites so far proposed for Atlantis, grouped by regions of the world. Please note that the features considered in <u>Table III.1</u> are schematized to the utmost. And this is done on purpose. The idea is to keep the reasoning simple, so that one is not easily misled.

We again recall that by the word "pillars" the ancients usually meant any important strait connecting two seas; by "island" they often meant what we nowadays call "continent"; by "true ocean" Plato probably meant the Pacific + Atlantic Ocean; and by "Outer Continent" or "True Continent" Plato probably meant the Americas, as most experts believe.

In the schematic diagram (<u>Table III.1</u>) below, we do not include the many other features of Atlantis that the philosopher describes in rich detail in his two seminal dialogues on the Lost Continent, and which only fit our siting, and no other so far proposed for Atlantis. The motive is to keep the reasoning simple and uncontroversial in order to have it serve as a sort of screening test to sort out the more promising sites for Atlantis. The finer details can be added later on.

Table III.1 - The Actual Geography of Atlantis Given by Plato in the Timaeus (24e–25a) [077]			
Two Pillars (Strait)	Island of Atlantis (Larger than Asia + Libya)	Many Islands in True Ocean	Outer Continent Ahead (True)

This preliminary screening allows us to discard the sitings which do not fit even these most basic requirements. We could perhaps have included other features such as: the tropical climate during the Ice Age; the many metals and gemstones produced by Atlantis; the huge population; the two crops a year; the precious and fragrant woods and herbs; and so on.

Other important features comprise: the elephants, horses, bulls, and other such mighty animals; the volcanoes and earthquakes; the worship of Poseidon and the Bull Religion; the fabulous abundance of gold and silver; plus the dozens of further items mentioned by Plato.

But this inclusion would have rendered this document cluttered and tedious, and we wanted to keep it simple as some sort of preliminary screening test, easy to check and validate. In this way, these basic requirements can be verified in depth in a rather simple manner, and a pre-selection made that is rather safe and sound. The other features just mentioned may be incorporated to this tabular comparison later, as wished. But the ones used here will have to do for now.

The Case of Cuba and the Caribbean Islands

Let us now try to fit actual locations to Plato's above description. For that purpose we base ourselves on the world map shown above and the nameless geographical features given by Plato and outlined in Table III.1 above.

We begin this section with Gibraltar Strait, the usual choice, and with Cuba, in the Caribbean region, which has been in the news a lot. The present analysis of course also applies to the other Caribbean islands, as well as to the nearby coastal regions of the three Americas.

Curiously enough, several researchers now contend for the equivocal priority of having first proposed the Americas, and the Caribbean region in particular. Even if we ignore the fact that Columbus himself was actually looking for the "Atlantic Islands", we are still faced with the reality that there were many proponents of this dubious identity ever since the times of the Conquest itself. [078]

In fact, the Antilles were believed to be the remnants of sunken Atlantis. These were believed to be located in the East Indies, which Columbus actually mistook for the Antilles. Among these early proponents we cite the very first chronists of America such as Fernando de Oviedo (1525), Father Bartholomé de las Casas (1527), Francisco López de Gomara (1552) and Pedro Sarmiento de Gamboa (1572), among several others of lesser importance.

Father Las Casas correctly identified America with the Outer Continent mentioned by Plato. And he explicitly affirms in his writings that the Caribbean islands – which he calls <u>Anegadas</u> ("Submerged") – "are the probable remains of Atlantis due to their extensive shoals (<u>bajos fondos</u>)".

Cuba is one of the preferred recent sitings of Atlantis, to believe certain researchers and the odd results they apparently got on the seafloor of the region. This site is among the most popular of all such ever since Cayce prophesied the return of Atlantis there, "starting in 1968".

The fact that nothing of the sort happened then or later has led several adepts – among them John White, of Pole Shift fame, and Graham Hancock and quite a few others – to become so disillusioned as to decamp towards more viable alternatives such as mine.

I really pity the lay reader, endlessly assaulted by all sorts of false claims and specious results such as the ones criticized here. And this is done not only by the hastier (or greedier) researchers themselves, but also by the press and other information media, always bent on misinforming the public and in deceiving the more gullible persons.

What is even more deplorable is the fact that some academics often engage in this unethical deception of the more gullible public, motivated by personal ambitions and by sycophantism.

However, we warn the dear readers that these odd Cuban results – which, by the way, have never been published, despite the several years that have elapsed since they were first obtained – are <u>geologically impossible</u>. You see, <u>these finds were made under 2,200 feet of water</u> (670 meters), whereas sea level only dropped 130-150 meters or so (430-490 feet) during the Pleistocene. [079]

It has been also suggested that this site actually slipped under, from shallower waters. But this is impossible. Even if such were the case, the artificial structures claimed for the site could never have been preserved in any recognizable way. They would have been shattered and buried by the piles of mud released by such a violent disaster.

What is even more incredible is the fact that such an uncanny find – actually made several years ago – simply vanished from the news in what is really a most mysterious, poorly explained riddle. The promised robotic photos and more detailed scans never materialized.

We eagerly await some further, promised disclosures. But until they are made, we remain most skeptical of these vaunted claims. And we advise our more commonsensical readers to do the same.

Any claim that specifically violates a well-established scientific fact should be looked upon with extreme skepticism by all, until it is independently verified by a number of further researchers. As they say, "extraordinary claims require extraordinary proof".

A case comes to mind, precisely in relation with the Caribbean region. A few years ago an individual named Aaron DuVal – allegedly the "President of the Egyptology Society of Miami" – claimed to have found sunken pyramids just off the Bimini Islands, near the Florida Keys. These pyramids were allegedly full of strange hieroglyphic inscriptions, golden crystal caps (pyramidions) and so on. In time, these pyramids had shrunk to a mere pile of stones pompously called "Scott Stones".[1080]

What is even worse is that these "stones" – whose actual photo can be seen here – turned out to be mere barrels full of cement dumped at the place in order to break the waves of the beaches there. The metal casing rusted away, and only the cement was left, simulating stone pillars. This fact has been denounced by several marine archaeologists. [1081]

But the news persists, as insistent as ever. We leave the decision to the dear readers, limiting ourselves to recommend a detailed analysis of the "stones" and of this article here. After this cautionary preamble, we pass to the geographical analysis of the Cuban region in question here. In the map linked here, Gibraltar is the narrow strait separating Europe from Africa at the left side of these two Old World continents. [1082]

As can be seen in the map just linked, the Caribbean region is placed right in front of Gibraltar, despite the fact that it can hardly be said to be located "close by", as Plato specifically affirms, according to most specialists.

The proximity of Atlantis to the pillars seems to be an inescapable reality which clearly does not apply here. And hardly can the Antilles be deemed to be placed on the antipodes of Europe, since it is only 60° from the meridian of Greenwich (London), rather than 180° or so, as it should, to be considered antipodal.

Moreover, where are the many islands beyond Cuba (Atlantis), which Plato specifically mentions? Where is the "true ocean" ahead? And what about the "Outer Continent" beyond? Is it really America itself? But does not the text of Plato suggest that it is far away ahead? With this, we pass to the analysis of the actual geographical data in comparison to Plato's data.

The results we get from a close inspection of the above map are summarized in Table III.2 next. As is clear, several things are grossly amiss here. Can Cuba – or even the whole Caribbean – really be said to be "larger than Asia and Libya put together"? Cuba is part of the tenuous strip of land placed in front of Central America in the map (the Caribbean Islands).

By "Asia", Plato very probably meant Turkey (Asia Minor), also so-called in antiquity. And by "Libya" he very likely meant the whole of Africa north of the equator, the portion already known in Plato's time. Are there really "many islands beyond" Cuba which would help ships to reach "the true continent beyond", and which they would have already reached, anyway?

Table III.2 - Results for Cuba & Caribbean Region			
Two Pillars (Gibraltar)	Island of Cuba, etc.. (Larger than Asia + Libya) ???????	Many Islands Beyond??? In True Ocean ???????	Outer Continent Ahead (America)

Is the Caribbean Sea or the Gulf of Mexico possibly the "true ocean" that Plato had in mind? Or should we instead conclude that Plato did not really know what he was talking about and was merely playing on words or freely inventing his features more or less at random?

Or, yet, did the philosopher mean something else despite the ardent hope of Columbus that the partly sunken continent he eagerly sought was actually located there, in the Americas, which he mistook for the East Indies down to the end of his troubled life?

Columbus was mistaken in his belief that the way to the East Indies was open in this region of the world, perhaps in Panama or Nicaragua. And it is not entirely impossible that it really was open in former epochs, by some sort of canal built by the Atlanteans, according to what some early traditions report.

Columbus actually mistook America for Antilia and the East Indies, which he aimed to reach. Should we also share his mistake, as so many researchers do, or should we look somewhere else for a more adequate site for Atlantis? Or is it a fact that Columbus actually knew that the fabled East Indies were indeed the remains of Paradise Lost and of the "Island of Atlantis", its unsunken remains?

Crete, Cyprus, Malta and Other Mediterranean Locations

Let us now tackle Crete, another all-time favorite, particularly within the academic community. This preference is due both to its famous volcano (Thera) and because the place is such a delightful tourist resort. Yes, academics and archaeologists are human too, and love spas.

The Thera volcano provides a highly convenient framework for the destruction of Atlantis, even though this site fails every other facet typical of the Lost Continent: wrong size, wrong location, wrong date, wrong traditions, wrong people, etc..

But the resort is charming, and the researchers love to do some well-paid vacationing with their families while at work on the site. And the Greek islands are among the best places in the world to enjoy a prolonged vacation or a sabbatical year. So, they cling to the place, and will never give it up unless they are forced to do so.

The present analysis also applies to Cyprus and to Malta and other Mediterranean islands and locations. These sites were recently again reconsidered as a prime location for Atlantis with some refurbished research currently being done along the more scientific canons of submarine research which we introduced starting three decades ago.

And it further applies to Syrtis, in Libya, and to "Troy" in Turkey, also often considered as possible sites for Atlantis by several researchers. And so to any other site in the Mediterranean region or in the nearby seas such as the Black Sea and the Caspian Sea, for instance.

Curiously enough, the most recent of the many proponents of Cyprus affirms that it fits essentially all of Plato's many clues given in his two texts on Atlantis. According to the author of this unscientific proposal "Cyprus fits 51 out of 53 features proposed by Plato".

But this is an obvious hoax which I have already denounced in detail as scientifically impossible. For instance, we fail to see how this may be possible at all, given the fact that Cyprus does not even comply with the most basic of exigencies outlined in the above passage of Plato's <u>Critias.</u>

As we shall be arguing next, Plato's main exigency for Atlantis is the one of it being placed outside the "Pillars of Hercules", no matter where this feature may in fact be located in this vast world of ours. Another basic requirement is of it being located in the Atlantic Ocean, not the Mediterranean.

One should also note that <u>none</u> of the ancient and the Renaissance explorers <u>ever</u> looked for the fabled Atlantic Islands inside the Pillars of Hercules, in the Mediterranean region. Were they all wiser or simply more foolish than these Atlantologists themselves are?

It is clear that, as its very name indicates, the legend of Atlantis is connected with the Atlantic Ocean, no matter what meaning this name may have had in the minds of the ancients. Plato specifically affirms this fact himself. So, regardless of how many features may actually fit any such Mediterranean theory, it has to cope with this requisite first of all.

We of course fail to see this as possible at all. Even if we accept that the "Pillars of Hercules" were those of the Bosphorus, as some traditions specifically affirm, we still have to cope with the reality that Cyprus and Malta and Crete, etc. are <u>not</u> Atlantic locations, no matter how we reinterpret the meaning of the term "Atlantic Ocean".

As we have just said, the word "ocean" (<u>Okeanos</u>, <u>Oceanus</u>, <u>Aśayana</u>), to the ancients invariably meant – since the times of Homer and probably far earlier – the idea of something that encircles or surrounds, more or less as does the <u>Serpent Ouroboros</u>. [1083]

The Ouroboros Serpent was the mythical (and mystical) counterpart of the Ocean itself, and its symbolic representation, in Classical antiquity. This quaint symbolism is originally Hindu, as we have managed to show. It belongs to the Serpent Shesha, alias Vritra or Varuna. These names – which date from Vedic times – actually mean "encircler", much as does the word "Ocean" itself.

This idea of "encircling" in fact applies to the Atlantic and the Pacific Oceans. These two oceans are actually coterminous and in fact encircle the Americas from one pole to the other. And the word "Atlantic" means "of Atlantis", as Plato himself affirms. So, strictly speaking, these two oceans are really one and the same, the "Ocean of Atlantis".

And this is precisely what Plato has in mind when he call his "Atlantic Sea" the "veritable Ocean" (<u>alethinos pontos</u>). Hence, we are actually allowed to look for Atlantis in both the Pacific and the Atlantic Oceans. But such is patently not the case with the Mediterranean Sea.

Of course, it is also difficult to see how Cyprus could have been tropical during the Ice Ages, when it is not so even now, in the present Interglacial. Today, temperatures have globally climbed by about 15°C or so, according to the most recent climatological research.

We will be discussing the case of Cyprus next, due to the novel features of the proposal of the alleged researcher who, by the way, apparently now gave up on his entire undertaking, since he simply vanished from the media, along with most of his undersea scans, after his bombastic expedition to the claimed site.

For the present analysis, we again resort to the world map already shown above, or any other map that the dear reader may prefer. Crete is the tiny island barely visible at the center of the Mediterranean Sea, just beneath Greece. The island of Cyprus is the even tinier island below Turkey, in the Eastern Mediterranean. These islands can better be seen in this map of the Mediterranean region linked here. [1084]

If we insist that it is essential to consider Plato's "as you say, when talking in public, Pillars of Hercules" to be Gibraltar Strait, his dialogues on Atlantis fail to make any sense at all, at least insofar as reality is concerned. If so, we had better drop the whole search, as we already stated.

So, let us all be open-minded and magnanimous, and provisionally consider the "Pillars of Hercules" in question here to be the same as the Bosphorus Strait, which leads from the Mediterranean to the Black Sea. For Crete, we do not even need to posit new "Pillars of Hercules" in the Greek islands, as some proponents of this site have done in the past. We might accept these.

The Bosphorus Strait is located near Istanbul (ancient Byzantium), which can be seen in the same map of the Mediterranean region linked above, between Greece and Turkey. Byzantium was the capital of the Eastern Roman Empire, which lasted until well after the onset of the Middle Ages. This capital commanded this crucial strait commercially and militarily. This strait allowed ingress to the Black Sea and to Eastern Europe, and was hence very strategic in antiquity.

With the advent of Christianity, Byzantium became named Constantinople, the "City of [Emperor] Constantine". King Constantine was of course the famous patron of Christianity. And Constantine was also the man responsible for the death of Paganism, which he outlawed in the whole Eastern Roman Empire, fiercely persecuting all those who preferred to profess it.

The Bosphorus was considered to be the site of the "Pillars of Hercules" even before the name of these famous features was transplanted to the region of Gibraltar, where it remains stuck down to the present time. In reality, bosporus or bosphorus (or bosporos or bosphoros, rather, the Greek words from which the Latin name derives) means "cattle passage, oxford" precisely because Hercules was said to have crossed there with the cattle he rustled from Geryon, in Erytheia.

In later times this name was attributed to the crossing of the mortal girl Io, the beloved of Zeus, in the shape of a cow. No matter what, these "pillars" may be considered acceptable by all but the hardiest of skeptics. We want to give all our competitors the benefit of doubt. With this, Crete may in fact be considered to be located "in front of the Pillars of Hercules".

So may Malta, and for that matter, Cyprus, if we are broad-minded and tolerant enough, as can be seen in the same map. And so may Syrtis, in Libya and Schliemann's phony "Troy" (or Hissarlik). (See map of Mediterranean region linked above.) But Morocco, another frequently proposed site, cannot, given the fact that it lies outside Gibraltar, and hardly in front of the Bosphorus. So, let us stick to the sites just mentioned, leaving Morocco for the next section.

Robert Sarmast and the Cyprus' "Discovery"

Let us now consider Cyprus, the object of the proposal recently made by Robert Sarmast, an Atlantologist who dedicated a considerable amount of time and, allegedly, money into this research of the seafloor in the region in his recent book: <u>Discovery of Atlantis </u>(Mt. Shasta, CA, 2003). Sarmast is a self-proclaimed researcher and has used a detailed study of the topography of the Mediterranean seafloor in the region of Cyprus done by oil prospecting companies working there.

Sarmast also claims that his Atlantis site accords with "51 out of 53 features given by Plato". Alas, Sarmast's research seems sorely flawed and doomed from the start. Besides, on reading his book it is essentially impossible to see how any of the claimed features of his site can ever be made to coincide with the ones given in detail by Plato: very extensive agricultural plains; abundant mineral resources; vast forests (Cyprus has always imported firewood and timber), and so on.

The fact that this site hinges, as the author himself admits, on the hypothesis that the Mediterranean Basin was dry as recently as 10 to 12 thousand years ago – the epoch of Atlantis' cataclysm – turns it into a virtual geological impossibility.

According to this author, the Mediterranean Sea was closed off from the Atlantic Ocean by a dam across Gibraltar. This dam, he says, broke off at the date of the Atlantean cataclysm, and a monumental flood "swallowed up" the whole region of Atlantis in a terrible day and a night of pain, very much as Plato himself affirms.

But how is this possible if this flooding, even if real, was necessarily extremely slow and gradual rather than sudden and violent as Sarmast thinks?

The fact is that this flooding of the Mediterranean Sea actually lasted a full millennium or two. This rate of filling corresponds to something like 6 millimeters per day, something hard to perceive in practice. Some researchers in fact propose far larger rates of filling – reducing the time of flooding to something like 20 years or so. Even then, this rate corresponds to only about 1 centimeter/hour.

An annoyance, certainly, but far less than a disaster such as the Great Flood described by Plato, which occurred in the space "of a single day and a night of pain". People would have ample time to evacuate the region, annoyed, it is true, but otherwise unharmed.

But there are other aspects of Sarmast's theory that are even harder to believe. Many, many thousands of competent marine geologists – both scholarly and lay – have studied the Mediterranean seafloor with all types of sophisticated equipment such as side-scan sonar, multiple beam sonars, ROVs equipped with TV cameras, minisubs, oceanographic ships and so on.

It is hard to believe that they all failed to observe what Sarmast – an amateur at best – claims to have actually discovered. And their verdict is unanimous: the Mediterranean Sea has been full since about 5.2 million years ago, that is, since Miocenic times.

But what is even more incredible is Sarmast's claim that – in order to adequately comply with his theory – the Mediterranean had to be neither full nor empty, but stuck in between these two extremes in an essentially perfect equilibrium.

According to this researcher (see his book, pg. 132f.), the Mediterranean Sea is about 3,100 meters deep in the region where he sites his "Atlantis", which is however located at a depth of 1,650 meters or, just about midway between the two extremes.

Moreover, this intermediate depth had to be essentially constant for many tens of thousands of years, in order to allow the Atlantis Civilization to flourish and develop from scratch, as it is said to have done. And then, this situation had to endure until the date of Atlantis' demise, 11,600 years ago, the date given by Plato.

Now, this is an essential impossibility in geological practice. If Gibraltar Strait is closed (forming an isthmus), the Mediterranean Sea fast dries up, as it is known to be filled from the Atlantic Ocean inflow, as Sarmast himself admits.

On the other hand, if the strait is open, the Mediterranean fills up in a matter of mere decades or at best a millennium or two, leaving no time for Sarmast's "Atlantis" to exist one way or the other. Once started, the process of opening feeds on itself (by means of a positive feedback) and is fast led to completion and the opening of the rather large channel.

As we all know, the burden of proof is incumbent on the proponent. So, we eagerly wait to see how Sarmast will account for this obvious inconformity of his would-be Atlantis.

After I had written the above piece, Sarmast has been in the media a lot with his expedition to the site of Cyprus, made with the help of an oceanographic ship. I wrote a Statement on that, which I posted in my Atlantis site, in order to orient my readers against what I consider both an obvious hoax and a possible scam. [o85]

As a serious researcher of Atlantis, I consider it my duty to the public to come out and to point out to them the more obvious scammers and charlatans. This subject is also being currently discussed in our Atlantis Forum, where the readers of this text may read and comment on this alleged discovery.

Sarmast's alleged "find" – of what he claims to be the Acropolis and the walls and Great Plain of Atlantis – was soon dismissed as a mere "mud-spilling volcano" by the specialists working in this region of the Mediterranean Sea.

The location of his "find" is, according to the GPS data he posted in his site, just off Cyprus, at a depth of 1,650 meters and more. But, in contrast to what he alleges, this deep region was never subaerial, at least during the last 5.2 million years or so.

This remote date precedes the rise of humans on earth. so, it could never have been the site of Atlantis, despite Sarmast's specious claims. By the way, the dramatic event that Sarmast shows in his site ("New animation file of the Mediterranean basin flooding", in windows media) embodies at least three or more gross errors (or impossibilities) which can only fool the more gullible persons; these are:

> • First, the alleged "sea of Atlantis" is only an inland lake distant and isolated from Gibraltar and from the Ocean. So, how could Atlantis ever have developed into a naval power whose ports were frequented by most nations of the world, according to Plato's detailed description?
>
> • Second, the dramatic "flood" event Sarmast illustrates in his site with an animation never happened. The filling of the Mediterranean Sea took tens or even thousands of years to occur, as we just pointed out above and, in more detail, in our Statement on it just linked. So, this is just another

illusion created by computer graphics but which in no way corresponds to real events taking place either in the times of Atlantis, as alleged, or 5.2 million years ago, as experts have unanimously concluded.

• It is a miracle that the isolated "sea" or "lake" of Atlantis would have exactly the right depth (about 1,650 meters below present sea level) in order to make Sarmast's "Atlantis" come alive the way he wants. The Mediterranean Sea – and most others, by the way – simply does not behave this way. As a myriad researchers have concluded from their detailed in situ investigations of the seafloor, it is either wholly dry or wholly filled, and never half-full, as Sarmast alleges. So, unless Sarmast is prepared to provide compelling evidence of what he idly affirms, his claims have to be considered rubbish, until proved by him or accepted by other independent researchers.

No Such Cataclysm Ever in the Times of Man

Ingenious as Sarmast's proposal might sound to the more gullible public, its main fault lies in the fact that no such cataclysm, even though possibly imagined by some inventive writers, ever happened in the Mediterranean Sea at all at the recent dates normally associated with Atlantis.

This is a well established geological fact, and it is rather foolish to insist on proposing a theory that is overruled by irrefutable scientific facts such as the ones attested by the ample sedimentological records now available from hundreds of independent researchers.

Moreover, Bob Sarmast further postulates serial openings and closures of the Mediterranean Sea at Gibraltar, with a dry Mediterranean Sea being catastrophically filled at the geologically recent date of Atlantis' demise some 11,600 BP. And Sarmast repeatedly affirms that this date is impossible to scientifically establish on empirical grounds. Is it really?

Robert Sarmast is really no scientist. Moreover, this allegation of his is, to put it bluntly, <u>false</u>. In fact, there is a host of viable scientific techniques, all quite reliable and accurate. Marine sediments are normally composed of an "ooze" full of fossil microorganisms such as <u>Globigerina</u>, whose carbonate shells can be quite adequately dated by radiocarbon methods and corrected by techniques such as dendrochronology, as is current nowadays.

The dating accuracy of this method is now better than a couple of decades, more than adequate for the present purposes. In practice, a drill-core is obtained from the seafloor by an oceanographic ship equipped with a coring rig. Each layer corresponds to a specific date, so that the history of any specific maritime spot can be determined in a very reliable way by Sedimentology. [1086]

When the region is dry (subaerial) no such globigerina sediments form, and the nature of the deposits is unmistakably different. The history of the Mediterranean – and in fact most seas – has been studied in this and other ways, invariably with the same results.

Basically, Gibraltar Strait was first opened some 10 Mya [Megayears ago]. It later closed again, but has remained open since about 5.2 Mya, as indicated by the ooze deposits collected directly on the Mediterranean seafloor. So, there can be no question of the Mediterranean Sea being dry or half full down to as recently as 11,600 years ago, the date of Atlantis' demise.

Again, if anyone proposes that such was indeed the case, despite the compelling contrary evidence, the burden of proof is incumbent on him or her. Until then, all we can do is wait for that proof, before we can even consider the region around Cyprus as a possible site of Atlantis. This region is under the 1,000 meters isobath, and hence far under the global lowering of sea level which in fact took place in the Ice Age, which was only about 130-150 meters or so.

Bob Ballard and the Black Sea Flood

Sarmast's flood story closely parallels the one of the so-called Black Sea Flood, which has also been in the media a lot the last few years. Alas, despite all the media hype – always bent on misinforming the public – this theory of the Flood is also similarly doomed from the start according to most specialists who do not have an axe to grind. [1087]

The present scientific consensus is that the Black Sea flooding, even if real, was very slow and gradual enough to be not at all catastrophic. On that, cf. here and here and here and here and here and here and here and here and here! [1088]

Actually, the whole Black Sea research seems to have been a contrivance devised by the American Navy in order to have an excuse to spy on a strategic location. The Black Sea is tactical to the Russian Navy, which uses it as the exit into the Mediterranean Sea for its ships and its nuclear subs. Hence the curiosity of the Americans who, even though the Cold War is long over, like to keep an eye on the Russians.

No matter what, the very expensive research – equipped with the Alvin Submersible, Navy ships and subs, etc. – was wholly funded by the American Government, a highly unusual precedent, to say the least. Moreover, Bob Ballard is a retired Navy officer. Some people even say that Bob Sarmast also is. But this seems to be intrigue, even though Cyprus too is a political sore spot.

Moreover, the hypothesis of the Mediterranean Sea flooding is invariably rejected by most experts, Creationists included. Now, this rejection by Creationists is curious, as they ardently seek any confirmation of the Biblical Flood.

Creationists generally consider the Flood to have taken place in the Near East region. What this means is that the Black Sea flooding, even if factual, is too local and too slow to satisfy even them. How could such a petty, local event ever be deemed universal? Reach the distant Americas? Have been so wildly exaggerated in its consequences by whoever wrote its biblical description?

No matter what, even if these local cataclysms – either the one of the Black Sea or that of the Mediterranean Sea – were in fact real, it is hard to see how they would come to be regarded as the Universal Flood. This, of course, in contrast to the brutal rise in sea level which in fact took place at the end of the Ice Age, which in my opinion was the true culprit.

Too many things are missing here for a connection of this event with the Universal Flood to be acceptable by any but the more gullible: the global character; the interminable tempests; the sudden floods and giant waves (tsunamis); the volcanic eruptions (conflagrations); the catastrophic nature; the universal diffusion of the myth, the widespread mortality, the correct dates, etc..

It is known that even if the Black Sea flood actually took place as claimed, sea level rise in the region – said to have occurred at the meager rate of one foot/day or less, that is, about one centimeter per hour – would have been slow enough to allow people and cattle to leisurely move to the obvious safety of the mountainous regions. [1089]

The same thing would also probably be true of the Mediterranean Sea, and even more so, given the fact that its basin is far larger than that of the Black Sea. So, one way or the other, these events were far from catastrophic, at least in the way claimed by Plato, the Bible and the other very extensive mythology on the Flood, a myth existing among essentially all peoples on earth.

But this event, if it ever occurred at all, even on the dramatic scale imagined by its proponents, took place several millions of years ago, when Mankind did not even exist at all.

Again, it is very difficult to accept that these relatively petty, localized cataclysms, even if real, would have had the impact the Universal Flood did in remote locations such as the Americas, Oceania and the Far East as a whole. Plato specifically speaks of a global, violent cataclysm of fire and water which took place "in a single day and a night of pain".

This type of global catastrophe is suggestive of a supervolcanism or a giant tsunami, in contrast to this gradual filling out of the seas, which took place in the course of centuries or even millennia. That these Near Eastern floods were not volcanic in nature is proved by the fact that no volcanoes exist in the regions concerned: Cyprus, Gibraltar, the Bosporus, Palestine, and so forth.

All in all, attractive as these hypotheses might seem to some, they must be discarded until proven and verified to have been as violent, universal and catastrophic as claimed.

Curiously enough, the tradition of the Black Sea Flood seems to have been recorded in the local Flood myths, even though it did not occur in the times of Man. It is also curious to observe that Sarmast, even though claiming to be a mythologist, did not avail himself of these myths on the Mediterranean Sea in order to support his bold thesis. One Flood myth from Turkey tells how: [090]

> **Iskender-Iulcarni (Alexander the Great)**, in the course of his conquests, demanded tribute from Katife, Queen of Smyrna. She refused insultingly, and threatened to drown the king if he persisted. Enraged at her insolence, the conqueror determined to punish the queen by **drowning her in a great flood.** He employed Moslem and infidel workmen **to make a strait of the Bosphorus**, paying the infidel workmen one-fifth as much as the Moslems got. When the canal was nearly completed, he reversed the pay arrangements, giving the Moslems only one-fifth as much as the infidels.
>
> The Moslems quit in disgust and left the infidels to finish the canal. The Black Sea swept away the last dike and drowned the workmen. The Flood spread over Queen Katife's country (drowning her) and several cities in Africa. The whole world would have been engulfed, but Iskender-Iulcarni was prevailed upon to open the Strait of Gibraltar, letting the Mediterranean escape into the ocean. Evidence of the Flood can still be seen in the form of drowned cities on the coast of Africa and ship moorings high above the coast of the Black Sea.

Smyrna is the modern Izmir, in Turkey, more or less near the mouth of the Bosphorus and the Black Sea. Many legends are told of Alexander the Great, often called Dulkarnain ("two-horned") in the region. This name perhaps arose from an undue association with the figure of Moses, another horned hero, like Alexander.

Legends are often transferred from one personage to another, and from one place to another, as seems to be the case here (parting of the Red Sea?). Curiously enough, the legend apparently works in reverse here, and it is the Mediterranean that is filled by the Black Sea, rather than vice-versa, as Bob Ballard and others insistently allege.

We also note that the feat of opening Gibraltar Strait is also here attributed to Alexander, rather than to Hercules, as is usually the case. But Alexander's date is too late to be of any avail in the case of Atlantis, as the fabled hero lived as late as the 4th century BC, far later than even the Creationists will ever accept as the actual date of the Flood cataclysm, let alone the Platonists.

As we already noted, this curious myth actually works in reverse, with the overflowing Mediterranean waters escaping into the Atlantic Ocean, rather than vice-versa, as Bob Sarmast proposes. It is not impossible that the Turkish Flood Myth actually originated from an attempt on the part of Alexander or some other real hero to enlarge the Bosporus Strait, with the catastrophic results reported here. Or maybe the event was actually transferred from some other region of the world.

It would be interesting to try to check the physical evidence of the sunken cities mentioned by the above mythographer. Do they really exist in the region? Or is it the case that Bob Ballard and Bob Sarmast and other such researchers are actually reasoning in reverse? Is this the true reason of their failure so far? Or is the myth sheer invention or contrived and specious?

One of the mainstay arguments of Robert Sarmast is that the existence of the myth of Hercules opening the Strait of Gibraltar could not possibly have arisen out of nothing, and must hence stem from actual facts, as most myths normally do. And I agree.

But if so, what of the myth just told? Should it also not be deemed real according to this type of reasoning? After all, Alexander is far more historical than is Hercules himself.

As we just said, myths are often transferred from one place to another and from one hero to some other. And so are heroes and gods. In fact, it seems that Hercules was originally a Hindu hero.

Moreover, Alexander is also credited with the miraculous crossing of the Red Sea, another fact that proves his early identification with Moses. And he is said to have built a causeway across the ocean in order to invade Tyre, more or less replicating the far earlier feat performed by Rama and Hanumant when invading Lanka.

The very myth of Hercules opening the isthmus of Gibraltar after his passage with Geryon's cattle was originally set in the Bosphorus and/or the Kertch Strait, the Black Sea's connection with the Sea of Azov, in the north (see map here). And this myth – which is encountered in one way or the other all over the world – in turn derives from identical ones of the East Indies, its ultimate source. [091]

The *Ramayana* and the Vadavamukha

The real source of the myth of Hercules opening the Strait of Gibraltar seems to have originated in Indonesia itself. There the story is told of the Krakatoa Volcano and the opening of Sunda Strait, which seems to have been a geological event in late Pleistocenic or early Holocenic times.

This story is told in the Pustaka Raja Purwa, the far-famed Javanese chronicle, one whose geological reality can hardly be questioned anymore. We comment this Javanese tradition next, and will not detail it here any more than this.

The ultimate source of the myths in question here is invariably the Ramayana, the charming Hindu initiatic romance. The Ramayana is allegedly the first epic ever written. As we have demonstrated, the Ramayana was in fact the source of the Iliad and several others such.

The Ramayana tells in detail, in one of its most important passages, how Rama and Hanumant built a causeway of floating stones (pumice) for the purpose of invading Lanka.

Lanka was, in the Ramayana, the capital of Ravana's worldwide empire. As such, Lanka was the true archetype of both Troy and Atlantis. This bridge is often misidentified with Palk Strait in Sri Lanka, the connection of the island to the Indian subcontinent. But this is the result of the substitution of Sri Lanka for the true Lanka, actually located in Malaya. And this strait is often called Rama's Bridge (Ramasetu or Setubandha) or yet, Adam's Bridge. [092]

This fact again shows how readily myths are transferred from one hero to another and from one place to another, much as was the case of Gibraltar and the Bosphorus, etc..

In the Ramayana, the story is also told of how Rama and Hanumant, after having destroyed Lanka, cut open the causeway that connected the island to the continent, opening the strait. The ocean, thus released, invaded the whole region causing it to founder under the sea.

In the Christianized and Muslim variants of the Hindu legend, this bridge (Ramasetu) was used by Adam when he was expelled from Paradise, theoretically located in the island of Sri Lanka. And this bridge was broken open in order to prevent him from attempting to return to Paradise.

A similar Flood story is also told of Troy and, as we well know now, of Atlantis itself. The story is also told of Tyre, where Alexander allegedly built a similar causeway to invade the fortified island in which the city was formerly located.

Curiously enough, Tyre's causeway actually exists, even today. Of course, this causeway was never built by Alexander, but by the Phoenicians themselves. This shows in practice how myths are often transferred to the realm of pseudo-historical reality, generally by design and artfulness intended to deceive the more credulous readers.

The Ramayana is an initiatic romance, a marvelously crafted novelistic account of the myth of Atlantis, its war, and its destruction by the Flood, just as Plato affirms.

As such, it also closely parallels the Iliad of Homer in essentially every detail. And these include not only the incending and subsequent sinking underseas, but also the great war, the abduction of the fickle queen by the villain, the terrible vengeance of the cuckolded king, etc..

Now, the true site of Setubandha is really the Malay Peninsula, which in fact leads from the Indonesian islands to the Asian continent as some sort of bridge or causeway (see map of the region here). A close comparison of these texts will readily show the uncanny parallels. [093]

But what is even more curious is the fact that this widespread myth originated from real geological events. These events are actually connected with the Flood and its probable causation by a supervolcanic explosion of the Krakatoa. And this disaster was also apparently the cause of the catastrophic end of the Ice Age as well, just as we have long been arguing.

This prehistoric supereruption of the Krakatoa was one of the largest such ever. According to experts, it was equivalent to fully 100,000 hydrogen bombs of one Megaton each, or about 10 times the whole world's nuclear arsenal. The explosion created a giant caldera fully 50 kilometers across, which opened Sunda Strait (<u>Selat Sund</u>a). This strait now sunders Java and Sumatra (<u>see above map</u>). [1094]

This much energy is clearly enough to destroy the entire world and to trigger an enduring Ice Age, as most scientists now realize. It is moreover estimated that the eruption of this submarine supervolcano carried over 100 km³ of vaporized oceanic water into the atmosphere, a value ample enough to generate the copious rains which characterize the Flood myth the world over.

The giant earthquakes created by the colossal explosion also generated the giant tsunamis reported in several traditions of the Universal Flood found worldwide, the Americas included.

These giant tsunamis probably lofted the continental glaciers, carrying them out to sea and speeding the end of the Ice Age. And this was compounded with the albedo reduction due to the deposition of soot and cinders shed by the volcanism.

As is now clear, mythical heroes such as Rama and Hercules are really mere personifications of volcanoes. So are doom-bringing gods such as Vishnu and Shiva and many others. These heroes or gods usually consist of twins like Hercules and Atlas, Rama and Hanumant, Shiva and Vishnu, Agni and Indra, and so forth.

These twins also invariably correspond to the two Pillars of Hercules, themselves really consisting of twin volcanoes. And twin volcanoes are a rarity, except in Indonesia itself, the epicenter of earth's so-called Fire Belt.

These two heroes in fact correspond to the two pairs of such pillars. One pair of pillars was dedicated to Hercules (in Gibraltar) and the other pair was dedicated to Atlas, in Indonesia. Actually, the true action took place in Indonesia, the main site of the Pacific Fire Belt. The pillars of Gibraltar were mere "mirror images" having no reality insofar as the events in question here are concerned.

Mt. Atlas is the true Pillar of Heaven. As such, it is really dual. And it is in fact located in Sunda Strait (the Krakatoa and Toba volcanoes). Gibraltar Strait is of course a purely virtual pillar, being no volcano and, even less, the "Pillar of Heaven".

The same is also true of the Atlas Range in Morocco, which is again not volcanic. Even the Berber natives of the region reject this identification, which is late and actually due to the Greeks and the Phoenicians, in their endeavor to fool the more gullible people.

Alternatively, one might consider that each of the two pillars in each world half was dedicated to one of the two twins, forming the observed pair. One should keep in mind that the two pillars represent the Twins, as in the astrological symbol of Gemini. [095]

So, it is only natural that we have two pairs of pillars, one in Gades (Gibraltar) the residence of Hercules; the other one in Malacca (Indonesia), the residence of Atlas himself, the elder Hercules.

The two heroes are here visibly confused, one with the other, Hercules representing Gadeiros or Geryon, and Atlas either the older twin or the junior one, depending on the account. In other accounts – for instance the one due to Diodorus Siculus – Hercules is specifically identified to Kronos, just as he was in the Orphic traditions. And Kronos is the elder Titan, often made the father or alias of Atlas.

The *Pustaka Raja Purwa* and the Opening of Sunda Strait

One of the most curious aspects of the legend of the opening of the strait by the hero – attributed to Hercules in Gibraltar and the Bosphorus in the Mediterranean, and to Rama in Sunda Strait (in Indonesia) and Palk Strait (in Sri Lanka) – is the fact that the myth is also found in the Javanese annals, exactly where the event actually took place.

The "hero" or "god" is of course the volcano, as we already mentioned. Even more exactly this volcano is the Krakatoa volcano, precisely the one which opened the giant rift which now corresponds to the Strait of Sunda sundering Java and Sumatra.

This event is told in some detail in the Pustaka Raja Purwa, a Javanese annal dating to the Middle Ages. But the story told there was actually obtained from earlier sources of an enormous antiquity. This story also figures, disguised under several different allegories, in several Hindu traditions, some of which dating from the Rig Veda itself.

David Keys, the sensationalist author, actually cites this very event as evidence of his catastrophic giant eruption of the Krakatoa of 535 AD, the one which allegedly decreed the end of the Byzantine Roman Empire with the Great Plague which it somehow allegedly caused. [11]

But, as I already pointed out, the giant eruption of the Krakatoa volcano in question here is actually the one which sank Atlantis, unfortunate enough to be placed in precisely this region of the world. This, unless we actually had two similar explosions of the ferocious Krakatoa volcano, a very definite possibility that only an in situ research may definitively confirm. [096]

As a matter of fact, this type of research has already proved that the Krakatoa volcano seems to have formed several such large calderas over the ages as the result of its many successive supereruptions, much as is the case with supervolcanoes everywhere, the Yellowstone included.

Actually, the colossal fiery cataclysm of the Krakatoa volcano in question here is by far more than ample to have triggered the likewise catastrophic end of the Ice Age some 11,600 years ago, the very date given by Plato for Atlantis' demise.

Several reasons prevent us from believing the reality of Keys' proposal. For one thing, the actual events of 535 AD were too small in scale to require such a huge supereruption. Second, the Roman Byzantine Empire continued to function down to far later times, in contrast to what Keys affirms in his book and his documentary.

But what really renders this association impossible is the fact that the opening of Sunda Strait is also commemorated in myths far earlier than the relatively late date of 535 AD. Such myths include the one of the Ramayana and that of Hercules just cited, and which both date from far earlier times. The Javanese chronicle in question, the Pustaka Raja Purwa, is worth quoting verbatim here:

> "A great glaring fire, which reached to the sky came out of the mountain... There was a furious shaking of the earth, total darkness, thunder and lightning. Then came forth a furious gale, together with torrential rain, and a deadly storm darkened the entire world... When the waters subsided, it could be seen that the island of Java had been split in two, thus creating the island of Sumatra."

It is interesting to note that, just as reported here, the islands of Java and Sumatra were originally both named Java. One of the islands was called Java Major and the other Java Minor. Quite often the two islands were not distinguished, and were called by the single name. This fact bespeaks their original unity, as also attested in the Javanese annal.

The name of Java is also extremely important. This toponym actually means "white" in Sanskrit. As such, Java is the fabled "White Island" which was deemed to have been the site of Paradise, as discussed further above. Moreover, the name of Java is related to that of the Javanas or Yavanas, that is, the white races.

This name – which assonates with the one of the Iaꜰones (or Ionians) – is also the name of the Greek people, which apparently also came from this distant region of the ancient world. This fact is of extreme practical importance, since it provides a direct connection between the Sea Peoples, ancient Greece, Taprobane (Java and Sumatra) and the former site of Atlantis.

We note that myths take place outside history, <u>in illo tempore</u> ("once upon a time", in Latin). Even when the events are historicized – as is so often the case – their dates have no meaning at all, and refer back to the primeval time which the Egyptians called <u>Zep Tepi</u> and the Australians call "Dreamtime". Hence, the annals just quoted actually refer to the ante-Diluvian kings of Java and their times, and cannot be historicized as David Keys is attempting to do.

No matter what, this Javanese chronicle apparently refers to the <u>Ramayana</u> events and, hence, to the story of Atlantis itself, extremely popular in the region of Indonesia. And it is indeed quaint to see the history of Atlantis obsessively told there as both sacred myth (<u>Ramayana Wayang</u>) and as actual history, all in the very site it actually took place a very, very long time ago.

These fascinating, surreal events in fact closely resemble a dream or nightmare, just as the Australians so aptly put it. And so do the Javanese, with their surreal puppets, which are no more than oniric shadows of a past long gone. But this nightmare is as inescapable as the rites we celebrated every Sunday, the very day in which the Terrestrial Sun [the volcano] flared up, destroying the whole earth, just as illustrated in my book's cover.

These nightmares refuse to go away, and constantly challenge us to solve the riddle that the Sphinx put to Oedipus, again a very long time ago: "decipher me, or I shall devour you!". And they will too, in time, whether deciphered or not, I am sorry to say...

Such is perhaps the reason why Herodotus affirms that "the Atlanteans never dream". Perhaps they are so afraid of nightmares as to be unable to sleep in peace without the help of sedatives. Better yet, they fear the Mare herself, the Submarine Mare that is indeed the Krakatoa and his brothers, who simply refuse to go away despite the pink eyeglasses that Darwin and Lyell force us all to wear with their panglossian doctrines on Uniformitarian Geology and Evolution.

Well, enough of day-dreaming. Let us return to Science and to the harsh, inescapable geological facts-of-life. Central to Sarmast's latest theory on Atlantis' demise, as we just said, is the fact that the Mediterranean basin suffered a catastrophic flood with the destruction of the Gibraltar "dam" which once closed off the Mediterranean Sea from the Atlantic Ocean.

This event, even if real, was necessarily too slow and too gradual to convincingly explain the catastrophic events universally associated with the Flood. Such was also the case with the Black Sea "flood" of Bob Ballard, as a lot of recent research has unequivocally demonstrated.

For that matter, it is also wholly unable to account for the violent destruction of Atlantis by Fire and Water, in the manner described in detail by Plato in both the <u>Timaeus</u> and the <u>Critias</u>. People could very easily flee the slowly rising waters (one foot or less a day), without ever running the risk of being "swallowed by the earth" as they were en masse in Atlantis, according to Plato's report.

All in all, it is apparent that the Mediterranean sites so far proposed for Atlantis seem to be utterly inadequate: Crete, Cyprus, Malta, Spain, and so forth. And the same is also true for the other circum-Mediterranean locations, as we will be arguing next.

Crete is by far the best bet, though itself impossible. Impossible for the reasons already pointed out: wrong date, wrong volcano, wrong geographical size, wrong location, wrong side of the pillars, and so forth. Hence, the best one may do is to forget the whole proposition.

Anyone who reads Plato closely will not fail to conclude that the prince of philosophers unequivocally spoke of an empire of continental dimensions destroyed by a supervolcanism. And this worldwide empire was clearly placed outside Gibraltar Strait and, very probably, antipodal to it. No matter what, Atlantis' vast dimensions would never fit inside the smallish Mediterranean Sea.

Starting to Bear Fruits

We sincerely hope that the next expedition planned by Sarmast to research the site he thinks to be the one of Atlantis has a greater success than had his past one or that of Koudriavtsev, the Russian who claims Atlantis is located in the British Shelf. After all, a find there would perhaps prove that Atlantis once had a colony or factory in the Mediterranean region, as it very possibly did.

But we were extremely skeptical on this, as nothing at all in Plato really fits the region of Cyprus or any others nearby. Besides, even in the unlikely event of the ruins of an Ice Age civilization being found there, who can guarantee that it was not a mere colony or a factory of Atlantis, rather than the real thing, as Sarmast so unfoundedly claims?

No matter what, I am extremely glad to see that my pioneering proposal of looking underwater for Atlantis rather than on dry land is starting to bear fruits and to become popular with today's Atlantologists: Hancock, Sarmast, Koudriavtsev, Collina-Girard, Ballard, Schoch, the Atlantis Team, Stephen Oppenheimer, the Flem-Aths, and a dozen other authors whom we could further name here.

These researchers have now all or mostly abandoned their former pseudoscientific views such as Pole Shift in favor of my own theory that Atlantis' demise was the result of the huge sea level rise which occurred at the end of the Pleistocene, as the result of the melting of the massive continental glaciers that then existed. [12]

Even in the unlikely hypothesis that they rediscovered this reality independently, they are obliged to give me credit for it, as I preceded them all by a full decade and more. This is demanded by scientific ethics, and is something that cannot be idly dismissed by anyone.

Who knows, people will also soon start to accept my location of Atlantis-Eden as well, and start looking in the real site where Atlantis has always lain: the shallow seas of the Indonesia continental shelves? I have so much confidence in this location of Atlantis that I am in the process of setting up an oceanographic expedition to look at the seafloor of the region for certain features which I have already diagnosed by means of alternative techniques such as outer space spying.

The Results for the Mediterranean Locations of Atlantis

The main results we just got for the sites in the Mediterranean Sea locations are summarized in Table III.3 below. Now, can these tiny islands truly be considered "larger than Asia and Libya put together", as Plato specifically affirms? Are there really any islands ahead of these that would help ships to get to the opposite continent beyond (Africa)?

Are these islands many? Are they really located in the "true ocean" which Plato explicitly mentions? Is Africa really the "true continent" that environs the "true ocean" all around? Can the Mediterranean Sea indeed be considered the "true ocean" that Plato had in mind? Why, and how? Was Plato really so sloppy in his description of the geography of Atlantis?

Even the allegation made by Bob Sarmast that Africa is the "outer continent" mentioned by Plato seems to be false, after all. Plato's description of this "outer continent" clearly places it out, in the ocean. Why would it be called "outer" if it lay inside the Mediterranean Sea?

Table III.3 - Results for Crete, Cyprus, Malta, Syrtis, etc.			
Two Pillars (Bosphorus?)	Island of Cyprus, etc.. (Larger than Asia + Libya) ???????	Many Islands Ahead ??????? In True Ocean ???????	Outer Continent (Africa) ???????

Besides, Plato and other ancient authorities reserved the name of "outer continent" to what seems to be the Americas, which in fact "contained" the Ocean, as we already affirmed. The other continents – Europe, Asia, Africa and even Atlantis – he and others dubbed "islands" in the sense of being encircled in whole or in part by water.

In my humble opinion, no amount of arguing – no matter how cleverly done – will ever convince any commonsensical, down-to-earth person that by "true ocean" (pelagos ontôs; alêthinon ponton), Plato is really referring to the puny Mediterranean Sea. [097]

Plato was no fool. And he specifically contrasted the Mediterranean with the "true Ocean" in the passage of the Timaeus quoted above in extenso. So, how can one believe that the two are in fact one and the same sea or ocean? Not even a child would believe this type of claim were it not put to him by a would-be authority reputed to know what he is talking about.

However, I well know that self-delusion is a sad fact of life, and that many people will let themselves be misled by this type of specious argumentation, if artfully done. Neither will I ever be convinced that these puny Mediterranean islands would be deemed "larger than Asia and Libya (Africa) put together" by Plato, the wisest of philosophers.

Were the ancients all that stupid? And did they all believe that the actual "Atlantic Ocean" – which the Phoenicians and the Carthaginians and even the Greeks themselves often sailed – was dark and somber and "innavigable" due to pumice and sargassos and seamonsters of all sizes?

Nor will I ever believe that Africa can be said to "encompass the Ocean all around", as Plato specifically affirms of the Outer Continent. Facts are facts, and no amount of clever argumentation will ever change them a jot, no matter how craftily conducted. Plato and others often referred to Africa and Europe as "islands", rather than "continents".

Rather than mere words, these "theorists" should be able to produce geological proof of their claims the way I did, rather than just artful arguments: viable geological mechanisms acceptable to all scientists; viable dates and locations; viable Ice Age climates, and so forth.

Now, Plato would have to be an idiot to be affirming things that everyone in his own time well knew to be lies or falsehood. However, if some are willing to bend Plato's words that far in order to make them fit their text, any result whatsoever can be had. But then, the philosopher's words would really mean nothing anymore, would they?

Such is the reason why I try to found my case on so much scientific proof, and insist on producing so much factual evidence for it: linguistic, geologic, traditional, and so forth, even at the risk of boring some of my dear readers to death.

And I try to do that, no matter how intrinsically logical my arguments might in fact seem to myself and to other specialists, so that the dear readers can check it all by themselves.

Returning to Sarmast's case. The "true continent ahead of the many islands" might be taken to be Africa, as this researcher actually does. But the fact is that these many islands are apparently lacking here, as can be seen in the map just given. Moreover, as I just said, how can Africa be said to encircle the whole ocean on the outside?

These are all important matters which, after I pondered them long enough, led me to reject any of these Mediterranean locations as possible sites for Atlantis, if the Lost Continent is indeed to be considered something real.

We hope to have convinced the dear readers that such is really the case here, no matter how aptly this case may be defended by someone. Only new facts of an incontrovertible nature may cause me – and hopefully most of my readers as well, I think – to change opinion on this crucial issue. It is true that Plato might be just plain lying. Or was just simply an ignoramus? But if so, why bother with Atlantis at all?

When one looks closely at the results summarized in Table III.3 above, one can see that even if one accepts that the Bosphorus is really the

"Pillars of Hercules" which Plato had in mind, nothing else fits the detailed description given by the philosopher.

I advise the readers to again use the table just filled above (<u>Table III.1</u>) as some sort of <u>yantra</u> or <u>mandala</u> in order to meditate the issue long enough, as the Hindus are wont to do. The truth is all out there, but must be thoroughly absorbed before it is fully realized.

And I believe that then, you too, dear reader, will probably come to the same conclusion that I and several others researchers of Atlantis also did: any Mediterranean location for Atlantis is sheer nonsense, if we are in fact decided to heed Plato's words on it.

CHAPTER 12 - THE CELTIC SHELF, MOROCCO AND TARTESSOS

> *In my opinion, the most serious argument in favor of the assumption that Atlantis had not been invented by Plato, is that the time when it vanished... the circumstances of its vanishing... coincide with the data which, no doubt, were inaccessible to Plato, on the time of the end of the last Ice Age and a substantial rise of the level of the World Ocean that accompanied it.*
>
> <u>Viatcheslav Koudriavtsev, Atlantis: New Hypothesis (2001)</u>
> [I first mooted out this important fact, as far back as 1982]

Another all time favorite candidate for Atlantis' location is the west coast of either Africa or Europe. Among these we name Tartessos (Spain), Morocco, the Celtic Shelf (Brittany, Ireland, Scotland and England), the North Sea and the Baltic Sea. These coasts have the great advantage of being located in the Atlantic Ocean itself. But this does not help much, as we shall see next.

Despite this reality, the sites in question here keep popping up in the news as possible locations for Atlantis. And the reason is that the astute Phoenicians, who first colonized this region of the world, recreated an illusory Atlantis in that region in order to fool the competition, who invariably attempted to follow them to the fabulous Cassiterides, the source of their precious metals, in the Far East.

For the purposes of the preliminary assaying being done here, these and other sites at the west coast of Europe may be bunched together. But we will leave the submerged island of <u>Espartel</u> (inside Gibraltar) for later, because of its novelty and its alleged scientific importance, which is in fact nil. [098]

The Celtic Shelf (<u>map here</u>) is located to the south of Ireland and of England, extending eastwards to the coast of France. The area of the Celtic Sea which covers the Celtic Shelf is considered to range from 48°N and 52°N to 4°W and the 1,000 meters isobath at the edge of the continental slope. It is bounded on the east by the English Channel, and on the south and west by the local continental slope. The major part of the Celtic Sea area is shallow and ranges between 100 and 200 meters in depth. [099]

Some shallower areas do, however, exist to the west of Cornwall (UK) and to the southeast of Ireland. There are also a number of relatively shallow banks encountered in the deeper parts of the Celtic Sea, including Labdie Bank, Jones Bank and the Great Sole Bank. These shallow waters indicate that the region generally lay above sea level during the Pleistocene Ice Age, when sea level was about 130 to 150 meters lower than presently.

A number of curious geological features of the Celtic Shelf such as seamounts, canyons and ridges generally extend all the way to the continental slope of Brittany. Features such as slopes, trenches, basins, iceberg scour marks, seamounts and banks render this submarine region rather unique. Sedimentologically speaking, the seabed of the Celtic Sea is composed of gravel and sand, becoming somewhat muddier in nature to the south of Ireland.

In truth, it is nice to see that the seeds which I have been sowing for such a long time are finally starting to yield fruits. Many Atlantologists of all shades are fast adopting my pioneering proposal that catastrophic sea level rise was the actual cause of Atlantis' demise, as can be seen in the above quote and many others such.

Some of these authors are even adopting my complementary proposal that the Flood is truly to be identified to the catastrophic end of the Pleistocene Ice Age and the catastrophic rise in sea level that resulted, a fact that gladdens my heart. They are also starting to accept this identification of mine of the cause of the Universal Deluge and of Atlantis' identity with Eden, the site of Paradise Lost. Too bad that they often fail to give me credit for these revolutionary finds!

Well, the consolation prize is that Atlantis is fast becoming a candent issue in the news, now that the riddle has finally started to make scientific sense to several experts, both maverick and academic. Hence, I am finally able to publish my research internationally, after having done it for a long time in Brazil and in my site. And I hope my pioneer research helps a lot in bringing Atlantis back to life.

After this short preamble, let us apply the features of Table III.1 to the regions in question here, the west coasts of Europe and/or Africa. First of all, we note that these regions can hardly be said to be located "in front of the Pillars of Hercules", as Plato specifically affirmed, being in fact at its sides.

Why wouldn't Plato, a peerless rhetor – called doctor mellifluus because he was deemed a supreme master in the art of expressing himself with perfect clarity when he wanted to do so – have said "at the sides of the Pillars of Hercules" or something to that effect, affirming instead that they lay "right in front of the Pillars of Hercules" as he actually does according to what we showed above?

Does not this assertion of Plato seem somewhat foolish, were these sites in fact acceptable? Moreover, the sunken portions of the regions in question here can also hardly be said to be "larger than Asia (Near East) and Libya (North Africa) put together", as Plato specifically affirms.

These sunken areas are at best only 1/20 (or 5%) of the total area given by Plato, as we show further below, with actual maps of the sunken region to prove our case. This is an insignificant proportion, which can be wholly dismissed in practice. As such, it might be forgotten and dismissed as of no consequence for the history of Atlantis which we are attempting to recover here.

The Many Islands Ahead

With this, we turn to another problem: the one of "the many islands ahead". Where, may we ask, are the many islands ahead of Ireland and Tartessos and similar locations which would have helped sailors to cross to the Outer Continent ahead, the Americas? The only islands on the way to America departing from the British Shelf are the ones of Newfoundland and those of the Caribbean Sea.

But these are in America, and are only reached after one actually arrived in Plato's "opposite continent". So, they did not really help much in crossing to America, as Columbus found out. It is true that the Azores are about midway to America, and could hence help the crossing.

But such is not the case at all. One of Columbus' predecessors, Martin Behaim – who attempted to reach the East Indies via the west even before the great explorer himself – actually attempted to make a landfall in the Azores. However, the maritime currents there were headed the wrong way, and he failed, being shipwrecked and almost dying in his failed attempt.

Columbus learnt this lesson very well. Instead, he departed not from Spain, but from the Canaries, rather than the Azores, taking advantage of the North Equatorial Current which circumvents the doldrums of the Sargasso Sea, and in fact helps the difficult crossing quite a bit. It is highly likely that the explorer had learnt the trick from ancient sources now lost or hidden in the secret vaults of Sagres School.

However, the Canaries can hardly be said to lie "ahead of the way" there. Actually, they are inconveniently off the way, as can be seen in a map. Such is particularly the case for sailors departing from the British Shelf region or the North Sea and heading for North America.

Most of these islands on the way – the fabled "Atlantic islands" – were ardently sought for centuries by hundreds of explorers, and never found except as actual misnomers such as Brazil (Ys Brazil) and Argentina, (Argyre, "the land of silver"); Septe Cidades (Antilia); San Brandán; Satanazes; Roillo; Salvaggia; Capraria; Madeira; etc..

Where are these islands to be found now, but as sore mistakes? We will return to this subject when we discuss the "Atlantic isles" as possible candidates for Atlantis further below.

Is the Atlantic Ocean – so much smaller than the Pacific – indeed to be considered the "True Ocean" to which Plato specifically refers twice in a row in his texts on Atlantis? Why would it be so named if it is not really the site of Lost Atlantis?

Sadly, the Internet site of Viatcheslav Koudriavtsev, the eminent Russian who so cogently proposed the Celtic Shelf and even led an expedition to the place, went off the air for some undisclosed reason. The more people engaged in the hunt for Atlantis, the faster the Lost Continent will be discovered, charted, researched and brought back to life in all its former glory.

Maybe the real reason was that nothing worthwile was found on the Celtic Shelf, despite Koudriavtsev's high hopes. It is also possible that he later found out that the Russian authorities who helped him out in the expedition were more interested in espionage than in really researching Atlantis. Life is hard, these Kali Yuga days...

The Celtic Shelf is actually rather small, as can be seen in the map linked above. See also the interesting article that comments this issue here. Its area is roughly equivalent to the one of the Iberian Peninsula, as can be seen in the map just linked. The area of that region is only about 500,000 km², roughly 1/20 (or 5%) of the area given by Plato for the size of the sunken continent of Atlantis. [↑100]

The actual area of the Celtic Shelf that was really subaerial in the Ice Age is far smaller (the 130 to 150 meter isobath, technically speaking), and is hence quite unlikely to have been a fit site for the Lost Continent of Atlantis, whose size is obviously far larger than this.

Very much the same conclusion also holds for Tartessos (part of Spain) which hardly sank at all (see Koudriavtsev's map here). The same also applies to the North Sea and the Baltic Sea, where the situation is very much the same, as can be seen in the map just linked. What is even worse is the fact that not only Ireland, but all or most of the Celtic Shelf region was wholly covered by ice during the Ice Age, as can be seen in the map of Ice Age Europe here. This map shows the entire British Shelf as an ice covered polar desert during the Ice Age. [101]

So, how could any substantial civilization ever develop there or anywhere else in Europe, which was then mainly desertic as this paleovegetation map dramatically shows?

The British Shelf is detailed in this Ice Age map of Ireland here. Its results are also applicable to Britain itself since it was from there that the glaciers advanced over Ireland. And this map also shows that the first humans only entered the region rather late, by about 7,000 BC or so. [102]

This date is desperately belated for a possible connection with Atlantis, which disappeared 2,600 years earlier, according to Plato. It is also apparent from this fact that the first humans had to wait for the end of the Ice Age to be over in order to start colonizing the British Isles.

Again, this fact suggests an ice covered region. And this is verified in situ in Ireland itself, where the scouring done in the rocks of the region by the glaciers can be observed even today.

In Koudriavtsev's map just linked, the areas covered by glaciers correspond to the areas in white. His estimate of the ice covering seems to be overly conservative in comparison to the more detailed, more precise maps just linked. In fact, most experts agree – based on the in situ evidence – that these glaciers extended further, to also cover the British Isles themselves, as just shown.

So, it is extremely hard to see how the Celtic Shelf could ever have housed Atlantis. Atlantis was tropical even at that time, according to the detailed report of Plato. Maybe this disappointing reality clarifies the disenchantment of Koudriavtsev with his research expedition to the British Shelf site.

Moreover, there are no volcanoes worth mentioning in this whole region. So, how could it have been destroyed by a supervolcanism and/or a giant tsunami of the type described by Plato?

Coconuts, bananas and scented woods – which abounded in Atlantis according to Plato – do not grow in this region even today, now that the local climate is far warmer than during the Ice Age. After all, temperatures rose globally by about 15 °C or more in average after the end of the Ice Age, according to the recent finds of experts on Climatology.

All in all, appealing as this proposal of the Celtic Shelf might appear to some local researchers, it seems that the theory of a West European Atlantis must be trashed.

With this, we turn our attention to Morocco, another nearby site long proposed for Atlantis. This identification has been done ever since Herodotus placed Atlantis and Mt. Atlas in precisely this region of the world. Plato was of course familiar with this fact, which he apparently disregarded in his writings, certainly because he realized the utter nonsense of the proposal.

It is true that Morocco benefits from the fact of having a few mighty volcanoes in the nearby Canary Islands, a site linked with the Isles of the Blest since remote antiquity. Besides, this region enjoyed a warm climate even during the Ice Age.

But we will see next that Morocco is no more than a second-hand replica, and that the place was artfully created by the clever Phoenicians as some sort of "mirror image" of true Atlantis. It was essentially desertic then, and hence unsuitable to house a mighty civilization of any sort.

This region of north Africa – called Mauritania by the ancient Greeks and the Romans – even had a "Mt. Atlas" according to Herodotus and others. Except that this name of the famous mountain is of a relatively late date, and derives from the Phoenician exploits in the region.

The Berber natives call the mountain by an entirely different name (Gebel Toubkal) and do not connect it with the legend of Atlas or Atlantis, which they also knew, by the way. According to the reliable <u>Encyclopedia Britannica</u> (sv. "Atlas Mts."):

> "The name [of the Atlas Mts.] was given by Europeans who supposed them to be the home of the mythical Greek god, and is <u>never</u> used by the native races" [my emphasis].

In fact, this appellative and its connection with Atlantis first figures in Herodotus himself (<u>Hist</u>. IV:184). But we believe that Herodotus and the other Greeks were merely reporting Phoenician (Carthaginian) legends on Hercules and Atlas, their two supreme heroes, whose exploits they unduly transferred to the region of Morocco.

As is known, these two heroes originated in Hindu and Phoenician and Pelasgian and Etruscan mythology, later passing to the ones of the Greeks and the Romans. Philo of Biblos, basing himself on the work of Sanchuniathon, a Phoenician priest, affirmed that Greek mythology actually originated from the Phoenicians. This was also the view of several other ancient authorities, Herodotus included.

The Dualism of Hercules and Atlas

Noel, in his justly famous <u>Dictionary of Mythology</u> (Paris, 1867) affirms that: "the Phoenicians, during their exploits in Mauritania (Morocco) seeing the lofty mountains of this country covered by snow and occulted by clouds, gave them the name of Atlas, thereby transforming the king who is the symbol of astronomy into a mountain whose head sustains the skies."

This curious myth closely parallels the one told by Ovid in his <u>Metamorphoses</u>. According to the poet, Perseus, on being ill-treated by the giant, showed him the Medusa's head, and Atlas turned into stone, huge as a mountain, and is said to bear the skies on his head and shoulders.

We believe that this curious myth – which is found even in the Americas, by the way, as just affirmed – allegorizes the actual transformation of people into stone which takes place when they are buried by volcanic cinders and become fossilized. This fact can be physically seen in Pompey and Herculaneum, where such fossilized "statues" are displayed to the fascinated tourists who visit the place.

We agree with Noel in that it was the Phoenicians and the Greeks who thus named the Atlas Mts. in Morocco. This event happened when they started to explore the region in the 6th century BC or so, with Hanno and Himilco, etc.. And the Phoenicians were, according to Herodotus and others, the instructors of the Greeks in many things, mythology and writing certainly among them.

So, they also handed this information – unknown to the Berber natives themselves – to the Greeks, who in turn passed it on to the Romans. But the dates in question are all too late to be of any use to those seriously searching for Atlantis rather than for illusions and mirages.

Moreover, this mountain is not even a volcano, and thus does not justify its naming as "Pillar of Heaven". This expression was an onomastic reserved for volcanoes, as we have already said. The idea of "Pillar of Heaven" is in fact closely evoked by volcanic plumes, which literally rise to the sky itself as if supporting it.

We have already illustrated one such gigantic instance, which evokes the shape of an "atomic mushroom". A close reading of all or most of the ancient references to such pillars will no doubt evoke the idea of a volcano and its plume, particularly in the smoke clouds which never abandon the summit of such mountains.

In Phoenician mythology, from which the Greek one on Hercules derives, the two heroes often figure as avatars of Atlas and Kronos. Kronos seems to be the alias of Hercules. And these two heroes or gods were often identified, for instance, in the Orphic Mysteries. [103]

Athenagoras (Pro Christ. 18:20) reports the curious Orphic cosmogonic tradition where Hercules is explicitly identified with Kronos (Saturn) and is said to have been the origin of all things through an egg he laid. So does Diodorus Siculus (Lib. III:52) who affirms that Atlas and Kronos (Saturn) ruled Atlantis after their father Ouranos was ousted by Kronos, who moreover castrated him.

These texts allow us to conclude, by comparison with the writings of Plato, that Hercules and Gadeiros are both one and the same hero. These reports and cosmogonies (cf. Eusebius, Praep. Evang. I:10) are all very obscure and extremely confused, so that it is difficult to make much sense of them, unless one is a skilled master in matters mythological. [104]

But what their myth finally amounts to is the identification of the twin heroes with the two races of Atlantis, as well as the two volcanoes, their ophiomorphic shape. In their disputes, the twins, like the two volcanoes of the Amerindian myths or the ones of other peoples, end up by causing the Flood and destroying the whole world.

In the text just linked, Eusebius quotes Sanchuniathon, the famed Phoenician priest, thus: "But the Greeks, surpassing all in genius, appropriated most of the earliest [Phoenician] stories, and then variously decked them out with ornaments of tragic phrase, and adorned them in every way, with the purpose of charming by the pleasant fables... and with these fables, as they traveled about, they conquered and drove out the truth."

The figures of the Greek Herakles and the Roman Hercules both ultimately derive from the one of Baal Melkhart, the great Phoenician god, and his twin and dual, Atlas. The two brothers are often confused and interchangeable, just as are the twins of all mythologies.

In reality, the two heroes imperson the two main moieties of the Greek nation, the Pelasgians (partly Phoenician and Etruscan) and the Aryans. The first component corresponds to the Dravidas (or "reds") and the second to the Indo-Europeans (Yavanas or "whites"). And the disputes of these two brothers in fact correspond to the War of Atlantis, as Plato expounds in his seminal dialogues.

Gades, Gadeira, Cadiz and Gadir

Gades or Gadeiros is in fact the Phoenician name of Hercules, as the twin brother of Atlas, according to Plato. This name means something like "cowherd, herdsman". Plato translates his name as Eumelos, which means something like "rich in cattle" in Greek. But the real meaning is akin to the one of the "Good Shepherd", who leads his people away from the site of Paradise destroyed. [13]

That the name of Gades or Gadeira is not specifically applicable to Cadiz in Spain is attested by the multitude of places named Gades, Gadir, Gadeira, Agadir and so on, applied to many regions of the Atlantic coast both of Europe and Africa frequented by the Phoenicians. The name of Gadeiros – which Plato affirms to correspond to the original language – is said to be Phoenician by Moreau de Jonnés, the great French exegete and mythologist.

According to him, this name means the same thing as "strait". But this etymology is only approximate. Even more exactly, this word means the same as the English "oxford" and the Latin <u>bosphorus</u> or <u>bosporus</u>, derived from the Greek <u>bosphoros</u>, that is, "the place where cattle ford". Better yet, the name means "the place where cattle are forded (or ferried by boats)". The Hindus call these places "ghats", a word akin to "gate" and, more exactly, to a strait or passage or pass.

This name is of great importance in Hinduism. It refers to the <u>Tirthankaras</u>, the saviors of mankind who effect the crossing from one era to the next, leading their people (or "cattle"). In other words, Tirthankaras are some sort of a Noah figure or, better yet, Moses, who created a ford on the Red Sea for his people to pass through during Exodus.

The name of Gades also translates the Hindu one of Kattigara, the Indian port which figures preeminently in every map of the region since the times of Ptolemy. Kattigara ultimately derives its name from the Dravida <u>kati-kara</u>, meaning exactly the same as "oxford" or "bosphorus", as the place where cattle are embarked in order to cross over the ocean.

We commented this Dravidian etymology in one of the endnotes, the next one. We note that the place in question here is ancient Indonesia (Taprobane or Kattigara), whose pristine language was precisely Dravida. Hence, the etymology just derived is not to be dismissed idly, as it is philologically perfect in every sense.

If so, it seems that we have located the exact site of the Far Eastern Gades, alias Tarshish or Tartessos. It was from Kattigara that the vast amounts of tin which rendered the Bronze age a reality was shipped to the Mediterranean region.

In relation to Hercules, the name of Gadeiros represents precisely this sort of thing, the time when he brought the "cattle" of Geryon to Greece, crossing the Bosphorus, in his tenth labor. The route is confused (purposefully) and is said to be across either (or both) the Bosphorus (in the east) and Gibraltar (in the west), betraying an early confusion of the two sites as being the "Pillars of Hercules". **14**

Several facts oppose Morocco's identification with Atlantis. For one, the whole region of the Sahara Desert – Morocco included – was an <u>extreme desert</u> during the Ice Age, as is easy to show, basing ourselves on <u>detailed paleovegetation maps of the region</u> such as this one here. [105]

Now, this is a fact, and not the result of any idle speculation. So, it cannot be dismissed by anyone, unless they are prepared to back up their claims with further finds that somehow invalidate the one just made that Morocco was a dreary desert during the Ice Age, the time of Atlantis.

Consequently, the region of Morocco could not support any productive agriculture and was hence mostly uninhabited and backwards. In other words, Morocco could hardly harbor a decent civilization, let alone the populous one of Atlantis, as described by Plato.

Moreover, the region of Morocco did not sink at the end of the Ice Age, as can be seen in this <u>map published in my Atlantis site</u>. Hence, Morocco does not at all fit Plato's report on Atlantis, since the philosopher explicitly speaks of the well-watered, vast lowlands full of rivers subsequently sunk by the Atlantean cataclysm. [106]

Even if we somehow discount this crucial detail, the region of Morocco is also by far too small, being about the same size as Spain itself. It is hence many times smaller than huge Atlantis, whose very extensive fertile lowlands were ecstatically lauded by Plato.

Again, the same geographical problems which arise for Spain and the North Sea also beplague the site of Morocco. This region can hardly be said to be placed "in front of Gibraltar Strait", and it would be clumsy of Plato – deemed both the prince of philosophers and of rhetors – to say so.

Furthermore, we are compelled to ask if the Atlantic is really the "True Ocean" specifically mentioned by Plato. Plato's reference was apparently done with regard to the Pacific Ocean, as we already demonstrated further above. Hardly would this expression fit the puny Atlantic Ocean itself.

Tartessos (Spain) has also often been proposed, and is once more back to the media, as a possible site of Atlantis due to the sad efforts of some Spaniards. But this is only an old confusion which can never be. This whole region was a dry steppe during most of the Ice Age, as can be seen in this paleovegetation map of Europe here. [107]

What this means in practice is that the region of Spain, like most of Europe, was totally unsuitable for agriculture during the Ice Age, and hence could not harbor a populous nation like Atlantis.

And the same observations made above also apply to the site of Spain itself, and of Portugal. As can be seen in this map, the British Isles (England and Ireland) were both extreme polar deserts during the Ice Age, the times of Atlantis. It is known that they were unpopulated then except perhaps by a few hunters-gatherers following the herds of large mammals characteristic of the Ice Age.

The same also holds in regards to the North Sea and the Scandinavian Peninsula, which were then either Extreme Polar Deserts or, even worse, simply covered by mile thick glaciers, as can also be seen in this remarkable paleovegetation map.

It is hence no surprise to observe that proponents of this site for Atlantis invariably place Plato's Lost Continent in later times, in the Neolithic and even after. But this is a Procrustean force-fitting that is most unfair, and which should be vehemently denounced by all serious researchers.

Disfigure Plato's words in such a drastic way, and the wonderful element is removed from his relation. Atlantis becomes an ordinary civilization of minor importance, located in the middle of nowhere and having no impact whatsoever on the past civilizations of Europe and the Near East. And if this is really true, why bother to look for it at all?

After this long but necessary preamble, we are able to finally apply the above results to reality, as shown in <u>Table III.4</u> below. As noted in this table, can we really say, as Plato did, that these regions are located in front of Gibraltar? Or are they some other such pillars we might far more reasonably find somewhere else?

Are the sunken lands of any of these regions really "larger than Asia and Libya put together"? Are there "many islands beyond", on the way to the Americas, helping the sailors get there?

The Azores are in fact more or less midway to America. But they hardly help anybody, being placed in treacherous waters and contrary winds and currents which lead to doom.

Many sailors have been wrecked by these perilous waters. Why would Plato affirm just the opposite then, and claim that they would be helpful to explorers on the way there? And why would Plato speak of "many islands" if the Azores really are a minor archipelago at best; puny volcanic rocks which were uninhabited until their discovery by the Portuguese in 1428? Hardly do these islands fit Plato's description of the "many islands ahead".

Table III.4 - Results for the Celtic Shelf, Morocco, Tartessos, Spain, etc..			
Two Pillars (Gibraltar) In Front ???????	Sunken Lands of the Region Larger than Asia + Libya ???????	Many Islands Beyond ??????? In the True Ocean ???????	Outer Continent Beyond (America)

Likewise, the Canaries can hardly be said to be placed "ahead of the way" to the Americas, unless Plato is supposed to have been unable to express himself with clarity. But the Outer Continent ahead does in fact seem to be America itself. However, the results in Table III.4 are too full of question marks to be deemed acceptable for a reliable identification of this site with Atlantis.

CHAPTER 13 - ANTARCTICA AND THE ARCTIC OCEAN

> *Men are not prisoners of fate, but only prisoners of their own minds.*
>
> <u>Franklin D. Roosevelt (1882–1945)</u>

The key to this theory is the preposterously unscientific idea that Antarctica used to be tropical (like Atlantis) down to about 12,000 BP or so, but then suddenly switched to a glacial climate, "in one dreadful day and night of pain", more or less as Plato states in his dialogues on Atlantis. The mechanism of this sudden climatic change is usually held to be the result of Pole Shift.

According to this hypothesis – originated by I. Velikovsky and first espoused by Charles Hapgood and Col. Mallory, but now championed by several researchers such as John White (<u>Pole Shift</u>, New York, 1980), the Flem-Aths and Graham Hancock (<u>Fingerprints of the Gods</u>, New York, 1995, etc.) – the crust of the earth suddenly shifted in relation to the mantle, so that Antarctica was taken from a temperate region down to the South Pole, where it fast became frozen and covered by ice.

Alas, several serious problems invalidate this theory. The pole shift they posit is apparently caused by an imbalance of the ice caps rather than, say, by an asteroidal or cometary impact of large enough proportions, as proposed by Flavio Barbiero and other researchers. But there is no proof or geological precedent of any sort whatsoever for such a remarkable event, one way or the other.

We already expounded in an endnote of the present section the crucial difference between Magnetic Pole Shifts, Terrestrial Pole Shifts, and Celestial Pole Shifts, all three of which are sorely confused by the Pole-Shiftists just pointed out.

What is more, Antarctica is now known for sure to have been under ice for at least a million years and probably more. This has been conclusively verified by the analysis of ice cores collected in situ in Antarctica itself.

Moreover, ice cores and other data (paleovegetation, lake varves, dendrochronology, paleontology, etc.) have unequivocally proved the fact that Pole Shift did not occur either at the date in question or any other in the past.

The evidence produced by Hapgood and Mallory – and adopted by White and Hancock among others – is now known to be both false and invalid. Their proposal derives from a gross misinterpretation of ancient maps such as the one of Oronteus Finaeus, where the icy continent is shown as far larger than it presently is.

But this is possibly the result of having been originally charted in the Ice Age, when its shelf glaciers extended wide, out into the sea. And Hapgood's proposals also derive from a gross confusion between Magnetic Pole Shift (real) and Terrestrial Pole Shift (impossible).

What Hapgood and his followers misinterpret as rivers are really large cracks and fissures in the huge ice sheets of Antarctica, and are in fact quite common in its marine glaciers even today. And it is false that these maps provide an accurate rendering of iceless Antarctica. They do not! The size is wrong (by far too large); the shape is wrong (split in two); and so are the other features as well, climate above all.

The case for Pole Shift became hopeless with the definitive establishment of the reality of the Ice Ages and the drastic lowering of sea level they cause. Moreover, it is hard to see how Antarctica would have been covered by ice in the short span of a single day and a night, when it is so extremely dry that snowing there happens at an immeasurably small rate.

So, their proposal that Antarctica got suddenly submerged by ice rather than by water is once again hopeless. The situation is so bad that most if not all of the former Pole Shift champions have now decamped in favor of more viable alternatives such as my own. White has publicly recanted from his former views on Pole Shift and his support of Edgar Cayce's "channeling", both of which he now considers untenable.

And Hancock, though somewhat ambiguous in his present stand, has visibly switched in favor of my own proposal of global sea level rise, as can be seen in his latest books such as Underworld, where the issue of Pole Shift is not even mentioned, by the way.

Moreover, as we have been arguing here, Pole Shift is both a physical and a geological impossibility. It is true that some ancient traditions apparently confused Antarctica with the Southern Land Unknown (Terra Australis Incognita).

And it is also true that Antarctica's continental size roughly fits the one mentioned by Plato in connection with Atlantis. But that is all there is to it. So do (roughly) many places on earth: North America, South America, Australia, India, and so forth.

This view on the Southern Continent was merely the result of the ignorance of the Renaissance geographers and navigators on the actual location and identity of Atlantis, its true archetype. Since both unknown continents were actually known to be located in the Southern Hemisphere, these researchers tended to confuse the two.

The ancient geographers tended to merge both into the enormous southern continent shown in Ortelius' world map just linked and in several others which I have uncovered.

One should keep in mind that in Science, as in everything, the burden of proof lies with the allegers. So, it is incumbent on the proponents of Pole Shift to prove their case, demonstrating the physical reality of their proposal with more than just words alone.

For instance, they could start by pointing out the evidence registered in the geological or the climatological records. And, of course, we would also like to have direct fossil evidence of human habitation of any kind whatsoever in Antarctica, something that is also sorely missing. Or that its climate was mild in the Ice Age, as they repeatedly claim.

Until then, we should let their case rest and be filed away in the already overloaded cupboards of dead files of odd proposals too badly contrived and poorly argued to be accepted by Science. Moreover, we already have enough <u>proven</u> catastrophes such as recurrent Ice Ages and cometary or asteroidal impacts to require a further cause which is not supported by any physical evidence whatsoever.

Curiously enough, both Antarctica and the Arctic Ocean have often been proposed as possible sites for Atlantis. This curious idea which has been revived over and over again perhaps derives from the ancient traditions which placed the site of Paradise precisely at the Terrestrial Poles, both north and south. Even as late as the Age of Navigation some cartographers such as Ortelius still tended to place Paradise at either the South or the North Pole, four rivers, tropical climate, and all.

It is weird that so many researchers even today place Atlantis at the South Pole rather than at the North Pole, where so many early geographers formerly did.

It is now known beyond reasonable doubt that Antarctica has been under ice for one or two million years. Hence, the idea that it was tropical down to 10,000 years or so ago, when Atlantis went under, is sheer folly which should be quickly abandoned by all sensible persons.

Moreover, as we will see next, Pole Shift is really a scientific impossibility which should be discarded as such by all those common-sensical persons who do not want to make fools of themselves.

This, even in the remote hypothesis that Plato had in mind its sinking under ice when he specifically affirmed that it sank away under the sea.

Why would Plato not say so if this were indeed the case? Why would he lie? The whole idea seems to be preposterous.

And this perhaps explains why, in one way or another, most of the former proponents of this foolish theory have now decamped towards my own one based on sea level rise and the volcanic cataclysms which indeed occurred at the end of the last Ice Age.

At least in one specific thing the Arctic Circle has a clear advantage over Antarctica. It is now under water, even though it was exposed (sub-aerial) during the Ice Age. In this regards the Arctic region might indeed be said to have sunk away under the sea, more or less as Plato affirmed in his dialogues. So, the Arctic seems a far more apt choice for the site of sunken Atlantis than Antarctica's folly.

Pole Shift and the Force of Sacred Traditions

The main problem with the polar regions such as the Arctic Circle and Antarctica is that they were both dismally cool and hence absolutely desertic during the Ice Ages. In all probability, not even the Eskimos would be able to survive in these regions during the Ice Age. Essentially no fish and no game would be available in these dreary, ice-covered expanses at that time. And agriculture would be impossible there, as is now quite clear to all who research the matter.

The force of the traditions which hold that Paradise was located at either or both of earth's poles is so great that even some great experts such as René Guénon – one of the best mythologists ever – firmly believed that Paradise is hidden somewhere under the Arctic glaciers, perhaps inside the hollow earth itself. So did B. G. Tilak, the famous Hindu guru who believed that the Aryans would have originated there, perhaps influenced by some current Nordic doctrines on this. [108]

Even today, some Theosophists such as Raymond Bernard and his theosophical adepts piously believe the reality of the Hollow Earth as the subterranean realm of the King of Shambhala, of Agartha, etc.. Moreover, Admiral Byrd is said to have died searching for the passage that would lead him into the inner realm of the King of the World, which he believed to be located at the North Pole. [109]

It seems to me – though we can never be sure in such mystical matters, as Einstein was wont to say – that these recurrent traditions have to do with Hindu myths on Mt. Meru, the Holy Mountain of Paradise, being located directly under the Pole Star itself. [110]

The same thing is also told of the Vadavamukha, the destructive volcano which leads to the interior of the earth, to Hell itself. Even Santa Claus – who lives at the North Pole as we all know – is somehow connected with this mythical polar abode. In our opinion these traditions are actually allegories of Atlantis as the cynosure around which all things whirl. But, who knows for sure?

No matter what, certain extremely popular authors – for instance, Graham Hancock – still defend, against all reason, the theory of Pole Shift which most former champions now execrate and publicly condemn as sheer fallacy.

As I demonstrate in an endnote, Pole Shift is both a physical and a geological impossibility. In effect, what Pole-Shiftists do is to sorely confuse Magnetic Pole Shift with Terrestrial Pole Shift. These are two entirely different things that have very little if anything to do with each other. Geologically speaking, both the mantle and the crust are solid.

Moreover, they are firmly anchored to each other, so that their relative motion is virtually impossible. Physically speaking, the Law of the Conservation of Angular Momentum prevents the crust from shifting from its actual position in relation to space, more or less as happens with a gyroscope. Earth's magnetic field is dictated by the earth's nucleus, which is molten and can hence move freely in relation to the mantle and the crust, more or less as a dynamo would.

In contrast, the position of the Terrestrial Poles is dictated by the motion of the crust in relation to the mantle, both of which are solid, and actually far stronger than steel in their rocky portions.

Mountains such as the Rockies and the Himalayas have "roots", just like teeth do. These roots firmly anchor the crust to the mantle, more or less as our teeth are fixed by their roots to the maxillas. Even if the asthenosphere were molten, as some experts unduly think, these roots would prevent the crust from slipping over the mantle.

They would serve as some sort of anchor even in the presence of a molten layer of magma. It is also a geological fact that the crust very slowly moves in relation to the mantle, as is now explicitly recognized by Plate Tectonics Theory.

But this motion is almost infinitely slow (a couple of centimeters a year at most). This relative motion is due to a curious phenomenon technically known as "creep", which we gloss in more detail in the footnote below, dedicated to the explanation of this curious phenomenon characteristic of solids. [15]

As is clear from this explanation, the current notion of Pole Shiftists may be discarded as ludicrous for all practical purposes. It is an utterly unscientific hypothesis which results from a most sorry mistake of Charles Hapgood and his many followers, who confused Magnetic Pole Shift and Celestial Pole Shift – which indeed do happen – with Terrestrial Pole Shift, which never does.

Once this crucial fact is realized, there is simply no way in which either Antarctica or the Arctic regions could have been tropical during the Ice Age, when global temperatures were fully 15°C lower than presently. This fact has now been proved beyond reasonable doubt in both Antarctica and the Arctic by direct research of ice cores drilled in situ.

It is indeed true that Pole Shift may indeed happen when the earth is tangentially struck by a huge asteroid or comet, more or less as happened when the Moon was formed some 4 billion years ago. In effect, it seems that such was actually the cause of earth's equatorial inclination of 23.5° in relation to the Ecliptic Plane, a curious anomaly which is hard to account for otherwise.

But why should one call this type of major cataclysm the effect of Pole Shift rather than the consequence of a major impact, the real event in cause here? Actually, some authors – among them Otto Muck, the great German scientist – postulate precisely this sort of giant impact as the cause of the demise of Atlantis in his famous book (The Secret of Atlantis, New York, 1979). So does Flavio Barbiero, his Italian follower of lesser fame but likewise great physical knowledge.

Muck's splendidly argued hypothesis is unfortunately rather unlikely to have actually occurred in reality. Such a giant impact would leave unequivocal traces even if it happened in a region presently under the sea. It would leave a layer of characteristic debris (tektites, rare metals, etc.), not to mention the giant impact crater itself, easily detected by its magnetic and gravitational anomalies.

So, for all practical purposes, this fascinating possibility may be simply dismissed and forgotten. The whole conception of Pole Shift apparently arose in deep antiquity. It is mentioned in detail by Plato in his remarkable Statesman. Even older references may be encountered in Herodotus and in the Egyptian and the Mesopotamian beliefs.

As late as 1637, Mercator and his school still drew maps of the North Polar Circle with the Four Rivers of Paradise and the possible entrance to the netherworld, where Paradise was actually said to be located. It is clear that bad habits die hard, if at all. [111]

This was a prevalent Middle Age misconception which originated from the Hindu traditions of an immense age, including the Vedic ones reported by Tilak. But these were heroic times now long past and long disproved by all kinds of contrary empirical finds.

Even the conception of the two Holy Mountains placed at the two poles of the earth is derived from the twin Merus (Sumeru and Kumeru), four rivers and all. But these are metaphors for the real holy mountains, which are in reality the two volcanoes associated with the two Pillars of Hercules. These two volcanoes are the Krakatoa and the Toba, which are actually both located in Indonesia, the true site of Paradise and hence, of Atlantis itself.

Turning now to the real geography of the Arctic and Antarctica as possible sites of Atlantis, let us apply the results so far obtained to both the Arctic and/or Antarctica, just as we did above for the other proposed sites of Atlantis. These results are summarized in Table III.5 below, in connection with Plato's lesson on the Lost Continent summarized in Table III.1 above.

Referring to the map of the world which we have been using here, it can hardly be said that either Antarctica or the Arctic Circle lie in front of Gibraltar Strait. But there is no better alternative choice here for the "Pillars of Hercules" than that of Gibraltar, which is the one these researchers themselves adopt. [↑112]

This frontal location affirmed by Plato does not seem to be the case either for the Arctic or for Antarctica in the map just given or any others. This, despite the efforts of Rand Flem-Ath and Graham Hancock and other proponents of Antarctica as the site of Atlantis. These researchers often choose distorted projections in an attempt to enhance their case, but all in vain.

Really, America seems to be interposed between Gibraltar and Antarctica, more or less as required by Plato. The Arctic seems to be located somewhat behind Gibraltar Strait, rather than "in front of it". But these distortions are the result of the cartographical distortions which have been used here, and really mean nothing much.

However, anyone taking the trouble to look in a globe of the world will readily see that both regions are not located "just in front of the Pillars of Hercules", as affirmed by Plato. Nevertheless, both regions indeed lie outside Gibraltar and hence may roughly be said to obey this requisite. It all depends on the person's opinion. As for myself, I do not think they really fit this requisite. But the reader may be more lenient.

Antarctica is a vast continent, and hence roughly fits the huge size specified by Plato. The same cannot be said of the Arctic region if we confine ourselves to the region which was actually exposed (subaerial) during the Ice Age. But then, someone might contend that the coterminous lands of Siberia and Alaska, etc. were part of the Lost Continent which sank away then.

Table III.5 - Results for Antarctica and the Arctic Region			
Two Pillars of Hercules (Gibraltar)	Sunken Lands of the Region Larger than Asia & Libya ???????	Many Islands Beyond ??????? In True Ocean ???????	Outer Continent Beyond (America) ???????

The Arctic region is shallow and was in fact subaerial during the Ice Age. But can one say that Antarctica is "sunken" under the ice, as some of its proponents allege? We do not think so. In no way can Plato's words be interpreted in this way. Plato affirms that Atlantis sank beneath the sea. Had he meant ice, he would have said so, we believe.

So, though in doubt, let us consider this requisite satisfied, if only roughly. Now, the Arctic region is coterminous with America. Hence, in no way can it be said to lie in the "True Ocean" which, according to Plato's description can only be the Pacific Ocean. Neither the Arctic Ocean nor the Antarctic Ocean – which not even deserves that name – can really be said to be the "True Ocean" of which Plato spoke.

Accordingly, we filled this item with question marks in Table III.5 above, until someone shows us otherwise. Again, in no way do we have "many islands beyond", leading to the True Continent (America). Hence, on these grounds, the Arctic, frozen or not, can be discarded as a possible location for Atlantis unless we postulate so huge a cataclysmic change that it rendered the geography of the whole world unrecognizable.

But if such is the case, nothing can really be said of the geography of Atlantis then or now. So, we filled this item with question marks, just as we did for the previous issue.

With this, we turn to Antarctica itself, which has staunch defenders even now, despite the scientific impossibility of this proposed site. Antarctica almost touches South America in its southernmost tip. There are no "islands on the way there", as Plato affirms. During the Ice Age, when sea level was considerably lower than now, the tip of South America was far longer, turning to the right and extending all the way to Antarctica itself along the Malvinas Plateau. [113]

Hence, what Plato affirmed can hardly be said to apply to the region at all, unless one admits that Plato spoke in riddles impossible to decipher or even understand at all.

The "many islands on the way" are, as we just said, clearly missing. Even if they existed they would hardly lead to the "true ocean" and to the "true continent", which would lie next to the site itself. Hence, in no way may either the Arctic or Antarctica be said to fit Plato's description of its actual location, in contrast to what many proponents of this site speciously claim.

Taprobane and the Atlantic Islands

> The true mystery of the world is the visible, not the invisible.
>
> Oscar Wilde

Another all time favorite candidate for Atlantis are the islands of the Atlantic Ocean: the Azores, the Canaries, Cape Verde, the Madeira Islands, Trindad, Bermudas, etc., etc.. Already during Classical antiquity some or all of these islands were identified to the fabled "Isles of the Blest" and their alias, the "Atlantic Islands" as soon as they were discovered.

The fabulous "Atlantic islands" were all deemed to be the remains of sunken Atlantis by all those in the know, Christopher Columbus included. No researcher ever doubted the reality of these fabled islands and, hence, the one of the Lost Continent whose remains were ardently sought by all sorts of gold-thirsty adventurers and explorers of these distant regions of the world.

Every island discovered in this western ocean was hopefully identified with the legendary "Atlantic Islands", or "Isles of the Blest". And these islands were universally considered to be the fabled remains of sunken Atlantis by all geographers throughout the Middle Ages.

Such ancient legends also abounded during the Renaissance, the Age of Navigation. For instance, we have the fabled discovery of these islands by mythical personages such as St. Brendan, or by the Archbishop of Porto, and several other such semi-legendary explorers whose myth of course survived down to the times of Columbus and even later. [114]

These islands were also identified with those of the East Indies (Indonesia) and with the ones of Atlantis itself. And they were named accordingly: Antilia, Cipango, Septe Cidades, Ys Brazil, Canaria, Capraria, Madeira, Cassiterides, Argyre, Thule, Sanbrandan, Satanaxio, Ilha Verde, Hiera, Kerne, and so on. Hence the host of islands so named both in the Atlantic and in the Pacific Ocean. [115]

Had the reality of the "Atlantic Islands" and their fabulous wealth ever been put to question by any geographer, the no-nonsense Jewish capitalists who financed these naval expeditions would never have put their money into the adventure, trading good income for bad.

As is clear, the name of "Atlantic Islands" derived not from the one of the ocean so misnamed, but from Atlantis itself, according to what Plato himself specifically affirms (Tim.114a).) [116]

In truth, the ocean in which these islands were believed to lay was named "Atlantic Ocean" – that is, "Ocean of Atlantis" – exactly because of the fact that it was believed to harbor the site of sunken Atlantis or, rather, its mountainous remains now turned into these islands.

This misnomer was the result of an ancient, widespread confusion, as we now comment. The ancients well knew that Atlantis was located in the Far East, in the ocean now called Pacific Ocean, but formerly called by names such as Outer Ocean, Ocean Sea, Eastern Ocean, Western Ocean or, more simply, Ocean.

Indeed, this ocean, the Pacific, was the Mar Oceano of which Christopher Columbus so insistently spoke, and of which he so wanted to become the admiral. Columbus had read Marco Polo closely. And he concentrated in the Genovese's ecstatic description of golden Cipango and its fabulous riches in gold and gemstones.

Columbus also knew of its location in the Mar Oceano (Lat. Mare Oceanus), the "Ocean Sea" of the ancient traditions. Polo's description ignited Columbus with gold fever. And this fact accounts for Columbus' determination to become the Almirante del Mar Oceano ("Admiral of the Ocean Sea"), a title which he would eventually earn from the kings of Spain.

Said otherwise, the ancients thought that the present Atlantic Ocean was coextensive with the Pacific Ocean, the true "Ocean of the Atlanteans". Hence, they named it accordingly to Atlantis, expecting to find the fabled "Atlantic Islands", its remnants, somewhere inside the wide expanse of that ocean which they firmly believed to extend all the way to the East Indies, exactly as did Christopher Columbus himself.

Their belief went so deep that they labeled every island therein discovered after these fabulous islands, which they well knew to be part of the East Indies, the remains of sunken Atlantis left behind when its lowlands sank away under the sea: St. Brendan, Antilia, Satanazes, Ys Brazil, Cipango, Septe Cidades, Candyn, Anguana, and the several others just mentioned further above.

Some of these fabulous islands – for instance the one of Satanazes – even retained in whole or in part the characteristic circular shape associated by Plato with Atlantis' capital city. Satanazes was often portrayed as a half circle, as if its other half had actually sunk away and disappeared under the waters.

And its curious tradition – the one of the sargassos and the huge hand which rose from the sea to carry ships and sailors under, directly to Hell itself – was likewise copied from East Indian traditions whose discussion unfortunately does not fit here.

The great admiral also correctly reasoned that the western ocean extended all the way to India, as Pliny specifically states in the passages quoted in the footnote below. So did Aristotle and Strabo and several other ancient authors of Plato's time and even a little later. This fact may also be seen in Toscanelli's map, which also shows several others of these legendary "Atlantic Islands". According to J. Siebold, a well-known specialist: [117]

> Long ago, Aristotle had said: "The regions round the Pillars of Hercules are in connection with the regions round India, and between them there is nothing but sea." Strabo [too] believed that by sailing with an easterly wind in the western ocean one "could reach the Indies". About 120 AD, the Roman philosopher Favorinus wrote that the same ocean which the Greeks knew as the Atlantic Sea was known in East Asia as "the Great Sea" [i. e., the modern Pacific Ocean].
>
> Roger Bacon and Albertus Magnus put forward similar views in the 13th century. In the 1470s, Paolo Toscanelli (1397–1482), the Florentine physician and cosmographer, was the earliest known medieval supporter of a westward voyage from Europe to the Far East to portray his theories cartographically. He contended that the Far East could be reached more directly by sailing west than by rounding the Cape of Good Hope and crossing the Indian Ocean.

Please note, in the above passage – written by a great expert on ancient geographical matters – that the Ocean we know as Atlantic was generally deemed one with the Pacific. It was supposed to lead all the way to the East Indies, exactly as Columbus believed. Favorinus asserts this identity of the two oceans, also explicitly identifying the "Great Sea" of East Asia (the Pacific Ocean) with the Atlantic.

And this name of "Great Sea" closely evokes the passage of Plato describing the "True Ocean" where Atlantis was located according to the prince of philosophers.

Toscanelli's letter and the map he sent to the king of Portugal in 1474 were highly instrumental in inspiring Christopher Columbus to attempt to reach the East Indies by sailing into the Western Ocean. This important letter is printed in full in the site just linked, and needs not to be quoted here. But the real original is missing, and this letter may have been forged, as some experts affirm.

This forgery was perhaps perpetrated by Columbus himself or, even more likely, by his son, Fernando, always bent on defending his father's much maligned memory. This type of thing was as common in antiquity as it is today. And the reason is always the same: money and ambition.

In one way or another, the letter and the map of Toscanelli reached Columbus. Or it may well be that the king himself made sure of that, intending to use Columbus as his secret agent, knowingly or unknowingly on the part of the famous explorer.

Columbus also received several other important documents, including the famous map of Martellus of 1479, on which a quaint monograph can be read here. This whole story is rather obscure. And it is so curious that several experts claim that Columbus was a Portuguese spy or secret agent bent on delaying the Spaniards, their competitors in finding the maritime route to the Indies. [↑118]

One such expert is Simon Wiesenthal, the erudite Jewish author whose curious book which we reference in the bibliography section of this book is well worth reading.

The ancients generally ignored the existence of the interposed Americas dividing the Ocean in two halves. This with perhaps only a few exceptions. For instance, Plato well knew of the existence of this divide of the Ocean, which he specifically names "Outer Continent" (Epeira, Peirata Ges).

This Greek name implies the idea of a land encircling the ocean all around, as we have already stated. But Plato was perhaps exaggerating a little bit, perhaps for initiatic reasons. The very name of the Ocean – a Sanskrit word meaning "which goes around" (aṣayana)– implies the idea of a sea or ocean which in fact surrounded the Americas, passing underneath them in the south, as the ocean in fact does.

But most people ignored this reality, and the myth of a great ocean extending all the way to the East Indies generally prevailed in antiquity. However, it is known that Magellan, the alleged first sailor and discoverer of this southern passage, apparently had a map of the entire region, to believe the words of Pigafetta, his famed pilot.

Every island discovered by the ancients in this great ocean was hopefully identified with the legendary "Atlantic Islands". And these mythical islands were also dubbed "Isles of the Blest", since they were believed to be the remains of sunken Atlantis, that is, of Paradise itself. In India, Paradise was deemed coterminous with Hades (Hell), and both were said to exist in a parallel dimension with the place itself. [16]

Similar legends also abounded later during the Middle Ages and the Age of Navigation, perhaps as a survival from antiquity. No matter what, they were a recurrent feature of the accounts of historians and geographers such as Herodotus, Strabo, Pliny, Plutarch, and so on.

The islands discovered in this ocean were also identified with the East Indies and with Atlantis, and named accordingly: Cipango, Kattigara, Antilia, Septe Cidades, Ys Brazil, Canaria, Capraria, Madeira, Cassiterides, Argyre, Thule, Ilha Verde, Hiera, Cerne, and so on. Most (or all) of these mythical islands were sited in the East Indies according to ancient authorities such as Pliny, Solinus, Ptolemy, and so forth.[↑119]

Several ancient maps – starting with the map of Ptolemy and perhaps even earlier – explicitly show the region of Indonesia as an extensive land of continental dimensions. This former continent is far larger than India itself and is attached to the south of Southeast Asia. [↑120]

One such is the map just linked above. In it, Kattigara is the great chunk of land shown at the extreme right of the map, and shaped somewhat like a giant cow's leg. And this continent or coast is now mostly sunken, precisely as was the case of the Atlantean continent itself.

Coincidences? Or were Ptolemy and Marinus, as well as Martellus and Solinus, drawing from Alexandrine sources actually dating from Pleistocenic times, the ones of Atlantis when the existence of this now sunken continent was in fact a reality?

As is clear, when the map of Ptolemy or the map of Henricus Martellus of 1479 are compared to the map of Atlantis published in our site, it is easy to see that the two sunken Indonesian continents closely correspond to each other in both shape, size and Far Eastern location. [↑121]

Now, how could Ptolemy and his contemporaries ever know this poignant reality that has only recently been rediscovered by advanced techniques such as outer space spy satellites and oceanographic ships and subs equipped with side-scanning sonar? Who drew this detailed chart of the Far Eastern regions so far before they were actually discovered by the Portuguese and other modern explorers?

We are of the opinion that these remarkably advanced maps were actually created by the Atlanteans themselves during the Ice Age, whose realities they charted in great detail and exactitude. And their inconsistencies with modern maps actually result from the differences which resulted from the huge rise in sea level which occurred when the Pleistocene Age ended and the glaciers melted away, running off to the sea.

What other explanations do we have for these uncanny, essentially impossible mapological and climatological coincidences? Sheer chance? But this is unlikely, as we have discovered dozens of such unique Ice Age features in other ancient maps which we discuss in detail in our work on ancient cartography.

The most economical explanation – and hence the only one acceptable according to scientific methodology and to Ockham's Razor Principle of Maximum Parsimony – is the hypothesis just pointed out, unless someone is capable of hitting on a better one and is kind enough to point it out to us all, countering the considerable evidence which I have just produced.

PART IV - PARADISE AND THE FAR EASTERN ATLANTIS

> *You don't reach Serendip by plotting a course for it. You have to set out in good faith for elsewhere and lose your bearing serendipitously.*
>
> John Barth, The Last Voyage of Somebody the Sailor

CHAPTER 14 - DIODORUS SICULUS ON ATLANTIS

> *The only good is knowledge and the only evil is ignorance.*
>
> <u>Socrates (469 BC–399 BC)</u>

In the present part of this book we concentrate on the remarkable texts of Diodorus Siculus and other authorities who wrote of Atlantis independently from Plato. And we also present in some detail the tabular comparison for our site similar to the ones we made above for the sites so far proposed for Atlantis by other researchers both previous to and later than ourselves.

This comparison concerns the physiography of Atlantis, that is, the main geographical features of its region. Our table has the advantage of being simple enough to leave no room for sophistries which often becloud the reasoning of most proponents.

This comparison of our proposed site was left for the end for a very good reason. The idea is that the dear reader should enjoy it as some sort of dessert, which we all reserve for the time when we are already satisfied eating the main courses.

Besides, the expectation is that the reader will by now have become familiar with our main arguments and, moreover, have realized the potency of our tabular method, even though it is extremely simple to apply in practice. We will see that, despite the fact that Plato's physiography is only utter nonsense when applied to the region of Gibraltar, it perfectly fits its dual in the Far East, Taprobane.

The assertion of many experts that Plato was the only ancient authority ever to speak of Atlantis is wrong. Homer, the first of the Greek poets, already spoke of Atlas holding up the Pillar of Heaven from the bottom of the sea five or six centuries before Plato ever did so.

Now, Atlas is the very personification of Atlantis itself as a mighty giant or Titan, as the "Pillar of Heaven" bearing up the skies on his back. Herodotus also spoke of the Atlanteans and of Mt. Atlas as the Pillar of Heaven a full century before Plato wrote his piece on the Lost Continent.

So did, in one way or another, Hesiod, Pindar, Theopompos, Orpheus, Apollonius, Diodorus Siculus, Aelian, Krantor, Strabo, Plutarch, Ovid,

Pliny the Elder and a host of other authors of Classical antiquity and hence more or less contemporaneous with Plato.

But even other nations such as the Phoenicians also spoke of Atlantis in terms comparable to the ones of Greek traditions. Sanchuniathon, a Phoenician priest (fl. 14th century BC), gave an early account of Phoenician Cosmogony which is visibly akin to the sacred history of Atlantis narrated by Diodorus. His writings, long denounced as late forgeries by several experts, have been thoroughly vindicated by the archaeological finds made in Ugarit and other places.

Though difficult and obscure, Sanchuniathon's account apparently takes the traditions of Atlantis back to the second millennium BC or even earlier, since he was basing himself on far earlier Phoenician traditions.

The earlier authors often spoke of Atlantis under alternative names such as Colchis, Phaeacia, Scheria, Aeaea, Hesperia, Elysium, Elysian Fields, Garden of the Hesperides, Tartarus, Hades, Erebus, Isles of the Blest, Hyperborea, Delos, and so forth.

The names differed, but the place they referred to was invariably one and the same: Paradise destroyed and turned into Hell or Hades, the gloomy Land of the Dead. In other words, this formerly paradisial land was no other than Atlantis-Eden itself.

Even the contribution of authors later than Plato – for instance, Diodorus Siculus and Pliny – is most valuable. These authors invariably based themselves on far older sources, now lost. These sources were usually repeated verbatim, as was the custom in those days.

Allegories, disguises and metaphors could well be the creation of the poet. But the facts themselves could not be tampered with, as these were rooted in tradition and in religion.

Pausanias, Pliny, Avienus and several other later Classical authors also disclose very precious information on the Atlanteans, as we shall be arguing in more detail next.

These authors often identify the Atlanteans with the White Ethiopians and the Libyans or Phoenicians, accordingly placing Atlantis either in North Africa (Morocco, Libya, Carthage, etc.) or in its dual, the Ethiopia on the opposite bank of the World-Encircling Ocean, its other moiety.

For instance, Pliny (H. N. 2:92; 6:36) specifically places the Pillars of Hercules (Columnae :) along with Mt. Atlas at the exit of the Red Sea leading into the Indian Ocean. Pliny is very probably identifying these Pillars of Hercules with the two peaks at the banks of the narrow Bab-el-Mandeb Strait, which was in fact often closed up by extremely perilous coral reefs that there abound. [152]

Pliny's allusion to an eastern Atlantis is somewhat garbled, as is invariably the case with this tabooed subject. So, he could even be referring to Taprobane itself, if by "Red Sea" he meant the whole Erythrean (or Indian) Ocean and by "Ethiopian Ocean" he really meant the Pacific Ocean. No matter what, the authorities that Pliny used here are visibly independent of Plato's.

Pliny also refers that Kerne (or Cerne) is placed "opposite" Ethiopia (contra sinum persicum cerne nominatur insula adversa aethiopiae) and "opposite" Mt. Atlas, in Mauritania. Now, the words he uses (contra; adversus) also express the idea of "antipodal". This type of double entendre was standard in antiquity when speaking of Atlantis' location, as we will be arguing below. ↑153

Kerne is apparently the same as Kerkenes, the capital of Atlantis according to Diodorus Siculus. Moreover, the double entendres such as the ones Pliny uses here – meaning either "facing, next to" or, conversely, "opposite, antipodal" – are apparently tied up with the antipodal location of Atlantis on the other side of the Ocean.

The very fact that Pliny's text is so obscure and so ambiguous proves the fact that the great naturalist, like so many other ancient authorities, was reluctant to divulge the well-kept secrets having to do with Atlantis' true location beyond the Ocean, at earth's antipodes.

Properly interpreted, some of these authors even specifically place this paradisial (or infernal) land in Taprobane (Indonesia), just where we have located Atlantis. Their information is often seemingly incongruous and chaotic. But their data are all convergent, and only start to make sense when properly culled and carefully collated one with the other, as an ensemble.

Rather than sheer myth, the places and personages just named are often no more than mere codenames and metaphors for Atlantis itself. Like its several other names, Atlantis is the appellative given the sunken continent by both Plato and Diodorus, among others.

But this onomastic term is also used by several other authors, Avienus, Proclus, Herodotus and Pliny included. However, we must always keep in mind that the subject matter of Atlantis' historical reality was the core of the secret of the ancient Mysteries.

Hence, it could not be openly divulged to the profanes except under a veil of impenetrable mythical or religious allegories and other similar disguises such as the ones we are presently discussing.

For example, Homer spoke of Phaeacia (or Scheria) as some sort of ghostly Atlantis turned into the terrifying Land of the Dead due to a punishment sent by Poseidon. Hesiod spoke of Tartarus as a semi-mythical place beneath the earth or located at its far fringes, beyond the Ocean and inaccessible to humans and loathed even by the gods themselves.

Diodorus, the erudite Sicilian Greek – given the cognomen Siculus ("Sicilian") for that reason – wrote several important passages on Atlantis, in his <u>Bibliotheca Historica</u>. Although his book dates from the middle of the first century BC, and is hence somewhat later than Plato's, his sources – now lost – are obviously much older than that, and are visibly different from the ones followed by Plato.

Once properly interpreted, Diodorus' information is congruent with the one provided by the supreme philosopher. This coincidence proves that at least some ancient historians believed that the story of Atlantis was based on historical fact and treated it as such.

Diodorus is one of the most important authors on Atlantis, being second only to Plato himself. Moreover, as a skilled, careful historian, the Sicilian author actually wrote on Atlantis in factual historical terms, very much as did Plato himself.

However, despite the importance of the information that Siculus provides, his treatise is seldom if ever mentioned by Atlantologists in general, who apparently ignore his invaluable contribution to the enigma of Atlantis.

It is for this reason that we now comment on Diodorus' remarkable work on the Lost Continent in some detail. To start with, Diodorus places Atlantis <u>on the far side</u> of the Outer Ocean, "at the outermost bounds (or fringes) of the earth". And these "outermost bounds of the earth" are clearly the East Indies according to ancient Greek and Egyptian sources, among others.

For example, Homer speaks of the Far Eastern Ethiopia as the dual and counterpart of the other one, placed in Libya (North Africa). This Western Ethiopia was so named because it too was inhabited by the White Ethiopians who invaded this region of the world in the dawn of time.

And it may well be that Plato actually had that invasion in mind, rather than the far later one of the Sea Peoples when he wrote on the Atlantean invasion of the Mediterranean region in his dialogues.

Actually, it was this assertion of Diodorus that made me look for the Lost Continent in its correct location, <u>beyond the Ocean</u>. And it was there, in Taprobane, the "Land of Gold", that I eventually found the now sunken remains of Atlantis, exactly as described by Plato: continental size, far eastern location, tropical climate during the Ice Age, vast forests, priceless mineral resources, etc..

In no way may the text of Diodorus Siculus be interpreted as meaning that Atlantis was located near the Euro-African coasts of the Atlantic Ocean. This is where most experts currently believe it was located by Plato. But this is at best a gross one-sided misinterpretation of the philosopher's text.

The Far Eastern location of Atlantis is specifically stated by Diodorus. This antipodal placement may also be true of Plato, whose text on this issue is ambiguous and very obscure at best. And it is certainly affirmed by Pindar, who places the Pillars of Hercules at the "ultimate fringes of the earth" (eschata).

The word pro used by Plato in his Greek original may mean both "opposite; in front of; facing; next to" as well as "antipodal; located on the opposite side of the ocean". Such is also the case with the Latin words adversus and contra used by Pliny, as we just saw above.

We will see next that many other Classical writers used similar ambiguous expressions, given the fact that they were forbidden by oath to divulge the true whereabouts of the formerly paradisial location turned into the gloomy Land of the Dead feared by all.

Though up to now invariably interpreted in the first sense, a careful collation with Diodorus and other authorities shows that, beyond reasonable doubt, it is the second sense that really applies to Atlantis. Besides, since there is no great island – sunken or other – right in front of Gibraltar, Plato would at best be misleading if he really meant the first of the two senses of the word pro.

It is also clear from both his text and the unique features of Atlantis that Plato really meant the distant location, rather than the near one. For instance, in one passage of his dialogues, Plato specifically affirms that the Atlanteans actually came "from a distant point in the Atlantic Ocean".

Now, this can only mean the farther bank of the ocean, as we just demonstrated. Why would Plato use the idea of "distant" if he really meant nearby Gibraltar? And why would he say the Atlantic Ocean if the Atlanteans in fact came from the European coast itself, as most researchers currently believe?

Again, why would the philosopher say that the Atlantic Ocean was murky and "innavigable" in the region of Gibraltar when even the school children of his day knew that the Phoenicians and other peoples regularly sailed this region of Europe both inside and outside the pillars?

While this affirmation is obviously wrong of Gibraltar, it is quite true of Sunda Strait and the region of Indonesia. There the land had in fact sunk away in a great cataclysm, just as affirmed by Plato and others, Diodorus and Pliny included.

And this volcanic cataclysm left behind mud shoals and sandbars formed by the deposited tephra, as well as the terrible darkness which is consistently mentioned in the ancient sources and which was obviously caused by the dust and smoke suspended in the atmosphere by the giant eruption.

Likewise, in his remarkable text on Atlantis, Diodorus Siculus specifically adds something to the effect that: "The Atlanteans, dwelling as they do in the regions on the fringe of the ocean, inhabit a very fertile territory." By "fringe" Diodorus, like Pindar and other ancients, generally meant the far end, the other bank of the Ocean, at the ends (or "fringes" or "wings") of the world.

"Fringe" (eschaton, epeira) is a technical term whose meaning must be carefully considered if we really strive to understand what the ancients actually meant by it. As is clear, the meaning of such geographical expressions changes a lot in the course of time due to the linguistic affectations such as metaphor, allegory, irony, metonymy, synecdoche, paradox, hyperbole, and so on.

Curiously enough, Isaiah explicitly affirms that the Jews (Israelites) came from "the ends of the earth" and, more exactly, from the "islands in the east". This is tantamount to saying that the Jews were among the Ethiopians who came in from the Far Orient; from the islands of Indonesia, crossing to the West either via the Ocean or, far more likely, along the Silk Road, via the Far East.

Isaiah even refers to these Israelites as "the righteous men from the East", probably a way of saying that they were the same as the Pious Ethiopians of Homer, Herodotus and Pliny. [17]

Such is perhaps the real reason why Dawn is invariably portrayed as winged, for instance, in the remarkable portrait of Dawn holding up the dead body of her son Memnon linked to here. We will return to this subject further below, when we discuss the real identity of the Eastern Ethiopia ruled by Dawn (Eos) and Memnon. [↑154]

A close study of the remarkable passage of Isaiah just linked will no doubt reveal that it in fact refers to the destruction of Far Eastern Atlantis by the vajra, that is, by the supervolcanism of the Krakatoa.

The Atlantean Origin of Agriculture

Curiously enough, Diodorus also enigmatically affirms that: "Corn (wheat and/or barley) is unknown to its inhabitants [the Atlanteans]." This piece of information, though strange, is extremely interesting. The Atlanteans are held to have been the inventors of agriculture, which most experts think started in the Near East with cereals such as wheat and barley, etc..

But when we look deeper into the matter the real reason readily becomes apparent. It is now known for certain that the first cereal ever to be cultivated was rice. As recently discovered, rice agriculture started in the Far East (China and the East Indies) over 15,000 years ago and more.

Besides, rice was reaped from the wild there as early as 25,000 years ago, as some recent archaeological finds of great importance have also demonstrated.

These dates were obtained by the Chinese and other scholars from actual grains of cultivated rice found in a sacrificial cache, in a well-known archaeological site. So, these results are direct, and cannot be validly questioned by anyone sufficiently knowledgeable in the matter.

Moreover, these rice grains were themselves radiocarbon dated not by the Chinese alone, but also by reputed Western laboratories, which are quite well-known and universally accredited, and are hence beyond any suspicion whatsoever.

So, like it or not, we must all learn to live with the reality that agriculture originated not in the Near East, as most experts think, but in the Far East, where this practice is attested far earlier in time.

This remarkable archaeological find also precludes locations such as Europe and the Levant, where wheat and barley are of course the staple crops, as is well-known. In these western regions, rice agriculture was unknown down to relatively late times, when it was later introduced from the east.

We have already quoted, in previous chapters of the present book, a text by the traveler Marco Polo affirming, with a great deal of wonder, that the people from East Asia ignored wheat agriculture, cultivating rice instead. And the reason for that is easy to realize.

Rice is typically a tropical produce. This fact further confirms the tropicality of Atlantis, just as unequivocally affirmed by both Plato and Diodorus. Moreover, the very word "rice" ultimately derives from the Dravida (arici), a fact that again attests the Indian origin of the world's most important cereal. Even the name of "cereals" derives from an early form of this Dravidian base (*sariči).

Why would the plant have an Indian name if it actually came from somewhere else? This Dravidian name is also the source of words such as the Latin <u>oryza</u>, the Greek <u>oruza</u>, the Italian <u>riso</u>, the French <u>riz</u>, the Portuguese <u>arroz</u>, the English <u>rice</u>, the Arabic <u>uruzz</u>, etc..

Hence, even though the Atlanteans apparently did not have wheat, as Diodorus asserts, they abounded in rice and other tropical crops, exactly as so forcefully affirmed by Plato. And since this useful plant's name is Indian (Dravidian), it is virtually certain not only that the plant itself but also its culture are ultimately Indian in origin.

Plato even mentions – by means of a detailed description, since these fruits were unknown in his time, and consequently had no Greek name – what several experts recognized to be coconuts and bananas. The fruit "having a hard rind, affording a drink and meat and ointment" is obviously the coconut, as no other known fruit does so.

And "the fruit which spoils easily and makes a very pleasant dessert" is quite clearly the banana. If these fruits were known in ancient Greece, they would necessarily have a Greek name, even if imported. And Plato would obviously have used their names instead of these clumsy descriptions.

This reality is also fast becoming apparent to most researchers, now that we have so unequivocally demonstrated the Far Eastern origin of agriculture, perhaps within Atlantis itself. Despite their archaic date, we believe, the Chinese samples just mentioned – and so the Korean, the Vietnamese and the Indian ones – are certainly not the earliest ones to be had.

These sites are, it seems, mere secondary gene-centers which imported rice agriculture, probably along with some others such as bananas, coconuts and pineapples, etc. from its source. The development proper occurred far earlier than that, very probably within Atlantis itself.

From Atlantis the seminal invention passed to the other "gene-centers" where the technique was adopted and adapted to the local conditions, perhaps via crossbreeding with local wild species, a common agricultural technique of a highly advanced character akin to Genetic Engineering.

It seems that it was only when they later moved to the temperate regions of the world that the survivors of the Atlantean cataclysm were forced to give up rice agriculture – by far more productive than wheat or barley – in favor of these less desirable local substitutes such as barley, oat, wheat, etc..

It is not impossible that the survivors of the Atlantean cataclysm had to develop these local cultures afresh, starting essentially from scratch. But they of course <u>already had the seminal idea itself</u>. The odds against an independent reinvention of agriculture are exceedingly small, and can be ignored for all purposes, as we have formally demonstrated with rigorous mathematical arguments.

However, if we accept the hypothesis of diffusion, the above mathematical objections are automatically eliminated and everything starts to make sense. Moreover, this apparent reinvention of agriculture probably happened in several different places in the world: China, Southeast Asia, the three Americas, the Near East, Europe, India and so forth.

It was this local redevelopment that created the illusion of an "independent invention" in the so-called "gene-centers". Their existence was long ago postulated by N. I. Vavilov and most other specialists who later adopted his ideas. These, though outdated, still survive essentially unchanged down to this day, at least in academic institutions and in the standard textbooks on the subject.

The Sanskrit name of rice is <u>java</u> (or <u>yava</u>), which exactly coincides with the one of the island of Java (in Indonesia). This name again corresponds to the designative of the white races in this sacred tongue of India: Yavanas. It is also from this name that the one of the Greeks or Ionians, as well as that of Javan, the son of Japheth, are derived.

This ethnonym is spelled as <u>IaFones</u> (with the fau, <u>F</u>) in Homer, a form that leaves no room for doubting a common origination in India. This fact proves beyond reasonable doubt the Far Eastern origin of the Greeks or Yavanas.

Curiously enough, in Greek traditions, the Titan Atlas is made the son of Iapetos, along with other Titans such as Prometheus, Epimetheus and Hesperus. Iapetos was considered by the Greeks to be their ultimate ancestor, via Prometheus and Deucalion, their Flood hero and the son of the Titan Prometheus himself. [18]

In the Bible (<u>Gen</u>. 10:2; <u>Jer</u>. 66:19; <u>Eze</u>. 27:13) Javan and his brethren inhabit the "isles of the gentiles". These mysterious islands seem to be precisely those of Paradise itself, Java included, which we have now identified with Atlantis. The Egyptians, and several other ancients too, often referred to these islands, which they often place in the Eastern Ocean, and reached via the pristine Suez Strait.

All in all, it is now apparent that the Greeks – like the other white peoples of Europe and the Near East, the Ethiopians inclusive – originated there, in Indonesia. Thence they later moved out to the Mediterranean region when their own homeland got destroyed and sunk by the Flood, very much as affirmed by Plato and other ancient authorities, Diodorus Siculus among them.

It is this early invasion of the Mediterranean region by the Ethiopians from the Far East that corresponds to the early one reported by Diodorus Siculus.

And it is also this pristine invasion, rather than the later ones by the Sea Peoples (13th–12th century BC) that corresponds to the one reported by Plato as due to the Atlanteans or that reported by Theopompos concerning the invasion of the bellicose Makhimos ("Warlike") who also came from beyond the Ocean.

Said otherwise, it seems that Plato too, like Diodorus and others, is here identifying the Atlanteans with the White Ethiopians. These White Ethiopians – who comprised the other "red peoples" such as the Libyans, the Phoenicians, the Berbers, the Guanches, the Celts, etc. – probably moved to the Mediterranean region far earlier in time.

But they later again joined forces with the Sea Peoples when these attempted their unsuccessful conquest of Egypt after having conquered most of the Mediterranean region and destroyed the formerly mighty Hittite empire along with the ones of Minoan Crete, Mycenian Greece, and so forth. [155]

The problem of when the early Ethiopic invasion from the Far East actually occurred is moot. Its date is lost in the mist of time, and is only told in myths such as the one of Atlantis. The event apparently corresponds to Hercules' tenth labor, the "red kine" of Geryon being no other than the hordes of the red races led into the region by the hero, from the distant Far Orient.

The archaeology of the region is rather tenuous, and has little to contribute, except by providing a terminus post quem (lower limit) for the Ethiopic (Berber) presence in North Africa. This date is now minimally set at about 3,000 BC or so.

This date is when the great civilizations of Egypt, Mesopotamia, Mycenian Greece and Minoan Crete first appeared in the Mediterranean region. But it now seems that these "White Ethiopians" originally came into the Mediterranean region from the east no later than 5,000–7,000 BC, apparently starting the Neolithic Revolution and the introduction of agriculture in the region.

The Celts and the "Pious Ethiopians" of Taprobane

Exactly the same information is also found in the sacred traditions of the Celtic peoples. These nations repeatedly affirm that the Celts – or rather, their legendary ancestors such as the Fomoré and the Tuatha Dé Danaan – came from <u>beyond</u> the ocean, which they crossed in ships.

It is the same with most Greek Classical authorities on the White Ethiopians, beginning with Homer and Hesiod, and continuing through Pindar, Mimnermus, Diodorus, Pliny, Apollodorus, and many others, as we shall be commenting next.

In this endeavor, we quote several passages of these authors confirming beyond doubt that the Garden of the Hesperides – and hence the Isles of the Blest, the site of Troy and the one of Atlantis – all lay beyond the Ocean, that is, in the East Indies themselves.

The dear readers who follow our argument closely will no doubt be convinced of this fact, much as we were ourselves after a protracted study of these remarkable ancient texts. And this argument is essential for our case on the Far Eastern location of Atlantis.

Some Celtic accounts (the <u>Mabinogion</u>, etc.) even specify that the Celts came from the region of Defrobani, which all experts agree to be a misspelling for Taprobane. Far more likely, the Celts and the Germans came in several waves, some by land, via the east, and some by sea, via the west.

But in all cases these early invasions are apparently connected with the White Ethiopians such as the Berbers and the Libyans, their close of kin.

As we shall be commenting next, Diodorus also specifically identifies the Atlanteans with the Ethiopians. These "Greeks" (or Whites or Yavanas) of the Far East are also the same as the Pious Ethiopians of Homer and the Long-lived Ethiopians of Herodotus, Pliny, Solinus, Strabo, etc..

These authors invariably describe these White Ethiopians as tall, blond and blue-eyed, and as residing in Taprobane and/or Serica. These names respectively mean Indonesia and China, the modern names of the two Far Eastern places.

The idea of "blond Chinese" might seem ludicrous at first, but it is now too well established to be denied anymore by anyone in the know. For instance, the ancient Greek vase commented above illustrates Eos (Dawn) picking up the dead body of her valiant son Memnon, killed by Achilles during the War of Troy.

Here, both Ethiopian personages are portrayed as white and tall, looking Aryan rather than Negroid or otherwise. The Ethiopians are also depicted as whites in the ancient Greek vases such as the charming ones illustrated in the Perseus Project and reproduced later below in the present book.

As is clear, these White Ethiopians, like the Trojans, their allies, had close contacts with the early Greeks. Actually, the War of Troy is just another allegory of the Great War of Atlantis. Unlike the Homeric one, however, Plato reported this war as real, rather than purely mythical.

It is perhaps worth mentioning that both the War of the Gods and the Titans as well as the one of Troy are said to have lasted for ten years. And ten is a number often associated with Atlantis and its ten princes, as reported by Plato.

This coincidence again tends to show that these White Ethiopians were in fact aliases (and allies) of the Atlanteans. And Troy was – in contrast to what most experts erroneously think – placed on the far side of the Ocean, which the Greeks had to cross, in order to get there.

Eos or Dawn (also called Aurora, in Latin) is, by the way, herself a white woman. Her name is also synonymous with "Easterner" or "Oriental", and was often applied to designate Indonesia (Eoos, in Greek, Eous in Latin). Now, this epithet really refers to the fact that Indonesia was the site of Paradise where humanity and civilization first dawned on the world, at the start of the present era.

As we just affirmed, Indonesia, the Eastern Ethiopia, was usually called Eoos in Greek and Eous in Latin, names which derived directly from the one of Eos (Dawn). This, in contrast to Western Ethiopia, in Morocco, its occidental dual and antipodal.

This fact alone should suffice to prove the fact that the War of Troy was conducted in the Far East, in the "Land of Dawn", alias Taprobane or Indonesia or, yet, Atlantis, its alias.

The Turkish counterpart of Troy, discovered by the amateur archaeologist Heinrich Schliemann in Hissarlik is, of course, no more than just an illusion. At best, Schliemann's Troy is only a shabby replica of its majestic Oriental archetype, as several competent experts such as M. I. Finley have denounced.

As Finley pointed out, nothing fits the Homeric description in the pitiful Turkish counterpart. And it is precisely there – in this Far Eastern Ethiopia beyond the Ocean – that the great heroes and adventurers such as Perseus, Hercules, Ulysses, Achilles, Jason and so forth went questing their prizes: Andromeda, the Golden Apples, the Golden Fleece, Geryon's cattle, the palladium, and so forth.

Now, why would these Greek heroes and adventurers all go so far away if this distant land were actually unconnected with pristine Greece, as most experts currently think?

In actual terms, these "blue-eyed Chinese" of Far Eastern Ethiopia are the Tocharians (or Yüeh-chi or Hephthalites or White Huns) of the Tarim Basin region of Western China, whose reality is now too well established to be denied by any but the most die-hard of academic specialists.

Some researchers stubbornly maintain, despite the massive evidence that I and others have long been presenting, that the Tocharians are Europeans who somehow penetrated all the way to China in antiquity. But the facts are now too unequivocal to be interpreted in this way anymore.

Among other things, their existence there far predates their presence in Europe and North Asia. So, this alternative may safely be discarded as unscientific since it is contrary to the recent empirical evidence. The geographer Strabo (Geogr. 1:2:24-28) comments the two Ethiopias of Homer (Od. I:22) in considerable detail. He quotes Homer as interpreted by Crates of Mallus and by Aristarchus thus: [156]

"The Ethiopians that are sundered in twain, the farthermost of men." About the next verse there is a difference of opinion, Aristarchus writing: "Abiding some where Hyperion sets, and some where he rises"; but Crates: "abiding both where Hyperion sets and where he rises". (Aithiopas toi dichtha dedaiatai, eschatoi andrôn, hoi men dusomenou Huperionos hoi d' aniontos). [157]

Both interpretations are valid, exactly as Strabo affirms. And they both mean precisely one and the same thing. The "farthermost of men" (eschatoi andrôn) means that the Ethiopians inhabited the two extremities of the world, one in the east, the other one in the west. The western extremity is the region of Gibraltar, properly called Hesperia ("Occidental"). The eastern extremity is Indonesia, the other Ethiopia. This identity is affirmed by Herodotus (Hist. 3.106), who uses the same word to describe East India. [158]

And this is Indonesia, formerly a part India itself. Herodotus also mentions the African Ethiopia, in the extreme occident, where live the White Ethiopians: "taller, handsomer and longer-lived than any other humans" (Hist. 3:114). Hesiod (Theog.731) likewise uses the same word to designate Tartarus as located in the "outermost fringe of the earth" (es-chata gaiês), where the Titans were confined by Zeus. ⁺¹⁵⁹

The Connections With Atlantis

If one carefully collates all these (and other) passages, the inescapable result is that the Titans are the same as the White Ethiopians, perhaps in their decayed state. In fact, there were two types of White Ethiopians, one moiety being pious and long-lived, the other one bellicose and short-lived.

Theopompos (Var. Hist. III:18) refers to them as Eusebes ("pious") and Makhimos ("warlike"). As we already mentioned, this contemporary of Plato even refers to the invasion of Europe by these White Ethiopians – whom he describes as "twice the size and twice as long-lived as the ordinary mortals". This early invasion is perhaps the one which Plato connected with the Atlantean invasion.

Theopompos also refers to the gloomy region in that outer continent which was inhabited by the Meropes. This darkness he attributes to a red haze suspended in the atmosphere, probably by a giant volcanism. The Meropes – a Greek word meaning "mortals" and, perhaps, "dead ones" – are in all probability the same as the Titans, the dead heroes whom Hesiod names "the blest".

The famous author also mentions the Elixir of Youth encountered in this gloomy land beyond the ocean. As is clear, this island or continent comprised two sections: one blissful and paradisial, the other one doomed and infernal. And such was precisely the case with Taprobane in Hindu traditions.

Collation with other Classical authorities shows that this continental-sized region is the same as the Isles of the Blest of the Homeric and other traditions and that the dark section corresponds to Tartarus itself as described by Hesiod, Virgil and others.

For instance, the Alexander Romances, so popular in the Middle Ages, tell the story of Alexander the Great's quest for the Elixir in the East Indies. There the hero also meets this terrible darkness, but fails in his attempt to obtain the Elixir, betrayed as he was by Andreas, his cook.

Once more we see that Tartarus (or Hades) is visibly located in the East Indies and, even more exactly, in its far eastern extremity, Indonesia or Taprobane, the site where the Titans lived. And this fact is confirmed by Pliny and Solinus, who also place the Pious Ethiopians precisely there.

In the passage just linked, Hesiod also places Atlas holding up the sky pillar in the region of Tartarus. And he adds that there the day changes over, with Day and Night crossing each other.

Tartarus is somber and permanently covered by dark clouds of smoke. And this permanent darkness can only be the result of a giant volcanism like the one of the Krakatoa volcano which we already commented. No other geological mechanism results in the permanent darkening of extensive regions of the earth, except giant meteoritic falls, which are, however, orders of magnitude less frequent.

This giant volcanism also covered the local seas with floating pumice stone, rendering them "innavigable", just as described by Plato and others. It is only thus that one may logically unravel the frequent allusions to the somber, innavigable "Atlantic Ocean" of the ancients.

It is perhaps more than a coincidence that Hesiod places this frightening description of Tartarus just after his description of the Titanomachia, the great war of the Gods and the Titans. Plato specifically identifies this terrible battle with the War of Atlantis. And this war, he says, ended in disaster for the two sides, with both contending armies swallowed up by the earth.

A close reading of Hesiod's description of the Titanomachia also reveals that it is indeed a personification of a supervolcanic eruption followed by caldera formation. In reality, we had two parallel events here mythically identified: the real battle of the two Atlantean moieties and its cosmic counterpart, the war of the twin volcanoes of the region, the Dempo and the Krakatoa.

Again, volcanoes are the only known mechanism – barring giant asteroidal and cometary falls – capable of accounting for the dreadful events there described by the great poet: fire, thunderstorms, rock-throwing, tephra covered seas, molten stone, somber darkness, earthquakes, etc..

The presence of Atlas, the Pillar of Heaven, at the site provides a direct connection with Atlantis and its Holy Mountain, the volcano. This volcanic interpretation is apparently confirmed by Strabo's description of Ethiopia, when he quotes Aeschylus' now lost <u>Prometheus Unbound</u> thus:

> "The sacred flood of the Red Sea with its bed of scarlet sands, and **the mere on the shore of Oceanus that dazzles with its gleam of brass** and furnishes all nourishment to Ethiopians, where the Sun, who sees all things, gives rest to his tired steeds and refreshes his immortal body in warm outpourings of soft water."

The "Red Sea" in question here is the Erythraean (Indian Ocean). The "mere on the shore of Oceanus" is apparently the Tritonides Marsh, the place where Atlantis allegedly sank, its Great Plain turned into a mere or marsh, the present Java Sea. It was this Great Plain which formerly provided an abundance of food for the Atlanteans, according to Plato's detailed description, in perfect correspondence to this text of Aeschylus.

The mysterious "dazzling gleam of brass" which covers this mere is very probably the same as the "mud" or "scum" (pelos) which covered the sea of Atlantis, as reported by the supreme philosopher. This "scum" is in fact formed by the banks of floating pumice stone, still fiery here.

The only difference between the two accounts is that in Aeschylus the pumice is still hot and flaming whereas it is already cold and petrified in Plato. Pumice is a very good heat insulator, so that, when ejected by a volcano, it remains in this fiery state for quite some time.

This sea or marsh (mere) covered with white pumice stone also evokes the Ocean of Milk of Hindu traditions, where the allegory is very much the same. And it also recalls the fiery "Sea of Glass" of the Book of Revelation (4:6; 15:2) as well as the "Gravelly Sea" covered with floating stones featured in Sir John Mandeville's curious Travels. [160]

Moreover, the reference to the Sun stopping to rest and bathe in that mere before resuming its daily trip indicates that this is the place of sunrise and sunset. Hence, this location is Lanka or Taprobane, the site of the ancient International Dateline according to Hindu sacred traditions.

As is now clear, all these ancient traditions coincide and cohere, and start to make sense once properly interpreted. It is certainly no sheer coincidence that they all converge exactly in the region where we have located Atlantis-Eden, the former site of Paradise.

Names such as "Ocean of Milk", "Gravelly Sea", "Sea of Glass" and "Brazen Sea" seem ridiculously childish and utterly impossible as a geological reality. But when their real nature is understood we see that this imagery is quite apt and, in fact, extremely precise.

Even the curious "floating stones" used for the construction of Rama's Bridge start to make sense, very much as do the "floating gravel" of Sir John Mandeville and the "scum" which covered the Ocean of Milk during its churning. Pumice stone is a sort of siliceous foam so light that it actually floats in water for years on end, forming the "floating islands" so often reported in the Indonesian seas.

All in all, we see that most such traditions are coherent when properly interpreted. Hence, Plato was obviously inventing nothing in his relation of Atlantis or even embellishing the fateful events which led to its destruction at the dawn of the present era, the Holocene.

Moreover, it is difficult to believe that essentially all the ancient authors would convene on a lie of such an importance in order to create an illusion of reality for a sacred matter which is in fact the very foundation of most religions, the world over.

Diodorus, Plato and the Two Hesperias of the Ancients

Diodorus explicitly affirms that Atlantis was located on the far side of the "Atlantic Ocean" of the ancients which, as we already demonstrated, embodied the Pacific Ocean as well. The existence of the interposed Americas was widely ignored in antiquity, down to the times of Christopher Columbus and Amerigo Vespucci, when the New World was discovered.

The only exception were the high initiates such as Plato and Diodorus, who knew better. For instance, Strabo, the famous Greek geographer, specifically affirms that the Atlantic Ocean was an empty waste stretching all the way from Europe to the East Indies.

Said otherwise, this means that the "Atlantic Ocean" – or even more exactly, "the Ocean of Atlantis" of the ancients – included both the Pacific and the Atlantic Oceans now so called.

The well-informed geographer specifically adds that it was only the enormous size of this ocean which prevented the ships from crossing it either departing from the East (the Pacific Ocean) in the Indies or from the West (the Atlantic) in Europe and in Africa.

Amerigo Vespucci was the first modern person to realize the Americas were an entirely new continent which effectively separated this wide Ocean into two different moieties. But down to the times of Christopher Columbus everybody firmly believed that one could reach the East Indies by sailing westwards into the Atlantic Ocean long enough.

To judge from the lesson of the early geographers such as Strabo, Eratosthenes, Pomponius Mela, Crates of Mallus, Anaximander, etc., the ancients widely believed that the Atlantic Ocean extended all the way to the Far East, to Cipango, Kattigara, China and the East Indies.

This possibility was also explicitly affirmed and confirmed by Medieval travelers like Marco Polo and Sir John Mandeville, as well as several Renaissance explorers and geographers more or less contemporary with Christopher Columbus, including Pierre d'Ailly, Paolo Toscanelli, Martin Behaim, Henricus Martellus, and so forth.

Christopher Columbus was actually inspired to make his voyages of discovery by the books and maps of these early geographers. And it was also their teachings which inspired me to look further beyond Gibraltar Strait for the real location of the Lost Continent.

The idea that Atlantis lay "just before" Gibraltar Strait, and hence near the European or the African coasts is <u>nowhere</u> stated in Plato's text. As shown above, this opinion is derived from a common misinterpretation of Plato's text, which is highly obscure and intentionally ambiguous, and which probably refers to the antipodes rather than to the neighborhood of Gibraltar Strait.

Even less is this proximity to Gibraltar stated in the remarkably similar text of Diodorus Siculus which we are commenting here. This, despite the false claims to the contrary of some self-appointed Spanish "scriptologists", whatever that obscure title might mean.

These researchers fail to realize the fact that by "Spain" (Hesperia), the ancient Greeks and Romans really meant two entirely different locations. One was Spain itself, in the Iberian Peninsula. The other one was Taprobane, the "Land of the Dead", on the opposite side of the world. This dualism corresponds to the one of Ethiopia, of which Homer affirms essentially the same thing.

True Hesperia was of course associated with the Hesperides or Atlantides, the seven daughters (and/or lovers) of Atlas. These were caretakers of the Garden of the Hesperides, where grew the fabled Golden Apples from which the Elixir was fashioned, and which hence also imparted immortality.

It is only natural that Atlas would like to keep his daughters (and/or lovers, as some say) near himself. Besides, this proximity is specifically affirmed by several authors, Hesiod and Pindar and Aeschylus and Apollodorus among them. Some of these authorities even affirm that the Garden of the Hesperides (or Atlantides) was located on the slopes of Mt. Atlas.

And they also affirm the fact that the Garden of the Hesperides was located beyond the Ocean, in the Far East, precisely where the sun rose every day in order to start the new day.

This fabulous garden was also the same as the Islands of the Blest, where the immortal dead heroes abide, free of toil and worries, enjoying an eternal life imparted by the Elixir of Youth. For instance, Hesiod (<u>Works,</u>

158-69) affirms of the Fourth Race – the heroes killed in the War of Troy – that they were placed there by Zeus, the son of Kronos: [19]

> Zeus the son of Kronos made yet another, the fourth race, upon **the fruitful earth (pouluboteira)**, which was nobler and more righteous, a god-like race of hero-men who are called demigods, **the race before our own, throughout the boundless earth**. Grim war and dread battle destroyed a good part of them... when it had **brought them in ships over the great abysmal sea to Troy for rich-haired Helen's sake**: there death's end enshrouded a part of them.
>
> But to the others, father Zeus, the son of Kronos, gave **a living and an abode apart from men, and made them dwell at the ends of earth (peirata gaiês). And they live untouched by sorrow in the Islands of the Blessed on the far shore of deep-swirling Ocean** (en Makarôn Nêsoisi par' Ôkeanon bathudinên), **happy heroes for whom the grain-giving earth bears honey-sweet fruit flourishing thrice a year**, far from the deathless gods, and Kronos rules over them; for the father of men and gods released him from his bonds. [↑161]

In the above text we have slightly amended the standard translation where required for clarity, and highlighted the more important passages. This remarkable text of Hesiod is however somewhat dense and difficult. It therefore requires some explanation, which we now give for the benefit of the dear readers unfamiliar with such subtleties.

The "fruitful earth" or "boundless earth" is the same as the peirata gaiês, located beyond the confines of the earth (œcumene) and the ocean. Please note that Hesiod explicitly places Troy beyond the "great abysmal sea", the Ocean. And this agrees with our conclusion given above.

Hence, all attempts to locate Troy in the Mediterranean region – Heinrich Schliemann's included – are sheer folly, inevitably doomed to failure. The idea here in Hesiod and others is too clear for that. The Greek heroes crossed the Ocean to get to Troy in order to wage war on it. There they mostly met their end, and it became the Land of the Dead, where they now rest in peace.

The Islands of the Blest are here said by Hesiod to produce "three crops a year". Such is the reason why it is called "the fruitful earth". Actually, the word used by Hesiod (pouluboteira) implies the idea of "yielding many crops", apparently in the same sense as commented above.

These multiple crops a year could only have been of rice, the most productive cereal. And they are also an exclusive feature of the East Indies – Java and Sumatra in special. This fact invariably caused great amazement in the Greeks who visited the distant region.

No other cereal produces that much grain and that many crops a year, a fact that did not fail to impress the ancient Greeks. Besides, were it not for its many volcanoes, the over-exploited soil of the region would fast become unproductive and sterile for lack of proper nutrients.

Please note that this translator (Hugh G. Evelyn-White) mistranslates Hesiod's text to read "the Islands of the Blessed along the shore of the deep-swirling Ocean", which we have correct to: "the Islands of the Blessed on the far shore of the deep-swirling Ocean."

The actual word Hesiod uses is par', which here literally means: "beyond, farther, against, before, opposite", rather than just "along, beside", its alternative meaning. This word is again a double entendre very similar to Plato's own. The word par' exactly corresponds to the term pro used by the great philosopher in the same context. And it is also likewise dual, meaning both "near, along" and "opposite, beyond".

So one may choose the actual meaning desired according to the context, which is quite clear here. Such is also the case with the ambivalent expressions (contra, adversus) used by Pliny the Elder in the same context, as we commented further above. We will also comment further similar cases next.

Strictly speaking, this word can be taken to mean either of the two above acceptions. The Greek word par' (or para) is cognate with the English "far"; Sanskrit para; Greek peran; Zend para, etc., all meaning the same thing. It is also related to the Sanskrit paradesha ("far country, beyond the sea"), from which the name of Paradise ultimately derives.

The profanes misinterpret the passage the way they are meant to, and place these blessed isles on this side of the Ocean. But the initiates, who know far better than this, interpret it otherwise, and look to the farther bank of the Ocean, to the site of real Paradise, "the distant country" (para-desha).

Homer and the Islands of the Blest

We believe that Hesiod was being obscure on purpose, as is invariably the case in connection with Paradise's location. However, Hesiod's text in the Theogony (v. 215, 275, 294, 335) leaves no doubt on the fact that the Garden of the Hesperides – located on the Isles of the Blest – were placed on the far side of the Ocean, "at earth's fringes".

Moreover, Homer's text on the Islands of the Blest, discussed next, also leaves no room for doubting that they were located beyond the Ocean, as we now show. Homer is here describing how Hermes (Mercury) is leading the souls of the suitors of Penelope, all killed by Ulysses, to the site of Hades and the Island of the Blest. Even though Homer also uses the same confusing preposition, his text is unequivocal. The word para is here used by Homer in precisely this sense of "beyond":

> "When they had passed beyond the waters of Oceanus and the rock Leukas, they came to [or passed] the Gates of the Sun and the Land of Dreams whereon they reached the meadow of asphodel" (par d' isan Ôkeanou te rhoas kai Leukada petrên, êde par' Êelioio pulas kai dêmon oneirôn êisan) [Od. 24:12]. [162]

The above text can again be interpreted in either of the two ways just glossed. So much so, that one can see the how the two translators quoted in the link just given actually use the two different alternatives. No matter what, Homer is specific on the fact that the Isles of the Blest – and hence Atlantis, its alias – lay <u>beyond the Ocean</u>. So are innumerous other Classical authorities equally specific.

Besides, who would be brash enough to question the authority of the prince of poets? The other features mentioned by Homer are also worth explaining in some detail, even though space is short here. The rock Leukas should not be confused with its corresponding feature in Greece used for the execution of criminals. Rather, it is its counterpart and archetype actually located in Paradise.

Leukas' name means "white". And this name is perhaps equivalent to the one of the Cyanean Rocks (or Symplegades). No matter what, it here designates the White Island, the name of Paradise in Hindu traditions (Svetadvipa). And it also refers to the white (or light grayish) pumice stone characteristic of volcanic islands such as those of Indonesia, the true site of Paradise.

The Gates of the Sun are the same as the Gates of Dawn. They are associated with sunrise and sunset, and the two straits from which the sun is said to enter and to exit this world and the nocturnal one. Their location is, according to Hesiod's just quoted, in Tartarus or Hades.

And this is confirmed by Aeschylus in the passage we just quoted. We will return to this theme next, when we discuss the myth of Shamash and Mt. Mashu, the Split Mountain of Paradise.

The Land of Dreams is also significant. This name closely evokes the <u>Dream Time of Australian traditions</u>. Dream Time is associated with the

Rainbow Serpent, an alias of the Serpent Shesha, and it is connected with the Wondjina, the beneficent white sprites which we think to be the dead Atlanteans, turned into ghosts after their demise. [163]

Curiously enough, the Australian Aboriginals – whose vivid memories of Atlantis we discuss briefly in the figures section (Part II) of the present book – affirm that, after the Flood, these white giants (Wondjina) ceased coming to their land to visit them, as they often did before.

The Wondjina apparently became extinct in the cataclysm, a fact that again suggests a close connection with Atlantis whose people likewise became extinct then.

Ulysses apparently passed this land of dreams (the Lotus-Eaters') in the course of his travels. If so, this fact proves the hero was sailing the South Seas, where this region is known to be located. We believe these "lotuses" and the "dreams" they induced consisted of hallucinogens such as opium and hashish, produced in the Indies since the dawn of time. Edible lotus is also produced there, though it lacks the narcotic properties mentioned by Homer. [164]

In any event, even though often poorly translated, Hesiod's text is unequivocal in that the Islands of the Blest are located on the Peirata Ges. This is the land which encircled the ocean on the outside, preventing it from spilling in outer space, according to the mythical views.

Hence, the poet could never be speaking of the European side of the Ocean in the above quoted text. This passage should be collated with that of Plato on the Peirata Ges, which we have already commented upon above.

This peripheral land – which should not be confused with Atlantis proper – is apparently America itself, which in fact separates the Eastern Ocean into two halves.

Some authors often confuse the Peirata Ges with the Isles of the Blest, as Hesiod is apparently doing here. But Plato carefully distinguishes the two sites in his two dialogues on Atlantis. It seems that the reason for the confusion lies in the fact that the two lands – America and the East Indies – were both portions of the extensive Atlantean empire.

As is known, this vast empire encompassed the whole Pacific Ocean. This fact was firmly established by the noted German archaeologist Leo Frobenius in the early 1900's and cannot be idly doubted. We already discussed this seminal find in our figures section, to which the interested readers are now directed if they somehow missed it.

It is also no mere accident that both Plato and Hesiod used double entendres (para, pro) in order to describe the position of Atlantis and the

Isles of the Blest. So did several other ancient authorities, starting with Homer, the very first and greatest of Greek poets, as we just saw.

This coincidence tends to prove both the essential identity of Atlantis and the Isles of the Blest as well as the fact that its actual position could only be given in equivocal terms such as the ones just commented here. It is also from such double entendres that the concept of two Hesperias, two Ethiopias and two Atlantises actually arose.

One side of the world was deemed the "mirror image" of the other. Every feature on one hemisphere had its exact counterpart on the other. Hence the two "Pillars of Hercules", two Straits, two Ethiopias, two Hesperias, two Atlantises, two Paradises, two Hells, two Troys, two Greeces, and so forth.

This fundamental dualism is masterfully expressed in the remarkable Egyptian vase discussed in our figures section, to which we again direct the interested reader. It is this very dualism of the world that is implied in Hermes' famous aphorism: "As above, so below."

By "above" is meant the idea of heaven, and by "below" the one of earth. But even this concept is dual, and we may interpret these two words as designating earth ("above") and hell ("below"). From this comes the widespread concept of the triunity of space: Heaven, Earth, Hell.

As usual, this is a Hindu connection dating from the dawn of time (Bhur, Bhuvas, Svar). The idea is so archaic that it even diffused to the Americas before the Beringian Bridge became permanently closed by the huge sea level rise which happened when the Ice Age ended.

We well realize that the above dualistic explanation might seem far-fetched to most of our readers, both lay and experts. But we have gathered several hundreds of similar examples which unequivocally confirm our above conclusion.

These traditions mostly date from remotest antiquity, and were considered sacred by most peoples, both in the New and the Old Worlds. The reason for this dualism designating both the "charred faces" and their "charred land" is easy to understand, now that it has been mooted out.

The ancient countries were named after the peoples which founded them. So, when the Eastern Ethiopians invaded Libya (North Africa) and settled there, they renamed it "Ethiopia" after themselves and their former homeland in the Far East. And the name stuck, in contrast to the former one, which somehow got lost with the passage of time.

These White Ethiopians again eventually settled in Abyssinia (Nubia), which later also adopted that name. And after they settled in Africa, their name was further extended to apply to all Africans, the Negroes included.

In time this origin was forgotten, and the name "Ethiopian" came to designate the Negroes and other dark-skinned peoples due to a widespread misinterpretation of its meaning.

The Greeks facetiously interpreted this name as meaning "burnt faces" (aith ops). But it really applied to the Ethiopic land, charred and devastated by the volcanism. The Greek word ops means both "land" and "face", a fact that clarifies the widespread confusion. But the latter etymology is too well attested to leave room for doubting its reality.

In Roman mythology, Ops is the earth goddess, the Great Mother of Cereals, who is no other than Atlantis itself. The Latin word also alludes to "riches, abundance", no doubt due to the far famed riches and abundance characteristic of Atlantis, the pristine Ethiopia. [↑165]

The Twin Ethiopias, the Two Hesperias and the Dual Spains

> *Science may set limits to knowledge, but should not set limits to imagination.*
>
> Bertrand Russell (1872–1970)

Celtic mythology on Paradise and the Islands of the Blest (Flath Inis) is as rich or perhaps even richer than the Greco-Roman. According to it, these mysterious islands were also inhabited by the mysterious Fomoré, who seem to be the former Atlanteans themselves.

The name of the Fomoré signifies "[people] of the bottom of the sea". Their ruler is Tethra, a visible alias and counterpart of Atlas or Kronos, the ruler of the Titans in the Isles of the Blest. And Kronos is, as we shall show next, no other than Yama (or Bali or Yamantaka), the figure of Shiva as the first god to die and to resurrect from the dead, as Atlantis is doomed to be.

Vanquished in the battle of Mag Tured, Tethra later became the Lord of the Dead. As such, Tethra again evokes Kronos, who does the same in Greek mythology. In fact, the two apparently correspond to Yama or Bali, who is the Lord of the Dead in Hindu mythology.

Yama (or Bali) also closely evokes the figure of Hercules, whom the Orphics again identified to Kronos himself. The only difference is that while in both Celtia and Greece the two figures are purely mythical, Yama is considered a real person in India, where no one doubts his historicity.

Actually, Bali ("Strong One") is a pseudonym of Ravana, the great monarch of Lanka's worldwide empire. And Lanka is the same as (archetypal) Taprobane, alias Atlantis. The name of Bali (or Bala or Balarama) also gave the Phoenician name of Hercules (Baal) as well as several others such (Belus, Bel, Bol, Belenus, etc.).

The Hindus consider Yama as a sort of god whose passion and resurrection they yearly commemorate, very much as we do the one of Christ. The Hindu story of the great dispute between Bali and Vamana is normally told in connection with Vishnu's fifth avatar, the one of the Dwarf (Vamana). Bali was defeated by Vamana, and became the Lord of the Dead, in Patala. But he periodically rises from among the dead, and comes up to visit the living on the day of his festival.

Hesperia (Spain), the Land of Sunset, was sometimes distinguished from its dual, Ethiopia, the Land of Sunrise. This one was located in the Far East, where the day starts by an ancient convention. This is explicitly affirmed in this fragment of Mimnermus (fragm. 10, Diehl):

> Helios... rises at dawn in the land of rosy-fingered Aurora (Dawn or Eos), where he abandons the Ocean and climbs to the sky. He is transported there, during the night, **across the waves**, in his charming concave bed made by Hephaistos, winged and fashioned of precious gold. He is speedily **carried, while asleep, over the surface of the waters, from the abode of the Hesperides to the Land of the Ethiopians,** where his speedy chariot and his horses are detained until the arrival of Dawn, daughter of Morning. Only then rises to his chariot the son of Hyperion.

This passage is quite unequivocal in its esoteric meaning. The sun sets in Spain (Hesperia) and during the night crosses the Ocean in the Solar Cup, until it reaches Ethiopia, the Land of Dawn, on the opposite bank of the great sea. Once there, the sun again rises from the Ocean, climbs to the sky in his winged chariot, and crosses over the earth, until it again sets, in Gibraltar.

This voyage is the nocturnal portion of the sun's daily trip around the earth. The diurnal trip is very clearly illustrated in the remarkable Egyptian vase we already discussed above in our figures section, in Part II. As is now clear, we actually had two Hesperias or Ethiopias in Classical antiquity, one on each bank of the wide Ocean.

Moreover, the Ocean was believed to be unimpeded throughout, reaching all the way from Europe to the East Indies, the Land of Dawn.

Or perhaps the sun was believed to round the Americas on the far south, more or less as later done by both Magellan and Drake. Otherwise, how could the sun navigate from one side of the Ocean to the opposite one, in Taprobane?

Very noticeably, the Greek myth derived from the Egyptian one just mentioned. And this Egyptian myth is of course far older than Greece, and even precedes the rise of that nation itself. But Egypt in turn obtained the myth from India, where it is even older.

In India, Dawn is called Ushas ("shiny, dawn, aurora"). This word is cognate with others such as Eos, Hestia, Vesta and so forth. Even the Latin Aurora (earlier form: Ausosa) ultimately derives from this very base. Ushas is a personification of the Great Mother.

Her figure dates from the <u>Rig Veda</u>, where she figures most centrally. Rather than the Morning Star itself or the Sun, Eos-Ushas is its terrestrial counterpart, the same as the Fallen Sun. And the Fallen Sun is really the volcano, as we now know.

Another ancient fragment – this time due to Stesichorus (<u>fragm. 6:1-4</u>, Diehl) – repeats essentially the same story as the one told by Mimnermus. But it adds that after crossing the Ocean (<u>Okeanoio perasas</u>), the sun reaches "the depths of Night, sacred and somber". The gloomy realm of Night was the same as Tartarus or Hades. And it is here placed on the opposite shore of the Ocean, in the East Indies, as usual.

What is perhaps the clearest allusion to the fact that the Garden of the Hesperides and the Golden Apples it contained lay beyond the ocean, in the Far East, is Apollodorus' account of Hercules' Twelfth Labor (<u>Libr. 2:5:11</u>). This labor consisted in fetching these precious apples from the Garden of the daughters of Atlas. [166]

It seems that Apollodorus here closely followed the account due to Pherecydes of Syros. Pherecydes is the famous pre-Socratic philosopher from Syros, and his version of the story was preserved by a scholiast of Apollonius of Rhodes. According to tradition, Pherecydes was the instructor of Pythagoras, having instructed himself in Phoenician books and traditions.

The extant accounts of Hercules' itinerary to Hesperia are all extremely garbled, to the despair of all the exegetes who attempt to decipher its real meaning. As if to compound the difficulty, Apollodorus identifies Hesperia to Hyperborea, which most experts believe to have been located in the far north, rather than in the west. But this is sheer exoterism intended to confuse the profanes.

Hyperborea is actually the same as Hesperia, the Garden of the Gods and the site of Paradise. Hyperborea is Apollo's Paradise, and is also called Ortygia and Delos. As we have managed to show, the Boreas in question here is not the north wind which blows from the Alps, but its Indonesian counterpart, also called Boreas or Aquilon by the Classical authors such as Pliny and Solinus.

The name of the Boreas derives from the Dravida vaṭa, where the ṭ is cerebral, and sounds like IE r. Hence, we had the following linguistic evolution: vaṭa > vara > bara > boreas. This wind blows from the north in the region of Taprobane, and is specifically designated Boreas or Aquilon by the Classical authors just named, along with others.

When the Etruscans moved from India to the Alps region in Europe, they brought along the name of their north wind, which they transferred to the local one. And it was thus that the confusion of Hyperborea's site became permanent. No matter what, Apollo being the Sun God, it is hard to believe that his tropical Paradise would be located in the chilly far north, as some experts believe.

Most exegetes were never able to make any sense out of these garbled accounts, and have given up the trip as purely mythical. But what interests us here is the fact that, in order to get to Hesperia, Hercules actually embarked in the Solar Cup, together with the Sun itself.

This he did in Mauritania, and then crossed the Ocean in it, until he got to the far shore, where the famous garden was located. Now, Mauritania is Morocco, near the region of Gibraltar. Hardly would the great hero embark in the Solar Cup, cross the ocean in it, and then return to Gibraltar in order to get to the fabled garden where the life-giving Golden Apples grew.

In an unusual attempt to solve the puzzle, some specialists have concluded that the Garden of the Hesperides was located on an island such as the Canaries, the Azores, the Madeiras, etc..

But even this forcing of the hand will not solve the essential difficulty. Both Pherecydes and Apollodorus are categorical in that <u>Hercules actually crossed the Ocean</u> to its far shore. Otherwise, why would the hero embark in the Ocean-spanning Solar Cup, as we just saw in Mimnermus fragment quoted above? What else can this remarkable tradition actually mean?

Moreover, the fabled garden seems to have been located on firm land rather than on a shore. In fact, it was said to have been located on the slopes of Mt. Atlas, itself situated on the shores of the Ocean rather than in its middle, as would be the case in this alternative.

Nereus' reluctance to reveal the site of the famous garden also betrays the secrecy surrounding the true whereabouts of Paradise. And such is also the reason why the accounts of authors such as Apollodorus and

Pherecydes, or others who have written on the matter, are so garbled and confusing.

Hercules' Twelfth Labor

This confusion is visibly purposeful. It closely parallels the ones of Plato, Homer, Hesiod, Apollodorus, Pliny and other ancient authorities such as the writers commented above. No one ever disclosed the secret of the Mysteries which remained unsolved down to the present time.

And, as is now obvious, this secret centered on the actual reality and location of Paradise and its identity with Atlantis itself as a worldwide empire of the former era, the Pleistocene. Paradise was wiped out so completely by the Flood that even its former memory was utterly forgotten, except in the sacred traditions of the Mysteries themselves.

Curiously enough, Hercules' twelfth labor is quite similar to the tenth, at least in matters of geography and location. Perhaps, the two labors are really variants of the same story, told under different allegories. In both cases the hero's itinerary is highly obscure. In both labors the hero crosses the wide Ocean in the Solar Cup in order to get to the place intended, and so on.

Nor is the identification of the Golden Apples of the Hesperides with the Golden Cattle of the Sun so preposterous as it might seem at first. Diodorus Siculus mooted out this fact when he remarked that in Greek, the word <u>mêlon</u> applies both to "apples" and to "cattle".

So, it is quite possible that the Golden Apples, the Golden Fleece and Golden Cattle (<u>phoinikes boes</u>) of Geryon all refer to an ultimate reality common to all these concepts.

Moreover, in Hindu mythology, these fabulous cows – the Cows-of-Plenty – yield not ordinary milk but the Elixir itself. And, as we already argued, both these "apple trees" and these "cows-of-plenty" are ultimately allegories of the volcano of Atlantis-Eden, as we just showed.

In its tame, normal mood, the volcano is the bringer of abundance and felicity to all. But when it goes berserk, it explodes and collapses, bringing death to its own children.

It is precisely this image which is often associated with the Great Goddess herself, generally a cow: Hathor, Nut, Isis, Kama-dhenu, Gauri, and so forth. And it is often the Great Mother herself who brings on the carnage of the Flood. Such is, for example, the case of Hathor-Nut in Egypt.

Returning to the theme of the Golden Apples proper. According to Pherecydes – here visibly followed by Apollodorus – these precious fruit were presented by Gaia (the Earth Goddess) to Hera, on the day of her wedding to Zeus. The goddess was extremely pleased with them, and had them planted in her garden, at the foot of Mt. Atlas.

Hera later charged the Hesperides or Atlantides – the seven daughters of Atlas – with taking care of the precious fruit. But the girls started to pilfer the golden apples, so that the goddess further placed a hundred-eyed dragon (Ladon) to watch the tree where these apples grew.

Supporting Apollodorus, Hesiod (Theog. 215) also refers to: "the Hesperides who guard the rich, golden apples and the trees bearing fruit beyond glorious Ocean" (my emphasis). The word here used by Hesiod perên ("beyond") leaves no doubt on the fact that the Garden of the Hesperides in reality lay beyond the Ocean, on its shore antipodal to both Spain and Gibraltar. [167]

However, this word is related with par' which Hesiod also used in a similar context, as we showed further above. The idea here seems to be exactly the same.

So, the best we can make of these incongruous pieces of information is that we had two Hesperias and two Gardens of the Hesperides. The real one was located in the East Indies, the true site of the Garden of Eden, and the fake one in Spain (Hesperia) in the region of Gibraltar.

Some mythographers further add that the Garden of the Hesperides was located quite near the place where the Titan Atlas supported the Pillar of Heaven, obviously in Atlantis itself.

Moreover, since this fabled garden is also an allegory of Atlantis itself as the Garden of Eden, we are again led to conclude that we also had two Atlantises: a real one in the East (Taprobane) and a phony one in Gibraltar, where most people think it was really located.

According to Apollodorus, in the course of his twelfth labor, Hercules crossed the Ocean in order to get to the Garden of the Hesperides. There he met the giant Atlas, supporting the sphere of heaven. Prometheus, whom the hero had earlier rescued, had advised Hercules not to go to the garden himself, but to ask Atlas to do so in his stead.

The cunning Titan gladly agreed to do so, if only Hercules would hold up the skies for him during his absence. Hercules also agreed, and cheerfully picked it up.

Atlas then went to the garden, plucked three golden apples and brought them back to Hercules. But then he changed his mind, and said he would deliver the apples to Eurystheus himself, leaving the task of supporting the skies to Hercules.

Hercules feigned agreement, if only Atlas would pick it up while he arranged the carrying-pad on his head. The Titan fell for the ruse, and Hercules simply picked up the golden apples, leaving Atlas with the ponderous burden which he was condemned to bear up on his back.

The Legendary Cassiterides and the Mysterious Source of Tin

This story of Hercules and Atlas taking turns in bearing up the world is extremely interesting. It shows their intrinsic dualism in this role as world-bearers, one on each side of the world. In fact, Atlas and Hercules correspond to the figures of Atlas and Gadeiros, the twins who, according to Plato's account of the myth, were the main rulers of Atlantis.

The disputes of the two brothers would eventually become very serious, ultimately leading to the Great War of Atlantis. This war was really a civil war pitting brother against brother, in this case the Dravidian moiety against the Aryo-Semitic one. These two races of India would later become the Pelasgians or Etruscans and the Greeks proper, of Aryo-Semitic extraction.

One of the greatest unsolved mysteries of antiquity concerns the sources where the Phoenician merchants obtained the vast amounts of tin which rendered the Bronze Age a reality. It is known that these sources were located in the Cassiterides, the fabled "Islands of Tin".

But the problem is that the astute Phoenicians never disclosed their site to anyone so that even today no one has any idea of where these mysterious islands were really located. Kultepe, a place in Turkey has been recently proposed. But the mines there are very meager, and could never do as the vast sources of the precious metal.

It is also pertinent to note that the Hesperides were sometimes identified to the Cassiterides As such, they were also confused with Tartessos, or Tarshish, the place where tin and bronze were also said to originate, and which many people confuse with Spain. But these were mere Phoenician lies intended to hide their true sources of tin.

Spain never produced a single ounce of tin, so that we are forced to look somewhere else for the true Hesperides or Cassiterides which sourced the crucial metal. Even the British Islands (Scilly and Cornwall) will never do, as the deposits there were only discovered by the Carthaginians <u>after</u> the Bronze Age was through. Besides, Cornwall is no island, and the Scilly Islands have no tin.

Hence, these islands or lands could never have provided the enormous amounts of tin which made the Bronze Age possible. Bronze is an alloy of copper with tin (about 10% of total) and cannot be produced without this important but rare component metal.

And it is also logical that bronze could only have been invented in a place endowed with the two essential metals: copper and tin. We must not forget that Plato specifically affirms that Atlantis abounded in all metals, tin included. So, Atlantis would be a prime candidate for this remarkable metallurgical invention.

We have also demonstrated in other, more technical works of ours that the true Tarshish – the place whence bronze and tin really came in antiquity – was located in Indonesia, rather than in Spain or England or some other Mediterranean location. Hence, the equation Indonesia = Atlantis is once again apparently inescapable.

Even today, most of the world's tin is produced in the region of Indonesia and Southeast Asia, also its probable main source in antiquity. Copper is also abundant there, and so are nickel and other precious and semi-precious metals. Moreover, no other ancient viable sources of tin but the Far East have ever been identified so far, all being too late in time or insufficient.

Even the name Tarshish – and hence Tartessos – really means "tin" in Dravida, the local language of Indonesia in antiquity. So does the name of Taprobane, itself composed of <u>tamra</u>, a name variously designating "tin, copper, bronze, gold" and other such dark or ruddy metals, and <u>parna</u> meaning "branch, bough, leaf, wing" and, by extension, "peninsula".

Hence, Taprobane was not only the Golden Bough itself, but also the fabulous "Peninsula of Gold" (or Tin or Copper). This name invariably applied to Indonesia, a fact directly attested in Flavius Josephus and innumerous other ancient authors. And it seems logical to conclude that the fabulous Golden Apples were produced in the Peninsula of Gold.

This place was also named Cassiterides ("Islands of Tin"), even though the actual site of these mysterious islands was never divulged by the Phoenicians, who held the monopoly of this lucrative commerce during the entire Bronze Age.

The name of the Cassiterides itself derives from <u>kassiteros</u>, meaning "tin" in Greek. But even this word in turn ultimately derives from the Sanskrit <u>kassita</u>, also meaning the same thing.

Where else but in India itself would the ancient Greeks – or the Phoenicians, their suppliers – have picked up the Indian name of the precious metal which they in fact imported from there? These are issues which, when closely meditated, leave no room for doubting the existence of a second Hesperia – or Tartessos or Tarshish or Cassiterides, etc. – in the Far East, in the region of Taprobane.

And its "western" location also becomes logical, as soon as we realize that, the world being round, beyond the farthest west lay the farthest east, and vice-versa. Euripides (<u>Hipp.742</u>) also refers to the Hesperides as located in the Far East: [168]

> **"To the apple-bearing shore of the Hesperides**, famous singers, would I go my way, there where **the lord of the deep-blue mere forbids further passage to sailors**, fixing the sacred boundary of the skies, **the pillar held up by Atlas**. There **founts immortal** flow by **the place where Zeus lay [with Hera]**, and holy Earth with her gifts of blessedness makes **the gods' prosperity** wax great."

Euripides does not actually say on which side of the Ocean the Hesperides were located. But that the far shore is intended is clear from his text. The chorus (who is speaking here) is saying they would like to be a bird to fly over to the other side of the ocean, where the true Hesperides really are, along with their precious Golden Apples.

Why would the chorus have to be birds to fly over to nearby, continental Spain, if they could get there by simply walking? Why would they have to get to the farthest, forbidden bounds of the Ocean in order to get to coterminous Spain?

This passage of Euripides is extremely interesting and is worth discussing further. In another passage of his <u>Hippolytus (1053)</u>, Euripides returns to the subject and adds that Theseus wants to banish his son to the outermost bounds of the earth: "Yes, to beyond the sea and the Pillars of Atlas, if I could, such is my hatred of you" (<u>peran ge pontou kai topôn Atlantikôn</u>). [169]

The word Euripides actually uses, <u>pontos,</u> is not really the Black Sea, as mistranslated by Kovacs, a place where the Pillar of Atlas never was. This word in fact designates the high seas in general, and the wide Ocean in particular. The Black Sea was the Pontus Euxinus, a particular sea, rather than the sea in general, the meaning truly intended here.

It is this sort of inaccuracy that often distorts the ancient texts beyond clear understanding. We also note an important issue connected with the Pillars of Hercules and/or Atlas. The two heroes and their pillars were often confused one with the other in antiquity.

In practice, each pillar of the pair was attributed to one of the two heroes. Or, as some sources suggest, it is also possible that the Pillars of Hercules were the ones of Gibraltar and their duals in the Far East, the ones of Atlas, the true ones.

The first alternative is far more consentaneous with fact. Euripides (480–406 BC) is prior to Plato (428–348 BC), so that there is no question of the philosopher having invented the myth of Atlas and Hercules or their pillars, which dates from a great antiquity in Greece and other places such as Phoenicia and Carthage.

The idea is ultimately derived from Hindu mythology, where one of the Pillars of Heaven is attributed to Krishna, the other one to Balarama, his dual and twin. From India this tradition passed to Egypt and then to Phoenicia, finally ending up in Greece and Rome.

But the myth of the Pillar of Heaven even reached the distant Americas, where we encounter it among the Aztecs. It also figures in the sacred traditions of the other Indians, for instance, the Tupi-Guaranis of Brazil and several other tribes. We comment the quaint Amerindian traditions on Atlas and the Pillar of Heaven in our figures section, to which the interested reader is now directed.

The Aztecs identified the two pillars of heaven to the two poles or trees erected by Quetzalcoatl and Tezcatlipoca in order to prop it up again, when it fell over the earth, destroying the world. This type of cataclysm is derived from Hindu doctrines on the yugas, the eras of mankind. It has to do with supervolcanisms and their debris falling from heaven, as if the celestial sphere had shattered.

An unequivocal proof that Hercules went as far as Indonesia in the course of his twelfth labor is afforded by a revealing event reported by Diodorus. According to this author, Hercules there killed Emathion, the king of Ethiopia, who had attempted to cut off his passage.

Emathion was the brother of Memnon, whom Hercules subsequently invested on the throne of Ethiopia. The two brothers were the sons of Eos and Tithonos, and their connection with the Far East cannot be doubted, now that we have pointed it out.

But Hercules' itinerary is, as we already said, terribly garbled, perhaps in an attempt to hide away the true location of Paradise. However, how could Hercules have met the two kings of Ethiopia had he not gone to the distant realm, in the Far East, in Taprobane, where the sun rises?

The Split Mountain and the Twin Tree of Life

The two trees in question here are the Tree of Life and the Tree of Death (or of Wisdom). These dual trees we encounter just about everywhere, including in Hindu myths. These the Hindus identify with the Ficus indica and the Ficus religiosa, which often grow together, one from the top of the other, as a sort of parasite.

In Greece, as in America, the Twins are also often represented by two poles (Gemini). Even the Cross or Rood is made of two crossed beams, one considered male and the other one female.

The universal diffusion of this myth is sufficient to prove its Atlantean origin, since it cannot be otherwise accounted for. Only in Pleistocenic times could the myth have diffused to the Americas as it did. Afterwards, the Beringian Passage got closed by the enormous rise of sea level that resulted, so that all further communication between the Old World and the New became impossible.

The "lord of the deep-blue mere" could be either Poseidon or Hercules, or even Atlas himself. The three figures are sometimes confused, as we have already affirmed. In fact, it seems that the three were often the same. Strictly speaking, Poseidon is the "Lord of the Sea", his trident symbolizing his triple aspect, similar to Shiva's (Trikaya, Triton).

Poseidon's figure ultimately derives from the Vedic one of Varuna, who performed the same task in pristine India. Atlas, who represents Atlantis, also fell and became a submarine deity, when his land got submerged. And Hercules was usually associated with the pillars as the impassable bounds which should not be crossed by any sailors.

Here, Euripides apparently ascribes this role to Atlas and his far-famed Pillar of Heaven. All in all, it seems that all the three gods in question here personify Atlantis.

The quaint passage of Euripides just quoted connects a series of items which are all associated with Atlantis and its terrible fate. Though obscure, these features figure in innumerable myths and traditions the world over. And this brings us back to the times of Atlantis, when such a universal diffusion was still possible.

And it further seems that Atlantis and its twin pillars in question here are located in the Far Orient, on the other side of the Ocean, in Taprobane. This "Pillar of Heaven" is in fact the Krakatoa volcano, which destroyed Atlantis and triggered the catastrophic end of the Pleistocene Ice Age. Its explosion and collapse resulted in its splitting into two "pillars" or "pylons", the ones of the Split Mountain of Paradise (Mt. Mashu), which we will be commenting next.

As such, this twin mountain also corresponds to the two pylons of the Gate of the Sun mentioned by Homer as a main feature of Paradise. And it also corresponds to the two trees or poles associated with the twin Tree of Life and the two Pillars of Heaven.

The "Pillar of Heaven" is actually an allegory of the Krakatoa volcano. And this volcano is also associated with Mt. Atlas, as the boundary of Atlantis which should not be idly crossed by anyone. This mountain was ripped open by the cataclysmic eruption and collapsed.

It thus got cleft into two halves, becoming the Split Mountain of Paradise of which so many sacred traditions speak. Now, this event is historical and actually figures in certain Javanese annals. It corresponds to the opening of Sunda Strait by a giant explosion of the Krakatoa volcano, followed by subsidence and caldera formation. This myth of origin was later unduly transferred to the Strait of Gibraltar, where it never occurred, at least in the times of Man.

We also note that both the Tree of Life and its dual, the Tree of Death are invariably represented as of an enormous size, reaching all the way to heaven itself. It is clear that this type of tree never really existed, and is merely an allegory for something else. The same can also be said of the Pillar of Heaven, its analog and counterpart.

And this something is really the giant plume of the volcanic eruption, which often closely resembles a tree, a giant mushroom, a palm tree, an umbrella or canopy, a pillar, and so forth. The prehistoric supervolcanic eruption of the Krakatoa generated such a giant "mushroom", as can be seen in this accurate computer simulation here due to Ken Wohletz, the reputed Los Alamos volcanologist. [170]

The Split Mountain of Paradise was directly connected with Mt. Mashu of Mesopotamian traditions. From it, Shamash the Sun emerged every day to start his daily celestial course, as illustrated in the figure just linked. This myth dates from the Epic of Gilgamesh, if not earlier. It is extremely old, and predates even the existence of Greece itself, let alone the myth of Hercules. [171]

The name of Mt. Mashu means precisely "split mountain" in Akkadian. Its name seems to be a translation from the far older Sumerian language. Curiously enough, Shamash is portrayed, in the figure just linked, holding up a saw in his left hand.

This is apparently a sort of rebus or wordplay. The word "saw" in Sanskrit is <u>krakata</u> (Drav. <u>krakača)</u>. And this name closely suggests the one of the Krakatau volcano (Krakatoa).

Sheer coincidences? Or are these metaphors intended to be clues, as we suspect they are? Shamash's saw also closely evokes the sickle of Saturn (Kronos), likewise toothed. With this sickle, Saturn perpetrated the Primordial Castration, an allegory of the giant Krakatoa volcanism and the collapse of the mountain which turned it into a giant caldera.

Given its early date in the east – where it is already attributed to Indra in Rigvedic times – it is impossible that the myth of opening up Sunda Strait, the true archetype of Mt. Mashu and of the Pillars of Hercules, actually dates from as late as the Middle Ages, as required by the theory of David Keys and Ken Wohletz which we just commented.

The myth of the Split Mountain is further discussed in our figures section, further above (Part II), in connection with the quaint pre-Dynastic Egyptian vase illustrated there. The interested readers who somehow missed this discussion are again directed to this section of the present book.

CHAPTER 15 - THE JEWISH ENCYCLOPEDIA ON THE TRUE SITE OF EDEN

> *The important thing in science is not so much to obtain new facts as to discover new ways of thinking about them.*
>
> Sir William Bragg (1862–1942)

The Jewish Encyclopedia is a mine of information on obscure passages of the Bible and other Judeo-Christian sacred traditions. And this reference has the advantage of having been written by orthodox Jews, whose faith and accuracy cannot be put to doubt.

So, the words of this encyclopedia can be trusted by both Jews and Christians alike. In their description of the Garden of Eden, its illustrious authors affirm: [↑172]

> The Targum Yerushalmi translates "Havilah" by "Hindiki" ("Hindustan", or India), and leaves "Pison" untranslated. Saadia Gaon, in his Arabic translation, **renders "Pison" as the Nile**, which Ibn Ezra ridicules, as **"it is positively known that Eden is farther south, on the equator". Nahmanides concurs in this view**, but explains that **the Pison may run in a subterranean passage from the northward.**
>
> Obadiah of Bertinoro, the commentator of the Mishnah, in a letter describing his travels from Italy to Jerusalem in 1489, relates the story of Jews arriving at Jerusalem from **"Aden, the land where the well-known and famous Gan Eden [i. e., the Garden of Eden] is situated, which is southeast of Assyria"... The first river, Pison, probably refers to the Indus**, which encircles Hindustan, confirming the Targum Yerushalmi.
>
> The second river, Gihon, is the Nile in its circuitous course around Ethiopia, connecting with the Gulf of Aden... **Some explain the difficulty of finding the courses of the rivers [of Paradise] by supposing that since the Deluge these rivers have either ceased to exist**, entirely or in part, or have found subterranean outlets.
>
> Indeed, the compiler of the Midrash ha-Gadol expresses himself as follows: **"Eden is a certain place on earth, but no creature knows where it is**, and the Holy One, blessed be He!, will only reveal to Israel the way to it in the days of the king Messiah."

We note that rabbi Ibn Ezra specifically places the Garden of Eden astraddle the Line of the Equator. Many Jewish authorities concur with this view, including rabbi Nahmanides, the illustrious Jewish explorer and mystic. So, this view should not be idly dismissed, unless there is a solid reason to do so.

The Authority of Thomas Aquinas

Thomas Aquinas, considered the most erudite of all Church Doctors, also places the site of Paradise at the Equator. In his justly famous Summa Theologica, Aquinas writes that: "The Garden of Eden is located at the Equator, in a most temperate place." [173]

And why should we doubt the erudite Christian doctor's teaching, since he obviously knew quite well what he was talking about? Some people objected to Aquinas that the Equatorial region was extremely hot, according to Aristotle, and hence unsuitable for Man's abode. To which Aquinas replied as follows:

> **Reply to Objection 4**: Those who say that Paradise was on the Equinoctial Line are of the opinion that such a situation is most temperate, on account of the unvarying equality of day and night; that it is never too cold there, because the sun is never too far off; and never too hot, because, although the sun passes over the heads of the inhabitants, it does not remain long in that position.
>
> However, **Aristotle distinctly says (Meteor. ii, 5) that such a region is uninhabitable on account of the heat**. This seems to be more probable; because, even those regions where the sun does not pass vertically overhead, are extremely hot on account of the mere proximity of the sun. **But whatever be the truth of the matter, we must hold that Paradise was situated in a most temperate situation, whether on the equator or elsewhere**.

Again, Thomas Aquinas also identifies the site of Paradise with "the Abode of the Blessed and the Empyrean Heaven". The "Abode of the Blessed" is of course the same as the Islands of the Blest of Classical Antiquity. And the Empyrean or Empyreum derives its name from the idea of "fiery" (Greek pyros). [174]

The Empyrean is not the Celestial Sphere itself, as most naive people believe, but really the same as Eden, the Terrestrial Paradise. And this region is actually pleasantly cool, rather than hot, as we shall be arguing next.

The idea of "fiery" – or, even more exactly of "burnt fat" associated with this name of the place – is in reality a reference to the Universal Conflagration which actually destroyed the site of Paradise, turning it from a place of abundance into a veritable Hell. Such is also the reason why the region of Paradise is called <u>Gomeda</u> ("land of fat cattle") in Hindu traditions.

The name "Empyrean" hence literally translates the Sanskrit <u>Gomedha</u> ("Bull Sacrifice"). This word plays with it and is actually an explicit reference to the fiery destruction of the place in the Universal Conflagration which was later followed by the Universal Flood.

The view that Paradise, though equatorial, was actually quite cool is explicated next, in connection with Tenasserim, whose name means just that: "Cool and temperate region."

Tenasserim is located in the Malay Peninsula and Sumatra, being hence localized in the very site of Paradise itself. Though equatorial, this region – being located over lofty, cool mountains – is in fact most temperate, just as Aquinas asserts. And he adds that:

> "In Paradise both conditions [being equatorial and temperate] were found, because, as <u>Damascene</u> says (<u>De Fide Orth</u>. ii, 11): 'Paradise was permeated with the all-pervading brightness of a temperate, pure, and exquisite atmosphere, and decked with ever-flowering plants.'" [175]

It was only later, in the Age of Positivism, that Paradise was transferred to Heaven, and turned into a purely spiritual unreality. But, as Aquinas affirms – and his text just quoted is worth reading very closely – Paradise was actually located on earth, at the Line of the Equator (or Equinoctial Line). It is for this reason that the Garden of Eden was called "the Terrestrial Paradise" and was represented in all maps as an actual geographical place, invariably located in the East Indies.

Curiously enough, the early medieval maps of the world – for instance the one of Beatus (776 AD) – explicitly show the Split Mountain of Paradise (as <u>Mons Synai</u> = Mt. Sinai) in the farthest east. It is placed among the Seres, in China and Taprobane, more or less in its correct location.

As is clear, the ancients well knew the actual location of the Terrestrial Paradise. We just forgot it, in the course of time, somewhere during the dark Middle Ages, when Pagan books were perfidiously burnt.

Many authorities, both Christian and Jewish, are of the opinion that Paradise, the Garden of Eden, was an actual region on earth. Heroes such as Ulysses, Hercules and even Alexander the Great sought to find both the place and the Elixir that was uniquely encountered there.

And so did Christopher Columbus, Ponce de León, Alvaro Nuñez Cabeza de Vaca, and a host of other such explorers both of the Age of Navigation and of modern times. Interestingly, most of these people were matter-of-fact, no-nonsense, commonsensical explorers and archaeologists, not easily fooled by the idle talk of Positivistic quacks such as Darwin and Lyell, bent on demoralizing Tradition.

We also note that one of the main objections refuted by Thomas Aquinas concerns the fact that the Mountain of Paradise "reaches up to the lunar orbit", according to Rev. Bede, and hence cannot be located on earth, since no terrestrial place does this. This fact is obviously true. But this belief derives from Hindu mythological traditions on Mt. Meru, which are of course somewhat exaggerated. [176]

This tradition has to do with the "Pillar of Heaven" and the fact that the volcanic plume of the giant eruption reached all the way to the sky, at least in the view of humans. Actually, this volcanic plume reached only to the upper stratosphere. But it really appeared to be some sort of celestial pillar, as instanced, say, by the remarkable NASA photo illustrated here. [177]

This spectacular photo shows the Etna volcano of Sicily (Italy) during its most recent eruption. This photo was taken from outer space by a NASA satellite. The triangular feature is the island of Sicily, and the land at right is the tip of Italy's "boot".

This photo dramatically shows why erupting volcanoes were called "Pillars of Heaven". The giant Krakatoa eruption which caused the catastrophic end of the Pleistocene Ice Age was actually thousands of times larger than this one here, as we already illustrated further above.

Such plumes often take the shape of a giant mushroom, of a palm tree or an ordinary tree, or an umbrella, a lotus flower, etc.. Hence their connection with the giant Tree of Life which grows in Paradise. This mythical motif is typically Hindu: Mt. Meru as the "Pillar of Heaven"; the enormous Jambu Tree which grows in Paradise, etc.. [178]

Another possible explanation of the lunar connection lies in the fact that the Nile and the other rivers of Paradise were traditionally held to arise in "the Mountains of the Moon". There were several mountains so named in antiquity, some in Africa, some in East Asia.

In Hindu traditions, the celestial rivers such as the Ganges – which are also often equated with one of the four rivers of Paradise – are said to fall from heaven (the moon, etc.). And the Ganges actually falls over Shiva's topknot, which is invariably decorated by the moon itself (Chandrashekhara = "whose crest is the moon").

Here, the moon symbolizes Cyclical Time, invariably associated with the great god. But it also symbolizes a volcanic crater as some sort of soma vessel, often containing a crater lake which serves as the source of the waters of the entire region. The shape of crater lakes is quite often similar to a lunar crescent, since volcanic craters, though circular, are normally slanted to a side.

Dante on the Location of Paradise

In his Divine Comedy, Dante too expresses the view that the Terrestrial Paradise was located at the Line of the Equator. In Dante's world conception – the one usual in esoteric traditions – the earth was a sphere stably placed in the middle of heaven. [↑179]

One should keep in mind that the Renaissance – to whose happening Dante was highly instrumental – was actually a revival of Pagan traditions, and a sort of revolt against the stifling Christianity of the time. More than just mythology, these ancient traditions centered on the secret of the Mysteries, themselves based on Atlantis and on Hindu cosmogony.

Small wonder then that Plato's doctrines and the revived Platonic Academy of Marsilio Ficino and Pico de la Mirandola, among others, were so instrumental in its flourishing, which essentially doomed the Middle Ages, leading to seminal events such as America's discovery.

So, it is to be expected that Dante's teachings are also basically Platonic in their esoteric contents. In Dante's allegory, the Line of the Equator passed through the mythical Jerusalem, where also passed the Meridian which crossed through the poles to the opposite side of the earth, where it passed through the Mountain of Purgatory.

At the two extremes of the Line of the Equator were, on one side the Ganges, on the other the Ebro, the river of Spain. Here was the site of the Pillars of Hercules, so that its duals, the Pillars of Atlantis, were located in the East Indies.

When it was noon in Jerusalem, it was midnight in Purgatory, 6 AM in India, and 6 PM in the Pillars of Hercules. Similar doctrines are found almost verbatim among the traditional teachings of Hindu geographers such as Varamihira, Aryabhatta and others, with Lanka substituting Jerusalem, of which it was the visible archetype.

Purgatory was in fact the same as the tophet or volcano of Isles of the Blest and the site of Paradise Destroyed. It was the place where impurities were purged, so that one might later enter heaven clean of all the sins accumulated during one's existence.

This doctrine is not really Jewish or Phoenician or Christian, but originally Hindu. It figures explicitly in the majestic <u>Mahabharata</u>, and is hence far prior to its Near-Eastern counterparts.

As is clear, Gibraltar is a dual of the true Pillars of Atlas, in the Far East. Jerusalem is here equated with Paradise and the Center of the World. But this Jerusalem is really a dual and antipodal of Purgatory. And Purgatory was placed in the actual site of Hades and the Isles of the Blest, the site of former Paradise (or, otherwise said, Atlantis).

It is clear that the Jews and the Christians both forced their hand a bit in order to make the actual Jerusalem of Palestine fit the pristine scheme of things where Paradise was in fact placed at the Line of the Equator, along with the true Pillars of Atlas, the ones of Sunda Strait.

The phony Pillars of Hercules, like the phony Jerusalem where Jesus died, both lie at about 35°N. But these are both just fictional Paradises, which only mirror the true ones, in the Far East.

As one of the mainstays of the Renaissance, Dante was – secretly, of course, as he was no fool – both a Gnostic and an initiate in the Platonic Mysteries. So, the great poet was quite aware of the secrets concerning Atlantis and its mysterious connection with Paradise. These mysteries he obscurely expresses in several passages of his famous poem, so widely read and so rarely understood in its Mystery connections which are ultimately related to Plato and the Pythagoreans.

It is quite clear that God would hardly have stationed Cherubs in Eden with fiery swords to ward off trespassers, if the Garden of Eden was not real and located somewhere on earth, and hence subject to trespassing by unwanted human intruders.

We have succeeded in tracing this myth back to India and in identifying these "fiery cherubs" with half-personified volcanoes. Volcanoes are very often associated with fiery genii such as Cherubs and Karibus. So, it is not unexpected to actually find them posted in Eden. [20]

Rabbi Nahamanides and the Jewish Traditions

The Jewish traditions on Paradise are now known to have originated from the Mesopotamian ones. There, too, the Karibus (or Cherubs) figure centrally as twin guardians of the way to Paradise and to the Tree of Life, which they protect.

It is hence logical to search for the site of Eden both at the Line of the Equator and the Far East, since the Bible affirms Eden to be located "in the Orient". And the Orient in question here is the usual one, the Far East.

This view is also supported by Mesopotamian traditions which hold that Paradise was located to the southeast of Assyria, in Mesopotamia. What this means is that the actual site of Paradise lies somewhere in the region of Indonesia, the intersection of the Line of the Equator and a line drawn from Mesopotamia to the Equator along a southeastern direction.

We also note that the region of Indonesia is called "the Belt of Fire" by volcanologists and similar specialists. This fact confirms the Indonesian location of Paradise, a reality likewise supported by all sorts of ancient traditions, both sacred and profane.

One such esoteric tradition was reported by Rabbi Moses ben Nahman (Nahmanides), whose views we already commented above. These sacred traditions are highly regarded by the pious Jews, who apparently all believe the geographical reality of the Terrestrial Paradise. And why wouldn't they, if its reality is a central feature of the <u>Book of Genesis</u>, their most cherished holy book?

Nahamanides – more correctly called Rabbi Moses ben Nahman, Nahamanides being the Greek version of his name – was a medieval Talmudist, exegete and mystic. Nahamanides was an ardent believer in the reality of Paradise, and cogently showed that the Garden of Eden was located somewhere near the Line of the Equator. For that purpose Nahamanides invoked the support not only of notorious Jewish scholars, but also of non-Jewish travelers and explorers.

Among the <u>proofs adduced by Nahamanides</u> is included the story of the Greek team of medical doctors led by a Greek scholar with the suspicious name of Aesculapius, who succeeded in entering the site of the Gan Eden while searching for medicinal herbs. Unfortunately, their presence there awakened the Cherubs who succeeded in burning dead the whole team of unwelcome prospectors with their fiery swords. [180]

This curious story is quaintly reminiscent of the episode of the Epic of Gilgamesh, concerning the visit of the hero and his friend Enkidu to the Forest of Cedars. This mysterious forest closely corresponds to the Garden of Eden. It is guarded by the ferocious Humbaba (or Huwawa), whose fiery glance closely evokes the fiery sword of the Cherubs of Eden.

The Humbaba is, as several scholars have recognized, an imperfect personification of a flaming volcano. These researchers are all fast being led to Indonesia and its many volcanoes, just as I proclaimed several years ago. In particular, it seems that Gilgamesh and Enkidu attempted to destroy the Humbaba monster precisely because it was causing the destruction of Paradise. [181]

Curiously enough, the author just linked notes that the beak of the Anzu bird – and hence presumably the one of the Karibu itself – was toothed like a saw. This curious saw evokes the one of Shamash, whose connection with the Krakatoa volcano we already pointed out. [21]

The name of the Krakatoa volcano means, as we already know, precisely the idea of "saw" in both Sanskrit and Dravida (krakata), the two sacred tongues of the region of pristine Indonesia. So does the allegory of the saw or sickle wielded by Shamash emerging from the Mountain of Sunrise. Shamash is not really the sun himself, but a volcano imaged after the day star. [182]

And we also note that Humbaba's searing eye also closely evokes Shiva's third eye, the urna. And the urna is itself a disguised replica of the Vadavamukha as the Fire of Doomsday. Moreover, Shamash's saw or sickle closely corresponds to the one which Kronos used in order to castrate his father, Ouranus.

In Hindu sacred mythology, it is Shiva's fiery glance which inflames Kama, the Hindu love god, who in turn becomes the Vadavamukha, which is enclosed by Brahma inside the waters of the ocean. Come Doomsday, the Vadava goes berserk and explodes in an inferno of fire and water, destroying the whole world.

It is curious to note the emphasis placed by Mesopotamian traditions on volcanoes, given the fact that no such features ever existed in this region of the world. Far more likely, the Sumerians brought over these traditions of Paradise Destroyed by volcanic fire when they came from there, and later handed them over to the Akkadians, the Babylonians and the other peoples of the region, the Jews included.

The story cited by Nahamanides was taken from the Jewish tale entitled Asaph the Physician. But this is in turn derived from the Greek myth of Zeus burning down Asclepius, the son of Apollo, for his prodigality in resurrecting dead humans by means of the Elixir.

If this identification is correct, the story really refers to the destruction of Paradise, Zeus' destructive thunderbolt being here equated to a volcano. And this again accords to sacred Hindu traditions, where the vajra ("thunderbolt" in Sanskrit) is in fact an allegory of volcanisms.

Volcanoes – and more precisely super-volcanoes like the Yellowstone, the Toba and the Krakatoa – are the actual agents which periodically destroy the world when the time comes for it. These global destructions are, according to Hindu sacred traditions, sporadically effected by the Vadavamukha, the "Fire of Doomsday".

And the Vadavamukha, also called the Fiery Submarine Mare, is really the ferocious Krakatoa volcano. Moreover, this volcano is precisely the "saw" or vajra which we just commented above and whose name means precisely "saw, sickle".

It is quite clear that Nahamanides was not confusing things, but merely decoding the Greek myth of Asclepius (Aesculapius) as a different allegory of the destruction of Paradise by a giant volcanism. Since volcanisms occur on earth but apparently not in heaven it seems that Nahamanides was actually justified in attempting to prove the earthly nature of the Terrestrial Paradise, the Garden of Eden of the ancient biblical traditions.

Curiously enough, this wisdom of the pristine ancients – who well knew the reality of the Terrestrial Paradise and of its catastrophic destruction at the dawn of the Holocene Age – was eventually replaced by the skepticism of later philosophers such as Aristotle and his school.

This positivistic un-wisdom culminated in more modern Victorian pseudo-scientists such as Darwin, Huxley, Hæckel and Lyell, who postulated the geological impossibility of phenomena such as the Universal Flood or the fiery destruction of Paradise, the so-called Universal Conflagration.

Their specious pseudo-science blinded us all to reality, causing all subsequent scientists and intellectuals to ignore the very ample and obvious geological evidence offered by earlier researchers such as the French Comte de Buffon and Baron Cuvier and the British William Buckland, among several other experts of note.

This ugly pseudo-science has held back the progress of Geology and Climatology for almost two centuries now. But it now seems that scientists are finally awakening to the unavoidable reality of global cataclysms such as the ones told in the universal traditions of global disasters of the Flood.

These cataclysms of fire and water are periodically caused by volcanisms and earthquakes, as well as by other causes, for instance asteroidal and cometary impacts. We hope that our writings on the issue have helped to shed some light on these ancient issues which are finally being recognized as actual reality.

The <u>Zohar</u> and Alexander's Visit to Paradise

Another Jewish holy book, the enigmatic <u>Zohar,</u> tells a different version of this story of Aesculapius (Asclepius). According to this source, the victims of the fiery sword of the guardians of Paradise were not Asclepius and his team of healers, but the disciples of Plato and Aristotle who, in the time of Alexander the Great, followed him to the site of Paradise looking for the Elixir.

Now, this tradition is very curious. Alexander the Great is widely held to have visited the site of Paradise in the East Indies and actually to have found – or almost, at any rate – the Elixir of Life. Aristotle is said to have been his master on such initiatic matters, and the ample documentation on their letters on this issue is available as an apparent testimonial to the fact. [183]

The letters themselves may be fakes, as is so often the case. For instance the correspondence of the Pope and Prester John or the one of Christ and Tiberius, are now known to be forgeries. But the events therein told are in fact mystic allegories concerning the reality of Paradise and its location in the East Indies. Said otherwise, these documents are verbal maps to the site of Paradise.

This fact is well-known to the specialists. But the connection with Plato and Aristotle mentioned in the <u>Zohar</u> draws attention to Atlantis, the central feature of the works of these philosophers, master and pupil.

Alexander going to the Terrestrial Paradise in search of the Elixir may be just a legend. However, Plato's report on the Lost Continent is not. As we now know, Atlantis is just an alias of the Terrestrial Paradise. Atlantis is – or rather was, as both were utterly destroyed – the Garden of Eden, precisely as Nahamanides correctly affirms.

The Tree of Life and the Elixir seem to be just a pleasant allegory or, better yet, an euphemism for collective death. A metaphor for the volcano which explodes and carries us all directly to Heaven and to Eternal Life when the time comes for it. Or to Hell, depending on circumstances.

Too many people believe this fact for me to put its reality in doubt. However, as a physicist, I can only follow it up to the physical event itself, and no further.

The events which allegedly take place afterwards are a metaphysical reality, better left for authorities such as rabbis and priests to investigate. No scientist can say they are wrong in their views. Nor can anyone prove them right.

No matter what, the Jewish mystics who wrote the Zohar and other such Jewish holy books were clearly well aware of the connection of the writings of Plato and Aristotle with Paradise and its destruction. So, since these philosophers specifically named this place Atlantis, it is tempting to conclude that they all were in fact identifying the two places, much as we have been doing for a long time now.

A variant of the Jewish legend in question here placed the entrance to Paradise in the Makhpelah Cave in Hebron, the alleged tomb of the Patriarchs. This cave is the same as the Cave of Treasures of certain apocryphal scriptures such as the Book of Adam and Eve. And it is also the Cave of the Seven Sleepers of Ephesus and several other such esoteric traditions.

This quaint tradition links back to the Cave of Illusion of the Ramayana, and to several other later counterparts. Another such cave is the one from where Shamash issues. This wondrous cave, which we already mentioned above, is described in some detail in the Epic of Gilgamesh.

This cave is the mundus, the gateway to the Netherworld which the sun uses in order to pass into this one. In one form or another, this mythical cave is found the world over. And the context is invariably the same: the connection with the Netherworld.

The Navajo Indians call it sipapu. And they depict it at the center of the world, which they also figure after the pattern of the concentric dvipas (or paradises) of the Hindu traditions, themselves replicas of Atlantis, as we comment in more detail in our figures section. [184]

The Incas called it Coricancha, "the precinct of the sun", the connection with the fabulous Eldorado. The ancient Egyptians also built a sort of sipapu inside the Great Pyramid, visibly with the same function of linking the Mountain of Sunrise and Sunset with the netherworld.

This Netherworld is also the same as Dante's Purgatory and the Hades of Greco-Roman traditions. It is also the same as the Islands of the Blest or the Patala or Atala of Hindu traditions. Said otherwise, this Otherworld is Taprobane, the netherworld of Pliny and other Greco-Roman authorities. And Taprobane should not be confused with Sri Lanka, a mere replica, as we already demonstrated.

According to the ancient traditions, this cave leads directly into the Holy Mountain and the otherworld below it. It is a sort of gate or yoni or vulva similar to the one of Tanit, the Phoenician goddess.

As Plato described it in his remarkable Myth of Er the Pamphilian, this cave or passage eventually bifurcates, with one wing leading down into Hell and the other one up into Heaven.

It is now clear that this sacred tradition is both universal and extremely ancient. And the very universality of the tradition unmistakably proves its hoary antiquity, dating from Pleistocenic times, when the intercommunication between the New and the Old Worlds was still possible, ceasing afterwards, according to current academic wisdom on the matter.

It also far predates Alexander, Plato and Aristotle, and even the much older Epic of Gilgamesh itself. Or even the Ramayana, the first epic ever, to believe the Hindu authorities.

This universal tradition can be traced back all the way to Atlantis and, hence, to Paradise itself. It refers to the Garden of Eden and the time when it was destroyed by its volcano. It is the hollow (or split) mountain known as Mt. Mashu or Mt. Meru, or Mt. Atlas in Pagan traditions or as the Cave of Treasures and Mt. Sinai of the Judeo-Christian ones.

In the Americas, this mysterious cave also becomes the Chicomoztoc of the Aztecs and the Tollán Zuivá of the Mayas. These names both mean Siete Cuevas in Spanish and "Seven Tombs (or Caves)", in English. The Greek philosopher Pherecydes referred to them as Heptamykoi, again meaning the same thing.

The passage of the tradition to the Americas could only have occurred via Beringia, during the Ice Age itself or shortly after. Otherwise, how can we account for its presence in the pre-Columbian religious traditions of both New World and Old World peoples: Amerindians, Hindus, Jews, Greeks, Muslims, Christians, Australians, and so forth?

Is it not arrogance on our part to doubt the concordant traditions of essentially all the ancient peoples on earth? Why should they all be deemed ignorant primitives, when it is now apparent that it is we, rather than they, that in fact ignore our prehistoric past and even up to now ignore the scientific reality of global geological cataclysms such as the ones of the Universal Flood and Conflagration?

This sacred esoteric doctrine on the yugas (or eras of mankind) was so long and so often persecuted that it is now utterly lost to most if not all people on earth, with the possible exception of the so-called "primitives": the American Indians, the Australian Aboriginals, the Melanesians and Polynesians, the Africans, and so forth.

Those Westerners in the know are afraid to believe these traditions, for fear of persecution and ostracism. Only the so-called "primitive" dare to preserve and to cherish their sacred traditions which we Westerners have relegated to the never-never realm of purely spiritual realities. But this situation is fortunately starting to change, now that people are again headed for loftier values.

The Pishon, the Nile and the Ganges

The view that the Pishon (or Pison or Phison) passes under the earth to become the Nile in Egypt was current in antiquity. Josephus, the Jewish historian, affirms this in his <u>Jewish Antiquities</u>.

So does Cosmas Indicopleustes who portrays this river doing just this in his famous map of the world before the Flood which we comment in some detail in our figures section (Part II of the present book).

This widespread notion ultimately derives from the identification of the Nile with its celestial counterpart in the Egyptian and other traditions. This confusion basically results from the fact that there are two different Niles, one running in Paradise and the other one in Egypt.

The Pishon River of Paradise is actually the same as the River of Milk. This river is also the same as the Celestial Nile which once flowed in Atlantis-Eden.

Now, the expert view of the above quoted rabbis expressed that "the difficulty of finding the courses of the rivers [of Paradise] by supposing that since the Deluge these rivers have ceased to exist, entirely or in part, or have found subterranean outlets" is also extremely interesting.

We have been able to locate these four rivers of Paradise precisely at the site where we have also located the lost continent of Atlantis: in Indonesia and its seas.

All these four rivers were in fact submerged by the Flood. But their beds remain essentially intact on the sea bed, where we have been able to locate them and to trace them in detail in the maps of the seafloor of the region obtained by NOAA and other institutions such as NASA, which we already commented further above.

And, guess what? These rivers are all four located exactly over the Line of the Equator, just as the rabbis just cited specifically affirm. This coincidence is of course too uncanny to be idly dismissed as accidental by anyone not prepared to prove this allegation with fact, rather than sheer opinion, as is usually the case in such matters.

As Plato recommends, mere opinions should never be accepted as a refutation of proven empirical or traditional facts. The opinion expressed by rabbi Obadiah of Bertinoro, quoted further above, that "the well-known and famous Gan Eden is situated... southeast of Assyria" is also in accordance with the ancient traditions.

For instance, the tradition on subterranean rivers feeding the paradisial ones of Taprobane is supported by the Tale of Sindbad the Sailor. And it is also reported by Plato in his Phaedo, where the four rivers of Hades are described in great detail.

The ancient Mesopotamian traditions placed Dilmun – their version of the Garden of Eden – in the South Seas, to the southeast of Mesopotamia. When one consults a world map, for instance, the one discussed in Part III above, it is easy to see that the site of Indonesia in fact lies directly to the southeast of Mesopotamia, just as rabbi Obadiah affirmed.

Actually, rabbi Obadiah did not say <u>how far</u> to southeast the Garden of Eden actually lay. And he actually meant a whole lot. All the way around the Indian Ocean and then across it to Indonesia. But this enormous distance could easily be sailed – and in fact was – from deepest antiquity.

This fact is now fast getting accepted by all specialists, after heroic researchers and adventurers such as Thor Heyerdahl proved its feasibility in actual practice. As is clear, all the manifold data given in the above quotation of the <u>Jewish Encyclopedia</u> exactly fit our location of Atlantis-Eden to an uncanny accuracy.

So, how can one doubt the reality of Paradise any further, now that we know that, just as stated in the <u>Midrash ha-Gadol</u>: "Eden is a certain place on earth, but no creature knows where it is."

Well, this assertion used to be true up to now. No one <u>knew</u> Eden's true location up to now. But we now know its location for sure, don't we? In Indonesia, where else? Or, more exactly, in Taprobane, exactly where the most ancient traditions always placed it.

CHAPTER 16 - THE CASE OF TAPROBANE AND SUNDA STRAIT

> There is a place where a stone god rose from the sea
> and a mountain opened up in the sky; and as the world
> heaved and compressed, there occurred sights and sounds
> of which today's foremost nuclear weapons designers
> scarcely dream. I know of a world which saw waves as
> high as skyscrapers. I know of a cloud that spread, globular
> and huge, and where it touched the earth and the sea, it
> converted men into gas.
>
> Charles Pellegrino, Unearthing Atlantis

Introduction

As we already warned the dear reader, we left the tabular comparison of our proposed site of Atlantis with Plato's text for the end for a series of good reasons. The main one is that we hope that by now, the reader will have realized the impressive power of this comparison method, despite its unbelievable simplicity.

Moreover, we also hope that by now the readers will have realized the fallacies of the sites so far proposed by other researchers of Atlantis, as well as become familiarized with the main geographical features of Plato's Lost Continent and its vicinal regions and, moreover, with the exquisite subtleties used by the ancient mythographers such as Plato and Diodorus, and others as well.

Above all, we expect that the readers will finish reading this book with a sweet taste in their mouth, considering our proposal as some sort of dessert which, we hope, they will hopefully find delicious.

No discovery, either modern or ancient, is as important as the realization that Paradise once existed on a certain place on earth where Civilization and Agriculture first developed. For, if Paradise was once a reality, this means that we humans were able to do it, and to live in peace and harmony. And if so, we can do it again, and again and again...

Pindar, Plato and the Pillars of Hercules

Many people think that Plato was the first author to report the innavigability of the Atlantic Ocean in the region of Gibraltar. This belief is erroneous. Pindar (518–438 BC), the great Greek poet, wrote in his Nemean Odes (4:65), almost a full century before Plato ever spoke of Atlantis that: "Beyond Gadeira, into the western darkness, there is no passage. Turn back and go no further…"

If one takes Gadeira to mean the neighborhood of Cadiz, in Spain, Pindar could only be speaking of the region of Gibraltar. The same is of course true of Plato, who affirms more or less the same thing. This belief is traditional, and dates from the remotest epochs.

Aristotle affirms the same thing in his Meteorologica (II:354a): "Outside the Pillars of Hercules, the sea is shallow, owing to the mud, but calm, for it lies in a hollow." Now, Aristotle, though a disciple of Plato, was a "no-nonsense" Classical authority, who did not believe in the traditions of Atlantis and even poked fun at Plato for having proposed something that could not be found anymore, a non-existent reality which could neither be refuted nor confirmed.

One thing is obvious. If these authors were talking of the region of Gibraltar, they were utterly wrong, as this type of thing never existed there. Gibraltar is a wide, deep strait. There are no shoals there or beyond it and, even less, sunken islands of any considerable size, let alone of the continental proportions stated by Plato.

Moreover, the cataclysm reported by Plato is quite obviously of a volcanic nature as we have already showed. And there are no volcanoes at all in this entire region. So, one is hard put to understand in geological terms how this region could have become darkened or covered with floating debris (pumice) or silted up so much as to impede navigation, features typically volcanic in origin.

Curiously enough, the same story was earlier told of the Strait of Messina, the one between Sicily and Italy. Again, this strait is wide and deep, and far from perilous. But this time, we at least have a volcano at play, the Etna, placed there.

The Etna volcano is active even today, and has erupted with violence over both the historic and the prehistoric past. So, the Etna could well have caused the darkness reported by Pindar and others.

The Strait of Messina was traditionally connected with Ulysses' navigation, as told in Homer's charming Odyssey, the famous Greek saga. This strait was identified by the ancient Greeks and Romans with the site of Scylla and Charybdis, the two perils faced by the great sailor.

Messina Strait was also connected with the Symplegades (or Cyanean Rocks), themselves floating islands which can only be explained as formed by floating banks of pumice stone, which are in fact produced when the Etna volcano erupts with sufficient violence.

And the Etna volcano was, accordingly, identified with Mt. Atlas, as the "Pillar of Heaven" for the reasons therein commented. Messina's strait was also identified with the two Pillars of Hercules, as attested, say, in Imbelloni's map commented in our figures section (Part II).

The two perils of the Odyssey, Scylla and Charybdis were the exact counterparts of the two Pillars of Hercules. Charybdis was a giant maelstrom always ready to devour the passing ships with their crews. And Scylla was a lofty rock inhabited by a terrible man-eating dragon. And this dragon was in all probability a fire-spitting volcano, the usual allegory.

These two features also closely evoke Calpe and Habila, the two pillars of Gadeira described by Avienus in his Ora Maritima. Their shape, he says, correspond to a cap and a cup, just as do the ones of Calpe and Habila.

In Hindu terms, these two geographical features correspond: Charybdis to the terrible Vadavamukha and Scylla to Mt. Meru, the Pillar of Heaven. We might also say that they correspond to the two Merus, the Sumeru and the Kumeru, likewise shaped.

In antiquity, it was often said that Atlas supported the heavens from the top of Mt. Etna, whereas Hephaistos, his infernal counterpart, had his forges underneath this mountain, whose lava was interpreted as the slag due to his smelting of the metals used in his works.

As is clear, the legend of Atlas, of the impassable strait and of the innavigable seas somehow got transferred, already in Classical times, from Messina Strait to Gibraltar Strait. Earlier still, this legend was said to apply to the Bosporus Strait, between Greece and Turkey, or to the Bab-el-Mandeb Strait, at the exit of the Red Sea to the Indian Ocean, as reported by Pliny the Elder.

Imbelloni's map just mentioned further lists several other straits early associated with Atlantis and the Pillars of Hercules (or Atlas). So, one sees that this tradition was transferred from one place to the other, as if to purposely confuse the profanes on the true location of Atlantis.

Once this fact is realized, it is easy to see that most, if not all sites thus far proposed for Atlantis and the Pillars of Hercules, its main geographical feature, are poor fits at best. For instance, Thera (and Crete) – an all-time favorite among Atlantologists due to its terrible volcano – has this prime feature but unfortunately lacks any viable strait nearby.

Its proponents had to force their hands and invent a would-be strait south of the Peloponnesus, considering Cape Malea as one of the Pillars of Hercules and Cape Tenaros as the other. But these two capes form no strait, but a wide bay, as a close inspection of a map of the proposed region will reveal. [185]

So much so that J. V. Luce – the noted classicist and another proponent of Atlantis in Thera – does not support this claim, and in fact avoids this odd identification, explicitly recognizing that the Pillars of Hercules were really associated with Gibraltar and the Atlantic Ocean.

Moreover, the ever attentive Imbelloni fails to list these would-be "Pillars of Hercules" in the Peloponnesus, another fact that attests their non-historicity.

Furthermore, it is highly unlikely that anyone in antiquity would ever seriously consider this broad passage leading nowhere as the site of the all-important strait flanked by the Pillars of Hercules, the impassable bound or limit leading to the Ocean of Atlantis, be it the modern Atlantic Ocean or some other coterminous water body such as the Pacific Ocean.

When we consider other proposed sites for Atlantis, the fit is even poorer. For instance, Cyprus, recently proposed by Robert Sarmast, lacks both the volcano and the strait. Hence, it is an extremely poor conformity to Plato's invaluable text. The same is also true of sites which have been repeatedly proposed over the centuries: Antarctica; Bolivia; Cuba, the Antilles and so forth.

These proponents often bend facts to make them agree with their pet theories, as in the case we just quoted. I, instead, decided to follow the counsel of Descartes, and attempt to frame a theory which best interprets the known facts and best agrees with the description of the ancient authorities: Pindar, Plato, Homer, Hesiod, Diodorus Siculus, and so on. This is the only scientifically acceptable strategy.

In my quest, I would tentatively adopt a site or propose an altogether new one, and then compare it to Plato's text and others. One of my tests consisted in filling the schematic table used in the present chapter and observing the empirical fit. And I did this over and over again, year after year.

And guess what? I finally came up with what can only be the real solution to the riddle, which fits both the known geological reality and the very detailed picture of them provided by the experts just named as well as the many other sources which I used in order to support my conclusions.

Pindar makes several other references to the impassability of the Pillars of Hercules and its shoals in his famous poems. So do many other ancient authorities. In fact, this widespread tradition survived down to the Renaissance and the Age of Navigation, until Christopher Columbus and other explorers completely dispelled the taboo. [22]

These dreary shoals or marshes are also mentioned in the Argonautica of Apollonius of Rhodes as the Tritonian Marshes, as well as in many similar passages of ancient authorities. And these traditions date from far before Plato's account of Atlantis and its impassable seas.

Another detailed account of this region is given by Avienus in his Ora Maritima. Avienus' description bears no resemblance whatsoever to the Spanish Gadeira or Tartessos, the region in question here.

Hence, it is again quite clear that these traditions referred not to the Atlantic Ocean now so named, but to the Ocean of Atlantis, whose true identity with the Pacific Ocean is obvious by now. Limitations of space do not allow us to pursue this fascinating subject here, and we leave this task for a fitter opportunity.

The actual region in question here is the East Indies (or Taprobane), the sole geographical fit. And these marshy seas full of shoals and lagoons are located there, in Indonesia, being part of the Pacific Ocean, then generally believed to be coterminous with what we presently call the Atlantic Ocean.

There, in these perilous seas, we indeed have all sorts of extremely dangerous shoals and extensive marshes that can only be crossed by the skilled native pilots.

It is very easy to become trapped or wrecked in these lonely marshes and shoals and there to die from hunger and thirst. This dreary region was – and in fact still is – plagued by the terrible Malay pirates, always ready to prey and execute whoever dared to sail these forlorn seas.

The True "Pillars of Hercules"

If Gibraltar was not really the "Pillars of Hercules" that Plato had in mind, as we just showed, to what pillars was the philosopher really referring, then?

In our prolonged study of this difficult problem, we came to note an extremely curious feature of Plato's text which would eventually lead us to the correct solution of the ancient riddle which no one had ever deciphered so far. Plato's text, which we already analyzed above, somehow seems to be the "mirror image" of the reality we actually have in Gibraltar.

According to Plato's text, we have:

- Narrow strait leading to the Ocean.
- Huge half sunken island of Atlantis forming impassable shoals in front of the strait and rendering the region "innavigable".
- Many islands beyond it, on the way to the Outer Continent.
- Outer Continent beyond, apparently the Americas.

In the region of Gibraltar we actually have:

- Narrow strait leading to the Ocean.
- No shoals or island of any substantial size, sunken or not.
- No "many islands on the way" to serve as entrepots to ships on the way to the continent beyond.
- Outer Continent = the Americas.

As is clear, nothing but the Americas themselves fits the bill here. As a matter of fact, we actually have the Azores Islands on the way to the Americas. But these tiny islands could never be described as "many". And its neighboring seas are too perilous to make them serve as entrepots for provisioning ships, as more than one explorer actually found out. Columbus, who was familiar with these reports, carefully avoided these islands on his way to America.

Even if we ignore the presence of the interposed Americas, as the ancients normally did, the actual geography of the region of Gibraltar is inadequate to assign a viable meaning to Plato's detailed description. Besides, one would then be hard put to provide an adequate "outer continent", since Asia was not considered a continent by Plato and others, but merely an "island".

We already demonstrated that Plato's text can be interpreted as meaning either "in front of, facing" or, conversely, "antipodal to". Taking the antipodal alternative, we also concluded that this strait was Sunda Strait, the true "Pillars of Hercules". Consider now the situation which obtains when we consider Sunda Strait as the true "Pillars of Hercules" which Plato had in mind. The situation now becomes:

- Narrow strait leading from the Ocean (Indian) to now half-sunken Indonesia, but formerly a huge continent.
- Huge half sunken islands of Indonesia forming impassable shoals.
- Many paradisial islands on the way (Indonesia, Melanesia, Micronesia, Polynesia) to render the long trip pleasant.
- Outer Continent beyond (America).

As shown by a comparison with Plato's discourse just quoted, the fit is now perfect. Indonesia is truly the remains of a huge sunken land, as we already showed. And such is the reason why Plato called Atlantis an "island" (<u>nêsos</u>), such being one of the etymons of the Greek word in question here.

And this is particularly the case when we consider the situation prevailing soon after the cataclysm, when the Atlantean seas were still covered with fiery pumice stone, a fact that closely evokes the perilous Symplegades met by both Ulysses and the Argonauts or, even more, the "mud" covered seas and shoals described by Plato.

Oceania's islands just mentioned are really myriad (literally). They not only provided passing ships with food and water but, above all, with the lovely native girls, who made the hearts of the tired sailors beat faster and set their minds to dream of Paradise.

And this time, the "Outer Continent" also comes out right: the Americas. So does the narrow strait in question, Sunda Strait, really opened by a giant eruption of the Krakatoa supervolcano. This event is the one really connected with the story of Hercules (a personification of the volcano itself) opening up a passage there, during his tenth labor, the rustling of Geryon's cattle.

Moreover, the two "Pillars of Hercules" correspond to the two volcanoes flanking Sunda Strait, the Krakatoa and the Dempo. One is a lofty mountain, and the other one a giant volcanic caldera, precisely corresponding to features such as Scylla and Charybdis or to Avienus' Calpe and Habila.

Though hard to believe, these coincidences are too exact and too inescapable to be attributable to mere chance. It is hence clear that Plato somehow heard ancient traditions from the South Seas which had been devised in connection with Taprobane and the demise of the once paradisial region.

Actually, such traditions abound in that distant region. And they date from remotest antiquity, having passed into the sacred traditions of a great many ancient nations.

For instance, these traditions reached Greece quite early in time. They actually figure in both the Odyssey and in the Argonautica, two of the earliest sagas of ancient Greece. These "Greek" navigations actually took place in the South Seas, as we already showed.

In fact, these two Greek epics – and several others such – ultimately derive from sacred Hindu-Buddhist traditions like the ones recorded in the Jatakas. They also figure in more profane texts such as the navigations of Sindbad the Sailor or in the even older Tale of the Shipwrecked Sailor of the ancient Egyptian traditions.

Even the famed Mesopotamian text of the Epic of Gilgamesh does so, particularly where the hero and his friend Enkidu sail to the Forest of Cedars or to Paradise (Dilmun), where he went questing the Elixir, very much as Alexander and other heroes would do later.

These tall tales are still current in the South Seas, whence the early sailors probably brought them to their own homelands in Greece, Rome, Mesopotamia, Egypt, Phoenicia, Israel and so on.

Once again, these uncanny coincidences are too close to be attributable to chance: floating islands, serpent kings, monstrous sea serpents and whales, perilous seas and maelstroms such as Charybdis and the Vadavamukha, and so on. And all of these are features which physically belong to Taprobane and nowhere else.

Actually, these traditions are so ancient and so widespread that they apparently date from Atlantis itself, when the memories of the cataclysm were still vivid in the minds of its scant survivors of the cataclysm. If so, it is even possible that the Greeks originally brought these sacred traditions along from Indonesia, when they moved out from the destroyed region of Taprobane into the Mediterranean one.

Moreover, Plato's report being based on the traditions of the Mysteries, it seems that they ultimately derived from these secret sources. Of course, Plato would never disclose their true origin. This would constitute a grievous crime in ancient Greece, one punishable with death.

So, the wise philosopher invented a plausible alternative, a romantic explanation in the figure of Solon and his visit to Egypt. This invention provided not only a believable source, but also a believable date which could not be checked in any direct way anymore, since Solon was long dead by the time Plato introduced this idea in his two dialogues on Atlantis.

Hardly would an Egyptian priest – at least one high enough in rank to be given knowledge of this most secret of Mystery traditions – confide them to a foreigner, a Greek stranger like Solon. In Egypt, as in Greece, this profanation of the Mysteries was forbidden by an oath which was never really broken by anyone. A further reason was the death penalty which ensued if anyone actually broke the sacred vow.

It is certainly for this very reason that Plato, like all others, never speaks openly of the true locations and the true traditions, entrusted only to the innermost disciples, sworn to perpetual secrecy.

Again, the fact that Plato does not speak in conformity to the geographical knowledge of his time, but in terms which are only true in the region of Sunda Strait is telltale of the fact that his true source were the traditional Mystery channels which actually date from the times of Atlantis itself.

It is foolish to suppose that the great sage would invent a lie which would fit the actual reality we are now disclosing, perhaps for the first time ever. Chancy coincidences are in reality a measure of our ignorance. The more "coincidences" we have, the more likely is a cause-and-effect relationship.

And when these coincidences start to pile up, as here, the astute investigator is obliged to stop and to start to look for this type of connection, just as we are doing here.

The Perfect Fit of the Indonesian Site

Observe, in Table IV.1 below how well the situation of Indonesia and Sunda Strait perfectly fits the one described by the prince of philosophers for Atlantis summarized in Table III.1 below.

Table IV.1 - Results for the Region of Indonesia and Sunda Strait			
Narrow Mouthed Strait (Sunda)	Huge Island Right in Front (Larger Than Libya and Asia) (Indonesian Atlantis)	Many Islands Ahead (Melanesia, Micronesia, Polynesia) in True Ocean (Pacific)	Outer Continent Beyond the True Ocean (America)

Please note that Plato's use of the word "island" (<u>nêsos</u>) here refers more to a sunken land of continental proportions than to a smallish piece of ground fully surrounded by water, the modern sense of the word, but not the ancient Greek one.

And this brings the match even closer than a simple island ever would, sunken or not. Consider now the situation that really obtains at Gibraltar, and which can be observed in a map of the region, such as the ones already presented in Part II further above.

Table IV.2 - Results for the Region of Gibraltar			
Narrow Mouthed Strait (Gibraltar)	Huge Island in Front (Larger than Africa and Asia ???????	Many Islands Ahead ???????	Outer Continent Ahead (America)

It is clear that, if indeed Plato's description refers to reality, the situation around Gibraltar Strait – summarized in <u>Table IV.2</u> above – offers no consistent solution.

Our proposed solution, instead, affords a most perfect fit to Plato's puzzling text. Were this the only evidence we have on the matter, we agree that the intelligent reader might remain skeptical. But there are further myriad proofs which we have uncovered, and which leave no room for doubting our solution of the so far unsolved riddle.

Plato and the Prehistoric Crossings to America

The vastness of the Pacific Ocean, pointed out by experts as impossible to cross in primitive embarkations in fact posed no insuperable barrier. As Thor Heyerdahl and several other enterprising adventurers demonstrated in practice, this ocean may be readily crossed in the giant sail-endowed rafts and proas of the Polynesians and other peoples of the South Seas region.

These ancient sailors were in no hurry whatsoever, and could hence enjoy the ride provided by the Equatorial Counter-Current which leads directly from Indonesia to Ecuador, in America. Plato, the great sage, explicitly avers that this crossing of the Ocean was a matter of routine even in Atlantean times. And he also reports that the Atlanteans had very advanced sail ships (triremes). [186]

In other words, Plato is telling of the ancient voyages undertaken across the Pacific to the distant Americas by the enterprising Atlanteans and their close successors, the Polynesians. Both the ancient Hindus and the Chinese merchants also had several advanced ships fully able to cross the ocean, particularly when speed was not an issue.

The crossing of the Indian Ocean from India to Indonesia and Southeast Asia has been a matter of routine since remotest antiquity. These voyages were also undertaken by the Aztecs, as we comment in the Codex of Totonicapán, which tells of one such trip by their shamans.

The ancient Greeks seldom if ever sailed the Atlantic Ocean, which they deemed gloomy and damned, according to the many legends that survive from antiquity. These were mere lies spread by Phoenicians, who thus preempted competition in their commerce with the East Indies.

In fact this cunning people transferred the legends of the South Seas to the Mediterranean region in order to discourage the competition, as ferocious then as now. By contrast, the Phoenicians, like the Greeks and Romans and other Mediterranean peoples such as the Minoans and even the Jews (e. g. Solomon's navy) currently navigated the Indian Ocean, which they usually accessed by way of the original Suez Canal, open since remotest epochs.

Such early navigations are also widely attested in the Egyptian and Mesopotamian records, and can hence be hardly questioned. They are also reported by Herodotus and other ancient authors. It is therefore far more logical to suppose that Plato was in fact speaking of the Indo-Pacific navigations, rather than of the far more unlikely Atlantic ones.

The Pillars of Hercules frequently figure in the Phoenician coins, for instance the ones shown in our Atlantis site and in this quaint illustration here. The second of the above illustrations of the Phoenician version of the Pillars of Hercules is highly interesting. The two pillars are shown in connection with a burning vessel and an olive tree. [187]

The burning vessel (incense burner) is a vivid allegory of a volcano. In fact, it is the submarine volcano associated with the Vadavamukha and, even more exactly, the Krakatoa volcano, as we argue in detail further above. The olive tree is in turn an allegory of the Tree of Life. As such, it represents the volcanic "mushroom" of the subaerial volcano, the Dempo volcano of Taprobane.

The conch is the attribute of Triton, and is an indirect reference to Poseidon, the Flood, and the terrible War of Atlantis. This symbolism is too complex to gloss here, and the interested reader is referred to our works on this symbolism, some of which are available in our Atlantis site just linked above. The conch symbolizes a whirlpool or maelstrom, as we show in detail there.

This curious submarine feature was familiar to the Greeks since the times of Homer and Hesiod. It was called Charybdis, being the terrible whirlpool which sucked down Ulysses' ship with all his crew. And this giant maelstrom is in fact the Vadavamukha, the submarine supervolcano of Taprobane, the ferocious Krakatoa.

In time, this legend got transferred to the Atlantic Ocean as the island of Man Satanaxio ("Hand of Satan"). This mythical island was the site where a giant devilish hand allegedly rose from the sea, dragging down the passing ships and their unlucky crews directly to Hell itself.

The burning pot and the olive tree are also associated with Poseidon (as the submarine volcano) and with Pallas Athena (as the subaerial volcano). The disputes of the two gods are actually an allegory of the Great War of Atlantis waged between the Atlanteans and the prehistoric Athenian Greeks. The burning pot of incense allegorizes the volcano and the olive tree the Tree of Life, that is the volcanic plume of the other one, its dual.

BIBLIOGRAPHY

1) Atlantis (General)

Andrews, S., Atlantis. St. Paul, MN, Llewellyn Publ., 2001.

Ashe, G., Atlantis, Lost Lands, Lost Wisdom. London, Thames & Hudson, 1992.

Beaumont, W. C., The Riddle of Prehistoric Britain. London, Rider & Co., 1946.

Berlitz, C., The Mystery of Atlantis. New York, Avon Books, 1969.

Berlitz, C., Atlantis the Eighth Continent. New York, G. P. Putnam's Sons, 1984.

Braghine, A., The Shadow of Atlantis. New York, Dutton, 1940.

Carli, Comte G. R., Lettres Americaines. Paris, Buisson, 1788.

Cayce, E. E., Edgar Cayce on Atlantis. New York, Paperback Library Inc., 1968.

Collins, A., Gateway to Atlantis. New York, Avalon, 2002.

Duncan, R., Atlantis. The Opening of the Field. New York, Grove Press. 1960.

Ellis, R., Imagining Atlantis. New York, Alfred A. Knopf, Inc., 1998.

Fears, J. R., (ed.), Atlantis, Fact or Fiction? Bloomington, IN, 1978.

Fell, B., America B. C.. New York, Pocket Books, 1989 (Rev. Edition).

Frost, K. T., The Critias and Minoan Crete. JHS (1909) 33:189-206.

Luce, J. V., The End of Atlantis. Great Britain, Thames and Hudson, 1969.

Mavor, J. W., Voyage to Atlantis. New York, G. P. Putnam's Sons, 1969.

Muck, O. H., The Secret of Atlantis. New York, Times Books, 1978.

Paschos, V., Atlantes Not The Gods. Athens, Museum of Atlantis Ed., 2000.

Plato, Timaeus and Critias. London, Penguin Books, 1977.

Ramage, E. S., Atlantis, Fact or Fiction?. Bloomington, Indiana Univ. Press, 1978.

Scrutton, R., The Other Atlantis. Sphere Books, London, 1982.

Spence, L., Atlantis in America. New York, Kessinger Publ. Co., 1997.

S. de Camp, L., Lost Continents. New York, Dover Publ., 1954.

Vitaliano, D. B., Legends of the Earth. Bloomington, Indiana Univ. Press. 1973.

Wellard, J. H., The Search for Lost Worlds. London, Pan Books Ltd., 1975.

Whitshaw, E. M., Atlantis in Spain. Stelle (IL), Adventures Unlimited Press, 1994.

Wiesenthal, S., Sails of Hope. New York, Macmillan, 1973.

2) Catastrophism, Ice Ages, Geology and the Flood

Bellamy, H. S., Moons, Myths, and Man. London, Faber and Faber, 1936.
Best, R., Noah's Ark and the Ziusudra Epic. Fort Myers, Enlil Press, 1999.
Bruce, F. F., Commentary on the Book of the Acts. Grand Rapids, Eerdmans, 1977.
Clube, V., and Napier, W., The Cosmic Serpent. New York, Universe Books, 1982.
Clube, V., and Napier W., Cosmic Winter. New York, Universe Books 1990.
Corliss, W. R., A Handbook of Geological Enigmas. Maryland, Glen Arm, 1980.
Donnelly, I., Ragnarok, The Age of Fire and Gravel. New York, D. Appleton, 1883.
Dundes, Alan (ed.), The Flood Myth. Berkeley, Univ. of Calif. Press, 1988.
Hœrbiger, H. and Philipp, F., Glazialkosmogonie. Berlin, 1913.
Kulp, J. L., Flood Geology. Journal of Am. Scient. Affiliations (1950) 2:1-15.
Tanaka, S., The Buried City of Pompei. New York, Madison Press, 1996.
Velikovsky, I., Ages in Chaos. Garden City, New York, Doubleday, 1952.
Velikovsky, I., Earth in Upheaval. Garden City, New York, Doubleday, 1955.
Velikovsky, I., Worlds in Collision. Garden City, New York, Doubleday, 1950.
Wenham, G., The Coherence of the Flood Narrative. VT (1978) 28:336-48.
White, J., Pole Shift. New York, Doubleday, 1980.
Wilson, I., Exodus, The True Story. San Francisco, Harper and Row, 1985.
Wood, R. M., The Dark Side of the Earth. London, Allen & Unwin, 1985.

3) Archaeology and Egyptology

Budge, E. W., Tutankhamen. New York, Bell Pub. Co., 1923.
Budge, E. W., The Book of the Dead. New Jersey, University Books, Inc., 1960.
Casson, L., The Ancient Mariners. New York, MacMillan Co., 1959.
Drege, J. P., and Buher, E. M., The Silk Road. Oxford, Facts On File, 1989.
Durant, W., Our Oriental Heritage. New York, Simon & Schuster, 1935.
Harden, D., The Phoenicians. New York, Fredrick A. Praeger, Inc., 1962.
Hodges, P., How the Pyramids Were Built. Longmead, Element Books, 1989.
James, S., The World of the Celts. London, Thames & Hudson Ltd, 1993.
Mercer, S. A. B., The Pyramid Texts, Volumes I-IV. New York, 1942.
Norman-Taylor, D., The Celts. New York, Time-Life Books, 1974.
Payne, R., The Splendor of Persia. New York, Alfred A. Knopf, 1957
Sitchin, Z., The Stairway to Heaven. New York, Avon Books, 1982.
Sprague de Camp, L., The Ancient Engineers. New York, Ballantine Books, 1988.
Time-Life, Age of God-Kings, 3000-1500 BC. VA, Time Life Books, 1987.
Time-Life, Barbarian Tides, 1500-600 BC. VA, Time Life Books, 1987.
Tompkins, P., Secrets of the Great Pyramid. New York, Harper, 1971.

Tompkins, P., Mysteries of the Mexican Pyramids. New York, Harper, 1976.
Torr, C., Memphis and Mycenae. Cambridge, Cambridge Univ. Press, 1896.
Wright, G. E., Biblical Archeology. PA, The Westminster Press, 1960.
Wright, R., et al., Gems and Minerals of the Bible. New York, Harper, 1970.

4) Sea Peoples

Ahlstrom, G. W., Who Were the Israelites? Winona Lake, 1986.
Albright, W. F., Syria, the Philistines and Phoenicia. CAH II, 2. Ch. 33, 1973.
Albright, W. F., The Sea Peoples in Palestine. Cambridge, 1975.
Barns, J. W. B., Five Ramesseum Papyri. Oxford, 1956.
Bennett J. et al., The Knossos Tablets. London, 1959.
Boardman, J., The Greeks Overseas. London, Thames and Hudson, 1980.
Bonfante, G., Who were the Philistines? AJA (1946) 50, 251-62.
Borghouts, J. F., Ancient Egyptian Magical Texts. Leiden, Brill, 1978.
Breasted, J. H., A History of Egypt. New York, C. Scribner's, 1933.
Breasted, J. H., Ancient Records of Egypt. Chicago, Univ. of Illinois Press, 1906.
Briquel, D., Les Pelasges en Italie. Rome, 1984.
Bryce, T. R., The Kingdom of the Hittites. Cambridge, 1999.
Burdajewicz, M., The Aegean Sea Peoples. Oxford, Oxford Univ. Press, 1990.
Cifola, B., Ramses III and the Sea Peoples. Orientalia (1988) 57:275-306.
Cornelius, F, Geistesgeschichte der Fruhzeit, vol. II, 2. Leiden, E. J. Brill, 1967.
Cornell, T. J., The Beginnings of Rome. London-New York, Routledge, 1995.
Desor, E., Lacustrian Constructions of the Lake of Neuchatel, Smithsonian, 1863.
Ehrlich, C. S., The Philistines in Transition. New York, E. J. Brill, 1996.
Fantar, M., Pheniciens et Carthaginois en Sardaigne. RSO (1969) 44: 7-21.
Friedrich, H., Velikovsky, Spanuth und die Seevölker. Berlin, Wörthsee, 1990.
Huxley, A., Achaeans and Hittites. Belfast, Belfast Univ. Press, 1968.
Lemche, N. P., Prelude to Israel's Past. Peabody Mass, Hendrickson, 1998.
Lewis, N., Greeks in Ptolemaic Egypt. Oxford, Clarendon Press, 1986.
Marangozis, J., The Pelasgians. Myths & Reality. Toronto, 2000.
Margolith, O., The Sea Peoples in the Bible. Wiesbaden, 1994.
Margolith, O., Where did the Philistines Come From? ZAW (1995) 107: 101-9.
Martin, K., Stele. Lexikon der Aegyptologie VI: 1-6, 1986.
Nibbi, A., Sea Peoples: A Re-examination of the Egyptian Sources. Oxford, 1972.
Nibbi, A., Wenamun and Alashia Reconsidered. Oxford, 1985.
Oren E. D., Sea Peoples and Their World. Philadelphia, 2000.
Prado, J. J., Invasion de la Méditerranée par les peuples de l'Océan. Paris, 1992.
Pugliese Carratelli, G. (ed.), I Greci in Occidente. Milan, 1995.
Santoro, N., Popoli del Mare. Santoro N, Bologna, 1980.
Velikovsky, I., Peoples of the Sea. Garden City, New York, 1977.

Woudhuizen, F., Language of the Sea Peoples. Amsterdam, F. Woudhuizen, 1992.

5) Mythology and Religion

Bellamy, H. S., Moons, Myths, and Man. London, Faber and Faber, 1936.
Bullen, J. B., The Sun is God. Oxford, Clarendon Press, 1989.
Burkert, W., Ancient Mystery Cults. Cambridge (MA), Harvard Univ. Press, 1987.
Campbell, J. and Moyers, W., The Power of Myth. New York, Doubleday, 1988.
Dundes, A., (ed.), The Flood Myth. Berkeley, Univ. of California Press, 1988.
Frazer, J. G., The New Golden Bough. New York, Criterion Books, 1983.
Gillon, A., Larousse Encyclopedia of Mythology. Paris, Larousse, 1987.
Graves. R., The White Goddess. New York, George Braziller, Inc. 1966.
Kirk, G. S., Myth, Its Meaning and Function. Cambridge Univ. Press, 1973.
Kirk, G. S., The Nature of Greek Myths. London, Penguin Books, 1990.
Wolkstein, D., and Samuel N. K., Inanna. New York, Harper and Row Publ., 1983.

6) Archaeoastronomy

Allen, R. H., Star Names, Their Lore and Meaning. New York, Dover, 1963.
Aveni, A. F., Skywatchers of Ancient Mexico. Austin, Univ. of Texas Press, 1980.
Blake, J. F., Astronomical Myths. London, Macmillan and Company, 1877.
Brown, P. L., Megaliths Myths and Men. New York, Harper and Row, 1976.
Krupp, E. C., ed., In Search of Ancient Astronomies. New York, McGraw-Hill, 1978.
Maffei, P., Monsters in the Sky. Cambridge, Mass., The MIT Press, 1980.
Neugebauer, O., The Exact Sciences in Antiquity. Brown, Brown Univ. Press, 1957.
Olcott, W. T., Star Lore of All Ages. New York, G. P. Putnam's Sons, 1914.
Pannekoek, A., A History of Astronomy. New York, Dover Publications, Inc., 1961.
Santilliana, G. de and von Dechend, H., Hamlet's Mill. London, Macmillan, 1969.
Temple, R. K. G., The Sirius Mystery. Rochester (VT), Inner Traditions, 1987.
Woolsey, J. M., The Original Garden of Eden Discovered. New York, 1910.

7) Crete

Alexious, S., Nikolas P., Ancient Crete. Athens, 1968.

Baikie, J., The Sea-Kings of Crete. London, 1926.

Bibby, G., The Testimony of the Spade. London, 1957.

Birchall, B., (ed.), Bronze Age Migrations in the Aegean. London 1973.

Cottrell, L., The Bull of Minos. Pan Books, London, 1955.

Evans, Sir A., The Palace of Minos. London, Macmillan, 1921-1935.

Fowden, E., The Early Minoan Goddess. JPR (1990) 3-4:15-18.

Furumark, A., Linear A and Minoan Religion. OpAth (1988)17: 51-90.

Graham, J. W., The Palaces of Crete. London, 1962.

Hägg, R., Marinatos, N., (eds.), Early Greek Cult Practice. Göteborg, 1988.

Hawes, C., and Hawes H. B., Crete, the Forerunner of Greece. London, 1909

Higgins, C. R., Minoan and Mycenaean Art. London, 1967.

Hood, S., Settlers in Crete c.3000 BC. Cretan Studies (1990) 2:151-158.

Marinatos, S., Crete and Mycenae. Athens, Greece, 1960.

Muhly, P., The Great Goddess and the Priest King. Expedition (1990), 32:3, 54-60.

Perez, R., Ringkampf mit dem Stier. Meriam (1959) XII:8-43.

Persson, A. W., The Religion of Greece in Prehistoric Times. Berkeley, 1942.

Rehak, P., The Aegean 'Priest'. Kadmos, CMS (1994) I:223.

Rouse, W. H. D., The Double Axe and the Labyrinth. JHS (1901) 21:268-274.

Ward, A., The Cretan Bull Sports. Antiquity (1968) 42:117-122.

Warren, P., The Origins of the Minoans. BICS (1969) 16:156-157.

Warry, J., Warfare in the Classical World. London, Salamander Books, 1980.

Willetts, R. F., Cretan Cults and Festivals. London, 1962.

Younger, J. G., A New Look at Aegean Bull-leaping. Muse (1983) 17:72-80.

Yule, P., Notes on Scarabs and Aegean Chronology. BSA (1983) 78: 359-367.

G. E. Mylonas, Mycenae and the Mycenaean Age. Princeton, 1966.

A. M. Snodgrass, The Dark Age of Greece. Edinburgh, Ire., 1971.

E. T. Vermeule, The Fall of the Mycenaean Empire. Archaeology (1960) 13:66-75.

J. Chadwick, Who Were the Dorians? PdP (1976) 31:103-117.

J. T. Hooker, New Reflections on the Dorian Invasion. Klio(1979) 61:353-360.

Z. Rubensohn, The Dorian Invasion Again. PdP (1975) 30:105-131.

C. G. Thomas, Found: the Dorians. Expedition (1978) 20:3:21-25.

P. G. van Soesbergen, The Coming of the Dorians. Kadmos (1981) 20:38-51.

8) Troy, Mycenae, Hittites

Andrewes, P., The Falls of Troy. Greece & Rome (1965) 12:28-37.

Blegen, C. W., Troy and the Trojans. London, 1963.

Drews, R., Argos and Argives in the Iliad. Classical Philology (1979) 74: 111-135.

Easton, D., Has the Trojan War Been Found? Antiquity (1985) 59:188-195.

Finley, M. I., Lost: the Trojan War, in: Aspects of Antiquity, N. York, 1969, 24-37.

French, E., A Reassessment of the Mycenaean Pottery. AS (1975) 25:53-75.

Garstang, J., The Geography of the Hittite Empire. London, 1959.

Güterbock, H. G., The Ahhiyawa Problem Reconsidered. AJA (1983) 87:133-138.

Hooker, J. T., Ilios and the Iliad. Wiener Studien (1979)13:5-21.

Leaf, W., Troy, A Study in Homeric Geography. London, 1912.

Mellink, M. J., (ed.), Troy and the Trojan War. Bryn Mawr, 198).

Mylonas, G. E., Priam's Troy and the Date of its Fall. Hesperia (1964) 33:352-380.

Minoan Thalassocracy: Myth and Reality. Stockholm, 1984, 183-185.

Nilsson, M. P., The Mycenaean Origin of Greek Mythology. Berkeley 1932.

Nylander, C., The Fall of Troy. Antiquity (1963) 37:6-11.

Page D. L., History and the Homeric Iliad. Berkeley, 1959.

Vermeule, E. T., Mythology in Mycenaean Art. Class J. (1958) 54:3:97-108.

Wood, M., In Search of the Trojan War. New York, Facts on File Publ., 1985.

Zangger, E., Ein neuer Kampf um Troia. Archäologie in der Krise, Munich, 1994.

ENDNOTES TO PART I

1   Many authors – some of them quite famous – have now adopted, even though they often fail to give me credit for it, the mechanism I originally proposed for the demise of Atlantis, viz. the end of the Ice Age and the sea level rise which then took place when the meltwater of the continental glaciers returned to the ocean.

Some of these authors, often journalists with no training whatsoever in either Science or Epistemology (the science of framing theories) formerly championed unscientific theories such as Pole Shift and an Antarctic Atlantis, despite the fact, now certain, that the southern continent has been under ice for over a million years.

Most, if not all, of my former hypotheses and arguments have already been amply confirmed by many sorts of finds and discoveries made by scientific investigators since I first proposed my Atlantis theory.

In particular, many scholars have now woken up to the reality of Catastrophism, and to the fact that Darwinian Evolution and Uniformitarian Geology are no more than sheer Victorian pseudo-Science at its worst, and rest upon nothing more than wishful thinking in attempting to deny the inescapable reality of the global cataclysms of which the ancient traditions so insistently speak.

I have also now made considerable further advances in the details of my theory on Ice Ages, one of the greatest scientific riddles ever. This updated theory is presented in our chapter on the Ice Ages. Many wholly new and unexpected empirical finds – among them the Heinrich Events and the Dansgaard-Oescher Events – have now been discovered, and thoroughly confirm my theory, as I comment in the chapter just mentioned.

Global cataclysms such as the Ice Ages and supervolcanisms of global proportions are now accepted as an inescapable reality which hits us all every once in a while, in intervals of 100 thousand years or so.

So are also giant meteoritic impacts like the one which annihilated the dinosaurs some 65 million years ago. These giant impacts – which probably extinguished Life on Mars and possibly Venus as well – are now thought to have caused some major extinctions which have occurred in the earth's distant geological past.

But the contribution apported by supervolcanoes and/or volcanic paroxysms still goes unrecognized, despite its great importance in Climatology. The frequency of these cataclysms is a whole order of magnitude larger than their extraterrestrial counterparts as is now known. So, the importance of these natural disasters in controlling the climate cannot be overstated.

Another of my seminal discoveries, which is now confirmed, concerns the date and nature of the cataclysm which caused the end of the Pleistocene Ice Age. This cataclysm was very probably a Heinrich Event, H0, as is fast becoming clear. And it was not only sudden and brutal, but occurred at the exact date stipulated by

Plato, that of 11,600 years ago. Moreover, this event also probably corresponds to MWP1B, given the fact that the date of the two events so closely corresponds.

So, it seems the great philosopher was right after all, despite the fact that most scientists still adamantly refuse to believe the reality of the Flood cataclysm or, even less, its identity with Atlantis' demise.

The nature of the cataclysm which caused the end of the Pleistocene Ice Age – the Heinrich Event just mentioned – also seems to be the result of the phenomena preconized by ourselves some 20 years ago, that is, the result of giant maritime invasions caused by giant tsunamis, themselves generated by explosive supervolcanic eruptions, as discussed in this text. Scientists have not yet wholly accepted this to be the real cause of Heinrich Events. But I am sure that they soon will, when they realize the importance of my discovery.

And this will come about when they realize the utter impossibility of the mechanism now held to have been responsible for these catastrophic events: the breaking open of giant lakes dammed by the glaciers themselves. As some geologists of great reputation have remarked, this damming by ice is geologically impossible. This occurs for several good reasons, one of them being the lack of mechanical resistance on the part of ice, which is by far too fragile for the purpose of damming so much water.

The reduction of global glacier albedo by volcanic soot deposition has recently been accurately measured by NASA's satellites. And it has been found to be so important as to be proposed as a possible cause for the termination of Ice Ages, just as we long ago predicted it would be. In other words, though in no way prophetic, our scientific predictions turned out to be remarkably accurate, the most stringent test for a scientific theory like mine.

In fact, these discoveries of mine are all rather obvious in hindsight, since they are so logical. And these proposals, though non-canonical, are strictly scientific. In time, I am sure that my theory will become, in whole or in part, a new paradigm uniting Science to Religion. This great synthesis seems to be forthcoming and to be what is really needed for the new millennium which just started, bringing new hopes and new vistas to all mankind.

We also note that the local traditions of Indonesia also tell of the opening of Sunda Strait in prehistoric times. This opening was done by a giant volcanic explosion of the volcano in its interior, the mighty Krakatoa. And some in situ researches, which we comment further below, also confirm the reality of this supervolcanic cataclysm, having verified that the whole region of Sunda Strait consists of giant volcanic calderas, some fully 50 kilometers in diameter, as demonstrated in Ken Wohletz' article linked here. [026]

These traditions were later transferred to the Mediterranean region such as Gibraltar and the Bosphorus straits, where they in fact never occurred, as no volcanoes exist in these regions of the world. These straits were opened in far earlier epochs, before the time of humans, as is now known for sure.

It is from this transference of myths that results the usual mistake of confusing these regions as the ones associated with Atlantis. When the Greeks and the Phoenicians, etc. moved from their pristine destroyed abode in Indonesia, they brought along their sacred traditions, which they transferred to the local features such as Gibraltar and the Bosphorus Straits, thus establishing and perpetuating the confusion of the sites.

The recent discovery of the tiny <u>Homo floriensis</u> in the Indonesian island of Flores – with a height of under five spans and a brain no larger than that of a chimpanzee, even though having what seems to be a modern braincase – is a dramatic confirmation of the fact that several human species have existed side-by-side on earth since earliest times. This in contrast to the currently predominant theories on human evolution such as Out-of-Africa and Multiregionalism, and even with Darwin's Evolution Theory itself, which preaches the survival of only the fittest of the species within a given geographical niche.

As some anthropologists determined, Flores Man apparently existed down to the end of the Pleistocene, some 11,600 years ago, and was apparently extinguished by a volcanic paroxysm in the region, rather than due to competition with other, larger hominids of the region (<u>Homo erectus</u> and <u>H. sapiens</u>).

This volcanic paroxysm was probably a part of the one leading to the catastrophic end of the Ice Age. In this context, the Flores hominid necessarily coexisted with the other hominids of the region: <u>Homo erectus</u>, known to have existed there since at least a million years ago and even more, and <u>Homo sapiens</u>, which migrated to that side of the world no later than 60,000 years ago, when its presence in Australia is first attested (<u>Mungo Man</u>). This date is close to the start of the last glaciation, so that this return to Eden may have been prompted by it. [027]

We often read that <u>Homo neanderthalensis</u> – a different species of humans which existed in Ice Age Europe and the Near East – became extinct some time before the end of the Pleistocene, some 30,000 years ago. Though this may be true in most of Europe, it seems that the Neanderthals survived till a much later period, in refuges such as the Iberian Peninsula and the Near East, where he even successfully mated with the other humans there.

There, these earlier humans survived down to the end of the Ice Age, when they apparently went finally extinct, at least as a different species or subspecies of humans. The same is also probably true of Cro Magnon Man. This hominid is sufficiently different from modern humans in both size and other physical features to warrant a classification as a different taxon, either as a species or a subspecies in its own right. It is foolish to confuse the Cro Magnons with the modern humans, as some people do.

Even though the Cro Magnons might have substantially contributed to our genepool it seems that, as a species or subspecies, they too actually became extinct at the catastrophic end of the Pleistocene. And we seem to be their decayed descendants, lesser in size and in brain, to believe both the paleoanthropological and the traditional evidence: the Cro Magnons, like the Neanderthals, were giants about 30% bigger and brainier than we modern humans are ourselves.

It is quite probable that the biblical reference to the fact that "there were giants on earth these days" actually referred to these giant human beings. The same probably holds in regards to the frequent references in the sacred traditions of many peoples – the Celts in particular – to the existence of "hobbits" such as gnomes and dwarfs in the region of Paradise, their primordial mythical homeland.

---

2   We well realize that all really novel theories such as mine sound a bit odd and even ridiculous when they are first proposed. Such was the case of Heliocentrism – which actually landed its proponents in jail. And such was also the case with the Relativity Theory, which was rejected by all scientists until some 15 years later, when Einstein finally gained the overt support of Sir Arthur Eddington, the famous British mathematician and astronomer.

Again, this was also the case of Heinrich Schliemann and his "Troy", which all archaeologists thought to be no more than sheer legend until he dug it out. Very much the same thing also happened with Alfred Wegener, the illustrious proponent of Continental Drift. And so with Louis Agassiz, when he originally proposed the reality of the Ice Ages. These examples could be multiplied almost ad infinitum, except for the risk of boring the dear reader.

We emphasize, once again, that our theory, in contrast to most, is strictly scientific and is founded on actual, empirically observed facts, rather than on speculation or on religion or tradition alone. In contrast, Theosophists basically derive their beliefs from Mme. Blavatsky, a Russian lady who moved to India in the 1860's, where she later founded the Theosophical Society, which enjoyed a considerable following among the intellectuals of her time.

Mme. Blavatsky was an extremely intelligent person, and soon amassed immense knowledge of Hindu and other esoteric traditions, which she published in books such as The Secret Doctrine and the Veil of Isis. Her writings seem an undigested version of the esoteric doctrines of Buddhism, Hinduism, and other religions and occult doctrines, mingled with some pseudo-science which she obtained from the geological and paleoanthropological textbooks of the time, which would all prove wrong in the course of time.

Pole Shift is a sheer unscientific fallacy that holds no water. It is impossible on both physical and geological grounds. These ideas originated with Edgar Cayce, the famous medium, and were later popularized by Charles Hapgood, an amateur researcher. These unscientific doctrines survive to date in bestselling writers such as John White and Graham Hancock. Rather than scientists, these authors are professional journalists, whose specialty is precisely rendering palatable to the public what are usually pseudo-scientific lies and propaganda.

John White has – along with most such proponents of the theory of Pole Shift, Charles Hapgood himself included – publicly recanted from his former views on this possibility, which he now recognizes as an impossibly unscientific misconception. Graham Hancock has now de facto dropped his former unscientific proposal of an Antarctic Atlantis in favor of my own hypothesis of a Far Eastern Atlantis, as his more recent writings unequivocally testify.

Immanuel Velikovsky was another unusual character and romantic researcher. Originally a Russian Jew and an émigré to the US, Velikovsky's wonderfully written books soon became the delight of all inquisitive persons who, in the 1950's, were discontented with the inconsistencies and paradoxes of Academic Science. Among these, I myself should also be counted, as his books opened my eyes to the faults of theories such as the ones of Darwin's Uniformitarian Geology and his infamous Theory of Evolution, likewise founded on precisely this false premise.

The problem with Velikovsky was taking the catastrophic events he proposed as the literal truth, actually occurring in biblical times. Moreover, as an orthodox

Jew, Velikovsky also believed the dates and events of the Bible such as Creation – ridiculously recent by any valid geological standards – to be actual facts which should be implicitly believed by all.

But Velikovsky's books – like the ones of Mme. Blavatsky and even of John White and Graham Hancock – are a very good read even today, so long as they are considered what they really are: pleasant, well written Science Fiction based on ill-digested, untenable pseudo-Science.

---

3   The two Atlantises referred by Plato and other mythographers actually correspond to the Mother and Son of the sacred traditions of most peoples on earth. In reality, the two divine figures – Mother and Son – really correspond to a succession, just as this type of myth implies. The Mother is actually the Great Mother of both Gods and Men, and corresponds to figures such as Isis, Hathor, Diana Multimammia, Durga, and so forth.

Lemuria proper, or Mu, never existed at all. The name of Lemuria derives from the one of the lemurs and was applied by the naturalists Haeckel and Sclater, etc., to designate the hypothetical landbridge across which the lemur (a primate) would have migrated from Africa to Indonesia or vice-versa. The name of Mu – which means "Mother" in Dravida – is often applied to Durga (Kali) in India. Kali is the Great Mother of which all traditions speak. And she actually impersons the older Atlantis, of which the "Son" was the virgin offspring.

Despite its inadequacy, we adopt the name of Lemurian Atlantis – or more simply, Lemuria – in order to designate the former Atlantis (the Mother) as distinct from the second one, the Son. As we said, the name and concept of Lemuria was misappropriated from Science by Mme. Blavatsky, who posited it as a mid-Pacific continent of vast extent where semi-spiritual beings first developed. However, despite its name, our Lemurian Atlantis (or Lemuria) should never be confused with the imaginary one of Blavatsky and other Theosophists.

Even at the risk of some repetition, in order to make it clearer to the dear reader, we recapitulate here the story of Atlantis from its inception, as we have been able to reconstitute if from a host of data both scientific and traditional. Man (Homo erectus) first migrated to Eden (Southeast Asia) soon after he appeared in Africa, at the start of the Pleistocene, some 2.7 Mya [Million years ago]. And Man apparently evolved in parallel both in Africa and in the Far East migrating back and forth as the Ice Ages came and went.

Conditions again became optimum in the Far East, and humans returned to it after the end of the Eemian Interglacial, some 115 kya [kiloyears ago], when sea level again went down, exposing Eden's Great Plain. This civilization flourished and eventually developed agriculture and civilization there, turning the region into the Garden of Eden. However, the Toba volcano went off 75 kya, in what was one of the greatest cataclysms ever.

Man barely survived it, being globally reduced to a very small number, ranging in the few thousand individuals. When local conditions eased, a few millennia later, humans returned to Eden, and progress was resumed anew. The first Atlantis – which we here name Lemuria (or Lemurian Atlantis) – is traditionally deemed the "Great Mother", whereas the second Atlantis is dubbed the "Son" in essentially all such traditions found the world over.

The Great Mother's "virginity" refers to the fact that she engendered all other civilizations on earth, without being "fertilized" herself, just as was the case with all subsequent civilizations on earth. The Great Mother is also the Mother of Cereals commemorated in personages such as the ones of Ceres, Demeter, Persephone (Kore), Annapurna, Saning Sari, and so on. The role of the Mother Goddess is discussed in detail by Sir James G. Frazer in his seminal Golden Bough (London, 1922). [o28]

Sir Frazer of course failed to solve the deep enigma posed by the Great Mother and her Golden Bough itself. But our solution of the riddle is rather obvious when all facts I adduce are considered. The name of Tamraparna (Sanskrit) or Tamaraparana (Dravida) actually means "golden bough" in those sacred tongues of India.

And the name of Ceres – like the one of cereals, actually derived from it – ultimately comes from the Dravida *sariči (or ariči) meaning "rice, cereal". From this base also derive words such as the English rice, Greek oryza, Latin cerealis, the surname of Saning Sari (or *sarici = "rice"), etc.. The fact that the name of "cereals" derives from Indian languages proves the origination of cereal agriculture there, in South India or Indonesia, where Dravida was spoken.

The Far Eastern origin of cereals such as rice – and even of Agriculture itself – also seems now proven by the early dates associated with rice culture in that region of the world, which are the earliest known so far. Rice agriculture is now archaeologically attested to have originated there as far back as 15,000 years ago, and probably even much earlier. Moreover, wild rice cropping is there attested to date from at least 25,000 years ago.

These dates are far earlier than the corresponding ones of the Near East. And they both date from the Pleistocene Epoch, the times of Atlantis, according to Plato. The first Atlantis – the Mother – was the one which started soon after the last Interglacial, the Eemian Period, which lasted from about 130 to 115 kya [kiloyears ago]. And it lasted down to the Toba cataclysm of 75 kya.

When the Ice Age started and sea level dropped by as much as 130–150 meters – which is usual during these epochs – the vast continent we have personally discovered and mapped in the region of Indonesia over two decades ago became exposed and subaerial. Rains almost ceased and the other regions such as Europe, the Near East and Africa became desertic, either as the result of desiccation or of being frozen and covered by mile-thick glaciers.

The humans who survived the cataclysm were forced out of these unbearably dismal regions into the newly exposed continent, which was tropical, pleasantly warm and, hence, pluvious and fertile. Agriculture thrived there, and Civilization eventually developed.

The Americas were then unpopulated, and humanity did not thrive there, at least to any great extent. Eventually, the first Atlantis – the Great Mother – rose to an apogee which is hard to diagnose in detail, at least until some more archaeological field research is carried out in the region, which has been neglected so far by most anthropologists and antiquarians of all shades.

This great luciferine civilization flourished for about 40 millennia, until the global cataclysm triggered by Toba's supervolcanic eruption wiped it off. The last glaciation – which also started more or less at this date – is now widely held to have resulted from this cause. In fact, humans were reduced to a scant few thousand people globally, and almost became altogether extinct, just as happened to several other animal and plant species.

The earth afterwards entered one of the direst Ice Ages ever, and full recovery of the site of Eden took several millennia. But it is easy to imagine the heights attained by this great civilization in that enormous span of time. No matter what, conditions eventually normalized in the region of Indonesia, and it again became paradisial. People returned, and progress was again resumed, this time for about 60 millennia or so, until the end of the Pleistocene.

This second Atlantis was eventually labeled the "Son of the Virgin", who is often held to have gone berserk and to have "devoured her own children". This is of course an allegory of the fact that the soil of the region of Sumatra – where the Toba Volcano is actually located – caved in into a giant caldera which literally swallowed the unfortunate people then living there. It is a feature of Indonesia that such tragedies occur again and again, "like some sort of recurring pestilence', just as Plato himself affirmed.

A similar tragedy would again occur at the end of the Pleistocene, this time caused by the no less ferocious Krakatoa supervolcano. The recent cataclysm there – though of far smaller proportions – well attests the changing moods of the Great Mother. Small wonder then that the Hindus call her Kali ("Black One"), an allusion not to her skin color, but to her somber, unpredictable temperament. This name has also to do with the eras (Kali = "Time", in Sanskrit, the sacred language of India), whose dire ends she and Shiva (Kala) periodically bring about.

The third "Atlantis" – this time a paler replica – would again occur in the Indus Valley region, the oldest and most impressive of the ancient civilizations so far known. Its demise occurred, above all, due to the desiccation of the whole region which took place at about 3,100 BC, due to the partial exhaustion of the great Himalayan glaciers which are in fact a meager relict of the Ice Age. This date corresponds to what the Hindus identify with the start of the Kali Yuga, which they place at 3,102 BC to the day and the hour.

These three "Atlantises" and their eras correspond to what the Hindus call the Trimurti (or Trinity). They also correspond to other triple features, for instance, Tripura, the "Triple City" destroyed by Shiva. As such, Tripura also evokes Shiva's trident and his "tripartite arrow", the one used in destroying Tripura. Above all, the three correspond to the three elapsed Eras of Mankind, with us presently living in the fourth, the Kali Yuga.

---

4 Tektites are glass beads and concretions resulting from giant meteoritic (or cometary) falls or, perhaps, from gigantic volcanic explosions as well, as was possibly the case here. These giant collisions scatter tektites far and wide, as in the above case. The ones in question here are called Indochinites, in an allusion to the region where they abound the most. Indochina is the name of Indonesia during colonial times.

The Indochinites have been dated at 750 kiloyears (one kiloyear = one thousand years). The explosion of Lake Toba took place 75 kyears ago. The even larger one of Lake Taupo in New Zealand took place at about 100 kyears ago or so. Mt. Yellowstone, now overdue for a new giant explosion according to experts, exploded some 600 kya or so ago. As is now becoming apparent to experts, volcanoes formerly thought to be extinct are now known to be merely dormant, and may wake up in time in colossal explosions fully able to destroy the whole world.

These supervolcanoes may trigger both the Ice Ages and their catastrophic terminations, just as we have long been arguing. These giant explosions, which mainly occurred in the region of Indonesia – volcanically and seismically the most active in the whole world – are large enough to trigger Ice Ages on or, conversely, their cataclysmic endings. However, whether one is indeed caused depends on other conditions, probably dictated by insolation (sunshine) and other such variables, astronomical or not, which modulate earth's climate.

As we just commented, the region of Indonesia has literally hundreds of active or dormant volcanoes. But it has been very little researched so far, mainly due to its remoteness and present poverty. Further research of the Indonesian region will – now that its connection with the birthplace of Mankind has been pointed out – certainly confirm the reality of what we are claiming here.

Indonesia is part of the Pacific "Fire Belt", and the extreme violence of its volcanoes, earthquakes and tsunamis has been recently attested by the colossal disasters which just happened there. Our predictions concerning the disaster-prone nature of the region of Indonesia have undergone an undesired confirmation with these recent disasters. We hope that they suffice to convince people of the reality of what we claim before it is too late.

Our research is strictly scientific and is based both on climatological and geological data, as well as on very detailed local traditions. Likewise, our views are the fruit of almost three decades of study of the myth of Atlantis-Eden from a strictly scientific, unbiased point-of-view. We have no axes to grind but the truth, and push no religious, scientific, philosophic or mercenary purposes, as most experts unfortunately do.

As the ancient Latins used to say, *Amicus Plato, magis amica veritas* ("Plato is a friend, but truth is an even closer friend"). It is our belief that the sacred traditions of the ancients embody prehistoric events in a highly stylized, codified manner. The ancients loved to play on words to convey the truth, as our present text demonstrates. Hence, all we have to do is to attempt to learn to decode these ancient myths and odd rituals in order to recover the embedded reality. But this is a difficult art which has taken me many years of study to master.

We note that the recent investigation of the prehistoric behavior of the Krakatoa Volcano done by Ken Wohletz, a volcanologist working in Los Alamos Laboratory (linked here), has dramatically confirmed our predictions made about two decades ago. The Krakatoa is really a supervolcano that has repeatedly erupted in an explosive way many times in the past, and particularly during the Late Pleistocene and the start of the Holocene, when the Ice Age was ending in a catastrophic way, apparently due to a volcanic paroxysm of some sort. [029]

As we already said, Wohletz was working in collaboration with David Keys, and hence tended to believe, along with him, that the giant Krakatoa eruption which caused the opening of Sunda Strait, as reported in the <u>Pustaka Raja Purwa</u>, occurred in the early Middle Ages (535 AD), decreeing the end of the Roman Empire. Now, this is a very recent, historical date, by any standards, and is hence hard to accept.

Moreover, the in situ research conducted by other volcanologists failed to confirm this recent date, in turn supporting the Late Pleistocenic and Early Holocenic eruptions which we just adduced. So, this recent date should be taken with a lot of caution, as it is unsupported by any direct or indirect volcanological evidence whatsoever, despite Keys' insistent contention.

This subject of course requires further volcanological research. But the fact is that this very recent date postulated by both Ken Wohletz and David Keys is actually impossible, given the fact that the legend on the opening up of Sunda Strait told in the <u>Pustaka Raja Purwa</u> and other traditions is far earlier than the medieval date of 535 AD they have been claiming on rather slight indirect evidence that seems very tenuous to ourselves.

Moreover, this legend also passed to Greece and Rome far earlier than that, another evidence of the utter impossibility of the relatively recent date in question here. No matter what, except for this delusion, Wohletz' computer simulation of the Krakatoa's supereruption is a peerless masterpiece of detailed information on this important matter.

And so is his article on it, just linked above. As can be seen in this article, there are several distinct calderas of the Krakatoa, obviously attesting several different prehistoric supereruptions of the terrible volcano, some possibly simultaneous or mutually triggered in a serial paroxysm. We eagerly anticipate their actual dating by some reliable method, perhaps sedimentological or in situ.

One should also observe in his article, the giant size of the "pillar of fire and smoke" which normally attend this kind of supereruption. It is this giant "pillar" – fully 50 kilometers high and 150 kilometers across – which gives the name of "Pillar of Heaven" to these singular geological features.

No one who closely studies the magnificent simulations of the Krakatoa prehistoric supervolcanic eruptions presented in that article and pauses to ponder them over will, we are sure, fail to realize the real nature of these giant "pillars" and "umbrellas" of which the ancient myths so insistently speak.

By the way, some experts write "Krakatau", where others prefer to write "Krakatoa". Which is the preferable form of the name? It is true that the Indonesian name of the famous volcano is Krakatau. But the European form is Krakatoa, a name which allegedly resulted from a misunderstanding on the part of a journalist working on its formidable eruption of 1883. This large eruption was the one that caused a giant tsunami which caused the death of fully 40,000 people (and probably many more) directly and due to its terrible aftereffects.

The name of the Krakatoa apparently derives from the Sanskrit <u>krakača</u>, meaning "saw" or "sword". This Sanskrit word ultimately derives from the Dravida <u>krakaśa</u>, also meaning the same. It is quite possible that the journalist who spelled the name as "Krakatoa" learnt it from a native using the more vernacular form krakaśa, which resembles "krakatoa" more than "krakatau".

As is clear, the Indonesian language merely uses a corrupt form of the ancient Indian name of the volcano. And why should one actually prefer the Indonesian form over the other, more vernacular one also obtained from a local language perhaps directly derived from Dravida or Sanskrit?

Be that as it may, it seems more reasonable to me to cling to the now more usual form of the name, "Krakatoa", as most experts have done. And the above etymology actually shows that its name and concept both date from a hoary antiquity, when these sacred languages of India were still spoken in the whole region of Indonesia. This evidence is further proof of the geological fact we just stated: the separation of Java and Sumatra by a giant explosion of the Krakatoa volcano long precedes the date given by David Keys and Ken Wohletz.

The above curious etymology of "saw" or "sword" apparently refers to the fact that the Krakatoa eruption actually separated Java from Sumatra, as if cut off by the action of a saw or a sword. This separation of the two islands is told in a great many myths of this and other regions. One is the legend of Hercules opening the Pillars of Hercules which, as we already saw, ultimately derives from the Indonesian historic traditions. Another is the Rigvedic myth on Indra opening up the bellies of mountains which we quoted further above.

Still another connected myth concerns the tradition of the Split Mountain of Paradise which we comment in more detail in Part III of the present book. In Mesopotamian mythology this myth concerns Mt. Mashu, whose name means precisely "Split Mountain". It was from this mountain that the sun (Shamash) was said to rise daily, in order to start the new day.

All this is of course an allegory of the successive Atlantean fiery cataclysms and the eras ("days") they decree. Curiously enough, Shamash, the sun, emerges from the Split Mountain with a saw in his hand. So, the connection with the Krakatoa volcano is very hard to deny, unless a better explanation is offered. This type of motif also figures in the Bible in the myth of Jahveh splitting, with his sword or scimitar, Leviathan or Rahab. [030]

This seamonster is the primordial serpent which the Hindus call Ahi or Shesha. And this serpent is an alias of the volcano itself so imaged because it sheds long threads of whitish pumice stone. This passage is quoted in full above, in the main text, and needs no repetition here. And its context is clearly connected with the Flood and the mass migrations it caused.

This curious Jewish myth is now known to have been copied from Phoenician and/or Mesopotamian mythology concerning Aleyan Baal, the mighty god who also performed a similar feat. Aleyan Baal is an alias of Hercules (Baal), so that these parallels are most perfect. But the clinching argument is afforded by the actual form of Indonesia in the region of Sunda Strait, between Java and Sumatra.

This region is the very one where the Krakatoa volcano exists now submerged under the waters of Sunda Strait. As can be seen in this map here, the land in the region resembles a giant with his sword (or saw) raised, in the act of sundering Java and Sumatra in the region corresponding to the Krakatoa volcano, the "saw". How can one scientifically account for, by means of empirically verifiable causes, such uncanny coincidences except as the result of diffusion from one place to another, even if academic opinion – so often erroneous – opposes this view? [031]

ENDNOTES TO PART III

5 In the <u>Subject Index</u>, at the end of the present book, we present a short Atlantean Glossary on certain of these essential terms used by Plato in connection with Atlantis. This glossary briefly glosses each term listed, but is far from thorough or complete. It briefly covers the essential terms having an initiatic character which were used as double entendres by the great philosopher; words such as "ocean", "island", "opposite", "outer continent", "Atlantic Ocean", "earthquake", "flood", "mud", etc..

In the text that follows we also gloss some of the terms which we deem essential for a proper understanding of Plato's texts. This explanation is extremely important for all who strive to understand what the prince of philosophers really meant by words and names such as these, when he used them in connection with Atlantis. After all, words change in the course of time, so that these terms all had, in his time, a meaning which is often radically different from what they mean nowadays.

The reader is also advised to research these terms and keywords in full, either on the Internet or in specialized treatises, glossaries and encyclopedias. Plato really wrote for the members of his Academy. Plato's disciples and colleagues were all initiates. When dealing with matters having to do with initiatic issues such as the secret of the Mysteries, Plato invariably used these double entendres and wordplays so that, while the profanes understood something, the initiates understood quite something else.

This procedure was standard in Greece with myths, initiatic sagas and romances such as the <u>Odyssey</u> and the <u>Iliad</u>, not to mention their many counterparts everywhere. For instance, what Plato and other ancients really meant when they said that "the island of Atlantis lay opposite to the Pillars of Hercules" is nearly universally understood to signify that Atlantis lay just ahead of Gibraltar Strait. But such is not the case at all, factually speaking, for a series of reasons which are easy to understand.

First, there were a great many "Pillars of Hercules", some inside, some outside the Mediterranean Sea. Even the Indian and the Pacific Oceans had their own "Pillars of Hercules". Second, the Greek word actually used by Plato (<u>pro</u>) may also mean "antipodal", rather than "opposite, facing, in front of". So, while the profanes got the wrong message, the true initiates understood the correct one, the idea of "antipodal".

We will return to this interesting topic further below. Again, when Plato referred to the "True Ocean" (or "Western Ocean", "Outer Ocean" or "Atlantic Ocean") he really meant not what we now understand by that term, but the "World Ocean" now so named, the sum total of all interlinked oceans. Even more exactly, by "Atlantic Ocean", Plato (and other ancients) usually meant the Pacific Ocean, rather than the Atlantic Ocean of today, deemed to be the eastwards extension of this "true ocean" then known from the east alone.

The name of the Atlantic Ocean – which eventually got permanently transferred to what we presently call by that name – is actually a misnomer resulting from some confusions we discuss in more detail next. And this confusion mainly resulted from the fact that most ancients ignored the existence of America, believing, much as did Columbus and other navigators, that the Atlantic Ocean now so-called extended all the way to the East Indies, where they well knew that the formerly paradisial "Atlantic Island" was actually located.

The very word "ocean" – originally derived from the Greek okeanos – ultimately comes from the Sanskrit aśayana and means "round-going", that is, "going around the earth, in a circle". This name alone should serve to prove our thesis sufficiently. But there is more, much more to it. As Plato affirms in his famous dialogues on the Lost Continent, Solon learnt the history of Atlantis from the Egyptian priests, and translated the names and corresponding geographical and geological features from that tongue into the Greek one.

Plato also adds that the Egyptians in turn did the same when they originally learnt the history of Atlantis from some undisclosed source whose identity he most unfortunately declines to specify. And we have, after a great many years of dedicated study, been able to identify this undisclosed source to India and its two main sacred languages, Sanskrit and Dravida. India's sacred traditions and holy books are both vast and extremely rich and detailed, particularly in what concerns the myth of Paradise Lost.

This serendipitous discovery has allowed us to reconstruct in detail not only the initiatic message of Plato's and similar texts on Atlantis, but even the geological and climatological reality of the sobering events the great philosopher so convincingly narrates. From then on, our work was mainly of "reverse engineering", reconstructing what the philosopher and others ancient authorities (Indian included) really meant by their cryptic myths, their sagas and their pseudo-historical narratives.

Were it not for this important discovery of ours, we would never have been able to decode these secrets and, even less, realized the unique geological reality of Atlantis' demise and its connection with Eden and the Flood. The very universality of these myths serves to prove their hoary age and the Pleistocenic date of their occurrence, which of necessity took place before the Beringian Passage got closed by the rise in sea level.

In the present chapter we also comment in some detail the issue of Taprobane, the true archetype of the "Atlantic Islands" or "Isles of the Blest". These islands were of old believed to be the remainders of Atlantis as both the paradisial abode of the blessed elects and the site of Hell itself. These islands were in fact the highlands of Atlantis, the mountains which remained emerse when the huge continent sank under the rising waters of the ocean at the end of the Ice Age, some 11,600 years ago.

Curiously enough, this is the exact date of the Atlantean cataclysm quoted by Plato, an uncanny coincidence, to say the least. The divine philosopher also specifically identifies this cataclysm with the Universal Flood, in a way which leaves little room for doubting the reality of the global disaster. In the present chapter we also collect and amplify the material on the Isles of the Blest and on the "Atlantic Islands", of which the island of Taprobane was perhaps the most important of all in antiquity.

Taprobane is even today believed to have been the actual site of Paradise Lost by the Hindus. Hence its great importance to all of us who seek Atlantis' whereabouts now that we know that the Lost Continent was in fact the site of Paradise Lost. The Dravidian Hindus also know this sunken continent by the name of Kumari Kandam, and affirm to have come from there, in the dawn of time, when it sank away, at the end of the last Ice Age, some 11,600 years ago.

In the present chapter we also review the many sites for Atlantis so far proposed by previous researchers, over the centuries. For the older authorities, our text is based in the detailed review of the subject made by L. Sprague de Camp, a great researcher of the theme of Atlantis. The themes of Atlantis, the Flood, and Paradise Lost have undergone a considerable revival in recent times, perhaps fostered by our own research on the matter, which opened new trends and new geologically tenable possibilities for Atlantology as a whole.

In consequence, a great number of authors – several of whom are accredited academics and scientists – have been writing on the Lost Continent and related matters. Many of these Atlantologists, some serious, some mere hoaxers, have published their research on the Internet, which holds literally hundreds of articles and homepages describing their claimed finds and allegations. We also include these modern authors in our list and in the present critical review in order, above all, to orient the average reader on the often questionable validity of their claims concerning Atlantis and its possible location.

---

6 We note that the curve on the site just linked records rises of 30 meters and more in under a few centuries or so. How much under is hard to tell from the data in question. In fact, the rise must have been far faster in order to cause the tropical corals to drown, rather than build up at the measure that sea level rose. For all we know, these rises may have been essentially instantaneous, due to meltwater pulses or massive Heinrich Events. Compare, f. i., the graph here, where the large rise at 11,600 years ago is virtually instantaneous. [122]

This sudden rise corresponds to what is technically known as MWP1B (Meltwater Pulse 1B), which is an essentially instantaneous massive injection of glacier meltwater. The cause of this pulse is uncertain, and is perhaps due to the breakaway of dammed lakes of glacier meltwater or, more likely, the carrying off to the sea of huge flotillas of icebergs, perhaps by giant tsunamis or similar maritime invasions.

We note that MWP1B probably caused the abrupt flooding away of the Sunda Shelf, as commented in this recent scientific article here. This sea level rise of 30 meters or more is known to have occurred within one or two centuries at most, and was very probably essentially instantaneous in nature. As the article just linked (and others related to it) shows, the whole of the Sunda Shelf was suddenly flooded by MWP1B; assuming its maritime character then, to become the South China Sea. [123]

The reader should observe that this meltwater pulse occurred at the exact date specified by Plato, of 11,600 BP [Before Present]. Hence, ordinary commonsense, as well as standard scientific practice (Ockham's Razor) require that we at least attempt to identify the two events. We also note that the article in question also demonstrates that this cataclysmic flooding of the Sunda Shelf resulted from the opening of Sunda Strait, which connected the Sunda Shelf with the Indo-Pacific Ocean.

The catastrophic opening of Sunda Strait was probably due to a giant eruption of the Krakatoa volcano, perhaps the very one which actually triggered MWP1B. This giant eruption broke off the Antarctic glaciers by means of the giant tsunami it caused in the Indian Ocean. At least one research team – that of Peter Clark from Oregon State University and colleagues – has concluded that the source of this MWP was the Antarctic glaciers and that the event is somehow connected with the flooding of the Sunda Shelf. Cf. also here and here and here and here and here and here. [124]

The cause and nature of this catastrophic event is still unexplained. So, it is tempting to identify these two simultaneous events with each other: the opening of Sunda Strait by the giant volcanism and the MWP1B, both of which occurred at the exact date given by Plato. We believe that we have the explanation of the events which led to the catastrophic end of the last Pleistocene Ice Age, which also took place at the exact date given by Plato: 11,600 years ago. We present a brief outline of the main geological events leading to the abrupt flooding of the lowlands of the Indonesian region here:

1) A supervolcanic eruption of the Krakatoa volcano, attended by caldera formation and the opening of Sunda Strait, created a giant tsunami in the Indian Ocean. This giant wave broke off the Antarctic glaciers, which then extended up to South Africa and Tasmania. Sea level then rose abruptly, by 30 meters and more (MWP1B) as these ice shelves drifted off to warmer seas.

2) The resulting crustal stresses of enormous potency caused by this extra water then triggered a veritable chain reaction of giant tsunamis, earthquakes and volcanisms, which fast destroyed the glaciers both on land and on sea. This is a positive feedback process which quickly led to the end of the Ice Age. The rafting of the North American glaciers was probably the consequence of the giant maritime invasions caused by these giant tsunamis.

3) The sudden flooding of the Sunda Shelf by the sea would be most disastrous to the people living on the whole expanse. It would flood the entire region, swamping out the paddy fields, and hence destroying the extensive rice crops and food sources of Atlantis mentioned by Plato.

4) As a consequence of this disastrous flooding, people would be deprived of their staple food, rice, and would starve en masse, in one of the greatest catastrophes ever to hit humankind. Such major human disasters are now well-documented, and can hardly be denied anymore. The recent disaster in Indonesia – one of the greatest ever, killing fully 400,000 people or even more – is proof sufficient that this whole region is disaster prone, and is periodically devastated by such major catastrophes since the remotest past.

There is also a considerable evidence of similar giant maritime invasions of a sudden, cataclysmic nature provided by geological features such as drumlins and scablands, particularly evident in the continent of North America. These features provide evidence of giant floods which somehow managed to loft enormous areas of continental glaciers, perhaps rafting them off to sea. [125]

The methods used to study the mechanism of sea level rise in question here do not record instantaneous events such as, say, giant tsunamis, but only determine the average values of sea level rise lasting long enough to cause coral reef drowning and stranding. Put otherwise, scientific curves are smoothened by averaging, and fail to record the sharp peaks associated with almost instantaneous changes wrought by sudden maritime invasions and tsunamis.

Actually, the uncertainty in the graph here is about ±25 meters, an enormous amount in sea level variation, which is normally measured in a few millimeters per century or so. The very fact that the end of the Pleistocene was attended by widespread mass extinctions of all sorts tells the tale of its sudden, catastrophic nature. Cf. also here and here and here and here. The last of these links is very interesting, as it provides solid evidence that the end of the Pleistocene was caused by a volcanic paroxysm of sorts, just as we have been arguing for the last two decades and more. [↑126]

We also note that the inescapable reality of catastrophic extinctions of global extension irrefutably prove the falsity of Darwinian Uniformitarian Evolution. Darwinian Evolution and Darwinian Geology are both Uniformitarian in nature, and cannot be amended in order to comply with the realities of Catastrophism. As a matter of fact, both the above aged Victorian doctrines were devised by Darwin and Lyell for the specific purpose of disproving the Catastrophist views of earlier researchers such as Baron Cuvier, Comte de Buffon and William Buckland who, of course, believed in the reality of the Flood as most well-informed persons presently do. [↑127]

Much as Darwinism once pretentiously ousted Catastrophism, Catastrophism now returns revived and triumphant in order to debunk Darwinian Evolution. Any attempt to save that doomed, outdated, unscientific Victorian theory is wholly specious, and must be faced as such by all persons interested in truth, rather than in convenience. This outdated Victorian theory is an offshoot of Polygenism, and was concocted in order to further the Colonial interests of the British Empire during the Victorian Age.

According to Sir Karl Popper, the basic requisite for a theory to be deemed scientific is that it be falsifiable. If a theory cannot be falsified, that theory is to be deemed unscientific, period. Darwinian Evolution and Darwinian Geology are both based on the Uniformity Principle, the main tenet of both. Moreover, this principle – postulated by the two scholars but never actually proved – is the very foundation of Darwinian Evolution Theory, even today taught in essentially all primary and academic institutions the world over. [↑128]

The Uniformity Principle frontally denies the possibility of global cataclysms of an unusual nature such as the Flood and the Ice Ages. But the reality of these global cataclysms is now established beyond any reasonable doubt. Hence, Darwinian Evolution has been irretrievably falsified by well-established geological facts and the only acceptable solution is to trash the whole theory as outdated and unscientific.

---

7   Hæckel's Lemuria is an unreal, gigantic landbridge which theoretically stretched all the way from Madagascar in Africa to the central Pacific region, far

beyond the Far East. This landbridge – which in fact never was – pretensely served to explain the diffusion of lemurs (a small primate) all the way from Madagascar in Africa to Indonesia, where they also abound.

Even worse is Col. Churchward's Mu, the huge sunken continent of the mid-Pacific. Most experts concluded that "Col. Churchward" was a fraud, and so were his alleged discoveries in the central Pacific region. Curiously enough, Hæckel's proposal is quaintly reminiscent of some ancient conceptions of Taprobane as a mythical sunken land in this (wrong) region of the world.

But Plate Tectonics Theory eventually rendered Hæckel's hypothesis superfluous, and it was finally discarded. Both Mu and Lemuria were fated to doom, as soon as geologists realized they never existed at all. With their scholarly demise, these fabled sunken lands soon fell in discredit among the public, and Theosophy soon lost its former popularity, except perhaps within certain circles of dedicated devouts.

However, it is quite possible that Haeckel and others – who made a lot of in situ research – actually heard the legends on sunken continents which are recurrent in the whole region of the South Seas. And so, they got their inspiration – as is so often the case – and decided to transfer Lemuria to the realm of scientific hypothesis. In fact, this is the way Science advances.

New proposals are tentatively accepted, tested out, and discarded as soon as they are found to be invalid. Curiously enough, the name of Lemuria seems to be connected with the dead ancestors. The name of the lemurs – the eerie nocturnal primates of the whole region – is derived from the one of the Roman ancestors, known as lemures, due to their spooky habits. The name of Lemuria is derived from the one of the feast (Lemuralia), where the dead ancestors of the Romans were commemorated. [129]

These dead ancestors are of course the same as the dead Atlanteans, killed en masse by the cataclysm which ended up submerging the whole place. This coincidence is extremely important. First, it shows the reality of the great carnage, in fact the one of the Flood. Second, the connection with Indonesia and the Far East cogently proves that these terrible events actually happened there. No matter what, it is interesting to observe the capricious way in which these proto-historical events keep coming back to us in such surreal ways.

---

8   These names respectively mean, in Latin or Greek: "Sea of Atlas" (Atlanticus Mare); "Sea of Cronus" (Kronius Mare); "Great Sea" (Mare Magnum); "True Ocean" (Alethinos Okeanos); "Ocean Sea" (Mare Oceanus); Occidental Ocean (Occidentalis Oceanus); Oriental Sea (Eous Mare) and, more simply, "Ocean" (Latin: Oceanus; Greek: Okeanos = "going around"). Another of its common epithets was Mare Externum ("Outer Sea").

Marco Polo, in his Travels, calls the Pacific Ocean – which he reached from China, via the Silk Road – by the name of Mar Ozeano ("Ocean Sea"). And the great explorer also explains that this Ocean Sea is the true ocean, the other seas and oceans being merely its arms or extensions. This fact shows where Columbus actually obtained the name of his Mar Oceano.

Columbus also named the Sargasso Sea in accordance with the ancient traditions on the Pacific Ocean as a sea loaded with dangerous sargassos (sea-reeds or kelp) strong enough to cause ships to wreck. This pristine tradition on the Sargasso Sea derives from India, as is so often the case. It has also to do with the "innavigable sea" of Atlantis as reported by Plato and others. In the famous Map of Ptolemy, this perilous sea is the Pacific Ocean, and is literally named <u>Mare Prasodum</u> ("Sea of Sargassos").

We will return to this theme further below, when we discuss the Ocean citing the ancient texts of Plato, Homer and Herodotus, among several other Classical authorities. In the Orphic traditions, Kronos (or Saturn) was usually identified with Hercules. Cf. Damascius, <u>De Principiis</u> 123b; Athenagoras, <u>Pro Christianis</u>, 18:20, and the comments on these passages made by Kirk and Raven in their seminal book on the pre-Socratic philosophers of ancient Greece.

This undeniable fact is of extreme practical importance. The twin figures of Atlas and Hercules, the two main rulers of Atlantis, are often confused. And this is particularly the case in relation to their famous pillars, attributed sometimes to one or to the other hero, or even to both of them. Atlas and Hercules are also the same as Atlas and Gadeiros, the twin rulers of Atlantis, according to Plato. Gadeiros is an alias of Geryon, himself the older avatar of Hercules, and he also seems to be the alias of Atlas himself.

These two personages ultimately derived from the ones of Krishna and Balarama, the two greatest heroes of Hindu mythology. In reality, we have two such pairs of pillars, one in Gibraltar, attributed to Hercules, and one in Indonesia (Malacca Strait) attributed to Atlas. The fact that these pillars were indifferently attributed to both Atlas and Hercules can be checked, for instance, <u>here</u> and in the many sources quoted therein. ⌐130

We will comment this crucial dualism further below in detail. Suffice it to say here that the true Pillars of Atlas are the ones of Indonesia, and that the ones in Gibraltar or in the Bosphorus, etc., are no more than virtual "mirror images" of no great importance. In fact, every such feature has its true archetype in the Far East, and its "mirror image" in the Far West, at the opposite side of the world.

It is strange to realize the close way in which Greco-Roman mythology and religion ultimately derive from Hindu archetypes. But this strangeness is merely the result of the widespread bias that human civilizations sprang independently from each other, which is false. It is merely the result of <u>opinion</u>, generally unscientific and unsupported by any evidence whatsoever.

In fact, the ancient traditions are full of detailed references to Civilizing Heroes and their civilizing influence: Cadmus, Hercules, Atlas, Aeneas, Neoptolemus, Cecrops, Oannés, Gilgamesh, etc.. Even the Americas are no exception to this rule: Sumé, Tamandaré, Jurupari, Quetzalcoatl, Viracocha, Bochica, and so on. Actually, it is apparently impossible to find a single tradition which ascribes the invention of agriculture and similar arts and techniques to purely local efforts rather than to those of outsiders.

As we said above, the word "ocean" (Grk. <u>okeanos</u>; Lat. <u>oceanus</u>) ultimately derives from the Sanskrit <u>asayana</u> according to Kirk and Raven and some other experts. The Skt. <u>asayana</u> means "round-going", and implies the idea of a water body encircling the earth all around, as the ocean in fact does.

In the ancient conception, the Ocean encircled the earth all around, like some sort of encircling ring (the Ouroboros Serpent). Even Homer depicts the world thus encircled by the Ocean (Il. 18:607, etc.). And so do many authorities, Plato included. Herodotus tells that "the ocean begins in the orient (east), where the sun is born" (Hist. 4:8) and that it encircles the earth (Hist. 4:36). Homer repeatedly uses the epithet of apsorrhoos ("which flows back into itself"), implying the idea of the Ocean's circularity.

Herodotus further adds (Hist. 1:202) that "the sea frequented by the Greeks (the Mediterranean?), that beyond the Pillars of Hercules – which is called the Atlantic and also the Erythraean (Indian Ocean) – are all one and the same sea." The idea is again of the circular ocean. These references to the Circular Ocean, often named Atlantean or Kronius, could be multiplied ad nauseam.

We note that the World Ocean in fact encircles the earth all around along the Line of the Equator but for small interruptions now bypassed in Suez and in Panama. The "earth" in question here should be understood as the Tierra Firme a concept which we clarify in more detail next. In some texts it corresponds to the Old World (Oikumene) and in others to the Peirata Ges (the Americas) of which Plato spoke.

Several other ancient sources also affirm that the sun is born from the ocean (e. g., Homer, Il. 7:422; Hesiod, Theog. 775; Mimnermus, fragm. 10, Stesichoros, fragm. 6:1, Apuleius, Flor. 6; etc.). The sun is invariably said to arise in pristine Ethiopia, the Land of Dawn. And this Far Eastern Ethiopia is precisely the site of Indonesia (Eoos), where the Ocean starts, according to Herodotus' passage just referred.

A close study of the above passages (and several others such) suggests the idea that the sun crossed the ocean after it set in Gibraltar, and then returned to the orient, where it rested overnight, and thence rose again in order to start the new day. Apuleius (op. cit.) affirms that the sun rises in Indonesia (India extra Gangem): "where the ocean returns upon itself and the sun rises" (prope oceani reflexus et solis exortus).

This world conception is discussed in our figures section, where we show an ancient Egyptian vase of the pre-Dynastic Period illustrating this curious belief. Justinus (Epit. 1:2:9) affirms that "Alexander invaded India aiming to extend his empire to the control of the Ocean and the Extreme Orient" (Oceano ultimoque Oriente). In other words, the Atlantic Ocean was apparently believed to extend all the way to the Orient, being coterminous and one with the Pacific Ocean, the "Ocean" proper.

Columbus, who closely studied these and other similar ancient passages, was thus amply justified in his belief that he could reach the Orient by sailing via the west, across the Ocean Sea. Cf. also the view on this of the Libro del Conosçimiento quoted and commented in the next section of the present chapter.

The Greek Dictionary of LSJ affirms that the Ocean "was conceived by the ancients as a *great river* [or stream or current] which compasses the earth's disc, returning into itself, apsorroos" (cf. Il.18.399; Od.20.65). The "earth" in question here is the Old World, composed of Europe, Asia and Africa. And they add that it was "later the name of *the Great Outward Sea*, opposed to the Inward or Mediterranean Sea". The Ocean was also called "sea" (thalassa, pontos) by the ancients, Plato also included, in order to avoid confusion with the River Ocean of Homer and other authorities. [131]

These erudite authors also quote (in Greek) a passage of Theopompos (Hist. Fr. 74 (a); cf. Aristotle's De Mundo 393a17) affirming that: "Europe, Asia and Libya (Africa) are islands that are surrounded by the circle of the Ocean" (tên Eurôpên kai tên Asian kai tên Libuên nêsous einai has perirrein kuklôi ton Ôkeanon). I comment upon this passage of Aristotle, along with several similar ones from other authorities including Plato himself in other works of ours, and will not delve into it here except to note the use of "islands" instead of "continents" in this and other places". [132]

No matter what, it is once again clear that the ancient conception of the Atlantic Ocean also included the Pacific and the Indian Oceans, and extended all the way to the East Indies. This, as if the Americas did not really exist or could somehow be crossed in Panama, at least by the sun and by heroes daring enough. Hence also derives the belief that the "Atlantic Islands" – which are the remains of sunken Atlantis, and were known to be situated in the Pacific Ocean – were somehow located in the western Atlantic Ocean.

Hence also Columbus' conviction that he could sail all the way to the East Indies by heading west, into the Atlantic Ocean. Blinded by the misconception that the "Atlantic Ocean" of today is the same one of which the ancients spoke in their sacred traditions, most researchers of Atlantis unduly confine their quest of Atlantis to the ocean now so named or, worse still, to the Mediterranean Sea where Atlantis never was.

Small wonder then that over two millennia and a half of such interminable searches for Atlantis have never resulted in anything other than illusions and deceptions to all. The same thing applies to Palestine, where an even greater research effort for the biblical Paradise has achieved exactly zero results so far. As is clear, no matter how hard one looks in the wrong spots, nothing will ever be found.

Suffice it here for us to point out that by the word "island" (nêsos) Plato and other ancients often meant what we now improperly call "continent". This word – which actually means "container" – they invariably reserved to the strip of land (Peirata Ges) said to encircle the Ocean all around on the outside, "containing it". And this strip of land in fact corresponded to the Americas, as we comment further below in the present chapter. Even more exactly, this Greek word often expressed the idea of "sunken land", more or less like the Skt. dvipa.

One should keep in mind that Plato invariably used the word nêsos (in the context of Atlantis) in contrast to the one of epeira or epeira ges. This word literally means "continent", in the sense of "environing land". But Plato's contrast of the two words actually suggests a dualism of sorts, one as "firm land" (chersonesos or cheronesos) and the other one as a "water land" or, better yet, a "sunken land" (nêsos).

As such, this "firm land" – which does not sink and hence remains "dry" (xêros) – contrasts with the "island of Atlantis" which does so. Now, this word literally means "peninsula" in Greek. And we believe that it ultimately refers to the Peninsula of Taprobane for a series of reasons. Hesiod refers, in his Theogony (117), to this "wide-bosomed Earth, the ever-sure foundation of all the deathless ones". This "ever-sure foundation" (hedos asphales aiei) is the unsunken portion of the "wide-bosomed earth" of Paradise (Gai' eurusternos+), which sank away, and where the gods originated, in the dawn of time. [133]

This passage is dense and difficult, but its meaning is unequivocal, now that the true message has been mooted out. What Hesiod is really referring several centuries before the times of Plato – and almost in the same words, by the way – is the sinking of Taprobane with only its "skeleton" remaining emerse, when sea level rose by fully 130 meters, at the end of the Pleistocene, some 11,600 years ago.

The Peninsula of Taprobane – also called Kra in the local languages – formed a sort of sternum (breastbone) which remained emerse when the lowlands of Atlantis disappeared under the waters. Hence its name as "firmament", meaning more or less the same in Latin (firmamentum). Such is really the meaning of the "divide of the waters" in the memorable text of Genesis.

We here limit ourselves to pointing out that the Sanskrit word kara from which derives the name of the Kra Peninsula is directly related to the Greek cheiros ("hand, claw, arm"). But it also designates the trunk of an elephant, in fact quite similar to the shape of the Malay Peninsula (Taprobane). From Sanskrit, the word entered the Greek language, being later converted, by means of a popular etymology, into the idea of cherros ("dry land").

---

9 The Greek words used here are all linked to Perseus Project. It suffices to follow their links in order to access not only their translations, but a vast amount of erudite dictionary glosses, commentaries, links to the actual texts, search mechanisms and so on, which are available in this reputable academic source. I well realize that these linguistic issues are obscure and difficult for most readers. They are exegetical in nature and are better left to the specialists who, like myself, delight in this type of Byzantine discussion. But I here furnish the necessary tools for those of our readers who might be interested in trying their hand at it in a more or less professional manner. [134]

It is also clear that, due to their immense difficulty, Plato's texts are sorely in need of a proper exegesis by a team of polymath experts, who are open-minded enough to accept the reality of the esoteric teachings he disclosed perhaps for the only time ever. Unfortunately, a proper exegesis of Plato's text has never been competently done before. But we firmly believe that even the average readers will be able to follow our own exegesis briefly given here (and done in more detail in other locations), if they only try hard enough.

The readers who find this type of issue intolerably tedious are advised to simply skip it for good or for the time being, returning to them later, when the opportunity arises. These readers should go directly to the geographical results summarized in Table III.1 and the others that follow it. Or they may read these linguistic passages perfunctorily, returning to them later when they feel like it. As long as they accept our conclusions, they will not miss much.

Antilia – whose name nowadays survives in the Antilles, so misnamed by Christopher Columbus himself – was the main of the legendary "Atlantic Islands" of the ancient traditions. The name of Antilia is allegedly a Latinized version of the original Portuguese or Catalan word anti-ilha, where anti means "placed opposite" and ilha means "island". But this name is really derived from ancient Hindu sources, perhaps via Greek and Latin ones just mentioned.

No matter what, Antilia means something like "counter-island" or "antipodal island" in any of these three languages. Antilia was in every sense the same as the legendary Taprobane and Septe Cidades. This the ancient mariners equated with the Isles of the Blest, allegedly discovered by St. Brendan in the early Middle Ages. These islands – often of continental extent and hence true continents in the modern sense of the word – the ancients placed in the farthest west, that is, in the coterminous boundary of the ocean with the farthest east.

And this is truly the other side of the world, the "opposite hemisphere", the Far East. Antilia in fact corresponds to Antichthon, the "counter-earth" or "antipodal earth" of the most ancient Greco-Roman traditions. Therefore, the names of Antichthon and Antilia mean precisely the same as "antipodal", that is, "feet opposed" (Drav. atti-illa or *anti-illa = "antipodal peninsula")

The Portuguese were among the first modern nations to systematically explore the Atlantic Ocean in search of the fabulous "Atlantic Islands". Actually, it was the Portuguese explorations which originated the Age of Navigation, when everybody started rushing to discover and appropriate the fabled "Atlantic Islands".

It is for this reason that most islands in the Atlantic Ocean bear Portuguese names: Antilha; Man Satanaxio (Satanazes); Açores; Madeira; Saya; Ymana; Ferro; etc.. On this issue study the interesting pages here and here by an erudite Portuguese-American researcher. The Portuguese were also the first to discover the maritime way to the East Indies, with Vasco da Gama and other such noted naval explorers. [↑135]

On the subject of Taprobane's connection with Antilia and Antichthon, cf. Ovid, Pont. 1:5:80; Pliny, Hist. Nat. 6:81-92; Solinus, Collect. 53:1-23; etc.. Pliny and Solinus specifically identify Taprobane with Antichthon, the now sunken continent of Pomponius Mela which we just commented. Cf. also this interesting article here. More references are further given in the Bibliography section of the present book, in the section on Atlantis. [↑136]

---

10 The sangams (or, better spelled, samghams) are the Dravidian literary academies of poets and mythographers, and their foundations and dissolutions are dictated by major earth cataclysms. We note that the date of the foundation of the first sangam of the present era was 9,600 BC. And this date is precisely the one given by Plato for the demise of Atlantis. Moreover, this date also exactly coincides with the catastrophic end of the Pleistocene, proving that Plato really knew what he was talking about. [↑137]

Dravidian traditions (Tamil) also affirm the existence of a sangam in a date prior to the one of the Universal Flood. This sangam was called Mahendramalai Tamil Sangam, a name which probably relates with the one of Mt. Atlas itself. Mahendramalai is Sanskrit and means "Great Indra Mountain", Indra being an alias of Hercules and /or Atlas, the heroes and first kings of Atlantis. We note that the Dravidian word for the Flood is "Piralayam" translated as "Great Deluge" in the site just linked.

This word corresponds to the Sanskrit <u>Pralaya</u>, meaning "Universal Dissolution", the opposite of <u>Kalpa</u> ("Creation"). These names refer to the periodic destruction and reconstruction of the world according to the geological or climatological eras, which the Hindus associate with the yugas. According to experts, the Dravidian word <u>piralayam</u> derives from <u>pir-al-ayam</u>, meaning "the fiery dissolution of the ancestral world". This quaint etymology is not ours, but is due to a Dravidian guru well versed in such things.

The Dravidian radix <u>pir</u>- also means "flood", just as <u>ala</u>- also means "sea". Dravidian tongues being polysemic, several other alternative etymons are also possible. But the one just given conveys the main gist of the etymology, far more detailed than the Sanskrit one, obviously derived from it. The Sanskrit word is conventionally derived from <u>pra</u>- ("fore") and <u>laya</u> ("dissolution"). But this etymology is apparently contrived.

In Dravida, <u>ayam</u> means "father, forefather, god, saint, brahman, pitri". So, what was in question here was a destruction by fire and water originating in the sea and destroying the ancestral world of the gods or pitris, our former ancestors. In other words, the catastrophic action of the fiery Vadavamukha – whose secret identity with the Krakatoa volcano we have discovered – is very visible in the above etymology.

As is clear, the previous world was destroyed by fire, rather than by water. Even more exactly, what we really had was a Conflagration followed by the Flood, in perfect accordance with the Puranic Doctrines on this phenomenon. In geological terms, what we really had was a supervolcanism – perhaps of global consequences – which triggered the end of the Ice Age, provoking the Universal Flood.

Some misguided Hindus tend to place their sunken continent of Kumari Kandam in the island of Sri Lanka, the one beyond the extreme south of India. But this is a widespread mistake resulting from a phony identity merely intended to deceive the profanes and the more gullible worshippers. The sacred traditions in fact identify Kumari Kandam with Taprobane, which is truly Sumatra, rather than Sri Lanka itself.

Other Hindu traditions place this site to the southeast of <u>Tamil Nadu</u>, the southeast region of India. Strictly speaking, Sri Lanka lies in that direction. But there are no considerable land extensions there, sunken or not. Hardly would Sri Lanka be described as lying to the southeast of India, rather than to the south of it, as can be seen on a map of the region. [↑138]

Moreover, the Dravidas are known <u>not</u> to have come from Sri Lanka, which is actually inhabited by the Sinhalese, who are themselves of Aryan extraction. But even these are non-native invaders who conquered the land which originally belonged to the Vedda natives of Sri Lanka. The idea of "southeast" apparently points to the location of true Lanka, in Indonesia. As can be seen in a map of the region, this is where Indonesia is located in respect to India: the Southeast.

The Dravidas – <u>or was it really the Aryans?</u> – only came into Sri Lanka rather late, in historical times, apparently sent there as Buddhist missionaries by King Asoka in the third century BC. The two nationalities dispute the land even today, and it is possible that the recent tendency to identify Sri Lanka with Kumari Kandam is really an attempt to justify the Tamil claim to the region. [↑139]

Perhaps the Sri Lankan Tamils reason that it is better a small bird in hand than a bigger one in the bush. But we take no part in the sore dispute which seems to be a further facet of the enduring strife between Dravidas and Aryans, which has lasted since the times of Atlantis. No matter what, the earliest name of the island of Sri Lanka, Para-Samudra closely suggests its identity with Sumatra. This Sanskrit name means "beyond the ocean", and later degenerated into the Palaisimundus of Greco-Roman sources.

But it could never apply to Sri Lanka itself, which is visibly not "beyond the ocean" for one starting from India, to which it is actually attached across Palk Strait. Actually, most experts hold that the name of Sumatra derives from Samudra, meaning "oceanic". Besides, the connection with "gold" also refers to Indonesia, formerly so-called, and not to Sri Lanka, which never produced a single ounce of the precious yellow metal.

---

11 David Keys, Catastrophe: A Quest for the Origins of the Modern World, Ballantine Books, New York, 1999, pg. 253. The Indonesian chronicle, Pustaka Raja Purwa (or "Book of Ancient Kings") is in fact little known in the Occident. It is however quite familiar to Indonesians in general. And its name is Sanskrit, a fact attesting its Hindu origin.

The word purwa is derived from the Skt. parva and refers to the Mahabharata main sections (parvan = "knot, division"). But this word implies the idea of "change", such as the phases of the moon or, more exactly, the era changes (yugas), which are dictated by major cataclysms such as the Flood and major wars like the Mahabharata War and the Ramayana War.

This word has also to do with the Wayang Purwa Theater. The Wayang is a theater where the shadows (wayang) of the puppets play the personages of the Ramayana, reenacting the events which led to the War of the Ramayana and the destruction of the place and the world by the Flood. Hence, a more adequate translation of the book's name would be "book of the kings who ruled at the time of the cataclysmic era changes" (i. e., the Flood). [140]

This interpretation of the word purwa is attested in the site linked here, which affirms: "Wayang purwa makes use of the purwa repertoire: the oldest stories about cosmic events and divine will are represented; the course of events is seen as being predestined, part of a cosmic law [dharma]." And it adds: "The Javanese word purwa means "beginning" or "first" and derives, probably, from the Sanskrit parwan, a word used to denote the chapters of the Mahabharata." [141]

In reality, the etymology of this word is very complex, as is so often the case with sacred etymologies in both Sanskrit and Dravida. Ultimately, the Sanskrit word parvan (or pūrva) derives from the Dravida parpa. And this Dravidian word in turn designates a separation or "bamboo knot", either of eras or of things such as Sunda Strait and the royal dynasties. Said otherwise, the word parvan (or purwa) really refers to the eras of mankind, of which the Atlantean era was the last one before the one in which we currently live.

---

12 The Internet is a mine of information on the subject of Pole Shift. Even Dr. Flavio Barbiero's attempt to save Pole Shift by positing large extra-terrestrial impacts does not seem at all viable, as per the criticism by Dr. C. Leroy Ellenberger and Dr. Paul Heinrich. Cf. the Internet articles here and here and here and here and here. Even if a major impact were able to cause Pole Shift – and I believe they indeed are, if large enough – the real cause of the disaster would be the impactor, not the resulting Pole Shift, which is just one of its secondary consequences. [142]

Moreover, its effects at such a recent date as 11,600 BP would be clearly discernible in the geological record (dust layer, impact crater, etc.). No such evidence is at all available. So, it seems safe to discard this cause for good. The other alternative – the one of Charles Hapgood that Pole Shift may result from an imbalance in the ice caps – is scientifically preposterous, and is not even worth considering. Most of its former proponents have now recanted from this position, as it is scientifically untenable.

We take advantage of this endnote to clarify the differences between Magnetic Pole Shift; Terrestrial Pole Shift; and Celestial Pole Shift. According to modern views, earth's magnetic field is engendered by the relative motion between earth's mantle and crust and the outer portions of the nucleus in relation to its inner portions. The nucleus is molten, and hence highly mobile in relation to the rest. Since it is metallic and hence electrically conductive, this relative motion between different portions of the nucleus generates electric currents which cause it to act as a dynamo, engendering a magnetic field which manifests itself as the one of the earth.

The Terrestrial Pole is earth's axis of rotation in relation to itself. This is fixed in relation to the earth's crust, and hence unchanging. Pole Shift of the type preconized by Hapgood, Hancock and White would consist of the abrupt motion of earth's crust in relation to the mantle. Since the two are solid and solidly anchored to each other, this motion is essentially impossible, except as the very slow result of creep.

A third type of pole is the Celestial Pole. We could say that this pole is the projection of Terrestrial Pole on the Celestial Sphere, which happens over the Pole Star. As the result of the Precession of the Equinoxes, the Celestial Pole changes over time, completing a whole cycle in 25,920 years. Since the inclination of the earth is fully $23.5°$, this motion is quite considerable. This motion was first directly measured by Hipparchos, according to the modern versions of history.

Far more likely, these celestial motions were measured a lot earlier in time, perhaps by the Atlanteans themselves. We show in other works that accurate computational devices such as the Great Pyramid of Egypt are in reality highly advanced astronomical computers originally devised in order to measure the Precession of the Equinoxes by means of a very clever artifice which puts to shame the techniques currently used by modern astronomers.

---

13 The word Gades or Gadeiros apparently translates the name of Govinda, one of the names of Krishna or Vishnu, as "the good shepherd" or "the cowherd" of Hindu traditions. In the <u>Rig Veda</u>, this name also applies to Indra and to Agni (Shiva in his fiery aspect, as Kala or the Vadavamukha). This Sanskrit etymology is complex, and cannot be fully expounded here. It relates to Gomeda-dvipa, "the Island of the Fat Cattle", one of the Hindu names of Atlantis. The name of Govinda is said by Monier to derive from gopêndra ("cow-lord"), which is also the real meaning of the name of Gadeiros or Eumelos.

And this is also equivalent to Skt. Pashupati ("Lord of Cattle"), one of the many titles of Shiva. This function of Shiva dates from the Indus Valley Civilization itself. The name of Govinda is further related to the Sanskrit gopa or gopala ("cowherd") and to Gautama (or Gotama), a name of Buddha meaning "desirous of cattle". Krishna (Govinda) is the twin brother of Balarama, much as Hercules (Gadeiros) is the twin of Atlas. One twin is said to be black, the other one white, both in India and in Greece. The idea concerns the two races, the Aryans being whites, and the Dravidas red or dark. [↑143]

The myth of the twins who dispute the "cattle" dates from the Rig Veda. In this hymnary this myth is told as the disputes of Indra and Vritra for the possession of the "cattle", a word which really means "people" or "armies", as we just said. One example is Rig Veda 10:108:3, where Indra is invited by the Panis to be "the herdsman of their cattle". As Marcel Bréal and other experts have recognized, this hymn was actually the (Vedic) source of the myth of Hercules and Geryon, which it closely parallels in many details.

Geryon is the alias and counterpart of Atlas as the elder of the twins. As we just said, the elder twin stands for the Pelasgians and Phoenicians, the predecessors of the Greek people later absorbed by the Indo-Europeans who invaded and conquered the whole Mediterranean region. Indra is the patron hero of the Aryans, and it is at least puzzling to see him being invited here to be the herdsman (or king) of the Panis. This luciferine Indian people has been identified by many experts as the predecessors of the Phoenicians (Poeni = Pani).

The ultimate etymology of the name of Gadeiros is also the Dravida gad-eru ("place where cattle are forded"). The first root is from #1109 gad ("to land, cross, ford,") and the second from #815 eru ("cattle"). The idea is both that of an oxford or, alternatively, a port or quay where people or cattle are embarked or disembarked. This last one is really the etymology of the word, which is connected with the Sanskrit ghat, a sort of quay or port or gate, generally located in riverbanks, where cattle was gathered to be forded over by a ferry.

In Hindu traditions, a ghat is the place in rivers where the worshippers bathe themselves in sacred ablutions. As we show in other works, this is a sort of ritual baptism. Now, Baptism is, as St. Jerome reveals, a ritual commemoration of the Flood as the event where people were drowned en masse. The idea of "oxford" and "ghat" is also connected with the name of Kattigara (or Cattigara) as the site of the famous strait (Malacca) or its dual (Sunda).

Kattigara is also the famous Indian port which figures in essentially all ancient maps ever since the one of Ptolemy himself. The name of Kattigara can be again derived from the Dravida #1123/1114 kati ("cattle") + #1109 kata, kar, *kara ("to embark, cross over, ferry") > kati-kara ("place where cattle are forded or ferried"). The idea is, as we already said, connected with the miraculous "Crossing of the Red Sea", which is really an allegory of the mass exodus from Lanka after its destruction.

Lanka is, of course, the same as Atlantis, being the capital of Ravana's worldwide empire. Lanka was destroyed by Rama and Hanumant, very much as Troy was destroyed by Achilles and Menelaos, and Atlantis was itself destroyed by a coalition of Greek armies. Ptolemy places Kattigara at 8.5°S; 180°E, which means the place is located near the Equator and almost opposite (antipodal) to the Canary Islands, where his longitude measurement started. And this was no sheer coincidence. [144]

The Canaries are the western counterpart of the Isles of the Blest, whereas its antipodal, Kattigara or Taprobane, is its dual and archetype, in the East Indies. Ptolemy's coordinates place Kattigara precisely in the site of Indonesia, exactly where we have located Atlantis. It is hence easy to see that Kattigara is the "mirror image" of the European Gades or Gadeira (Cadiz), its western replica. Kattigara corresponds to the Pillars of Atlas, whereas Cadiz, its dual, corresponds to the Pillars of Hercules. [145]

It is clear that the Phoenicians borrowed the word Gades (or Gadeira or Kattigara) from Dravidian India. The Sanskrit equivalent of this word is precisely tirthankara ("ford maker"), a key concept in Hinduism, being the title the Jains apply to their Saviors. But this Dravidian word can also be derived from #1416 kad- ("herder, guardian, keeper") + #815/917 eru ("ox, bull, cattle") > kad-eru ("cattle keeper, cowherd").

Hence, as applied to places, the name Gadeira means "oxford", and when applied to people it means "cowherd, shepherd" and, even more exactly, "oxforder". Proto-Dravidian k- usually passes into the Indo-European tongues as g-, these two gutturals being often confused in these tongues. The name of Kattigara exactly correspond to the one of the Strait of Bosphorus (Greek bos-phoros = "cattle forder"), which derives from the myth of Hercules crossing there with the cattle he rustled from Geryon.

The same myth concerning Hercules crossing the Bosporus Strait with Geryon's cattle also applies to Gibraltar Strait, which is also associated with this myth, as we already told above. So is the Red Sea (Bab-el-Mandeb Strait), in connection with the Crossing of the Red Sea by the Israelites. Except that the "Red Sea" in question here is really the Erythraean Ocean (Indian), whose name also means the same thing in Greek.

In other words, the Hebrew myth, like the Greek one, in fact derives from Hindu traditions on the crossing of Malacca Strait in Indonesia, as we already argued. This story is told in both the Ramayana and the Rig Veda, and is immensely older in India than its counterparts just mentioned. Curiously enough, the name of Hercules can also be derived from Dravida, where it means the same as Gadeiros or "Cowherd".

We already commented this fact further above, which we now complement here. In that tongue we have #1980/2814 čer-, her-, er- ("to fence, herd, gather, collect") + #1810 kulai ("herd, cattle, bunch") > her-kulai ("cowherd, cattle herder"). Also, cf. the Skt. kula ("herd, cattle, crowd, army") and Drav. #1971/1915 kuli ("ox, cattle, crowd"). The etymology of the name of Hercules or Herakles is unclear both in Greek and in Latin, and is deemed to be substrate.

Some experts think his name derives from the Etruscan hercle, of unknown meaning. No matter what, the usual etymology "glory of Hera" (Grk. Hera-kleos) is sheer folly, as already recognized by a great many experts. Hera was in fact a ferocious enemy of Herakles, the adulterine son of her husband, Zeus, by the charming nymph Alcmena. It is also clear that the Etruscan name of Hercules, Hercle, is close enough to the Roman and Greek ones to provide an adequate Dravidian etymology, particularly now that we know that Etruscan is a Dravidian tongue, as I demonstrated in my work on the decipherment of the Etruscan language. [146]

In other words, it seems that both the name and the myth of Hercules ultimately derives from India, being connected with the figures of both Shiva and Vishnu, as "the Lords (or Herders) of Cattle" (Paṣupati, Prajapati). The above Dravidian base, her- or čer, is also distantly connected with the Engl. "herd", the Skt. ṣardha; the Lith. kerdzus, the Germ. heerde, etc.. A related etymology is the Port. cerca, Lat. circa, etc, where the original sense of "to surround, encircle, fence out, guard" is preserved.

This base is also connected with Drav. #1509 kiṣkinda, meaning "surrounded (or fenced) place". This word figures in the Ramayana's fourth book, Kiṣkinda Kanda. Kiṣkinda is the site of the famous Pampa Lake, truly the site of Paradise, as "a fenced (hedged) place". Unfortunately, space does not allow the full discussion of this fascinating motif, which is closely connected with Atlantis as the site of Paradise Lost. Suffice it to say here that the description of Pampa Lake in the Ramayana closely evokes Plato's description of Atlantis as full of tropical trees, fruits, perfumes, incenses and flowers of all sorts. [147]

Not even the elephants are missing in this charming paradisial place. I suspect that the red dust said to cover the Ryshyamukha Mountain is really gold dust, suggesting an identity with Indonesia (the Aurea Chersonesus or Taprobane of Greco-Roman traditions). This region is also said to be tranquil, peaceful and free of evil, as Paradise also is, according to most traditions.

And it also seems to me that the miraculous waters of the Pampa Lake are those of the Elixir itself. Curiously enough, this pleasant Paradise is said to be western, as can be seen in the link just given. In other words, this Paradise – fenced or moated just as Atlantis also was – seems to be Sukhavati, the Western Paradise of Buddha Amitabha. And this idea connects with the one of sailing westwards, into the Atlantic Ocean, just as Columbus attempted to do, in order to reach the East Indies.

The name of Pampa Lake ultimately derives from the Drav. #3949 pampa ("expanse, ocean, marshy field"). The idea here is really the one of a flooded expanse turned into a sea, more or less as happened to Atlantis itself. Even more exactly, Pampa Lake seems to correspond to the Great Plain of Atlantis flooded and turned into a marsh or lake or sea, exactly as Plato reports in his dialogues on the sunken continent.

The Dravidian origin of the Ramayana's toponyms which I just mooted out is telltale of its origin in Dravidian India, rather than in Aryan India, as usually thought. In fact, it now seems that most if not all Hindu mythology and religion was adopted by the Aryans from Dravidian India. Even more exactly, the Ramayana, like other similar traditions ultimately originated in Indonesia, the pristine abode of the Dravidas.

---

14 The metaphors used in this myth are actually derived from the sacred tongues of India. In Sanskrit, the words gana and kula mean both "herd, cattle" and "horde, multitude, army". The story of Hercules (Herk-kula = "cattle-herder") driving away with Geryon's cattle is in fact an allegory of the mass exodus from the destroyed region. In the Bible, this story corresponds to the one told in Exodus, where Moses assumes a role akin to Hercules as "the Good Shepherd" who leads his people away from Paradise Lost.

The name of Eumelos can also be interpreted as meaning "Good Shepherd" in Greek. And, as Plato himself discloses, it is also the equivalent of Gadeiros. Rather than a Phoenician word, this term derives from Dravida, as gad- ("cattle") and iru ("to go; lead"). In other words, the name of Gadeiros also means "cow-herder". It is apparently again related to the name of Geryon, the cow-herder whose cattle Hercules stole, in the course of his tenth labor.

The name of Geryon derives from a Greek word meaning "elder, senior". But it also relates to the Dravida če-eru-on, apparently meaning something like "he who herds red cattle". This red cattle is people; red people, as we already said. And the "herds" are the ones of people leaving the site of Paradise Destroyed under the guidance of the Good Shepherd variously named.

The figure of the Good Shepherd is extremely ancient in India, where it already figures in the Rig Veda (1:164:31; 10:177:3, etc.). Cf. also endnote 13, above, where this subject is pursued. As such, this name translates the one of Vishnu as Govinda, also meaning the same thing. This name also corresponds to the one of Hercules himself. As we have just shown above, the name of Hercules – of unknown etymology – ultimately derives from the Dravida. This name, which literally means "cow-herder", like the one of Gadeiros, was later distorted into Herakles ("glory of Hera") by the Greeks, in a false etymology.

In Greek traditions, this mass exodus from Paradise Lost is beautifully illustrated in the famous Elgin Marbles, stolen from the Parthenon of Athens. This event was also commemorated in the great procession of the Panatheneas by the Greeks. Its is certainly more than a coincidence that Plato and his commentators (Krantor, etc.) also identify this festival with the Great War of Atlantis and the mass exodus from the destroyed region.

The same story is also told in the charming Ramayana, in connection with Lanka, and in the Mahabharata in connection with the one of Dvaraka, the fabled capital of Krishna. The twin Hindu heroes, Krishna and Balarama and/or Rama and Hanumant are the visible counterparts and actual archetypes of Atlas and Gadeiros (Hercules), who take turns holding up Heaven and the Pillars of Hercules.

---

15 Creep (or cold flow) is the slow motion phenomenon which occurs in the solid state itself. You can observe this phenomenon in action by pushing the tip of a sharp knife into an ice cube. If you push long enough, you will see the tip of the blade penetrate the ice cube. Try to do it faster, and the ice cracks. What happens is that the ice crystal ahead of the tip melts under the pressure, and then recrystallizes when it is finished passing. [↑]**148**

Exactly the same thing happens in the interface between the crust and the mantle, where the huge pressures create a semi-molten plastic layer known as asthenosphere. The asthenosphere is a very thin layer of only slightly mollified rock, and would never allow the solid crust to move relative to the likewise solid mantle. [149]

We also note that the molten sections of the mantle and crust under volcanoes are highly localized phenomena contained in the so-called "magma chambers" where the molten rock (magma) is withheld. I am sorry to say, the proponents of Pole Shift are generally all of them – Einstein, Velikovsky, Hapgood, Flem-Ath , and Hancock, included – totally unfamiliar with even the most basic tenets of geological theory. Their proposal is utterly unscientific and should be dismissed by everyone with a bare minimum of knowledge and rationality.

It is true that Antarctica has drifted away from Pangea and that it was once tropical, as attested by its immense deposits of carboniferous coal. But this drift was very slow and was the accumulated result of several hundreds of millions of years of extremely slow drifting. Antarctica is now known for sure to have been under ice for a million years and more, and is hence wholly unsuitable as a possible candidate for the site of Atlantis, a tropical paradise according to Plato.

---

16 In Sanskrit, Paradise was called Svarga (or Svarga-loka). It was also called Trinaka, Trivishtapa, Nakaprishta, Indraloka, etc.. Loka means "place, world" in Sanskrit and normally designates Paradise as the Otherworld. There the three realms of space – Heaven, Earth, Hell – meet and congregate, in parallel dimensions. The three realms just mentioned are all three called loka or triloka ("triple world") or tribhuvana (idem). Their location and geometry is often disguised. And so are the names, which vary a lot: Mahaloka, Janaloka, Taparloka, Indraloka, etc..

This disguise is really intended to baffle the uninitiated profanes, to whom such things are never disclosed. Hence the scorn of Pindar for them. Heaven, the Celestial Paradise, is the abode of the gods (devaloka). Hell (Patala or Atala), is inhabited by the devils (asuras or titans). And earth is of course the abode of us humans.

The connection of Taprobane with the number three (tri-) ultimately derives from the name of Tripura, the "Triple City" destroyed by Shiva. Tripura is really the same as Lanka (destroyed by Rama) and as Atlantis, also a triple city. Curiously enough, Taprobane was identified as the Island of the Blest, the site of Paradise, both in Hindu and in Greco-Roman traditions. Pliny and other Greco-Roman authors refer to Taprobane as the site of the Otherworld.

Actually, Taprobane was the site of the three realms of Triple World. In Hindu traditions, the three worlds were deemed to lie side-by-side, in different, though collateral dimensions. Alternatively, they were also thought to lie all three on a vertical axis, with Heaven above, and Hell below, as mirror images of the earth itself.

Hence the usual identification of its location with the Pole, a symbolism that has often led to the misplacing of Paradise in the Arctic or in Antarctica. The Greco-Roman traditions on Paradise closely parallel the Hindu ones, from which they ultimately derive, just as is the case here. A good description of the Greco-Roman conception of the Triple World is given in this excellent site here. [150]

Curiously enough, the Greeks often called the Isles of the Blest (Makaron Nesos) or Elysian Fields (Elysion pedon) by the name of White Islands (Leuke or Leukades). These paradisial islands should not be confused with their counterparts in Greece, which are mere replicas of the true ones, on the far bank of the Ocean, as we already demonstrated.

Originally located in the extremities of the earth (the Far East or Far West) by Homer, the site of Paradise (Elysium) and Hell (Tartarus) was eventually moved to heaven above and hell below. This Greek name, Leukades, is in fact a translation of the Hindu name of Paradise (Svetadvipa) meaning exactly the same thing in Sanskrit. Curiously enough, this name is also found in the Americas, for instance in the Yvymaraney of the Guarani Indians of Brazil or the Aztlán of the Aztecs, names which also mean "Pure Land", meaning "white".

The Tucanos – another tribe of the Brazilian Amazon region – have a similar conception, and identify Paradise with the "River of Milk" (Apiá Kondiá), again using the same idea of "whiteness". The "whiteness" of this place is associated with the fact that Paradise (Atlantis) was fully covered with a sort of white shroud of pumice stone and volcanic cinders on the occasion of its destruction. The "River of Milk" also figures in the Greek traditions, the Milky Way being its celestial counterpart.

And this idea also figures in the Judeo-Christian traditions on Paradise as the River Pishon, whose name actually means the same thing in Dravida, as we argue in detail elsewhere. It also seems that the River of Paradise was also the same as the River Styx, its infernal counterpart. As is clear, it is quite impossible that all these astounding coincidences are due to chance alone.

Actually, the Greek word leukas in fact expresses an idea of "pallor; grayness; ashy". This is associated with death and cinders allegedly from the many dead incinerated at the place. But the real reason was the thick veil of volcanic cinders which covered the whole region like a shroud on the occasion of its destruction. This symbolism is also the one embodied in the white veil of brides, as I comment in more detail in my Atlantis site. [151]

ENDNOTES TO PART IV

17   Cf. Isa. 41:1-9: "Thou, Israel… whom I have taken from the ends of the earth." Note that the Jews equate the East with the old, the islands and the righteous, etymons which all evoke Atlantis. It is important to note that this agrees with our conclusion that the Jewish people were the same as the Yüeh-chi (please note the close assonance with "Jewish") or Tocharians from China and Mongolia.

This assertion is of crucial importance in this matter of establishing Jewish origins, given the fact that it comes from a canonical Jewish source of indisputable authority, the prophet Isaiah. The symbolism of the Four Corners of the Earth is intimately connected with earth's fringes. In fact, these four corners allude to the four straits which delimit the earth at the Four Cardinal Points: Gibraltar in the west; Sunda in the east; Bering in the north; Magellan in the south.

These four corners figure centrally in Jewish mysticism. They are represented by the four fringes (zizit) of the tallit and the arba' kanfot worn by the orthodox Jews while praying, as an emblem of their national identity. The four zizits are each formed of four threads of blue twined to four white ones. Blue symbolizes the sea, being the emblem of Tarshish, as elucidated by St Jerome. And the white symbolizes the White Island which is no other than Java itself (called Svetadvipa = "White Island" in Sanskrit). [186]

The blue dye with which the zizit was dyed came from the "isles of Elishah", which, we believe, were the same as the one of Elysium. This, rather than Sicily, its alleged source, which of course never produced such snails. The true dye seems to be indigo blue, produced in the Indies.

It is important to realize that the word "fringes" (or "ends" or "wings") used here had a very specific significance among the ancients in general. It is used in the same sense in the Bible (Job 38:13; 37:3; Psa 139:9, etc.), where the word (kanaph) designates the uttermost parts of the ocean. [159]

This is the realm of night and of dawn, where the sun starts its daily trip by an international convention dating from times immemorial. This hoary convention probably dates from the days of Atlantis, the only ancient nation equipped for such remarkable implementations at such an early epoch in time. As a worldwide empire of navigators, the Atlanteans soon developed a need for such a universal grid, very much as is the case today.

We believe that the "wicked" whom Jahveh shook out of the "wings of the earth" with his mighty thunderbolt are the Atlanteans themselves, turned evil and corrupt after their decay, and hence discarded by God. If so, we have again mustered the authority of the Bible itself in support of our view that Atlantis lay there, in the East Indies, in the Land of Dawn and Sunset, where the sun both dies and rises again daily.

The "wings" or "ends" in question here are visibly earth's fringes, the place where east meets west, on the far bank of the Ocean. Where else would earth's ends or fringes be located but there? And we further believe that the idea of "wing" used here is an esoteric allusion to the name of Taprobane, whose Sanskrit name

(Tamraparna) signifies exactly "golden wing" (or "golden bough" or "golden peninsula"). This idea is also coupled to the one of "extremity": an arm, a wing, a branch or bough, the fringe of a piece of cloth, a long peninsula, etc..

The Book of Job – perhaps the oldest and the most "pagan" of all biblical texts – is a mine of information on issues having to do with Atlantis and its destruction by the vajra (volcanism) in the dawn of time. Curiously enough, most exegetes (see Commentary here) misinterpret the "wings of Dawn" of Psalm 139:9 as a reference to sunbeams shining through the clouds in early morning. [160]

Such naturist interpretations, so current in the 19th century, are now utterly outdated and were hence generally abandoned by the more knowledgeable experts. But the idea here seems clear enough: "If I take the wings of Morning and dwell in the uttermost parts of the sea." Morning is Dawn, and has wings in most ancient traditions, Greek in particular, as illustrated in the figure of Eos mourning her dead son Memnon shown further above.

As most Indologists well know, in antiquity the day started by convention in Taprobane, that is, in the East Indies, the Land of Dawn. The ancient texts – both Classical and otherwise – are full of references to this fact. And it is also reasonable to believe that the new day starts at the divide of the world where East meets West, and the sun's circuit is completed.

Malachi (4:2) makes a very curious reference to these "wings" which is quite revealing of their true identity. The prophet is talking of Doomsday, when the "Sun of Righteousness" will again arise with its wings, bringing healing to the righteous and fiery death to the wicked. This Sun of Righteousness is also the solar disk we see shining between the horns of bovine deities such as Shiva, Kronos, Ammon, Hathor, and so on.

We believe that this "winged sun" is the supervolcano which brings Doomsday to the world according to Hindu traditions (Agni). The just, it is believed, will then be rescued, and will in fact become immortal, as a reward for their piety. This image of the Winged Sun is of enormous antiquity. For example, it is found in the Rig Veda as the one of Vena, the true archetype of the Phoenix. We also have the Winged Disk in the religious symbolism of Egypt, Mesopotamia, Persia, Aztec Mexico, and so forth. [161]

---

18 The true etymology of the name of Iapetos is unknown in Greek, according to Junito Brandão, the great expert on sacred etymologies. Brandão denounces the customary derivation from japtein ("to throw") as false. The genealogy given by Hesiod (Theog. 507) substitutes Menoetius for Hesperus as the brother of Atlas. Like Diodorus, Hesiod also gives Ouranus and Gaia as the parents of the Titans.

We believe that the name of Iapetos ultimately derives from the Sanskrit yā -pati, meaning "lord of the moving ones". The first root is related to yahva ("moving waters"). But its basic form (yā) is related to Eng. "go" and means "to go, wander, err". This word is also an onomastic of Agni, Indra or Soma in the Vedas. We believe that this word was also the source of the name of Jah or Jahveh, the Jewish god who, like these Vedic deities, was also both the Lord of the Flood and of these errant nomads.

This sobriquet also apparently designates Varuna and Poseidon as the "Lord of the [Moving] Waters" (Idas Pati). Varuna, like Poseidon and perhaps even Jahveh himself, was the lord both of the waters and of earthquakes and volcanoes. As such, the name clearly refers to the Flood as a giant tsunami perhaps impelled by the super-eruption of the Krakatoa volcano, alias Vadavamukha or "Fiery Submarine Mare".

The name of the Yavanas (or "Greeks") also means "restless, ever moving" (yahva), being also related to javana ("a fleet horse or horseman"). As such, this onomastic term apparently refers to the early Tocharians (or Yüeh-chi), the nomadic White Huns from the Far East who were the ancestors both of the Jews and other early nomads such as the Ethiopians, the Celts, the Etruscans, the Greeks and other tribes of early Sea Peoples.

Their relationship with horses is curious, as it suggests the main feature of these feared barbarians: their ability to aim and shoot arrows while riding at full speed. Likewise, the connection with Poseidon and Varuna again suggests a direct nexus of the Yavanas with Atlantis and its demise by fire and water.

This would again imply that the two adversaries in the Great War of Atlantis, the Athenians and the Atlanteans, were both "Greeks" or Yavanas. In other words, the War of Atlantis was actually a civil war fought between the two moieties of the great nation, the Dravidas and the Aryans. The word "Greek" is related to "gray" and refers to the fact that this people was connected with the Atlanteans as the "hoary people", the Ancestors (or rishis) of the previous era of mankind.

The radix vana is likewise telltale of a connection with Atlantis and Paradise. This word means "forest, grove, wilderness, solitude" and, by extension, "a foreign or distant land". This word literally corresponds to the Skt. paradesha, whence derived the word "paradise" as a far country, placed on the far bank of the ocean. In this connection, the name of the Yavanas may literally be interpreted as meaning: "the wanderers from a distant land" or, even more exactly: "the nomads originated from Paradise."

---

19 The name of the god the Greeks called Kronos and the Romans Saturnus (or Saturn) is variously spelled: Kronos, Cronus, Cronos, Kronos, etc.. We attempt to respect the original spelling in the quotations we cite, for reasons of fidelity to our sources. Hence the different spellings found in our text, which may confuse the lay reader.

But it is impossible to maintain a perfect coherence in the spelling of Kronos' name, even though we normally prefer the Greek spelling just used. We recognize that this incoherence is perplexing, but are unable to solve the problem, which is better left to the more qualified experts.

The Latins (Romans) often used the form Cronus, their way of spelling the Greek name of Kronos, even though the god's Roman counterpart was called Saturn. Kronos is a very important god. But the etymology of his name is unknown, a fact that attests the foreign origin of the god, probably Pelasgian or Etruscan.

In Greece, Kronos presided over the Kronia festival. This is the equivalent to the Latin Saturnalia, the antecedent of Carnival. In Greek mythology, Kronos is a Titan, the son of the sky-god Ouranos and the earth-goddess Gaia. Kronos attacked his father, and castrated him, assuming the rule of his worldwide empire which Diodorus specifically identifies with Atlantis.

To avoid the same fate, Kronos devoured his children as soon as they were born. The only exception was Zeus, the youngest, due to his wife's ruse, who fed Kronos a stone wrapped in the child's swaddling clothes. After he grew up, Zeus treated Kronos the way he had treated his own father. Defeated and ousted, Kronos became the ruler of Hades, the netherworld. But he was later freed by Zeus, and became the ruler of the paradisial Isles of the Blest.

The great war between the gods, led by Zeus, and the Titans, led by Kronos is, as Plato explains, an allegory of the Great War of Atlantis. In other versions, the Titans were led by Atlas himself, perhaps emphasizing the identity of the two Titans. Diodorus also affirms that Kronos was the twin brother of Atlas and the co-ruler of Atlantis. Diodorus further adds that Zeus was the son of Kronos, and that he made war on his father, whom he defeated and ousted from the throne.

As is now clear, the account of Atlantis given by Diodorus is more or less coherent with the one given by Plato and other mythographers. The etymology of the name of Kronos is highly obscure. The connection with Khronos ("Time") is merely popular, and probably derives from his connection with Shiva (as Kala = Time).

No matter what, the above etymology is linguistically invalid, and is merely popular. But Kronos was often associated with a past era of mankind, the Golden Age. Kronos devouring his children is an allegory of Atlantis' volcano in fact doing so. The Great War is the War of Atlantis, and the Golden Age refers to the antediluvian era of Atlantis, which completed its allotted time, and had to be destroyed.

Some experts have proposed that the name of Kronos ultimately derives from the one of Shiva as Karana (or Krana, meaning "Creator" in Sanskrit). Others have pointed out the connection of his name with the radix KRN, of words such as "crown" (Latin <u>corona</u>) and "horn" (Latin <u>cornus</u>, Hebrew <u>karan</u>). And it is perhaps more than a coincidence that Kronos is often depicted as a horned god akin to Cernnunos (Celtic).

Kronos is also connected with the figure of Lucifer, another horned deity. The Orphics identified Kronos – or Khronos, rather – with Hercules. As such, the god was often portrayed as a giant dragon or serpent. In this connection, Kronos seems to be an alias of the Serpent of Eden. The story of Kronos and Zeus just told is all too similar to the one of Bali and Vamana to be explained away as a sheer coincidence.

All in all, both stories apparently correspond to a mythification of the Great War of Atlantis. Even the horned figure of Kronos is probably derived from India, where Shiva, his probable archetype, is often so portrayed, as illustrated next. Already, the <u>proto-Shiva of Harappa</u> bore a pair of buffalo horns whose similitude to Cernnunos has previously been noted by several experts.

<u>Yamantaka</u>, the alias of Shiva as Bali and/or Yama is also often portrayed as a horned god. The actual symbolism of horns is somewhat difficult. It is not exclusively a male emblem, as the Great Mother (<u>Hathor</u>, Isis, Io, etc.) also often bears such horns, usually with the solar disk shining between them. [162]

We believe that the horn symbolism has ultimately to do with the Horn-of-Plenty. If so, the real allusion is to the Pillars of Hercules and/or Atlas, the two volcanoes of Atlantis. These volcanoes insured the local fecundity of the land due to the rains and the perpetual fertility of the soil that they insured. Hence the connection with the Great Mother of Cereals and with Saturn, as the "inseminator" (sator) who introduced agriculture. This feat is often attributed to Osiris, Ouranos, Yama and other such civilizing gods.

The fact that some Sea Peoples such as the Sherden and the Tjekker (or Tjakkar) wore helmets decorated by feathers or by a pair of horns having the sun disk in between is telltale of the connection of this symbolism with the Far East, where their islands were located. The same is also true of the Egyptian divinities such as Hathor and Khnum, etc., where the occult symbolism of their curious headdresses is once again precisely the same as here. [↑163]

The Tjekker are the Tocharians, as several experts have recognized. Among these experts we name Prof E. Desor, whose wonderful book is referenced below, in the Bibliography. The word Tocharian figures in Sanskrit as Tukhara (or Tukkhara, etc.). This ethnonym is derived from the Dravida togaru meaning "red". This base has forms such as dora, meaning the same. By extension, this name means "pink, rosy" and hence "dawn". As such, the name applies to the ruddy races of the Far East, the Land of Dawn (Homer's "rosy-fingered Aurora").

The form dora is highly interesting. It closely evokes the name of the Dorians, that is, the Indo-European Greeks. The Tjekker are also mentioned in the Wen-Amon story of the 11th century BC. The author recalls visiting the city of Dor, which he calls "a town of the Tjekker". As is clear, the early Greeks, like the Sea Peoples, were a mixed stock of more or less white-skinned peoples comprising the Aryans (whites), the Dravidas (reds), the Semites, and so forth.

A Sanskrit-Tocharian bilingual inscription identifies the Sanskrit tokharika and Tocharian kucaññe ("Kuchean"). If so, the Tocharians are identical to the Kusheans or Ethiopians, at least in language. This identification is extremely interesting, as it places the Ethiopians both in the Far East (Xinjiang region in China) and in the west (as the Dorian Greeks, the Libyans, etc.). Once more we see that the Greeks were originally divided into two moieties, one Aryan, the other one Pelasgian or Dravida. It was these two moieties who fought the Great War of Atlantis, clearly a civil war.

Sandars (see above link) traces the Tjekker to the Troad (Asia Minor), and identifies this people with the Teucri, perhaps displaced from there by the Trojan War. But the Trojan War is really an allegory of the Great War of Atlantis, so that the Tocharians were first displaced from Atlantis into China and Southeast Asia, later moving from there towards the west (Asia Minor, Greece, Celtia etc.)

Sandars also suggests a connection of the Tjekker with the hero Teucer, the traditional founder of Salamis in Cyprus. It is suggested that the Tjekker may have come to Canaan from the Troad by way of Cyprus. The name of Teucer (Grk. Teukros) also embodies the idea of "red", being applied to madder, whence a red dye is extracted. The two feathers on the Tjekker headdresses correspond to those worn by the hoplites (lancers) of the Greek armies. Their long spears, rounded shields, short swords are also typically Greek. And their ships closely resemble those later found in the Aegean region.

It is also clear that the Sea Peoples came to the Mediterranean region and to central and west Europe in several waves. And they came both by land via the east (through the Silk Road) and the west (across the ocean). The first such wave occurred in the 5th millennium BC, or earlier, and corresponded to the Ethiopians and the Celt-Iberians, as commented above.

Another wave corresponded to the Hyksos, and started at about 1,700 BC. A third attempt – this time unsuccessful – occurred with the Sea Peoples proper, at about 1,200 BC. But these barbaric invasions, often peaceful, but invariably with the intention of settling on place, occurred down to Classical antiquity, and even later, in the Middle Ages, with Attila and other leaders. These peoples were of mingled stock ranging from Aryan to Semitic to Turkish, etc.. And they adopted a host of names which utterly confuse the specialists: Avars, Abars (Hebrew?), Asii, Hephtalites, Kushans (Ethiopians), Jujuan, Sacae, Tochari, White Huns, Yüeh-chih, etc.. It is quite clear that Plato had one of these invasions in mind.

The two horns or feathers of the headdresses of the Sea Peoples ultimately symbolize the two Pillars of Hercules. And the "sun" rising in between the two horns symbolizes the fiery volcanism, as shiny as the day star itself. Other nations of the Sea Peoples (Peleshet or Palestinians) wore plumed headdresses whose symbolism is again just the same. Their colorful feathers vividly portray the giant volcanic eruption and its fiery plume.

It is certainly more than a coincidence that some Egyptian gods such as Bes also wore feather headdresses. And Bes was deemed to have come from Punt, the Egyptian counterpart of the Islands of the Blest, which the heroes and pharaohs inhabited after death. The Sea Peoples also included the Teresh (or Tursha or Tyrshenoi or Tyrrhenians), that is, the Etruscans.

This fact is telltale of a connection with the East Indies and the Dravidas, as revealed by their Dravidian tongue. Luckily, I managed to decipher the hitherto mysterious language of the Etruscans in very complete detail, providing compelling Dravidian etymologies for all its rather ample known vocabulary, which presently encompasses over a thousand words.

My results have been published, and are currently available in the Internet, at the disposal of all interested parties. Up to now, Etruscan, like Pelasgian, its Greek counterpart, was universally considered an undeciphered "linguistic isolate" having no known connection with any other linguistic families anywhere.

This seminal discovery of ours provides an insofar unsuspected connection of the early Mediterranean and Near Eastern civilizations with the East Indies, their probable source. As soon as our deciphering of Etruscan is realized and recognized by the academic experts, a thorough revision of the current doctrines on the rise of civilization will be required.

Such changes of paradigm take time to be implemented. But they will be done, in time, as truth is inescapable, once discovered. What this discovery means is that that the existence of Atlantis and its location in the East Indies can hardly be doubted anymore. Otherwise, how can one reasonably account for the now inescapable fact that the early peoples of the Mediterranean region originally came from the distant Far East?

20 The figure of the Cherubs (or Karibus) originated in Mesopotamia, probably with the Sumerians who handed the tradition to the Akkadians. The Karibus were the terrible guardians of the temples and palaces in Sumer, and Babylon. Similar sentinels existed in Assyria and guarded the Tree of Life. The Karibus were winged, eagle-headed angelic deities.

The meaning and origin of the Akkadian word karibu and its Jewish equivalent cherub is highly controversial. Some experts affirm that their name means "one who intercedes" or as meaning "knowledge" or "wisdom". Others say the word means "strong ones". We believe that the ultimate etymology of this word is Indian, as is usual with such mystery names. [164]

In fact, the word "cherubim" is distantly related to "griffin", which it closely resembles. And this word is in turn derived from the French griffon, in turn derived from the Latin griffus and the Grk. gryps. This Greek word is related to the idea of "grip, grab, gripe, hooked".

The Greek word applies to eagles and griffins due to their curved beaks and claws. And it also applies to hook-nosed people and to hunchbacks. But the myth of griffins, cherubims, karibus, etc., apparently derives from the Hindu one of Garuda, the eagle of Vishnu. The (Sanskrit) name of Garuda is generally derived from the radix grī ("to devour, swallow"). But this etymology is contrived. [165]

The real source is Dravida, whence the word ultimately derives, as is so often the case with Hindu sacred names. The eagle Garuda is also connected with Garut-mat or Garutmān ("king of birds"). Garut means "bird, winged". The suffix mat (or mad) is ill-explained, and perhaps refers to the Elixir (mada). Hence, garut-mat = the "bird of the Elixir". In fact, the main function of the huge bird was dispensing the Elixir.

Garut-mat is a very important figure in the Vedas. For instance, the Rig Veda (1:164:46) affirms: "God is one. The sages call Him by many names. They call Him: Indra, Mitra, Varuna, Divya, Garutmat, the celestial universal sunbird. They speak of Agni, Yama and Matarishvan." The Veda also calls him Vena. Garut-mat (the eagle Garuda) is hence the same as the Phoenix and the Thunderbird or Sunbird of other traditions.

As an alias of Agni, the Bird is the Vadavamukha, the Fire of Doomsday, the all-devouring volcano. Hence its connection with God and with the Elixir and, above all, with the all-devouring Central Fire of which the Pythagoreans spoke. It is also in the same spirit of "all-devouring fire" that we must interpret the name of Garuda as meaning "devourer".

Ultimately, the word garut- derives from the Dravida #1362 karu ("griffin, eagle, vulture"). With the Dravidian connective -tt, the word becomes karutt > Skt. garut, later changed to Garuda. With the connective -pp it becomes karupp, and yields cherub, karibu, griff-on, griff-in, etc..

The word "intercessor" means an angel or guardian spirit. The idea may be connected with the idea that Cherubs and angels in general established a link between earth and heaven, intermediating our prayers to the gods. In this sense, Karibus correspond to the smoke of sacrificial fires and, even more exactly, that of volcanoes, which did just that when they destroyed the site of Paradise.

The Mesopotamian word karibu derived from the Dravida, with which Sumerian was closely linked. In Dravida we have #1278 karippu, meaning "fiery, scorched, sun-scorched, singed, iron, black, blackened, black-haired, crow". This etymon often applies to the Todas, just as it also did to the Sumerians themselves. This base is directly related to #1395 karupp- meaning "black, demon of darkness, black person". This word is also identical with the name of the Ethiopians, whose meaning is precisely the same.

The mythical idea here is that these peoples, originally whites or reds, were charred by the volcanism, turning black or charred. This myth is intimately connected with the fate of the Atlanteans, literally so charred. This story has of course very little to do with racial affairs, being a matter of historical fact.

These "Ethiopians" were really whites or reds, rather than blacks, as the name was later used. This epithet also applied to their land, in fact charred by the volcanism. In this sense, the epithet also applied to Egypt (Kemet = "the black land"). And it also designated the Waste Land (Terre Gaste) of the Arthurian Cycle. As such, this land again corresponds to the one of Atlantis, wasted by the volcanism.

Ultimately, this legend corresponds to the one reported by Plato on the Atlanteans, and in the Bible (Gen. 6) of the Sons of God mingling with the Daughters of Men, and breeding hybrid offspring. Here, the "Sons of God" are the Atlantean (reds or whites), whereas the "humans" are the dark races of the region of Indonesia (Atlantis): the Negritos, Melanesians, Australoids, Veddoids, etc.. Some of these natives are very obviously crossbreeds of Aryanoids and Negroids, as several experts have already mooted out.

---

21 Cf. also here, where the subject of the identity of Humbaba with volcanoes is told in more detail. The story of rabbi Nahamanides and his placement of Eden in the Far Eastern region is amply commented in Jewish sources. Some of the more interesting documents on them can be perused here and here and here, as well as in the other Internet documents which we already linked in the main text. [166]

---

22 In his Nemean Ode 3:21, Pindar affirms: "It is not easy to cross the impassable (abatan) sea beyond the Pillars of Hercules, which that hero and god set up as famous witnesses to the furthest limits (eschatas) of seafaring. He subdued the monstrous beasts in the sea, and tracked to the very end the currents (rhoas) of the shallows (tenageôn), where he reached the goal that sent him back home again, and he made that land known. My soul, towards what foreign headland are you turning my voyage?" [167]

This interesting passage deserves some comments. I have slightly corrected the excellent translation of Diane Svarlien, made for Perseus, in order to render it both clearer and more accurate. These shallows or shoals are probably the impassable ones of Atlantis as described by Plato. And the streams or currents are probably marine, rather than riverine as suggested by the word "stream" used by Diane Svarlien.

So, Hercules apparently followed a maritime current down to its end. And this maritime current seems to be the Equatorial Counter-Current which flows from Indonesia to Ecuador in America and vice-versa. In other words, it seems that Hercules actually crossed the wide Pacific Ocean all the way to Indonesia, the farthest bound of navigation. But it may also be the case that Hercules was sailing the Indian Ocean, where a similar countercurrent also exists along the line of the equator.

Please note that Hercules' navigation only makes sense in the Pacific or the Indian Ocean, and not at all in their Atlantic counterpart. Hercules followed the sun's path, and hence navigated along the Line of the Equator. This fact again confirms our interpretation of Pindar's riddling text.

Eschatas is a technical term referring to earth's fringes, as explained in Part IV, below. This term specifically applied to the Far East, where the East ended, and the West really started. This word leaves little room for doubting that Pindar was truly referring to the East Indies. These were the goal of all such navigations, Columbus' included. And this word, eschatas, is more or less synonymous with Paradise, meaning "the far off land beyond the ocean" (Skt. paradesha).

The "foreign headland" is again probably the Malay Peninsula, an integral part of Taprobane. Pindar's words here are somewhat malicious and are intended to both enlighten the initiates and confuse the profanes. The "monstrous beasts of the sea" are a recurrent feature of Indonesia, and refers to the formidable whales formerly abundant there. The goal which sent Hercules back home are the true Pillars of Hercules, the ones of Taprobane. And these are the two volcanoes just named, the Dempo and the Krakatoa.

The Pillars of Hercules were often compared to a trophy won by a wrestler or a poet. Similar "trophies" were erected as tokens of a great victory or conquest just as Hercules did upon his victory over the Trojans (cf. Isoc., Speech. and Lett. 5:112; 10:67). Quite often, two such pillars were erected, one by each of the two contending parties. We thus see that the two Pillars of Hercules and/or Atlas apparently commemorate the Great War of Atlantis, being thus intended as testimonials of its reality. [168]

In the above link, Isocrates tells how Hercules erected his famous pillars as a token of his victory over Troy. And true Troy, we recall, was located on the far bank of the Ocean. Schliemann's "Troy" in Turkey is merely a shabby replica of the magnificent golden city described by Homer. We also showed that the story of Troy was taken almost verbatim from the far earlier Ramayana, the great Hindu epic.

These two pillars were erected, Isocrates affirms, on the two continents of Asia and Europe. This would apparently indicate that the Pillars of Hercules were erected at the Bosphorus Strait, where Asia in fact meets Europe. But this is a phony pair of pillars of no great importance.

True Troy is Atlantis and the two Pillars of Hercules in question here were posted one in Europe (Gibraltar) the other one in Sunda Strait (Sumatra or Taprobane). Isocrates' affirmation clearly precludes the usual localization of these pillars, one in Africa, the other in Europe, since he specifically names Asia.

The word tropaiôs means "which causes the enemy to return", as some sort of scarecrow. The idea is that these trophies corresponded to the point where the enemy was thwarted and caused to go back (cf. R. Jebb, Comm. on Soph. Ant.,

l. 141 and C. T. Lewis, sv. tropaeum and LSJ sv. tropaion). But they also marked the farthest point reached by an explorer or adventurer (Hercules, etc.) in his navigation. Such is clearly the sense of the Pillars of Hercules, one on each side of the Ocean he crossed.[169]

The name of Anostos or Strophaios ("no return" and "which causes one to return") was often given to Cape Malea. This cape is not really the replica situated in the Peloponnesus, but its true archetype, the Malay Peninsula (Malea = Malay = Malaya = Malacca). In Greece, this geographical feature was normally associated with Cape Anostos (or Strophaios = Tropaios) and the Pillars of Hercules, according to Pindar, etc.. But these pillars or tokens were in fact placed in the East Indies, the true site of Troy. The ones of Greece were a mere replica, rather gross at that. This fact untangles the confusion made by Galanopoulos and Bacon in their book on Atlantis commented above, which proposes Crete as the former site of Atlantis.

To be more precise, these two real "Pillars of Heaven" were the two volcanoes at the Strait of Malacca, in Sumatra, the true site of Atlantis (and Taprobane, Lanka, Troy, Malea, etc.). Only volcanoes can really be considered "pillars of heaven" for the reasons we already adduced. This fact of course excludes a great many phony Pillars of Hercules and/or Atlas, the ones in Morocco and in Greece's Malea in particular.

Now, why would a volcano be named "victory-bringer"? This is an interesting riddle, which we believe to have been able to solve. According to Plato, the volcano of Atlantis – the one we have identified as the ferocious Krakatoa – exploded right during the War of Atlantis, swallowing the whole capital city and its people, and destroying the rest of Atlantis' mighty kingdom.

As the result of Atlantis' demise, the Greeks became victorious and hegemonic from then on. In other words, it was the ferocious volcano (or something the Greeks did to it) that brought the victory to the Athenians in the Great War of Atlantis, more or less as reported by Plato. What this could really be is a very good question whose investigation does not fit here.

Very much the same thing is also reported in relation to the War of Troy, itself an allegory (metaphor) of the War of Atlantis. According to the Iliad, the instrument of the Greek's victory was the Trojan Mare. And this equid is in fact another allegory of the volcano, the Vadavamukha. The Vadavamukha is the Fiery Submarine Mare of Hindu mythology. And the Fiery Mare is the same as the Mare of Troy, likewise the causer of its doom.

Curiously enough, the goddess Athena was also called Minerva in Latin. And we showed that this name means "Fiery Mare" or "White Mare" in Dravida (min-arva). It is perhaps no mere coincidence that Plato makes of Leucippe ("White Mare") the mother of Cleito, the wife of Poseidon and co-founder of Atlantis. The Fiery Mare is the Vadavamukha, alias Submarine Mare. The Submarine Mare is in turn the allegory of the Fire of Doomsday.

The mare or volcano periodically goes berserk, destroying the whole region, sometimes along with the rest of the world. This happened at the Universal Flood which, as we demonstrated, is both the flood which destroyed Atlantis in the course of a single day and night, as well as the abrupt maritime invasion technically known to geologists and oceanographers as Meltwater Pulse One B [MWP 1B]. We comment this important topic further above in the present book, showing that this geological event was in all probability Plato's Flood itself.

Isocrates (436–338 BC) was a contemporary and compatriot of Plato (428–348 BC), both of them being born in Athens. Hence, Isocrates' highly informative disclosures on these Atlantean matters – though highly encoded – are extremely important.

Isocrates' writings derive from independent sources and unequivocally show that Plato was not inventing anything, but just disclosing long held traditional teachings professed by the Greeks ever since the times of Homer and Hesiod. So much so, that Isocrates, a very conservative historian, developed a great scorn for Plato and the Platonic Academy, due to their indiscretion on these sacred matters.

Isocrates is hence a key figure for understanding Athenian thought in Plato's time, the 4th century BC. As already commented in some detail, Greek mythology and religion derive most directly from the Hindu and the Indonesian ones. So do the traditions on the War of Troy, the Iliad being an almost verbatim copy of the beautiful Ramayana, down to a matter of detail.

For instance, both romances are initiatic in character and both concern the kidnapping of the fickle queen; the great war waged by the cuckolded husband; the final, thorough destruction of the vast empire by Fire and Water, ending with the final flooding and submersion of the majestic city; the mass exodus from the destroyed place, etc... And it is well-known that true Troy in fact lay beyond the Ocean despite the contrary opinion of most experts. [↑170]

Lanka – the paradisial capital of Ravana destroyed in the Great War of the Ramayana – is an alias not only of Troy, but also of Atlantis itself. If it is already difficult to believe in the reality of one Flood and one submerged continent, imagine the difficult in having to believe in several different Floods destroying different Terrestrial Paradises, one per tradition.

The extant academic doctrines on the prehistoric human past consensually hold that the different human civilizations evolved in essential isolation from each other. So, they either hit on the idea of Paradise and its destruction by the Flood by chance, or as the result of a consensual lie, or from the direct observation of an actual geological event.

It is unrealistic to believe that such uncanny, literal parallels could ever arise as the result of chance alone, rather than by diffusion, the only possible explanation of the universality of these myths. But if we can accept the reality of a prehistoric civilization advanced enough to rove the whole world preaching their sacred religion, false or not, the existence of Atlantis is demonstrated ipso facto.

If, instead, one accepts the reality of the Universal Flood reported by most cultures of the world, the geological reality of the universal cataclysm is automatically proved, and so is the dramatic story of Plato and, for that matter, the one of the Bible and other such sacred traditions. So, the inescapable reality is that Paradise in fact existed, and was destroyed by the Flood, which sent its people out, in a great worldwide diaspora.

Now that we have shown that both the Greeks and the Pelasgians, their former enemies, came from the sunken continent of Sundaland, in the Far East, these uncanny parallels find a compelling, natural explanation: They are all the result of diffusion, rather than chancy coincidences.

And this is by far the most conservative alternative, the one we are compelled to accept according to Ockham's Razor, one of the pillars of Modern Science. Evading this problem, as has been done so far by the academics of all countries, will just not work anymore.

We note that Isocrates also mentions that the victory over Troy was jointly accomplished by Hercules and Telamon, a fact supported by other Greek mythographers (cf. Apollod. 2:6:4, Ovid, Met. 11:194, Hom. Il. 5.640-643, etc.). Note, in these passages that Hercules, to whom Telamon builds a trophy, is called Alexikakos ("averter of evils") or Kallinikos ("glorious victor"). [171]

These names mystically refer to a trophy or pillar (of Hercules or Atlas), as something that averts the enemy and is connected with victory (nike). This headland or cape variously named Anostos, Strophaios or Malea is hence one of the pair of Pillars of Hercules and/or Atlas, both again the same as the Pillar of Heaven. And Malea is Malaya, rather than its Greek counterpart.

Therefore, the tradition of the Pillars of Hercules and their connection with Atlantis (Troy) visibly dates from Homer or even earlier, and cannot be said to be an invention of Plato or Diodorus, at all.

Now, Telamon is an alias of Atlas, in his role of "pillar of heaven". Telamon's name is Etruscan, and means "bearer headland" or "pillar headland". It is formed from the same root of Atlas (a-tala) followed by mun ("headland, cape"). This headland or cape is clearly the same as the Pillar of Heaven. Telamon and Hercules apparently correspond to the twin figures of Atlas and Gadeiros, the co-rulers of Atlantis according to Plato.

So, we see, from the stories just told, that the two heroes formed a pair of twins who probably corresponded to Hercules and Atlas, the two brothers ever disputing hegemony with each other. The destruction of Troy by Hercules and Telamon (Atlas) or by Poseidon and Apollo (Ovid, Met. 11:194) is hence an allegory of the destruction of Atlantis in the (civil) war of its two main kings, who are precisely Atlas and Hercules (Gadeiros). [172]

We already noted above the essential identity of Atlas (or Kronos) and Hercules (Gadeiros). This type of dualism is typical of Hindu religion, where the Twins are represented by Shiva and Vishnu. But the two are also two successive avatars of the god.

According to Hindu beliefs of extreme antiquity, the god descends in an avatar (incarnates) in order to save the world from the former god (himself), turned old and corrupt. He defeats and kills his evil self, and assumes the rule of the new era. In time, the new hero or god grows old and corrupt, and history repeats itself.

In practice, the hero or god stands for his nation and people, generally the Dravidas and the Aryans or their many aliases everywhere. Theoretically, the two take turns in ruling the world, each the antithesis of the other as devas and asuras (God and Devil).

SUBJECT INDEX

A

Academy
Plato's school of philosophy in ancient Athens. Revived by Marsilio Ficino in the Renaissance, to which it was instrumental 19, 159, 274, 314, 344

Achilles
The greatest warrior on the Greek side in the Trojan War. Achilles killed Hector, but was later killed by Paris, the brother of Hector ... 113, 245, 246, 328

Acropolis
The fortified summit of ancient Athens. A replica of Atlantis.................. 189

Apples of the Hesperides
Wedding gift to Hera by Gaia. Furnished the Elixir which imparted immortality to its lucky possessors... 261

Argonauts
The companions of the hero Jason in the quest for the Golden Fleece. Their name means 'sailors of the Argo (ship)' 58, 290

Athena
Pallas Athena. Tutelary goddess of Athens. Greek name of Minerva 98, 128, 129, 295, 343

Athens
Capital of Greece in east-central Greece..................... 18, 297, 301, 331, 344

Atlantic Islands
Mythical islands of the Atlantic Ocean. They were in fact located in the Pacific Ocean, of old deemed coterminous with the Atlantic Ocean since the existence of America was widely ignored .. 19, 39, 41, 45, 105, 119, 163, 165, 170-171, 180, 185, 209, 226-228, 230, 315, 322-324

Atlantis
A famous kingdom in Classical Mythology whose real existence was first disclosed by Plato.......................... ii-ix, 1-11, 13-27, 29, 31-33, 35-39, 40-56, 58, 60, 62, 64, 66-80, 82, 84, 85, 87-90, 93-108, 110-116, 118-121, 123-125, 128-132, 134, 136, 137, 140, 143-152, 154-163, 165, 168-171, 173-177, 179-191, 194-196, 198-213, 215-230, 233-245, 247-251, 254-258, 261-264, 267, 268, 274, 275, 279, 280, 282-292, 294, 295, 297, 303, 304, 306-310, 314-317, 320, 322-324, 326-339, 341-345

Atlas
In classical mythology, a titan famous for his strength. The Pillar of Heaven, who bore the sky on his back. Identified with Mt. Atlas (qv).............. 21, 33, 41, 56, 58, 62, 64, 65, 69-71, 88, 89, 92-95, 99, 100, 104, 105, 121, 123, 124, 129-134, 136, 140, 145, 146, 149, 150, 160, 173, 176, 197, 198, 211-214, 234-236, 242, 248, 251, 257, 259, 260, 262, 263, 265-268, 275, 286, 319, 320,

E

Eden, Garden of

Elgin Marbles

Elysium

Erebus

Erytheia

Ethiopia

Ethiopians

F

Flood

G

Ganges River

Geryon

O

Ocean
In antiquity the world was circled by a stream of water, the River Oceanus.
iii, 1, 6, 12, 15-18, 20, 31, 33, 35, 38, 39, 43-45, 51, 56, 58, 62, 72, 73, 78, 81,
90, 91, 97, 100, 103, 105, 106, 111, 113, 114, 116, 117-124, 127, 133-135, 138,
140, 143, 145, 148, 152, 154, 158, 160-166, 168-172, 174-179, 182-185, 187-
189, 193-196, 201, 203, 204, 206, 209, 214, 215, 217, 218, 220, 225-230,
235-239, 242-245, 247, 249-255, 258-262, 265, 267, 277, 283, 285-290,
292-295, 303, 314, 315, 317, 319, 320-322, 324, 326, 329, 330, 334, 336,
339, 342-344

Oceanus
A Titan, ruling the watery elements. The Ocean personified... 113, 160, 185,
227, 248, 249, 254, 319, 320

P

Pacific Ocean
The largest ocean in the world. Same as the 'Ocean of Atlantis' or 'Atlantic
Ocean' of the ancients 6, 7, 15, 17, 44, 45, 55, 69,
91, 106, 115, 118, 119, 122-125, 138, 140, 152, 160, 163-165, 169-171, 177, 185,
215, 225, 227, 229, 236, 250, 255, 287, 288, 293, 314, 317, 319-322, 342

Persephone
Or Proserpine. Goddess of vegetation, and queen of Hades. Daughter or
junior avatar of Demeter or Ceres (qv), the Corn Mother....................... 308

Phaeacia
Land of the people who entertained Ulysses during his wanderings. A
ghostly alias of Atlantis 4, 235, 236

Phoenicia
An ancient nation of the eastern Mediterranean Sea... 11, 74, 130, 175, 266,
299

Phoenix
A mythical bird that periodically burns itself to death and then resurrects.
The Phoenix is an allegory of Atlantis and its fated rebirth 335, 340

Pillars of Hercules
Two famous rocks often misidentified as those of Gibraltar (qv) ....
iii, 41, 56, 71, 78, 82, 89, 92, 95, 97, 99, 113, 126, 130-132, 136, 150, 152, 154,
160, 161, 168, 173, 175, 176, 178, 184-187, 205, 207, 215, 224, 225, 228, 235,
238, 256, 266, 274, 275, 285-290, 294, 312, 314, 321, 329, 331, 338, 339,
341-343, 345

Pindar
Famous Greek poet. First to refer to the Pillars of Hercules vii, 10, 69, 172,
234, 238, 239, 244, 251, 285, 287, 288, 341-343

Plato
Greek philosopher of the 7th cent. BC. Considered the Prince of
Philosophers. Wrote the Timaeus and the Critias, the two famous dialogues

Pleistocene

Poseidon

Prometheus

Ptolemy, Claudius

Pyramid

S

Saturn

Scylla and Charybdis

Siculus, Diodorus

Suez Canal

T

Taprobane

Virgil
The celebrated Latin poet, the author of the Aeneid, which tells how the Romans came out of Troy after its destruction in the Great War vii, 10, 247

Z

Zeus
Roman name Jupiter (qv). Defeated the Titans and assumed the dominion of the world.................... 47, 81, 149, 186, 247, 252, 262, 265, 278, 329, 337